The Spanish Crown and the Defense
of the Caribbean, 1535–1585

Paul E. Hoffman

The Spanish Crown and the Defense of the Caribbean, 1535-1585

Precedent, Patrimonialism, and Royal Parsimony

Louisiana State University Press
Baton Rouge and London

Copyright © 1980 by Louisiana State University Press
All rights reserved
Manufactured in the United States of America

Designer: Patricia Douglas Crowder
Typeface: VIP Aster
Typesetter: Graphic Composition, Inc.

The author gratefully acknowledges permission to reprint sections of this book published previously in slightly different versions as "The Computer and the Colonial Treasury Accounts: A Proposal for a Methodology," in the *Hispanic American Historical Review* (Copyright © 1970 by Duke University Press); and "Diplomacy and the Papal Donation," in *The Americas* (Copyright © 1973).

Illustrations 8 and 11 are reproduced with permission of the British Library, London; Illustration 9 is reproduced with permission of the Archivo General de Indias, Seville, Spain; Illustration 10 is reproduced with permission of the Real Academía de la História, Madrid.

Published with the assistance of the Council on Research, Louisiana State University.

LIBRARY OF CONGRESS CATALOGING IN PUBLICATION DATA

Hoffman, Paul E.   1943–
  The Spanish crown and the defense of the Caribbean, 1535–1585
  Bibliography: p.
  Includes index.   1. Spanish Main.   2. Caribbean area—History, Naval.
3. Pirates—Caribbean area.   I. Title.
F2161.H7   972.9′02   79-16864
ISBN 0-8071-2427-3

To my parents
Louis Frederick Hoffman
Ella Cook Hoffman

Contents

Preface **xiii**

I   Introduction **1**
II 1535–1547. The Precedents Take Shape **20**
III 1548–1563. Naval Warfare Creates Its Own Precedents **63**
IV 1564–1577. A System Takes Shape **109**
V   1578–1585. The System Refined and Neglected **175**
VI Summary and Conclusions **213**

Appendix I. Methodology **237**
Appendix II. Raw Data on Available Militia Manpower Pools **261**
Glossary **264**
A Note on the Citation of Archival Sources **267**
Notes **271**
Bibliography **297**
Index **305**

List of Tables

1. Component Parts of Yearly Costs of Convoy Escorts and Coastal Patrols, 1568–1585 (in Ducats) **19**
2. Mean Yearly Costs of Various Types of Defense by Geographic Areas, 1535–1547 (in Ducats) **22–23**
3. Spanish Losses to Corsairs, 1536–1547 **26**
4. Estimated Average and Maximum Strengths of Militias, 1535–1585 **42**
5. Crown Shipments of Small Arms and Munitions, 1535–1563 **44**
6. Militia-Related Expenditures, 1535–1585 (in Ducats) **45**
7. Militia Military Actions, 1535–1563 **47**
8. Nominal Strengths of Caretaker Garrisons, 1535 to Installation of Regular Garrison, If Any **48**
9. Temporary Stationings of Military Personnel in the Indies (Non-Fort Towns), 1535–1585 (Royal Funding) **50**
10. Proposed Strengths of Temporary Garrisons, 1542 **50**
11. Spanish Losses to Corsairs, 1548–1563 **66**
12. Spanish Losses to Corsairs Around Española, 1548–1560 **68**
13. Mean Yearly Costs of Various Types of Defense by Geographic Area, 1548–1563 (in Ducats) **72–73**
14. New Spain Subsidy for Havana Fort Construction, 1558–1578 **99**
15. Spanish Losses to Corsairs, 1564–1577 **113**

16. Mean Yearly Costs of Various Types of Defense by Geographic Area, 1564–1577 (in Ducats) **124–125**
17. Florida Military-Mission Posts Established and Abandoned, 1565–1574 **142–143**
18. Temporary Antilles Garrisons Installed by Menéndez de Avilés, 1566–1568 **144**
19. Crown Shipments of Arms Primarily for Use by Militias, 1563–1585 **149**
20. Munitions Shipments from Spain to the Indies, 1563–1585 **151**
21. Mean Yearly Costs of Various Types of Defense by Geographic Area, 1578–1585 (in Ducats) **176–177**
22. Corsair Attacks, Militia Initiatives, and Militia Successes in Battles with Corsairs, 1564–1585 **201**
23. Spanish Losses to Corsairs, 1578–1585 **211**
24. Relative Importance of Defenses as Measured by Mean Yearly Expenditures in Ducats. **214**
25. Relative Geographic Distribution of Defenses as Measured by Average Yearly Cost (Amounts in Ducats) **215**
26. Category Codes **250**
27. Geographic Categories **252**
28. Computer Card Layout **253**
29. Units of Account and Currency, Values in Maravedís **255**
30. Maravedí Value of the *Peso de Cuartos* at Santo Domingo, 1554–1578 **258**
31. Maravedí Value of the *Peso de Cuartos* at Puerto Rico, 1554–1578 **259**

List of Illustrations

Illustration 1. Total Defense Costs and Total Incidents of Violence by Corsairs, 1535–1585 (Amounts in Ducats) **12**

Illustration 2. Corsair Incidents by Geographic Regions, 1535–1585 **13**

Illustration 3. Topical Distribution of Defense Spending Expressed as a Percentage of Mean Yearly Spending **14**

Illustration 4. Geographic Distribution of Defense Spending Expressed as a Percentage of Mean Yearly Total Spending **15**

Illustration 5. Corsair Routes and Cattle **117**

Illustration 6. Voyages of the Indies Fleet, 1568–1574 **130**

Illustration 7. Voyages of the Indies Fleet and Its Squadrons, 1574–1577 **134**

Illustration 8. Santo Domingo Under Attack by Sir Francis Drake's Forces, 1586 **156**

Illustration 9. Havana, Showing Fort and Projects for Fort and Boom at Entrance to the Harbor, post–1580 **160**

Illustration 10. San Juan de Ulúa, *ca.* 1580 **164**

Illustration 11. Cartagena Under Attack by Sir Francis Drake's Forces, 1586 **168**

Illustration 12. Voyages of the Indies Fleet and Its Squadrons, 1578–1585 **187**

Illustration 13. Years Covered by Treasury Records Used **246**

Preface

THIS BOOK had its origin in a stubbornly held belief that for me, if for no one else, a proper understanding of the particular had to begin with an understanding of the general. The result of that belief and nine years of work is a study which I believe to be comprehensive but not definitive. This book is comprehensive in that it is based on an examination of all of the treasury records, 1535–1585, for the Casa de Contratación and some nineteen other treasuries, seventeen of them from the Caribbean area, and of all the correspondence and related papers for the same period and area. It is also comprehensive because it seeks to present major patterns of change over time, space, and topical categories. But this book is not definitive because it does not provide every detail of every event, nor answer every question that could be asked about events and men's motives, nor, finally, provide documentation for every decision or even every payment the crown made for defense. The first two limitations arose from the practical necessities of publishing and, to a lesser extent, from the third limitation, that of the sources. Some documents that once existed no longer rest in the Archivo General de Indias or in the Archivo General de Simancas. That they may exist in some other archive, or even in some unlikely corner of those great storehouses of history should be a spur to further monographic treatment of events that are summarized here. It is my hope that those who may undertake such monographic treatment in depth will profit, as I have, from the perspective that this book seeks to provide.

I would like to thank the University of Florida, the University of Wyoming, Louisiana State University, the National Endowment for the Humanities, and the St. Augustine Restoration Foundation, Inc., for their support of the research and writing of this book. My debt to the archivists of the Archivo General de Simancas and the Archivo General de Indias is almost too great to express in mere words. I am particularly indebted to Doña Rosario Parra, Directora of the AGI, for favors large and small too numerous to mention. Individuals who have provided encouragement, suggestions, and criticism at critical times include Dr. Roger Daniels, Dr. Roger Williams, Dr. Robert J. Parks, Dr. Eugene Lyon, Dr. John J. TePaske, Dr. Richard Boulind, Mr. Albert Manucy, and Mr. Luís Arana. I am particularly indebted to Dr. Lyle N. McAlister, who directed my graduate training, and Mrs. Patricia Smylie, who provided the foil that helped me get this monster under control. Barbara, Philip, and Stephen will each know why I want to thank them for love and patience.

Many other people have helped me in my work and wanderings in Spain. To each of them, as to those just noted, I express my gratitude. I ask my readers to absolve all of them and all of those named of any responsibility for this book and any errors it may contain.

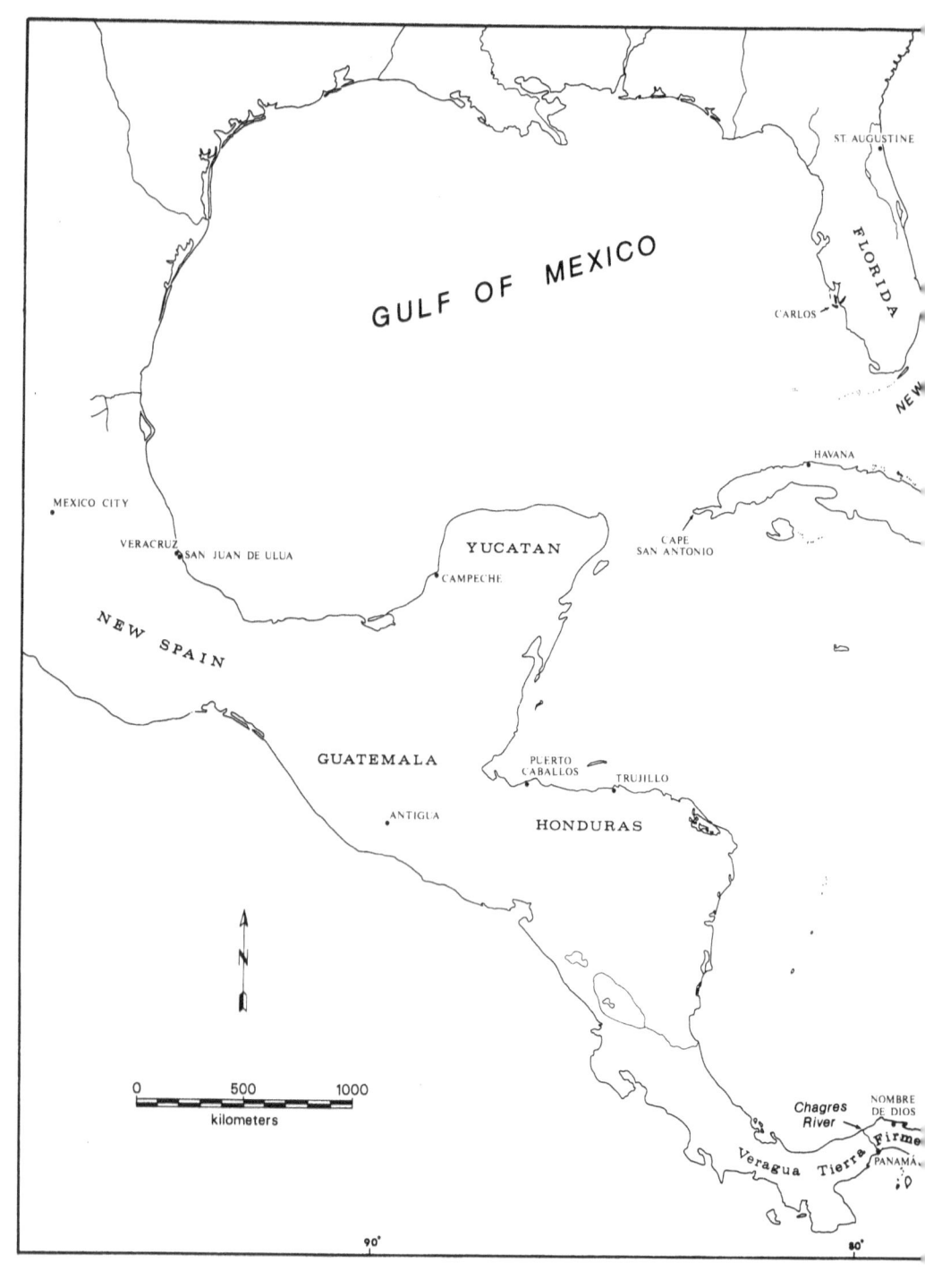

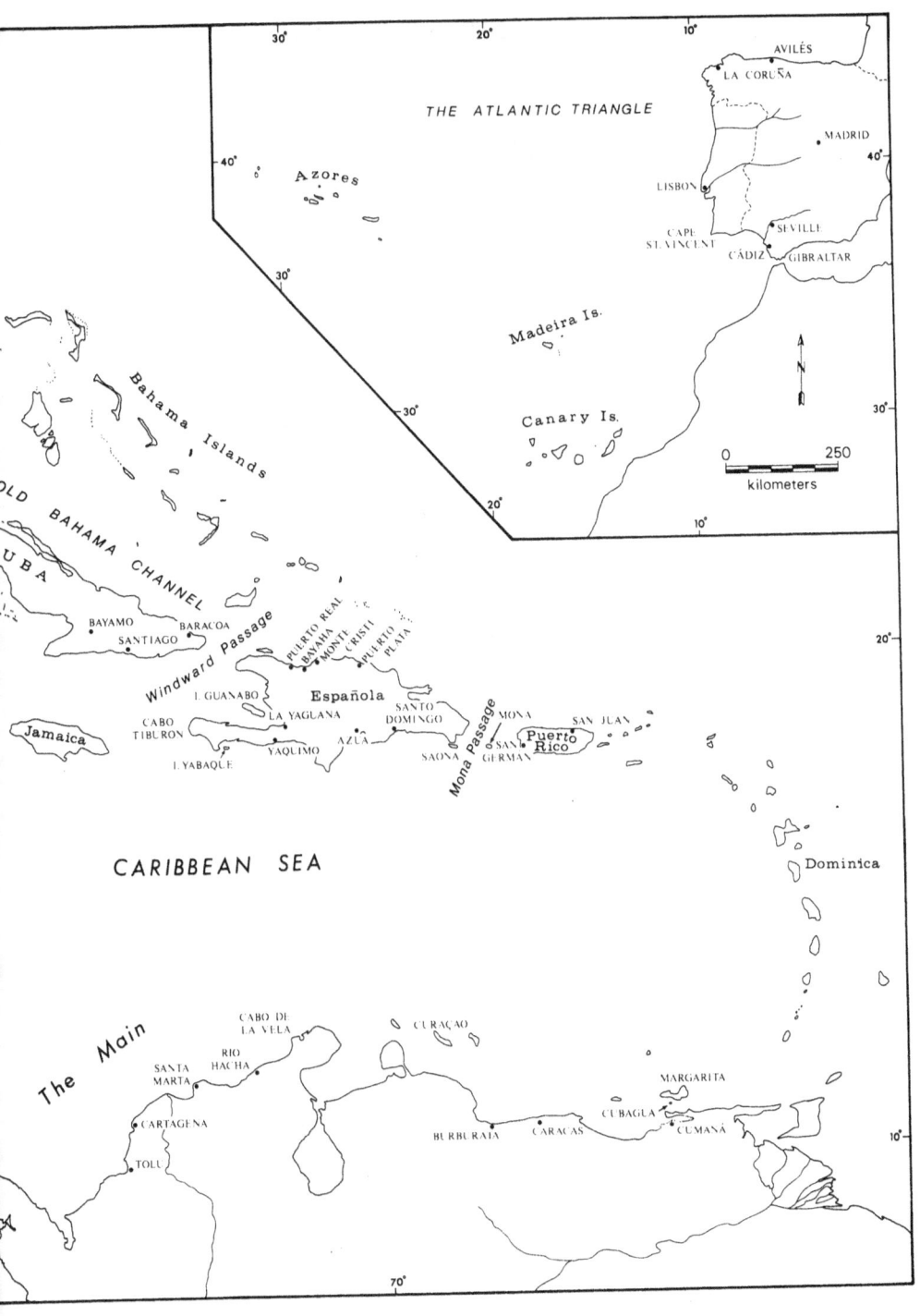

The Spanish Crown and the Defense
of the Caribbean, 1535–1585

Chapter I

Introduction

EVERY SCHOOLCHILD in the English-speaking world used to learn of the heroic exploits of Sir Francis Drake, while in some parts of Spanish America parents used to threaten disobedient youngsters with "El Draque." Children of both cultures thus learned the same legend—the legend of Drake's English daring and of Spanish terror in the face of his bold attacks. The Drake legend is the epitome of a larger legend shared by both cultures of Spanish military failure and timidity in the face of attacks by bold corsairs. Curiously enough, historians who should know better have repeated the substance of both legends down to our own day.

Much of the development of the Drake legend comes from English writers who have not asked why Drake abandoned the safety of the sea and the opportunities that it gave for escape to attack the mule trains coming overland on the Isthmus of Panama in 1572, nor why he took the great risk of sailing to the Pacific in 1579, nor why he used over a thousand men in his attacks on Santo Domingo and Cartagena in 1586. Each of these actions points to a military reality on the Spanish side that made it necessary for Drake to resort to imaginative, if sometimes very risky, tactics in his efforts to secure quick wealth. Spanish sources describing that military reality have been ignored, even by Spanish authors.

The power of the legends to mislead even careful scholars is well illustrated by an article on the defense of the Indies by Roland Hussey. He characterized Spain as "unequal to the task" of resisting the corsairs, the term applied to all non-Spaniards sailing in the Indies who did not have licenses from the Spanish crown. For the period before 1586, Hussey concluded that "since neither the crown revenues nor sovereignty were greatly endangered by the prevalent sacking of minor towns and seizures of coastwise shipping, Spain . . . spared little effort for the protection of America. Resistance in the Caribbean to about 1586 was therefore slight."[1]

Even a casual reexamination of the sources that Hussey cites suggests that he is wrong. The analysis of events that follows shows that although the "effort"—measured by royal spending for defense—was slight compared to the effort expended in the crown's European wars, it was adequate for dealing with the corsairs. Indeed, by about 1580 Spanish defense had gained a slight advantage over the corsairs, a fact indicated by declining numbers of attacks on ships and towns in the Caribbean.

Not only is Hussey's interpretation open to question on the basis of the sources he used, it is also in need of revision in light of the data found in a number of excellent studies published after he wrote. Hussey had available to him the general history of the Spanish navy prepared by Cesáreo Fernández Duro, Clarence Haring's and Gervasio de Artinaño y de Galdácano's studies of the institutional aspects of the Indies trade, a number of biographies such as James A. Williamson's of John Hawkins, and also a number of books more or less contemporary with the sixteenth and early seventeenth centuries such as Antonio de Herrera y Tordesillas' history of the Indies and Joseph de Veitía Linage's study of the operations of the Indies trade.[2] Also available by 1929, when Hussey wrote, were Herbert E. Bolton's studies of the borderlands, Woodbury Lowery's history of Spanish Florida to 1574, and Irene A. Wright's history of Cuba during the sixteenth century.[3] Only a fragmentary picture of the defenses of the Indies is found in these works. Many aspects of the story remained untold, a deficiency that Hussey only partially corrected with his own research. Subsequent publications supplied some of the missing detail, but none provides a satisfactory general synthesis.

Between the publication of Hussey's article and the early 1950s, the most significant publications touching on the history of the defense of the Indies were Irene A. Wright's collections of documents relating to English voyages and A. P. Newton's *The European Nations in the West Indies*.[4] Wright's volumes supplied much Spanish material and revealed for the first time some of the measures that the Spanish took in response to raids by English and French corsairs. Newton attempted a general history and supplied details not found in earlier works. Unhappily, the format of the series for which he wrote precluded the use of footnotes or an informative bibliography to guide the reader to his sources and to suggest additional lines of investigation. Nonetheless, Newton's work was an advance from Hussey's article.

With the 1950s came a group of studies from the School of Hispanic American Studies of Seville and the publication of Huguette and Pierre Chaunu's *Séville et l'Atlantique, 1504–1650*.[5] Except for Guillermo Céspedes' work on the *avería*, the studies issued at Seville concentrated on the fortifications and other monuments of the Caribbean's major ports.[6] Valuable for their illustrations and for their use of long neglected primary materials, they nonetheless lacked a larger historical focus and tended to concentrate on the developments of the seventeenth and eighteenth centuries. The work of the Chaunus proved so monumental in scope that few scholars have done much with it except to mine facts from the notes that accompany the tables in Volumes II–V. Those notes provide a running commentary on the military and economic situation of the trade with the Indies and come closer than any previous study to showing the interrelationship between coastal patrolling, convoys, and other forms of defense.[7] However, the Chaunus were primarily interested in the institutional and economic aspects of the convoy system, not its military role. Thus that important and complex story has remained untold until now.

During the 1960s, the attention of historians concerned with Latin American colonial history shifted to socioeconomic events or to the history of the expansion of Europe. John H. Parry's excellent works on the *Age of Reconnaissance* and *The Spanish Seaborne Empire* are examples of the latter trend.[8] The seaborne empire volume in particular attempted to incorporate the latest as well as the older secondary writings in its discussion of defense, but because of the limitations of that literature Parry was unable to provide a satisfactory overview of defense for the period of interest here.

Recently Kenneth R. Andrews has added to this literature with his book *The Spanish Caribbean: Trade and Plunder, 1530–1630.*[9] As his subtitle suggests, he finds the answer to the question of why the Spanish failed to occupy, develop, and defend the Lesser Antilles and the Guayana coast (which thereby became available to other nations for colonization) in the combined effects over time of trade—principally Spanish but also by foreigners—and the plundering activities of European corsairs, of whom the English seem the most important for his story. Together these forces drove the Spanish to the western Caribbean, leaving the eastern Caribbean open to non-Spanish penetration after 1620.

Like most of Andrews' work, this book combines careful use of mostly secondary sources and printed documents with interesting hypotheses. But as he admits, it is written from the point of view of those who attacked the Spanish Empire rather than from the vantage of the defenders. Consequently for the pre-1586 period it is only a small improvement over previous syntheses.

In short, until now the defense of the Indies could be studied only in part through a number of books dealing with key figures in the story, the institutional aspects of the convoy system, fortifications at the larger ports, and a few attempts at a general synthesis of that literature. The field thus remained in need of a reexamination of the primary as well as the secondary sources and of the writing of a new general survey of the defense of the Indies from the Spanish perspective.

This study aims to supply that need, although it is based on primary sources far more than on secondary literature because I found that the secondary works were either wrong or provided only the most fragmentary details for this period. The Chaunus' work is, of course, the exception to this statement, although some of its data were found to be incorrect when the same or additional primary sources were examined. Even so, this study stands in debt to the Chaunus for numerous facts mined from their notes and for the inspiration that their methods and breadth of vision provided.

Explanatory Factors

The history of the defense of the Spanish Caribbean down to 1586 is the story of the establishment of a series of precedents and of the subsequent emergence from them of a system of defenses. The precedents and the system were shaped by at least eight factors: (1) strategic geography; (2) the evolution of military technology down to 1586; (3) diplomatic and other events in Europe; (4) the concept and politics of the king's obligation to defend his subjects and their interests (that is to say, patrimonialism); (5) the changing state of the crown's fiscal affairs, which helped to shape a system of defenses characterized by the parsimonious spending of royal funds; (6) the population resources of the Spanish Caribbean; (7) the availability of various types of war matériel; and (8) the changing pattern of the corsairs' activities. Of these factors, patrimonialism (number 4) and parsimony (number 5) were the most important determinants in decision-making and hence in the history of defense. The other factors played various roles, as the next few pages of this introduction will make clear. All of the factors will reappear to some degree in the text that follows.

The strategic geography within which the story of defense unfolds was determined by the interaction of four elements: physical geography, the technology of the sailing ship and navigational instruments, weather patterns, and history. Physical geography provided the Spanish with only a few good ports in the south of Spain and in the Caribbean. Patterns of prevailing winds dictated the use of an Andalusian port, tended to dictate the route used by most ships seeking to leave the Caribbean, and determined the general routes to be followed in crossing the Atlantic Ocean. As it happened, the latter route was marked on the south by the Canary Islands and on the north by the Azores, each located at the approximate latitude at which shipping should sail for the fastest journey to and from the Caribbean. Within the Caribbean, the position of the Antilles and the fact that the prevailing trade winds were from the northeast meant that a shipmaster wishing to sail from the north coast of South America (the Spanish Main) far enough north to catch the prevailing westerlies that would take him to the Azores and so to Andalusia had two options: either he could try to beat eastwards against the trade winds (or tempt fate during the periods of variable winds when the trade winds were slack) to make use of the Mona Passage or the Windward Passage, or he could reach across the face of the trade winds to use the Yucatán Channel and Florida Straits. Once on the northern side of the Antilles, the winds were more favorable for his voyage, although the difficulties of navigating the Bahamas and the Bahama Channel diminished the benefit thus gained. Sailing for Europe from the Antilles was somewhat easier than from the Main, but even so many skippers preferred to run westward (downwind with the trade winds) to use either the Windward Passage or the Yucatán Channel rather than try to beat northeast from northern Puerto Rico or eastwards to and through the Mona Passage. In the Gulf of Mexico, prevailing northwesterly winds forced ships to sail in a great arc from the coast of New Spain to near the mouths of the Mississippi River and then southeast for the Florida Straits. In short, it was easy to get into the Caribbean, but hard to get out.

The technology of sailing ships and the navigational instruments available in the sixteenth century dictated that these natural patterns of wind and current, land masses, and islands be used wherever possible. No ships could point very well, which placed them at a great disadvantage when trying to tack into the face of the trade winds in the Caribbean. Because ship designers still made ships rounder as they made them larger, and roundness, as against length and narrowness, makes a ship even less able to point, the introduction of larger ships about midcentury in response to increasing volumes of trade and government bonuses for their construction meant the gradual abandonment of the old routes from the Main to Spain via the Windward and Mona passages. Instead, shipping from the Main used the easier route through the Yucatán Channel, around Cuba, past Florida in the Bahama Channel, and so to Spain. Once at the latitude of the Florida Straits, the sailor found more favorable winds and the Gulf Stream to help carry his ship beyond the zone of contrary winds.

Navigational instruments limited the seaman's ability to find his position, thereby increasing the importance of natural aids to navigation. The sailor could determine latitude but could not find his longitude except by dead reckoning, by the use of a compass preset for a given area, or by running down a latitude until he came to land, whence he could shape his course by coastal navigation. Thus shipping tended to hug the shore and to use strategically located headlands, such as the Capes of the Algarve, and islands, like the Canaries and Azores, as bearing points. As did the winds, so, too, the technology of navigation restricted the movement of ships to a relatively few routes.[10]

Weather patterns also played a part in determining the pattern of oceanic commerce. The hurricane season was known to the Spanish by the end of the fifteenth century, and this knowledge regulated the departure of ships from Spain and the Caribbean well before the royal orders of 1543 and 1562 formally established the pattern of two fleets each year, departing from Spain in January (later March) and August, and from Havana in May or June. Similar patterns, although less restrictive, governed sailing in the area of the triangle formed by the Azores, the Canaries, and the Straits of Gibraltar (hereafter called the Triangle). There the winter storms of November to February generally made sailing too risky. That same pattern of Atlantic storms also dictated that corsairs, no less than Spaniards, leave the Caribbean early in the fall of each year to return to Europe, if they had not left during the spring. Along the Main, from Cartagena to Nombre de Dios, winter storms from December to March often prevented shipping from sailing north and east for other parts of the Caribbean. At San Juan de Ulúa, New Spain, winter storms from the north and northeast posed dangers for ships at anchor or attempting to sail to Havana. The net effect of these weather patterns throughout the Atlantic world was to set up two sailing seasons: a spring season from early March to mid-July and a fall season from late August to late November. Most shipping moved during these periods. Economic life in the Caribbean and its hinterlands (which included Peru) moved to this rhythm.

The scarcity of deep-water ports in southern Spain and especially in the Caribbean and accidents of history other than navigational instrumentation and ship design further restricted the pattern of sailing. The Chaunus have explained the historical reasons for the selection of Seville, rather than Cádiz, as the terminus of the Indies trade.[11] In the Caribbean, conquest and occupation were heavily influenced by the harbors that the Spanish found. These ports, like the vital passages out of the Caribbean and the navigational marks provided by the Canaries, Azores, and Capes of the Algarve, were the places where shipping and hence wealth were concentrated.

The concentrations of wealth in a few ports, in coastal shipping serving those ports, in the narrow waters of the passages of the northeast Caribbean, and in the Triangle set the geographic zones in which the raiding corsairs were to seek targets and thus determined the areas where the Spanish needed to develop defenses. For both parties in that struggle, the problem was to employ weapons, manpower, and tactics that would give an advantage against whatever the enemy was using. The result was an arms race within a set of geographic constraints that applied to both parties because they shared essentially similar technologies and wished to benefit from the same economic system (although in different ways).

This basic pattern of defense zones determined by geography, history, and Spanish economic activity was augmented after the corsairs began to trade with residents of the Caribbean in defiance of the empire's navigation laws. Most of this trade occurred in areas somewhat removed from the main centers of Spanish commerce because it centered on the exchange of hides and other local products for various European goods. This illegal trade thus complicated the defense problem by adding other ports, coastal zones, and shipping routes to the area of military activity.

Changes in military technology constitute a second, but relatively unimportant factor explaining the history of the defense of the Indies. The most important change, and the one having the most impact on the events considered, was the evolving use of artillery. Cannon became more common and of larger calibers with greater range and hitting power. In Europe, the first of these changes placed an army attacking in the field at a disadvantage, even if it had artillery of its own, and thus caused the conversion of land warfare into a series of maneuvers and sieges with very few pitched battles in the open field. One result of this development was the evolution of new types of fortifications designed to give maximum protection to their walls by providing glacis and maximum flanking fire by using the geometrically designed cavalier and its variants. Improved fortifications in turn stimulated the development of larger calibers, greater range, and greater hitting power in artillery.[12]

In the Indies, the absence of large armies made possession of artillery a less important factor in determining the outcome of a pitched battle. Nonetheless, residents of the towns sought artillery, believing that its possession would give them the defensive advantages that European armies derived from it in pitched battles. Interest in the new style of fortifications came late and was in large part limited to projects initiated by the crown and designed in Europe. The most notable example was the fort built at Havana between 1558 and 1580.

At sea, the increasing use of artillery was contemporary with the use of larger ships. Yet neither the corsairs nor the Spanish relied on guns for victory at sea. Every battle that did not result in boarding was broken off because there was no other way to force an enemy to surrender.[13]

No important changes in ship design affect the history of the defense of the Indies, although it may appear that corsairs and Spaniards alike were actively developing new types. Only one new design was used in the Indies: the galleyed galleon, used in the Indies Fleet (Armada Real) from 1567 to 1580, and even it was based on the *galeaza* and smaller, oared sailing ships long used in Europe. Instead of developing new ship designs, both sides made innovative selections from available types according to their perceptions of tactical needs.

The third explanatory factor that must be considered is diplomacy and other events in Europe. Karl von Clausewitz's famous observation that diplomacy is war by other means was no less true in the sixteenth century than it is today. Diplomacy was particularly important because the definition of the extent of the Spanish Indies and the terms under which other Europeans might gain access to them were the issues around which the colonial sides of Europe's wars revolved. At issue were two different but complementary questions. One had to do with the rights of sovereigns other than the rulers of Spain to establish claims and colonies in the New World, especially North America. The other had to do with the rights of the subjects of those sovereigns to enjoy access to the trade of the Spanish empire in America on the same terms as Spaniards or, in a larger context, on the same terms of access as they enjoyed relative to the commerce of Spain herself. The failure of diplomacy to resolve these issues between 1535 and 1570 led to the breakdown in the Caribbean of the traditional distinction between war and peace and hence to unprecedented levels of royal spending for defense after 1563. This failure and its consequences will be discussed below.

The fourth factor affecting defense was the existing set of assumptions about the crown's responsibility to defend its subjects and their interests (as well as its own interests) and the political conditions that arose from those assumptions and modified them during the years studied here. The secondary literature is far from clear about the traditions that governed the crown's response to its subjects' calls for aid during wartime. Apparently the crown had always had some responsibility to provide for their defense, but the form which that obligation took varied with time. At the beginning of the fifty-one years covered in this book, the crown clearly felt that legislation was the way it should provide for defense. However, this didactic approach proved unsatisfactory because the failure of its subjects to fulfill the law meant that the crown's interests—chiefly in the form of cargos moving across the Atlantic—as well as those of the subjects, were exposed to attack by the corsairs.

Consequently, the crown began to assume an increasing part of the defense load in order to safeguard its own interests as well as to satisfy the petitions of its subjects. But there were limits to the crown's willingness to bear the costs, limits imposed by the crown's conception of its role in defense, especially on the seas, and its need to use its money for other projects having higher priorities. The crown was not the embodiment of the national interest as that concept has come to be understood in the nineteenth and twentieth centuries and so did not have to act in support of the "national interest." Thus one must always look for the crown's interest when considering its response to petitions from its subjects for the benefit of royal funds to pay for defenses. The money was the king's to use as tradition, dynastic interest, and paternalism might suggest. The public—that is, the subjects—had only a few traditional claims on those funds. The trick was to convince the crown that it, as well as its subjects, would derive benefits—be they material, moral, or prestigious—from a given defense project.

The success of any group of subjects in persuading the king to use his money for their benefit depended on their ability to use the political structure of the empire to place their case before the monarch and to influence him through his ministers. Some evidence of this political activity appears in the numerous instructions to advocates (*procuradores*) and in the occasional references to the connections of residents of the Indies with powerful persons at court, but the details of the patron-client relationships and the other facets of the patrimonial system that helped petitions become actions are not to be found. Nor are there any studies of the ways in which patronage connections were necessary for political success, whether by individuals or groups. The importance of such connections is shown by the success of Santo Domingo in obtaining royal funds during a period when this colony was of declining economic and strategic importance, while Cartagena, which was rising in importance in both categories, was unable to get much royal money. Of all the parts of the puzzle assembled here, this was the one whose outline is clear but whose details are obscure. Its existence can only be stated on the basis of the other pieces of the puzzle that outline it.

The fifth, sixth, and seventh factors affected the execution of the crown's decisions and will be commented on at greater length at appropriate points in the text. For the moment it is sufficient to note that the crown's penury or richness (factor 5) did affect the decisions it made, most notably during the 1540s. Similarly, the number of men available in the Indies (factor 6) for militia duty affected the entire history of defense, eventually forcing the crown to create garrisons of paid soldiers at certain key but sparsely populated ports. The availability of supplies (factor 7) was also important in determining the history of defense, but the reader will not find a detailed examination of why certain types of matériel were not available at a given time. This is a problem that would lead to places and circumstances far removed from the story to be told here. It is enough to know that matériel was not available.

The eighth and last factor to be considered here is the corsairs' activities, activities embracing illegal trading as well as raiding. The raids and incidents of trading were the immediate causes of or excuses for the military activities studied. No previous study has attempted to answer comprehensively the questions: where and when did attacks occur? how many were there? what were the reactions to them? what was the geographic and temporal extent of illegal trade? Without answers to these questions, the history of Spanish defense makes little sense. Because the changing pattern of corsairs' activities is such an integral part of the history of defense, it is covered in more detail in the text.

Descriptive Statistics

Examining the pattern of corsair activities and writing the history of defense involve a similar problem: seen in the particular, the events are overwhelmingly numerous and apparently meaningless because of a lack of interconnections other than those provided by geography and their evident relationship to European wars and diplomatic discussions. Corsair activities comprise scores of incidents, while defense involves nearly as many decisions and the actions following from them. It is difficult, on the basis of Spanish documentation, to determine whether collusion among the corsairs accounted for the evolving pattern of raiding and trading. Similarly, only a few documents discussing all of the defenses of the empire exist in the archives, and, as will be shown, their recommendations were not followed in every detail and thus provide little help to the historian trying to relate events to one another in meaningful patterns. The problem, then, is to subordinate the details of corsair raids and of Spanish military responses to frameworks that will give the details meaning as parts of patterns of behavior.

Statistical descriptions of *royal* defense spending provide the basic

Illustration 1 **Total Defense Costs and Total Incidents of Violence by Corsairs, 1535–1585 (Amounts in Ducats)**

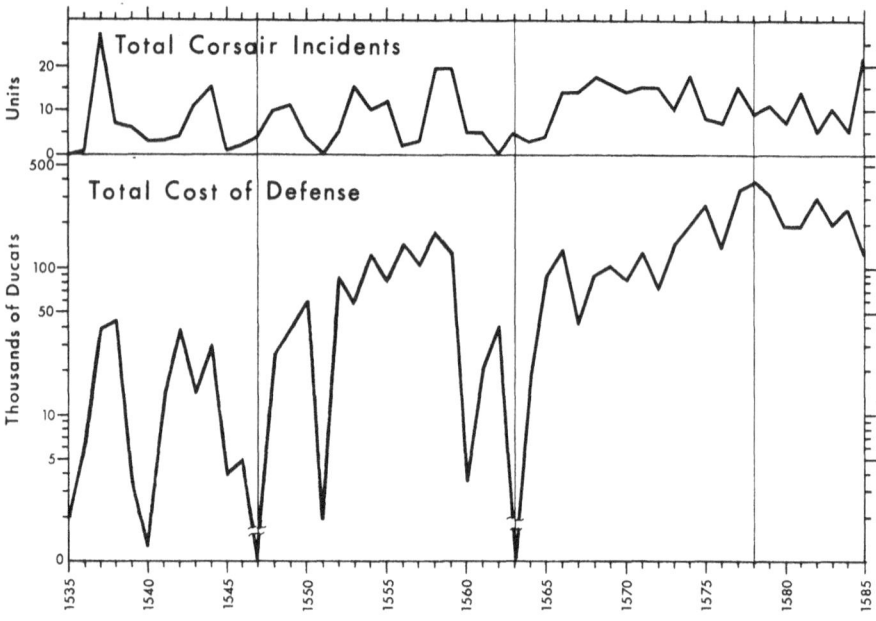

frameworks for this study. Examination of a graph (Illustration 1a) of the crown's total yearly expenses, 1535–1585, suggests that there were at least six periods of spending (measured from trough to trough), which, as might be expected, correspond roughly to the pattern of corsair activity as it too might be measured statistically (Illustrations 1b and 2).[14] Three of the first five periods, or peaks on the graphs, correspond to periods of European war (1535–1538, 1542–1544, 1552–1559) well known to historians. A fourth, the peak of spending from 1547 to 1551, is accounted for by a little-known Franco-Portuguese naval war off the Iberian Peninsula between 1548 and 1550. The remaining peak, 1560–1563, reflects a similar period of naval war off Spain, in this case against North African pirates. Study of the events indicates that the first two periods should be combined into a single period, because the break between them is due to the ill-kept truce of 1538–1542. The next three peaks should also be combined because of the importance during those years of naval patrols, an importance that translates into a pat-

Illustration 2 **Corsair Incidents by Geographic Regions, 1535–1585**

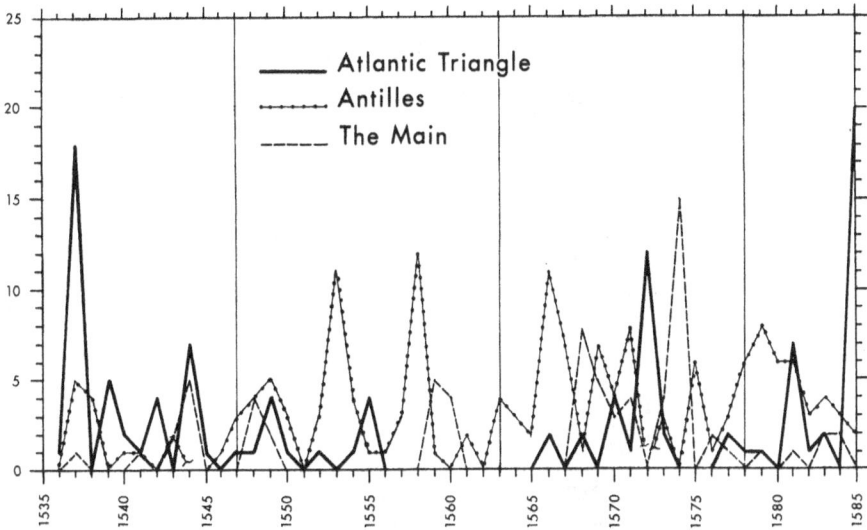

tern of mean yearly spending for defenses different from that in the previous period. These considerations account for two periods, 1535–1547 and 1548–1563. The remaining two periods used in this study, 1564–1577 and 1578–1585, are obtained by dividing the next segment of the graph at 1578, the peak year for spending and the year in which galleys were introduced into the defenses of the Indies. To contemporaries, they made a great difference, and indeed the statistical pattern of mean yearly expenses is different for the 1578–1585 period from that of the 1564–1577 period.

In sum, study of the events reduces the six periods initially indicated by the graphs to four sets of years: 1535–1547, 1548–1563, 1564–1577, 1578–1585. During each of these periods, royal spending for defense displayed a unique pattern, defined by the mean (or average) yearly costs of various types of defense (Illustration 3) and their geographic distribution (Illustration 4). These four patterns are the frameworks that allow the writing of a history of defense that is given form by the frameworks and at the same time serve partially to explain how and why those particular patterns of royal spending developed.

The reader will note that nothing has been said about the costs to

Illustration 3 **Topical Distribution of Defense Spending Expressed as a Percentage of Mean Yearly Spending**

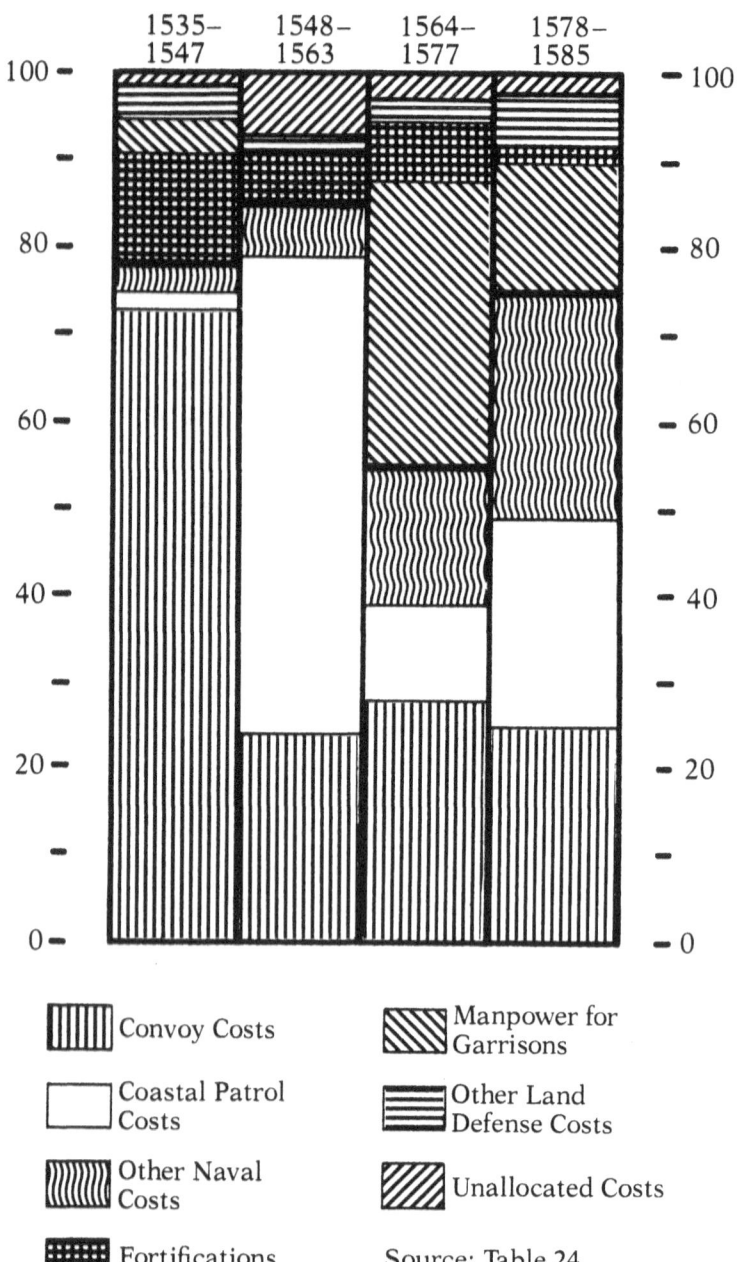

Illustration 4 **Geographic Distribution of Defense Spending Expressed as a Percentage of Mean Yearly Total Spending**

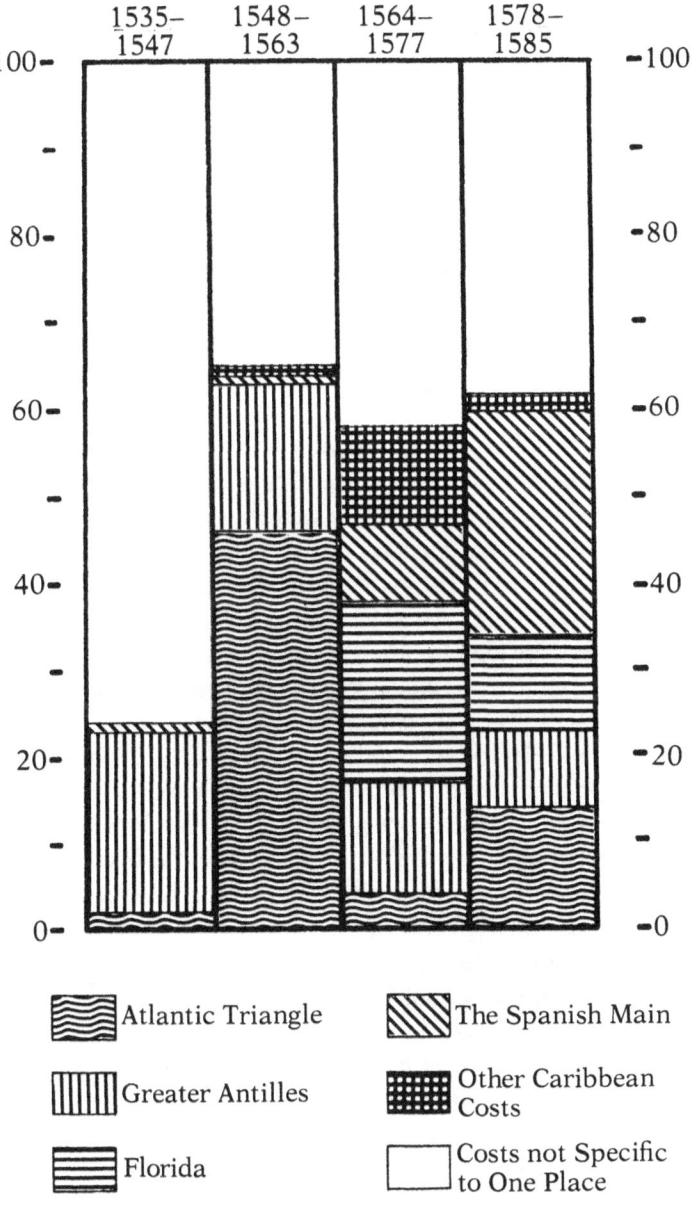

Source: Table 25

private persons of various types of defense. These costs have, of necessity, been omitted because there is no way to find out what they were and any estimation would be an exercise in imagination. The only records we have of private expenses are those of the *avería*, which were not used for this study because my concern is the evolution of state policy and the corresponding expenditures of the king's money. Accordingly the reader should bear in mind that all figures given in this study, including those for "convoys," are limited to what the crown spent. The total cost of the defense of the Indies in this period, to all parties, was more.

Any periodization and resulting set of patterns derived from numbers, however much that periodization is informed by a careful study of events, will necessarily prove to be a procrustian bed for some historical developments. Only the statistically naïve would expect otherwise. Yet this fact does not vitiate the usefulness of such patterns in explanation. That this is so is shown by the fact that of all the types of defense studied here for all of the various parts of the empire, only the history of fortifications fails to fit the gross periodization used, and then only at the division between the second and third periods.

Statistical description of complex events may have other limitations arising from the vagueness of sources or their absence for key years and from difficulties in precisely categorizing items. In this study, the data for corsair raids seem to be complete and reliable until the mid–1560s, after which reports become increasingly less precise as to time and place, tending instead to report global figures or the simple fact that there had been raids. This problem is worst for reports coming from the Main and for reports dealing with illegal trade, wherever it occurred. But despite the lack of specificity in some post–1563 reporting on corsairs, the magnitude of their activities in given areas at particular times is evident, and that is enough for understanding how the corsairs' activities affected defense and were affected by it.

Similarly, the magnitudes of royal defense spending are not much affected by a lack of treasury accounts for some years (see Appendix I) or by problems in categorizing costs, except in the case of the Indies Fleet, which served a variety of functions, being at some times a convoy escort, at others a coastal patrol, and at still others a fleet-in-being in port awaiting assignment. An ideal analysis of costs would establish a daily cost per ship for each of these uses, for each time they occur, and proceed to apportion costs accordingly. This was not done for this study because of the near impossibility of determining exactly how many men were on a given ship at any given time. Instead, the costs of crew salaries and other expenses that seemed to span a number of voyages, and hence a number of different uses of the Fleet, were categorized as costs of "general purpose" naval forces, with only those costs of repairs and victuals that could be clearly determined to have arisen from a cruise for a particular purpose being apportioned to the category in question (convoy escort or coastal patrol).[15] Because of this procedure, the cost figures for convoy escorts and coastal patrols are less than they would have been if the ideal had been followed. In all probability, however, the figures retain the same ratio to one another and to the total costs of defense as figures derived by the ideal method, and thus may be used, with caution, as guides to changing patterns of defenses.

This qualification of the reliability of the figures for convoy escorts and coastal patrols is greatest for the third period because the Indies Fleet performed both roles during those years, whereas after 1578 much of the coastal patrolling was done by galleys whose entire cost can be categorized without any reservations. Table 1 presents a breakdown of these figures by category and type of squadron (ad hoc local squadron, galleys, Indies Fleet, contribution to the *avería* for escorts other than ships of the Fleet), thus showing the extent of the problem during each period.

The third period also presents problems with the Indies Fleet's figures because the accounts of its treasurer for the period 1568–1572 are missing except for one subordinate's account. During those years, the fleet was actively engaged in patrolling and convoy escorting, but the costs of those activities, even in the limited sense noted above, cannot be fully reconstructed from other documents.

Still another qualification of the cost figures in all categories should be noted. No attempt has been made to place a value on items taken from inventories and used, unless those items were purchased for inventory, in which case the cost of purchase was categorized as "central supply." The value of these inventory items is included in the grand total for each place where such purchases were made. Because of this procedure, all the figures given for royal costs are minimums.

Readers inclined to damn quantitative history in all its forms may have concluded by this point that the numbers presented here are without utility. That critique overlooks the fact that the magnitude of the numbers and the ratios of those numbers to one another are what is important about numerical patterns. The changes in magnitude and ratio that the figures reveal, even with some qualification as to their reliability, are too great to be due entirely to the quality of the documentation and the criteria for categorization. Nor are the changes in magnitude due to the "price revolution." Price data assembled during this study show only modest increases in the prices the government paid for military goods and services. Unfortunately the data were not complete enough to allow the construction of a price index that could have been used to deflate spending totals. Moreover, the historical changes that the changing patterns of spending describe can be checked by reference to traditional literary sources and found to be accurate. The patterns of royal defense spending thus perform their purpose of guiding the historian to the more significant developments, thereby allowing him to place the myriad events that constitute the raw material of the story in proper relationships to one another and in historical perspective. That the patterns also provide some of the explanation of those events is an additional benefit.

Finally, a word about the definitions of two words used frequently in this study. *Defense* refers to Spanish use of military means to guard their empire and enforce its navigation laws in the face of attacks by other Europeans. Frontier warfare with Indians and police actions against communities of Cimarrons are thus excluded from this study except for the war with the Cimarrons of the Isthmus of Panama during the period when they were allies of John Oxenham and his men (1577–1579). The *Indies* refers to the Caribbean and the sea-lanes to it from Seville and Cádiz, and thus includes the waters of the Triangle. Events in the Pacific and the expedition to the Straits of Magellan, 1581–1584, are excluded from this study on the grounds that they had limited consequences for the development of the fight between corsairs and Spaniards, a fight that occurred almost entirely in the Atlantic and the Caribbean.

Table 1   Component Parts of Yearly Costs of Convoy Escorts and Coastal Patrols, 1568–1585 (in Ducats)

Year	Convoy Total Including Fleet Costs	Non-Fleet Costs	Fleet Costs for Convoys	Coastal Patrol Total Including Fleet Costs	Non-Fleet Costs	Fleet Costs for Coastal Patrols	Total for Indies Fleet	Non-Allocated Fleet Costs
1568	25,616	25,616	0	8,998	519	8,479	50,434	41,955
1569	55,805	17,995	37,810	7,196	14	7,182	46,109	1,117
1570	34,009	9,067	24,942	1,293	0	1,293	27,316	1,081
1571	33,991	33,991	0	2,783	2,783	0	0	0
1572	696	0	696	2,956	117	2,839	21,835	18,300
1573	100,449	42,389	58,060	15,548	0	15,548	73,956	348
1574	33,947	16,527	17,420	55,494	0	55,494	120,705	47,791
1575	85,386	20,869	64,517	19,308	0	19,308	165,123	81,298
1576	53,862	15,500	38,362	32,172	0	32,172	95,148	24,614
1577	64,487	10,710	53,777	29,300	15,207	14,093	147,688	79,818
1578	117,717	89,547	28,170	93,827	25,762	68,065	214,865	118,630
1579	82,530	16,350	66,180	103,744	33,318	70,426	169,334	32,728
1580	76,902	30,066	46,836	34,527	33,665	862	75,549	27,851
1581	39,066	36,762	2,304	48,308	48,149	159	6,829	4,366
1582	29,162	27,825	1,337	62,348	62,348	0	148,100	146,763
1583	0	0	0	16,202	16,202	0	105,364	105,364
1584	30,533	30,000	533	70,928	68,141	2,787	138,675	135,355
1585	49,480	49,480	0	51,220	49,154	2,066	2,867	801

Chapter II   **1535–1547.**
The Precedents Take Shape

THE YEAR 1535 was the last year of peace that the Indies were to experience during the sixteenth century. Omens of the renewal of war were numerous, the first reaching Spain in February in the form of reports that French ships were arming to raid Spanish shipping. Most ominous of all was the report that Pope Leo XII had told Francis I, king of France, that he was not bound by Pope Alexander VI's bulls of donation, the nominal basis for Spain's claim of an exclusive right to explore and exploit the New World. The pope's advice and the February reports were probably the only intimations the Spanish had of Jacques Cartier's second voyage. Yet even without knowing of that voyage, the Spanish could have seen the challenge to their interests in the Americas. That it came at the same time that Charles V and Francis I were disputing the ownership of Milan was used by Antoine Perrenot, later Cardinal Granvelle, as part of an unsuccessful last-minute attempt to prevent a European and colonial war by trading Charles's rights to Milan for Francis' renunciation of trade and exploration in the Indies.[1]

The empire entered the war with considerable experience in dealing with military threats. Much of that experience was codified as royal law setting out the duties of private persons to provide for their own defense. Laws covered most aspects of the protection of commerce and had been supplemented in earlier wars by the voluntary actions of the merchants of Andalusia, whose *avería* on trade provided the funds to equip a series of coastal patrol squadrons. Ever jealous of its authority, the crown had supervised the collection and administration of the *avería* and the use of the squadrons, but had contributed no more than the *avería* due on the value of royal shipments. In short, the *avería*'s coastal patrols were private operations under royal supervision. The same could be said of the militias of the Indies, although they did not exist as formal organizations before 1540 despite the traditional legal requirements that each *vecino* have arms and use them to defend himself and his king's territory. Like the *avería* organization, the militias depended on the voluntary cooperation of the individual, even though royal law and administrators might seek to coerce him into providing for his own defense.

Because of this body of law and practice placing the primary burden of defense on private shoulders, the crown was reluctant to spend its own funds for the defense of the Indies. Nonetheless, as the pattern of corsair raids developed and petitions for help came from the Indies and interest groups in Spain, the crown changed its attitude and began to authorize funds for land defenses. It was less willing to support naval defenses, although here too the course of the war, the failure of private persons to carry out their legislatively assigned defense responsibilities, and petitions by its subjects caused the crown to spend money to protect its funds crossing the ocean and gradually to realize that its interests as a shipper and as sovereign required that coastal patrols be funded from the royal treasury rather than by private interests. This realization came just before a new period of maritime hostilities made defenses essential once more.

The Pattern of Defense Spending

The result of these evolving attitudes and of historical accidents was a pattern of spending (Table 2) in which two treasure fleets absorbed large amounts (73 percent of mean yearly expenditures), while lesser amounts were spent on fortifications (13 percent of mean yearly expenditures) and caretaker garrisons (4 percent) and almost nothing (2 percent) on coastal patrols. Passive defenses, which required the enemy to attack before they could be brought to bear, thus dominated the picture (97 percent of mean yearly spending). Aggressive defenses able to

Table 2   Mean Yearly Costs of Various Types of Defense by Geographic Areas 1535–1547 (in Ducats)

Place	Total		Land Total		Man Power		Fortifications		Artillery	
Empire Total	15,234	100%	3,253	21/100	654	4/100	1,914	13/100	276	2/100
Triangle	336	100/2	0		0		0		0	
Caribbean Total	3,405	100/22	3,234	95/99	654	19/100	1,914	56/100	257	8/93
Antilles Total	3,139	100/21	3,061	97/94	649	21/99	1,914	61/100	253	8/92
Puerto Rico	817	100/5	817	100/25	131	16/20	654	3/34	24	80/9
Santo Domingo	2,267	100/15	2,188	97/67	519	23/79	1,260	8/66	182	56/66
Cuba	56	100/<1	56	100/2	0		0		46	83/17
Non-Antilles Total	265	100/2	173	65/5	5	2/1	1	<1/<1	4	4/1
The Main, Total	101	100/1	9	9/<1	5	4/1	1	/<1	0	
Cartagena	1	100/<1	1	100/<1	0	0/0	1	100/<1	4	44/1
Santa Marta	8	100/<1	8	100/<1	5	56/1	0		0	
"Venezuela"	164	100/1	164	100/5	0		0		0	

00/00 should be read: the first number is the percentage of total costs for a given area spent for the type of defense in that column (reads across). The second number is the percentage of the total for that type of defense spent in that place (reads down).

Naval Total		General Purpose		Convoys		Coastal Patrols		Place
11,829	78/100	435	3/100	11,140	73/100	250	2/100	**Empire Total**
268	80/2	0		112	33/1	153	45/61	Triangle
97	3/1	0		0		97	3/39	Caribbean Total
5	<1/<1	0		0		5	<1/2	Antilles Total
0		0		0		0		Puerto Rico
5	<1/<1	0		0		5	<1/2	Santo Domingo
0		0		0		0		Cuba
92	35/1	0		0		92	35/37	Non-Antilles Total
0		0		0		0		The Main, Total
0		0		0		0		Cartagena
0		0		0		0		Santa Marta
0		0		0		0		"Venezuela"

seek out the enemy received little royal support, although the privately developed coastal patrols in the Atlantic Triangle continued to demonstrate their value, as did those funded with the crown's money in the Caribbean.

In the Caribbean, the crown's spending concentrated on the Antilles (21 percent of total). Within the Antilles, most money was spent at Santo Domingo (15 percent), with lesser amounts at Puerto Rico (5 percent) and on the island of Cuba (less than 1 percent). This asymmetry in the areal distribution of royal expenses arose from a complex series of events in which corsair incidents, patrimonialism, strategic considerations such as population and wealth, the lack of local stone supplies, and a host of other factors played a part.

The Corsairs

The war that began in March 1536 lasted until the fall of 1544, with only the interruption of the ill-kept Truce of Nice from June 1538 to July 1542. French attacks on the communities and commerce of the Indies made all previous raiding in the Triangle and the lone raid on the Indies of 1528 seem like parlor games. Spanish losses were most numerous early in the war, as were the expressions of alarm and pessimism over the fact that the Indies were no longer secure behind the broad Atlantic. Once this fact was beyond dispute, these cries died down, although raids in areas not previously touched revived them. The continuation of raiding during the truce was also a cause for alarm because it suggested a breakdown in the traditional rules of war. Contemporaries should also have been alarmed by the beginnings of French direct illegal trade, but they were not, perhaps because it seemed to be a part of the war.

Although the raids were not unexpected, they produced reactions ranging from the gloom of the Seville merchants over the loss of three ships in December 1536 and January 1537 to the plea for action sent by an official in Panamá, who professed to be convinced that the successful capture of a ship off Nombre de Dios early in 1537 was a prelude to French attacks in the Pacific, delivered by way of the Straits of Magellan.[2] Other examples of the emotions aroused by these attacks are the decisions taken in 1538 to build new forts in the towns of the Indies—even though a coldly rational assessment of the military situation had recommended no new forts except at Santo Domingo—and Charles I's initial order to fit out a large fleet to attack the Cartier-Roberval expedition in its ports or as it emerged from them. Only fiscal reality dissuaded him from this action. Thus from the monarch on down, the initial actions of the French corsairs evoked strong, partially irrational responses among Spaniards.

During the second phase of the war, 1542–1544, raids do not seem to have been quite as much of a shock. Even the successful raids during the summer and fall of 1543 on Cubagua, Santa Marta, Cartagena, and Santiago de Cuba and the nearly successful attack on Havana by a fleet of four ships and over 300 men did not raise unusual alarm. Apparently people throughout the empire had become reconciled to the fact that the Atlantic was no longer a barrier to invasion. Their energies were directed to combating attacks and devising better defenses for the future rather than expressing anguish over the unexpected. Exaggeration and emotional pleas continued to appear in the documents, but they always seem to be parts of carefully developed plans for enlisting royal sympathy and action, usually on requests not connected with defense.

Yet another reason for the increasing acceptance of the fact of war may be found by studying the actual number of corsair raids (Table 3). Over the thirteen-year period from 1535 to 1547, at least sixty-six ships, not counting various small coastal craft not reported or only partially reported, were taken by corsairs.[3] Forty-one were seized off Spain, roughly half that number in the Antilles, and only ten on the Main. The Central American and Gulf coasts remained free from corsair activity. Towns were attacked some twenty-two times, but only fifteen raids were successful. Clearly the greatest danger to shipping was in the Triangle, followed at a distant second by the Antilles. In the Antilles, the most dangerous places were the Mona Passage, Havana, and the northern coast of Puerto Rico. The Antillian towns were the objects of the initial attacks between 1535 and 1538 but were less disturbed from 1542 to 1544. The reason for this shift and for the decrease in losses to the corsairs (except for 1544) was the development of a system of defenses that met the challenge.

The passage of time also revealed that the number of corsair ships was not as great as first reports had suggested. The largest concentration of raiders was the twenty-five sail reported off the Capes of the Algarve in the fall of 1537. Subsequent squadrons ranged between five and ten ships. In the Indies, the largest raiding party consisted of six sail, of which only four were large ships. Most of the damage was done

Table 3 **Spanish Losses to Corsairs, 1536–1547**

Year	Atlantic Triangle		Antilles			The Main			Totals	
	Ships Taken	Largest Corsair Group	Ships Taken	Raids on Land	Largest Corsair Group	Ships Taken	Raids on Land	Largest Corsair Group	Total Ships Taken	Total Raids on Land
1536	1	5							1	0
1537	18	25	5	2	2		1	2	24	2
1538		?	4	3	?				4	3
1539	5	1+		1	?				5	1
1540	2	1	1		1				3	0
1541	1	+	1		1		1	1	3	0
1542	4	10							4	0
1543		4+	2	2	3	2+	5?a	6	4+	7?
1544	7	11	+	1	3	5	1	6	12+	2
1545	1	1							1	0
1546		+	1	1	1				1	1
1547	1?	+	3	1	1				4	1
Totals	40?		17+	11		9+	6?		66+	17?a

+   designates a generalized report without specific numbers or my inference of incidents from incomplete documentation.

a   Only three raids on towns on the Main can be documented for 1543, but an additional two may have occurred in the fall, according to a report of 1544.

by single ships; only the sieur de Roberval's squadron of 1543 had more—the six just noted.

In short, the end of novelty, adjustment to a wartime psychology, realization of the actual risk run and of the small number of corsairs, and improved defenses took the edge off the alarm and gloom of townsmen, seamen, and royal officials alike.

Passing almost unnoticed amidst the raids and reactions to them was the development of illegal trade. From the time of Christopher Columbus' return from his first voyage, the crown had issued a series of navigation laws that required all persons and ships bound for the Indies to register and obtain a license from the Casa de Contratación at Seville.

Any person, merchandise, or ship found in the Indies without that license was considered to be there illegally unless they came from the Canary Islands, to which slightly different legal norms applied during the periods when they were permitted to trade directly with the Indies. These Spanish laws had first been given international force by the Treaty of Tordesillas, which made them part of the territorial settlement between the Spanish and Portuguese crowns. No comparable agreement existed with either the French or English crowns, not that such agreements would have meant much to subjects of either crown, who would surely have followed the example of the Portuguese seamen who violated the Tordesillas agreement by appearing at Española in 1514. Treaties, and investigations such as one made in 1535, to the contrary notwithstanding, the Portuguese continued to appear at irregular intervals, claiming to have been forced off course on their ways to or from Brazil and Africa.[4] In many cases their cargoes were confiscated by the crown's officials, but in others the Portuguese were allowed to sell some of their wares in order to buy provisions for the continuation of their voyages. This was a quiet trade and did not involve threats of violence by the traders.

In contrast to the peaceful Portuguese trade, the first recorded examples of French trading involved the implicit threat of violence. In August 1543 and October 1544, French ships traded at Cabo de la Vela, apparently selling goods stolen from Spanish ships captured off or near that town.[5] These French assays of illegal trade occurred at a time when the Spanish seemed about to open their trade to the French in return for territorial concessions as part of the Peace of Crépy-en-Laonnis (see below, page 64). Set against that background and the obvious use of force to bring about the trade, these incidents did not alarm the Spanish crown. Illegal trade by the French, like that of the Portuguese, did not seem to be a major problem before 1548. Accordingly, defenses were oriented to protecting towns and ships against raiders.

The Defense of Commerce

The basic legislation governing the defense of commerce had been developed in the 1520s when the danger to Spanish shipping was confined to the Triangle. In July 1522 the crown issued a set of armament requirements, graduated according to tonnage from a minimum of eighty tons, for ships in the Indies trade. These rules were intended to ensure that each ship could be defended against boarding parties. In combination with the coastal patrol squadron which the merchants of Andalusia had established the preceding year, this new law should have provided an adequate defense for commerce in the Triangle, but it did not. Four years after it was issued, the crown ordered that ships sailing to and from the Indies had to travel in groups of at least ten ships, with Seville and Santo Domingo being designated as assembly points. These groups were to be escorted from the Azores to Seville and from Seville to the Canaries by the *avería's* squadrons. In effect, a system of convoys had been created in the Triangle.[6]

The legally mandated system of ship armament and group sailings was not followed in practice except for the outward voyage from Seville, and even then frauds in armament were practiced. Ships whose artillery and other weapons had passed inspection might sail without them or with the weapons so stored as to be useless in the event of an attack. On the return voyage, ships left the Indies without the required weapons and frequently without any formal inspection by local officials. Even ships that may have sailed as a group could not always keep together, nor could properly armed ships always keep their weapons abroad if the need arose to lighten the ship. The result, from the 1520s to the early 1540s, was that poorly armed ships arrived singly or in small groups (two to four ships) at the Azores, where they were easy prey for the corsairs.

To remedy this state of affairs, the merchants and crown had cooperated in the development of the *avería* system of coastal patrols. These squadrons of two to three ships were designed to drive corsairs from the Capes of the Algarve and the coast of Andalusia and to go to the Azores to meet groups of merchantmen and escort them to San Lúcar. In general the squadrons performed their function well, but conflicts between the crown and the merchants arose because the crown invariably wanted the squadrons used at times and in places in which many of the merchants, who paid most of the cost of the system and partially controlled it through two representatives on a three-man board, had no interest. For example, in early 1535 the crown tried to get the merchants to fit out a squadron to meet the threat of ships said to be fitting out in France to raid Spanish commerce. The merchants responded by suggesting a method of financing that would have placed a very heavy burden on the crown's remissions from the Indies. Unwilling to accept those terms, the crown let the matter drop.[7]

Despite the problems that this system of ship armament, group sailings, and merchant-crown–controlled coastal patrol squadrons had shown, the crown reinstituted it after war had begun in the spring of 1536. Events during the next two years further revealed the inadequacy of such measures, causing first the crown and then the merchants to turn to convoys not only in the Triangle but also for the return voyage from the Indies. The stage was thus set for the introduction of convoys when war was resumed in 1542.

Neither the *avería*'s patrol squadron commanded by Diego López de las Roelas, which patrolled off Andalusia and the Algarve from July to November 1536, nor the squadron under Miguel de Perea, fitted out at royal expense at Málaga and used to escort a group of merchantmen to the Canaries in early 1537, were able to prevent losses among Spanish ships returning from the Indies via the Azores. Perea's capture of one French ship, from a group of three that had attacked him while he was refitting at Palma, was hardly compensation for losses such as the 100,000 ducats that the French took from a single ship that they caught alone in the Azores. That loss probably led to the decision of early 1537 to send to the Indies a new, larger patrol squadron commanded by the courtier Blasco Núñez Vela to gather treasure and return it in what was in effect a convoy, rather than leave the squadron on patrol in the Triangle. Perea's subsequent return to Cádiz for reinforcements and refitting did not supply the need for effective patrols in the Triangle, for his squadron too was sent off to the Indies to strengthen the first. Indeed, the only defense that shipping coming from the Azores received during the spring and summer of 1537 was that afforded by the Portuguese royal navy, which was in the Azores awaiting the returning East Indiamen.[8]

With the coming of fall, the crown ordered yet another patrol fleet but found that the Casa could not raise the money for it. Again, the Portuguese lent some protection to Spanish shipping, now under orders to wait at the Azores for an escort before proceeding to Spain.[9] An effective system of maritime defenses was still to be found.

The reliance on ad hoc measures continued, however, for the balance of the war. During the spring of 1538, outbound shipping was forced to await the sailing of ships armed by the *adelantado* Hernando de Soto for the conquest of Florida, while the Casa attempted to find ships to form a new patrol squadron for the Azores-Capes route. The reason for that patrol squadron appeared safely off San Lúcar in March. Núñez Vela and Perea had run the gauntlet from the Azores without incident, bringing home some 230,000 ducats in private remittances in addition to the crown's revenues.[10] The new squadron was disbanded before it was even ready to sail, but Perea's battered ships were held while the Casa sounded out the merchants on using them, at *avería* expense, to patrol in the Triangle. The merchants were agreeable but also wanted to send Perea to Havana, whence he would return as an escort for a convoy of ships.[11] Like the crown, they had concluded that the system of the 1520s, with its heavy reliance on private obedience to legislation and hit-or-miss escorting in the Triangle by small squadrons of warships, was not adequate for the defense of commerce under the conditions that had developed in the Triangle during the late 1530s. Modifying the crown's idea of a treasure fleet, they were prepared to institute transatlantic convoys under the control of the *avería* deputies.

Conclusion of the Truce of Nice (July 14–16, 1538) removed the need for naval defenses. Nonetheless, they continued to be discussed because of dissatisfaction with the measures taken up to that time. Among others, Núñez Vela was asked for his views, which he gave in a long memorandum that incorporated the best of recent experience. He suggested that the basic defense of the ships in the Indies trade should remain the individual ship, armed to a higher standard than that set in 1522 and sailing in groups of at least six ships. In addition, he argued for a squadron of nine ships, each up to 200 tons burden, to patrol in the Triangle. Once a year, three of those ships would be sent to the Indies to escort home all merchantmen who wanted to make the run. On the way to the rendezvous point, this squadron could patrol the Antilles, thereby satisfying the demands being voiced in the Indies for coastal patrols.[12]

Because of a lack of records, it is not known what decision the crown took on this recommendation, yet it clearly was a sort of blueprint for the policy that developed after 1541. In the interim, commerce resumed its peacetime pattern of unrestricted sailings, although the use of groups may have continued. Continued also were ad hoc measures for dealing with the corsairs who appeared prior to 1542. A French raider in the Azores in 1539 was countered by sending an armed caravel to warn and escort inbound shipping. But an English raider off the Capes in

1540 went undisturbed because the merchants refused to pay an *avería* to support a squadron and the Portuguese crown would not send its ships against him.[13]

News of the preparation of the Cartier-Roberval expedition set the decision-making apparatus in motion once again in a kind of replay of the events of 1537–1539, with the exceptions that in this case a study of convoying preceded the decision to fit out the crown's treasure fleet and the merchants eventually won the right to fit out their own convoy.

Because the objective of the French expedition was not clear at first, the crown sent out orders in the fall of 1540 for reports on how best to defend commerce. If replies were received, they must have suggested a reluctance on the part of the merchants to put up money for increased armament and the convoying of shipping. But because the French threat was growing more serious with each mail from the north, in March 1541 the Council of the Indies resorted to the precedent of 1537 and ordered the crown's revenues held in the Indies in anticipation of the arrival of another royal treasure fleet, which would protect them against Cartier. The emperor then decided to use this fleet to attack Cartier, but that plan was abandoned because it would have cost too much.

Preparations for a treasure fleet were resumed in the fall because it was clear that peace would not last much longer in Europe. Uncertainty about the size and purpose of the squadron, continued fiscal problems resolved only by resorting to loans, and general supply problems delayed preparations. By mid-May 1542, when Martín Alonso de los Ríos was appointed captain-general, the squadron had shrunk from ten ships to four, with two caravels as escorts. Delays still continued, compounded by the taking of accounts at the end of July. The fleet finally sailed at the end of August. The long delays were an omen of the fleet's eventual failure to bring back large amounts of money.[14]

While Alonso de los Ríos made his way along the track of his predecessor, Núñez Vela, war broke out in Europe and with it the renewal of raids on Spanish shipping in the Triangle and in the Indies. To meet this problem in the Triangle, the crown ordered a coastal squadron to be paid for with *avería* funds. Four ships and a *patache*, under the command of Captain Rodrigo de Gatapenda, sailed on October 10 for Madeira to recover cargoes and passengers put ashore there by shipmasters obeying royal orders to deposit both unless their ships could come to Spain in a group of well-armed ships. From Madeira the squadron passed to the Azores, returning to San Lúcar in early 1543.[15]

The cost of Gatapenda's squadron led to a political skirmish between the crown and the merchants. At their insistence, and to mollify them because French corsairs had taken ships on the Andalusian coast left "naked" by Gatapenda's departure, the crown reduced the *avería* from 6 percent to 4 percent. Sensing their advantage because of the crown's penury and hence its dependence on the *avería* for patrols in the Triangle, the merchants next demanded some of the ships that the crown had ordered prepared to go to meet Alonso de los Ríos for escorting merchantmen to the New World. The crown gave in, ordering two of Gatapenda's four ships retained at Seville to escort a group of ten merchantmen to the Canaries. The rest of Gatapenda's ships were hastily refitted and sent to sea under the command of Hernándo Blas.[16]

Blas spent the next three months patrolling in the Azores until, on the eve of Corpus Christi, he met the convoy of Alonso de los Ríos. The combined fleets arrived at San Lúcar on June 4. Much as many merchants had suspected, the Casa immediately seized all private shipments carried by the fleet.[17]

The ships detained at San Lúcar to escort the merchantmen to the Canaries were placed under the command of Captain Juan López de Isasti. He sailed with a group of at least ten ships, probably in March or early April. On the way to the Canaries he captured a French ship and its prize but was unable to prevent the escape of three *pataches* that had been with the ship. Isasti apparently continued on his way until the merchantmen were safely beyond the Canaries. He then sailed to Madeira, where he picked up monies deposited by shipmasters. He returned to San Lúcar early in June.[18]

The return of the Alonso de los Ríos fleet and the Isasti patrol led to another political struggle between the crown and the merchants over the form of the defense of commerce and who would pay for it. The merchants had already secured a further reduction in the *avería* to 2.5 percent, but they now pressed for the right to collect this on the remissions just brought back by Alonso de los Ríos. The crown indignantly rejected this idea, pointing out that it had spent a great deal of money for the fleet. It did not add, although it might have, that the squadron had not brought back as much money as had been expected, so that the proportionate costs were very high. Undaunted, the merchants next asked the crown for permission to set up their own convoys to the Indies, using an *avería* to pay the costs of escorting warships. As bait for the approval of this scheme, from which the crown would benefit like any other shipper, they promised to pay for a patrol fleet in the Triangle that summer. Already preparing to grant the merchants' request for a *consulado* (merchants' guild) as part of a general reform of the administration of the Casa de Contratación, the crown agreed.[19] The convoy would provide security at a lower cost than the royal treasure fleets had been able to do, even when those costs were forced upon the owners of seized funds in the form of an *avería*.

The orders that instituted this new convoy system were drawn up by the *licenciado*, Gregorio López, *visitador* of the Casa de Contratación, on August 9, 1543, and ratified by the crown in October. These orders fused earlier laws governing ship armament and group sailings with the fiscal device of the *avería* and the military device of the escorting warship. The minimum size of ships allowed to make the crossing was raised to 100 tons, and the Casa and shipmasters were enjoined to see that all ships were armed according to the formula of 1522. For the duration of the war with France, ships so armed were to sail in two groups of at least ten ships each, one to sail in March and the other in September. Each group would be escorted by a warship whose owner would be compensated by an *avería* on the goods carried by the group for cargo not carried and for the additional expenses of soldiers and weapons. This escort would convoy the ships to the Caribbean, sailing directly for Havana. There it would wait for three months, cruising for corsairs if its captain wished, while shipping assembled from the Main and New Spain. At the end of that period it would sail for Spain with the ships that had gathered at Havana. Shipping gathered at Santo Domingo did not have to go to Havana to join an escorted group but was required to form its own convoy by selecting one ship to be partially unloaded, with twenty soldiers and their gear taking the place of the cargo thus removed. In both cases, the escort's lost freights and additional costs were to be paid by an *avería* on the goods escorted.[20]

In a related reform designed to free the Casa's officials from judicial matters so that they could carry out their administrative duties, the Council of the Indies approved the formation of a *consulado* by the merchants of Seville.[21]

Even before all the details of this new plan were worked out, the ships in the Isasti squadron, augmented by one of Blas's ships, had been resupplied and sent out to patrol the coast and Capes in an effort to provide security for half a dozen ships reported to be coming from Santo Domingo. Isasti reached the Azores in October, but his death soon afterwards caused the squadron to return to Seville, where it was discharged from duty.[22]

The first of the new convoys sailed on November 3, 1543, with Blasco Núñez Vela, now viceroy of Peru, as its commander as far as Nombre de Dios. Only one warship, a converted merchantman, accompanied the convoy. The longer the Consulado thought about that, and the more information it obtained on the funds awaiting shipment in the Indies and the numbers of corsairs there or rumored to be fitting out for the Indies, the less happy it became. It requested, and the crown approved, the sending of two more ships to join the escort for the Havana-Spain return. By early 1544, the reinforcement had grown to three ships, which were to carry matériel to arm another two. In addition, the squadron was to stop at Santo Domingo to take under escort all ships returning to Spain from there.[23]

It was one thing to plan, another to execute. Bad weather, an accident to one of the ships, and demands for an immediate patrol to the Azores to pick up 100,000 pesos de oro left there by a merchantman resulted in the two good ships being sent there during May and June. Upon their return, they were refitted and sent off in August to meet the convoy coming in from Havana. The fact of that voyage was then used by the merchants to fend off a royal suggestion that additional ships be fitted out to protect commerce against three French galleasses that were in transit from Marseilles to the Channel ports. As a backup, the merchants suggested the Portuguese royal fleet, a suggestion that the crown followed up on.[24]

Shortly after the merchants thus rebuffed the crown, the second convoy under merchant auspices sailed under the command of Juan López de Archuleta. It apparently made the prescribed run to Havana, gathered shipping there, and returned, arriving in 1545.[25]

The merchants, no less than the crown, could be subject to unusual fears for the safety of remissions from the Indies. Thus when it was learned in mid-September that six French ships had attacked two Aragonese ships off Cape Santa María, Portugal, the deputies decided to fit out four ships to reinforce the escorts bringing in the fleet. The Portuguese had replied by that time that they were willing to use a royal galleon and four caravels to clear the Capes and escort the convoy safely into a port in the Algarve, but they declined to allow the galleon to go to San Lúcar, citing the dangerous coast as an excuse. Because of earlier troubles with the Portuguese over the taxation of monies in transit

1535–1547. THE PRECEDENTS TAKE SHAPE

through Portugal, the proposal to use the Portuguese escorts was apparently dropped in favor of fitting out up to six ships for a quick trip to the Capes. In fact, only one ship, the *Santa María*, seems to have been sent. The 1543 convoy and her escorts returned to San Lúcar without incident at the end of November.[26]

The signing of the Peace of Crépy-en-Laonnis (September 18, 1544) brought a temporary end to French commerce raiding off the Iberian Peninsula, but it was soon resumed because of the continuation of the Anglo-French side of the war and renewed French hostilities against Portuguese shipping sailing for Brazil and Africa. Although Spanish ships were not supposed to be attacked because Spain was a neutral in both conflicts, the crown and shipping interests at Seville could not be sure that the French would respect their neutrality. Consequently, when the numbers of French ships began to rise in 1546, the crown received a memorial from the Consulado on the subject of convoys and the protection of commerce. The Consulado now found that both the convoy system and coastal patrols supported by an *avería* were intolerable financial burdens on trade and that the convoy restricted the free movement of shipping. So far as the merchants were concerned at this juncture, they would prefer an *avería* that might pay for the costs of extra artillery and soldiers aboard underloaded merchantmen. Perhaps amused by this sudden shift in merchant policy, the crown pressed for additional statements about convoys and other methods of defending commerce, but the Casa and the Consulado ignored those requests. They were satisfied with the crown's temporary orders to send ships to the Indies in groups and to require ships to gather in, arm at, and sail from the Azores as a group.[27]

Having made up its mind that the *avería* should be ended, its accounts wound up, and surplus property sold, the Consulado not only neglected to comment on the defense of commerce but also ignored royal hints that a coastal patrol squadron might be in order in view of reports of French ships arming to attack the West Indiamen. Such hints were sent in September and December 1546 and January 1547.[28]

The actual presence of French raiders off the Capes in March 1547 caused the Consulado to change its position. It now agreed to a royal order to fit out a caravel to go to the Azores to warn inbound ships to wait there until a squadron of two ships and a caravel could be sent to escort them to San Lúcar. Preparations were begun, but the ships were soon taken over by the crown for use in a squadron that was to take arms to Licenciado La Gasca for his use in Peru and for arming ships for his return from the Isthmus of Panamá with the booty from suppressing the Pizarro Rebellion.[29] No patrol squadron got to sea that summer.

At the same time that it ordered the Casa and Consulado to fit out a patrol fleet for the Triangle, the crown ordered the Casa to reinstitute the convoy and to see that all ships arriving in the Azores that spring gathered, armed themselves, and sailed to Spain as a group. Individual ships that missed the group were to unload their bullion at the islands and report the size of escort required for their safety. The Casa at once objected, sending Prince Philip a copy of Gregorio López' order and stating that to follow it would mean that the ships then ready (mid-April) would have to wait until September to sail. Moreover, the Casa did not have a "warship" at hand. It had just sent orders that the seven or eight ships then at San Lúcar were to sail. Reluctantly, the crown approved this recommendation but told the Casa to see if two or three more ships might not be gotten ready in fifteen days to join the others, thus making a group of ten ships. All were to be armed according to the Formula of 1522.[30] Thus the net result of this exchange was to reestablish the group-sailing requirement with a minimum group of ten ships.

The rule remained in effect during 1548, although at least three merchants thought they might obtain permission to send five ships as a group. In asking for advice on this request, the crown specifically asked whether granting that permission would do harm to other merchants' interests;[31] the Casa's reply is not recorded. The question suggests how far some merchants had come since 1546, when they all rejected the restrictions that the group and convoy systems put on their normally free-wheeling activities. This is the first hint of the "monopoly mentality" that characterized the system after about 1570.

The crown's willingness to pay the costs of a patrol in the Triangle in December 1547 was the first indication of a shift in policy concerning the funding of patrols. Consideration of this question must have begun in 1546 when the crown reopened the question of the convoys and other means of defending commerce. Unfortunately, the documentation for the decision has not been found.

Although the steps leading to the abandonment of reliance on the *avería* cannot be fully stated, the reasons for it seem clear from the events just discussed. During the late thirties and early forties the crown had found that it could not depend on the merchants to agree with it about the need for patrols in the Triangle, the area of greatest danger to shipping and hence to royal funds crossing the Atlantic. Royal interests in the safety of these funds were, in effect, up for veto whenever the merchants felt that their economic interests would suffer more from the collection of an *avería* than from possible loss of cargo to raiders. Although it shared merchant interest in having cargoes assessed as lightly as possible to pay for defense, the crown apparently felt that it could not allow any remittance to itself, whether in money, bullion, or tropical products, to be lost. Nor could the crown ignore the duty of the sovereign to take steps to protect commerce, even from itself.

The single escort convoys of 1543 and 1544 had been steps in the direction of providing a cheap, secure form of shipping under wartime conditions but had had the defect of not including all ships returning from the Indies and in particular those coming from the Antilles. Moreover, the Consulado could exercise a veto, as it did in 1547. The alternative policy of a royal treasure fleet was costly. After the seizure of 1538, merchants had been reluctant to ship funds on the fleet of 1542. The seizure of those funds as well had foreclosed future possibilities of getting merchants to ship on a royally funded fleet and of paying some of its costs as freight and *averías* on the value of their cargoes. The crown could not afford to send such costly fleets for just its own revenues on a regular basis and could not afford to receive its funds at irregular intervals. Caught between the conflicting goals of a cheap defense of commerce and a desire for the safety of its remittances from the Indies, the crown was finally being forced to use its own funds to provide for the protection of commerce in those areas where shipping was in greatest danger. This decision solved not only the problem of defending shipping in the Triangle but also answered demands from the Antilles for a patrol fleet there.

Coastal Patrols in the Indies

In the Indies, the crown's reliance on private persons for the defense of its interests included the defense of commerce under the rules and changing conditions just noted and the use of militia troops as the backbone of the defense of the towns and cities of the area. But just as the crown had found the private defense of commerce unsatisfactory in the Triangle, so too in the Caribbean royal officials found that the crown's resources were needed to defend shipping against raiders. Realization that royally paid garrisons were needed to supplement the militias did not come until after 1547, however.

Interest in coastal patrol squadrons for the Caribbean can probably be dated from the first patrol, fitted out at Santo Domingo in 1528 to chase the lone French raider of that year, although the subject was not mentioned in the decade of peace that followed. War and the losses of shipping that resulted (Table 2), the disastrous fate of the ad hoc patrol squadron fitted out at Havana in March 1537,[32] and the brief appearances of the Núñez Vela and Perea fleets—with the apparent result that corsairs were not to be found where the fleets were—all served to revive the topic. So too did the loss of a ship off Española in 1540.

The first proposal for a permanent patrol force in the Antilles came from Diego Cavallero, an important merchant and resident of Santo Domingo with well-placed relatives at court. He proposed that three lead-sheathed caravels be based at Santo Domingo, with a system of convoys to protect oceanic shipping moving between Seville and Santo Domingo. Three years later the Audiencia of Santo Domingo took up his plan, requesting first two and then four ships. Havana, meanwhile, had imposed an excise tax on meat with the objective of accumulating a fund that would allow it to buy its own galliot for use against raiders.[33]

The crown's reply to the requests from Santo Domingo was to authorize discussions and whatever the Audiencia might think best—a formula that the judges interpreted to mean authority to fit out squadrons when necessary, using royal money. The first occasion when a patrol seemed appropriate occurred in March 1543. Two French ships and a *patache* appeared off San Germán and took four caravels on their ways from Santo Domingo to the salt pans near Cubagua (probably Araya). To counter this menace, the Audiencia sent out Captain Eugenio de Carrión with two ships, two caravels, and 250 men. The French were intercepted and the larger of what proved to be two ships was captured, along with forty crewmen and 2,000 pesos worth of cargo. The caravels chased the *patache*, but it escaped. Triumphantly, the treasury officials predicted that the corsairs "will not pass here so facilely as they have until now."[34]

This idle boast was given the lie by events during June and July, when corsairs took all the towns of the Main plus Margarita and Cubagua for good measure. True enough, they did not attack off Española.

A sequel to French raids on Cabo de la Vela was the fitting out of the escort of the 1543 convoy for patrol duty by that city, which evidently hoped to recapture some of the ships and goods lost to the French and felt that the cause justified an unauthorized loan from the royal treasury. Unluckily, the captain of the ship was killed by lightning, which also damaged the masts. Thus the ship's subsequent encounter with French ships near Santa Marta resulted in a standoff for want of vigorous command and adequate equipment. Reporting this incident, the residents of Margarita asked for a patrol fleet for their area.[35] As with all their subsequent requests for a patrol fleet, this one went unanswered.

No further coastal patrols, or proposals for patrols, were made in the Caribbean until June 1547. Once again the appearance of a corsair in the Mona Passage prompted the Audiencia of Santo Domingo to order the fitting out of two ships, but the squadron did not sail because it was learned that the French had left the area.[36]

Thus in the Caribbean, as in the Triangle, the failure of shipmasters to arm their ships properly, to stay in groups, and to fight when attacked led to the search for some other method of protecting commerce. When it was not provided by a series of ad hoc patrol squadrons fitted out in a frequently futile effort to catch corsairs after they had committed their crimes, nor by the escorts for the convoys—which had other purposes and which were but briefly in the area—the residents of the Antilles turned to the crown for the funds for a permanent patrol squadron. By 1547, the crown was inclined to grant that request.

The Militias

The militias were the other device that the crown created to make use of private resources for the defense of the Indies. Because the crown continued to rely on the militias until after 1563 and because certain aspects of the topic cannot be discussed with reference to just the 1535-1547 period, the discussion that follows will encompass events to the end of the 1550s and population considerations to 1586. The reader wedded to neat periodizations will pardon these unavoidable deviations from the overall scheme of the work.

The legal bases of the militia were vague during the sixteenth and even the seventeenth centuries. Juan de Solorzano names two general bases: self-defense, formalized into a medieval Castilian law making it an obligation of each resident of a town, and the obligation of subjects to respond to a call to arms when the king was personally in the field in their area. By extention, the latter applied when the crown's agents were directing defensive military activities on its behalf, although in that case Solorzano notes the elements of appeal to duty, hope of reward, and coercion present in the creating of military forces. On that same practical level, the great jurist recognized that even though it was a subject's legal duty to bear arms in a brief defensive war in his immediate area without any payment of his expenses, in fact the crown had to pay for the defense of the kingdom. Practice had thus converted the crown's obligation to pay for an extended campaign into its obligation to pay for any campaign and had changed the *encomendero*'s duty to maintain horses and armed retainers in proportion to the value of his grant into no greater obligation than that of any other subject.[37] The beginning of these changes is observable before 1586.

As early as 1528 the inhabitants of Cubagua and Santo Domingo demonstrated that they understood that they were obligated to defend themselves and the interests and possessions of their sovereign at their own expense.[38] As will be shown below, at other times and places the residents of other towns in the Caribbean demonstrated the same understanding of their military duties.

The crown made militia duties an explicit obligation of residents of the Indies in a *cédula* of October 7, 1540, in which it directed its officials throughout the Caribbean to organize militias, to see that they drilled every four months, and to require that individual householders keep appropriate small arms. At the same time, it instructed the Casa de Contratación to try to find a contractor(s) to supply the weapons that the militias would need.[39] In subsequent years, the crown instructed its officials to drill the militia and made provisions for the forced sale of weapons to residents who lacked them.[40]

Implementation of royal orders for the militias was nominally the responsibility of the town council of each town, acting in concert with or under orders from the local royal officials. The published resolutions (*acuerdos*) of the Havana council provide examples of the process from the 1550s onwards. But governors—and at Santo Domingo the president of the Audiencia—tended to take over this function because of the growing unwillingness of many militiamen to perform their duties and because, later, the governors became captains-generals.[41]

Indeed, it was one thing to legislate a militia, but quite another to make it effective. To be effective, the militias required enough men, weapons, discipline, and leadership to perform well, especially in battles against equal numbers of corsairs. These characteristics were lacking almost everywhere in the Caribbean to one degree or another, with the result that usually outnumbered, outdisciplined, and outled militias soon ceased to offer more than perfunctory resistance to the corsairs.

The key to the militia system was numbers. Population figures from the Caribbean towns during the sixteenth century are few and frequently unreliable where they do exist. Only Juan López de Velasco's figures for ca. 1574 provide a complete survey of the area prior to 1586.[42] Yet even this scattered demographic data can be impressionistically summarized into a table (Table 4) that makes the basic problem brutally clear: prior to 1560, only Santo Domingo could muster more than 200 able men and boys. By 1585, the largest force that could be assembled from local manpower was approximately 500 men. Forces of that size were available on the Isthmus of Panamá, at Havana, Santo Domingo, and Cartagena. But to assemble such numbers, all available men had to be gathered from entire provinces or, as at Havana, from entire islands.

Additional men were available in most communities if blacks, Indians, and transients were armed. Blacks and transients seem to have been viewed with suspicion, the former because of fears of arming slaves (the free black community seems to have been small), and the latter because they might become a "fifth column" within the town in the event of attack.[43] Nonetheless, both groups were recruited for the militias upon occasion. The use of blacks as auxiliaries to the white militias is recorded for Havana (1555, in the defense against Jacques de Sores), for Puerto Rico (1557), for Cartagena (1560, 1572), and for Santo Domingo (1583). Transients were probably included in the militias at most ports, but a record exists only for Santo Domingo (1583).[44] Indians were used at Santa Marta (1548) and Curaçao (1570).[45] In short, although blacks and white transients provided a large potential reserve of manpower for the militias, the latter were ordinarily composed only of white, locally resident males. That manpower base was clearly inadequate.

There is little direct evidence about the quality of the militias' leadership. If there were royal officials in a town, the militia was normally led by the highest ranking among them. In other cases the town council selected a leader, probably subject to the approval of the troops. Prior to the 1560s few royal officials seem to have been former soldiers and even fewer had been officers, a situation that was probably true among the civilian population as well. Thus the typical commander of militia units was probably not unlike the governor of Cartagena who, in the

Table 4   **Estimated Average and Maximum Strengths of Militias, 1535—1585**

Place	Average	Maximum	Notes
San Juan, Puerto Rico	50–80	150–200	Tended to increase in later decades.
Santo Domingo	450–500	1000+	Numbers decline after 1550s. Maximum dependent on trade conditions and transient population.
Havana	100	500	Havana manpower rises from c. 25 to c. 250 over period, but not all men are available. Maximum based on 1586 musters.
Vera Cruz Coast	200?	Unknown	Could draw on central New Spain.
Campeche	20–50	100	Maximum based on 1586 muster.
Honduras Coast	50–100	Unknown	
Nombre de Dios	Unknown	700+	Maximum based on men coming from Panamá.
Cartagena	200	300+	Average supplies from c. 1560 onwards.
Santa Marta	30–50	Unknown	
Río de la Hacha	c. 50	Unknown	
Cubagua	100	Unknown	Average is for 1530s and 1540s only.
Margarita	c. 75	Unknown	

Source: Appendix II.
Qualifications: Averages reflect numbers of men at musters, but not all were armed. Maximums include large numbers of transients and could be increased by 50% – 100% by arming blacks and Indians and by stripping nearby towns of men.

attack of 1559, went home to lunch and a siesta when the corsairs failed to attack during the morning, only to be routed from his home and the city when the attack came during lunch. Less common were men like the governor of Havana who managed to rally his few forces to counterattack Jacques Sores in 1555. Nor should it be forgotten that these essentially civilian-led militias had officers who shared the same motivations as their men to avoid loss of life and property in battles with equal or superior enemy forces. The collapse of the militias during the 1550s is final, if indirect evidence of the poor quality of their leadership.

1535–1547. THE PRECEDENTS TAKE SHAPE 43

Down to 1563 the militias were poorly armed because of strict royal control over the importation of weapons into the New World. Individual immigrants were usually allowed to take a number of daggers, swords, and firearms for their personal use, but no importations of guns as merchandise were allowed except in 1537–1546, 1553, and 1563, and even then the merchants had to sign a contract with the crown that specified the numbers and types of weapons to be sent to the Indies. But none of these contracts seems to have resulted in shipments of weapons to Santo Domingo (1537, 1563), the Main (1537), or Peru (1553), probably because most residents of those areas could not have afforded to pay the price a merchant would have had to charge to make his expenses and a profit.[46] Nor were many weapons made in the New World, with the possible exception of pikes or pikelike pole weapons that could have been made by any blacksmith.

In the absence of a commerce in weapons, the crown had to fill the role of supplier. At first it insisted on supplying weapons only to its forts (Table 5), where they were available for emergency use, but with the passage of the years, it came to see that the most effective method of arming the militias—and the cheapest from its point of view—was to order the Casa de Contratación to send weapons to various towns for forced sale to residents who lacked arms (see Table 6 for the crown's gross disbursements for all aspects of militia arming and training). The first shipment made under that policy was in 1557 (Table 5), although at least one shipment was supposed to have been made as early as 1539.[47] The shipment of 1557 brought limited improvements to the armament of the militias in question but did nothing for the smaller towns, whose militias still had to make do with whatever weapons they could buy or make. Nor did the crown's shipments of weapons deal with what proved to be the Achilles heel of the militias: a lack of powder with which to practice. An attempt to solve that problem was not to come until after 1563.

The results of this lack of an effective policy for supplying the militias with arms were reported from the Indies at every turn. Typical of the reports of the 1540s is one from Puerto Rico (1541), which states that the militia was drilling regularly but lacked arms.[48] During the 1550s the reports become more precise as to numbers of different types of weapons, revealing that the majority of the men carried pikes but usually lacked the shields and armor appropriate to the pikeman of the times, while lesser numbers had matchlocks or, rarely, crossbows, and only a

Table 5 Crown Shipments of Small Arms and Munitions, 1535–1563

Shipments of 1537, 1542, 1545

	Santo Domingo, 1537	Puerto Rico, 1542	Havana, 1545
Crossbows	63	0	24
Matchlocks	65	20	0
Thrusting Weapons	209	0	?
Matchlock Powder	800 lbs.+	100 lbs.+	?
Lead	?	?	600 lbs.
Other	Saltpeter, Sulfur		Saltpeter, Sulfur

Shipment of 1557

	Santo Domingo	Cuba	Vera Cruz	Cartagena	Panamá	Nombre de Dios
Matchlocks	292	48	24	50+	47	43
Pikes	1000	130	120	120+	88	262
Matchlock Powder	2500 lbs.	1200 lbs.	525 lbs.	525 lbs.+	1506 lbs.	326 lbs.

Table 6 Militia-Related Expenditures, 1535–1585 (in Ducats)

	Caribbean	Puerto Rico	Española	Cuba	Central Amer.	Tierra Firme	Cartagena	Santa Marta	
1535	75		75						1535
1536	19		19						1536
1537	353	153	199						1537
1541	19		19						1541
1542	7	7							1542
1543	6	6							1543
1548	112			112					1548
1549	10			10					1549
1552	41					41			1552
1556	27	27							1556
1557	2,914								1557
1558	33					33			1558
1561	75	75							1561
1564	4	4							1564
1568	760	41	52				354	313	1568
1569	39	39							1569
1570	115	7		108					1570
1573	145				145				1573
1576	88								1576
1577	71	21			29				1577
1580	34				34				1580
1582	18	18							1582
1583	82				73				1583

few rich persons kept horses and the weapons of the mounted lancer. Figures from Santiago de Cuba (1559) and Puerto Rico (1557) show that the ratio of thrusting weapons (swords and pikes) to firearms was between one to one and two to one, probably closer to the latter than to the former.[49] These were not unusual ratios, since many European armies still had even higher ratios of pikemen to matchlockmen, but they show that the militias of the Indies were not as well armed as many of the corsairs, who seem to have used firearms almost exclusively, with swords to finish off enemies wounded or scattered by their volleys. Moreover, the figures do not state the condition of the firearms nor the skill of their users, both important determinants of the outcome of a skirmish and both factors in which the corsairs usually had a great advantage.

Because there were relatively few militiamen and because there were not enough weapons even for that few, the record of the militias to 1564 was mixed, at best. Despite the general order of 1540, most militias did not drill on a regular basis, even during wartime. Militiamen did, however, stand guard on a regular basis, particularly at night. The system used at Havana seems to have been typical. Upon receipt of news that corsairs were sailing for the Indies, the governor and town council agreed to establish watches at the Morro and the "old town." Additional men were placed in the fort to supplement the warden and his servants. Counterrounds (*sobrerondas*) were provided. All watches and counterrounds were rotated among the residents for the duration of any war or other crisis.[50] At Santo Domingo, the distance of the Punta Caucedo from the city caused the Audiencia to hire watchmen to man an observation post there during the wars of the 1550s. By 1560, the use of hired watchmen at other ports was being urged because keeping watch placed a burden on residents.[51]

Drilling and keeping watch were important for developing discipline and preventing surprise attack, but of course the real tests of the militia system came in armed conflict. Initially the militiamen did fairly well, but by 1543 the corsairs were mounting more successful attacks; in some cases the militias fled without firing a shot. By the 1550s the pattern was well established: faced with equal, much less superior odds, the militiamen preferred to preserve life and movable property by fleeing into the countryside rather than fight on the beaches before the towns. The results of this pattern are summarized in Table 7. It should be noted that most of the successful corsair raids occurred against very small towns, isolated ranches, or sugar plantations whose defenders

Table 7   **Militia Military Actions, 1535–1563**

	Antilles			Main			Central America			
	Corsair Attacks on Land	Militia-Initiated Actions	Militia Success	Corsair Attacks on Land	Militia-Initiated Actions	Militia Success	Corsair Attacks on Land	Militia-Initiated Actions	Militia Success	
1535	2			1						1535
1538	3		1/2							1538
1539	1									1539
1541	1			2						1541
1543	2		2	2						1543
1544	1			1		1/2				1544
1546	1									1546
1547	1			2		2				1547
1548				1		1				1548
1550		1	1							1550
1552	1				1	1				1552
1553	4+				1	1				1553
1554	5	1	1/2	1						1554
1555	3			4						1555
1556	1		1							1556
1558	4	1					2		1	1558
1559	3		1?	6			2		1/2+1/2	1559
1560				1						1560
1561							1		1/2	1561
1563	1	1	1/2+1/2							1563

The numbers under "Corsair Attacks on Land" are actual attacks involving landings or attempted landings.
"Militia-Initiated Actions" includes cases where the militia attacked corsairs on land, usually watering or otherwise not expecting attack because no hostile action had preceeded the militia attack.
A "1/2" under "Militia Success" indicates a successful counterattack by the militia after an initial defeat by the corsairs. A 1 or multiple indicates that the militia drove off an attack.

were simply overwhelmed by superior numbers, firepower, and discipline. However, among the figures are the raids on Cartagena (1543, 1559) and Havana (1555).

The crown was forced to face the unreliability of the militias after 1563. When it did so, it had a number of precedents on which to draw for solutions. All involved royal funding and appeared before 1560. Con-

Table 8 **Nominal Strengths of Caretaker Garrisons, 1535 to Installation of Regular Garrison, If Any (Date indicates beginning of service)**

Place (Date of Construction of Fortification)	Warden	Artillerymen	Servants and Watchmen	Emergency Increase During These Years	Garrison Installed
San Juan, Puerto Rico (1533)	1 (1540)	1 (1541, Fort) 1 (1542, Morro)	? 1 Drummer (1576)	1542–43, 1555, 1556 1557, 1558, 1559, 1566–68	1582
Santo Domingo (1505?)	1 (1523)	1 (1535?) 1 (c. 1554, Water Battery)	5 (1535)	1538–39, 1542–44, 1548?, 1553–59, 1566–68	
Puerto Plata (1566)	1 (1567?)	1 (1581)	?	1566–68	
Havana (1538; 1558)	1 (1540)	1 (1542–48, 1550–1556, 1571)	2 (1552–56)	1556, 1565–69	1571
San Juan de Ulúa (1535?)	1 (1553?)	6–8 (1569–73, ?)	?	1569–73?	1581?
Trujillo, Honduras (1567?)	1 Captain (1567)	Fortified Town			
Cartagena (1565?)[a]	None	1 (1568?)	None		
Cumaná (1538)	1 (1540–41)	None Known			

a. Built by the city.

1535–1547. THE PRECEDENTS TAKE SHAPE   49

sideration of those precedents begins with an examination of the history of the caretaker garrisons.

Garrisons

Besides the militias, some port towns were defended by royal fortifications and in consequence had caretaker garrisons paid for from the royal treasury. Uniformly small in size, with fewer than ten men including the servants of the wardens, these caretaker forces nonetheless performed significant services. They maintained the munitions and weapons inventories as well as the fortifications. Because wardens and artillerymen possessed military experience and skills often lacking among even the militarized population of the Indies, their presence produced a limited feeling of security among the civilians. The caretaker garrisons thus provided moral as well as material support for the local militias.

A detailed examination of the history of each of these caretaker groups would be out of place here. The important facts about the number and type of men in each are provided in Table 8, which also includes information about when the caretaker forces were augmented and replaced, if at all, by full garrisons of soldiers and artillerymen. Table 9 provides information on temporary caretaker garrisons and temporary stationings of soldiers.

The need to supplement the militias and caretaker garrisons was recognized quite early. In 1538–1539, Blasco Núñez Vela provided the Council of the Indies with an appraisal of the military situation in the Caribbean, which was the complement of his memorandum about naval defenses. In his view, any force of 300 or more men could take any coastal city, regardless of how large it was, how well organized and armed the militia might be, or how extensively the town was fortified. An outnumbered militia could not be expected to hold its ground or any fortification. Rather, he believed that the militia should (and would) put up such defense as it could and then retire to the countryside, where the goods and families of the men could be dispersed and hidden, thus frustrating the efforts of raiders. A force of enemy intent on conquest could be dealt with by a fleet and reinforcements sent from elsewhere in the empire.[52]

Núñez Vela's opinion was based on militia actions during the late 1530s. When, therefore, the Spanish became aware of the large number of men and quantities of matériel being gathered for the Cartier-Ro-

Table 9   Temporary Stationings of Military Personnel in the Indies (Non-Fort Towns), 1535–1585 (Royal Funding)

Place	Artillerymen	Watchmen	Soldiers
Santiago de Cuba			50 (1566–68)
Puerto Caballos, Honduras		1563–64, 1567	? (1578)
Nombre de Dios		1569, 1579–81, 1583	100 (1569)
			80 (1571)
			60–90 (1572–73)
			40+ (1577)
			? (1583)
Santa Marta	1 (1563–76)	1+ (1565)	
Río de la Hacha	1 (1543 only)	(1554, 1559)	

berval expedition to Canada, they began considering sending a fleet or some other form of aid to the Indies. As an alternative to the fleet, the Council of the Indies proposed that troops be sent to four key ports (Table 10). Subsequent developments and continuing problems with the availability of money and men caused the Council to scale down the force to be sent and shift the troops to the Antilles—the area thought most likely to be attacked by the French.[53]

By the time these views had been formulated, Cartier was on his way to Canada and a larger war in Europe was underway. The next year French ships, which the Spanish said were under Roberval's command, attacked Santiago de Cuba, Santa Marta, Cartagena, and Havana. Only the latter would have been defended with a garrison had the Council's plan been followed.

The proposed garrisons of 1542 passed into history, but the idea that led to the suggestion remained: that invasion or the clear threat of invasion by forces capable of seizing and holding part of the empire should be met with the urgent dispatch of large numbers of soldiers.

Table 10   Proposed Strengths of Temporary Garrisons, 1542

Place	First Proposal	Second Proposal
Puerto Rico	50 matchlockmen	80 matchlockmen
Santo Domingo	100 matchlockmen	50 matchlockmen
Havana	50 matchlockmen	25 matchlockmen
Nombre de Dios	150 matchlockmen	None, but organize the militia and fortify the harbor

Source: AGI, Patronato 267, No. 1, R. 13, document 5.

This was a variation on Núñez Vela's basic insight: that the militias could not and would not do battle with any force large enough to deprive the militiamen of overwhelming numerical superiority. Subsequent events proved this insight to be correct. To deal with the problem thus created, the crown resorted to the creation of what were intended to be temporary garrisons; before 1565, it was able to carry out that policy (Tables 8 and 9), but afterwards the garrisons became permanent.

Fortifications

The geographic distribution, and to a certain extent the size, of the caretaker garrisons were a result of the history of fortifications. The locations of forts and their form were in turn determined by royal attitudes towards funding and by events. Prior to 1537, the crown, although not always its officials, pursued its policy of seeking to use private resources, principally those of *adelantados* charged with fortifying towns founded under their contracts. But with the beginning of attacks on the towns of the Caribbean and the resulting petitions for fortifications, the crown authorized a series of defensive works. It finally drew these individual projdcts into a general scheme in 1542, in the face of the threat posed by the Cartier-Roberval expedition and the outbreak of war in Europe. And yet both before 1542 and afterwards, the crown could not always get city and royal officials to spend the money that it had authorized! Nonetheless, enough royal money was spent for fortifications to make that the single most costly form of defense developed in the Indies before 1548.

Except for the works at Santo Domingo, none of the fortifications built during this period was substantial according to later standards. All were variations on the medieval castle's basic strategic design, which provided protection for the assembling and arming of soldiers who would then sally to attack the enemy. Although already an anachronism in Europe because of the development of siege trains of artillery, this type of fortification was appropriate to the Indies where the attackers could make little use of artillery and had to land on a beach, with all the disorder and vulnerability which that action entailed. The few artillery emplacements built during these years were the result of the realization that gunfire might prevent corsairs from reaching ships anchored off towns. Much less attention was given to using artillery to obstruct landing beaches. However, the increasing use of artillery in these special situations did not change the fact that defense against an enemy who had successfully landed remained in the hands of the militia, which needed a place to assemble and arm before meeting the attack. Simple fortifications served this essential military role. In addition, they served as displays of the crown's sovereignty and provided a sense of security for the residents of exposed seaports.

A few structures to shelter men and supplies should have resulted from the on-going conquest. But by 1533, when the first comprehensive plan to fortify the Indies was sent to the crown, only Jamaica, Cumaná, Santo Domingo, and Puerto Rico had fortified "strong houses" as a result of the contracts signed with *adelantados*.

A first, tentative step away from this policy may be found in the formula used to pay for a new fort authorized for San Juan de Puerto Rico in 1533. The Crown contributed four-fifths of the cost, with the city supplying the other fifth.[54] The fact that this was a tentative step and not a change in policy was shown by the crown's reaction to the general plan for fortifications laid before it by Gonzalo Fernández de Oviedo, chronicler of the Indies and warden of the fort at Santo Domingo.

Oviedo proposed the fortification of Dominica, the landfall of ships entering the Caribbean. Puerto Rico's newly authorized fort was, he said, badly placed but should be completed and complemented by a structure on the Morro. San Germán and Mona should be fortified to prevent corsairs from seizing them for bases in the heart of the shipping lane to Spain. Santo Domingo required additional fortification on the seafront as well as a wall around the fort grounds. The ports of Azua, Salvatierra de la Sabana, Puerto Real (Cap Haïtien), Puerto Plata, Havana, Point Morant (Jamaica), Sevilla la Nueva (Jamaica), Nombre de Dios, Puerto Belo, the mouth of the Chagres River, Cartagena, Santa Marta, Coro (Venezuela), and Cubagua should be fortified. To round out his grand design, Oviedo proposed the fortification of the Straits of Magellan and of Bermuda.[55]

At the time Oviedo made this proposal, two of the nineteen ports that he mentioned had or were building forts at royal expense, while four (Cartagena, Coro, Cubagua, and Sevilla la Nueva) were to be fortified under the *adelantado* contracts. A seventh, Santa Marta, was soon to be contracted out to an *adelantado*. Because there seemed to be no urgent reason to fortify the other dozen ports, the crown deferred action except to order Viceroy Antonio de Mendoza to build a fortified wharf at San Juan de Ulúa (1535) and to authorize Oviedo to wall the fort grounds at

Santo Domingo using funds from an excise tax and from the collection of debts due to the royal treasury.[56]

However, in the Indies local officials took matters into their own hands and rebuilt the fort at Cumaná (1533), built a fort on Margarita (1534), built earthworks around Cubagua (1534), and made repairs to the tower at Santo Domingo (1534).[57] Royal funds were used for all of these projects. Thus by 1535 slightly over half (ten of nineteen) of the ports had some sort of fortification either built or to be built, and the crown's funds had been committed to the construction of fortifications.

Probably little more would have been done to fortify the Indies had not war in Europe brought French raids in the Caribbean. Corsair attacks during 1537 on shipping off the Isthmus of Panamá, Havana, and Santiago de Cuba and on the towns of Havana and La Yaguana evoked petitions for fortification from Nombre de Dios and Havana and a reminder of his own plan from Oviedo.[58] In response, the crown negotiated a contract with Pascual de Andagoya, a city councilman (*regidor*) from Panamá then at court, for the construction of a fort at Nombre de Dios and ordered Hernando de Soto to build a fort at Havana while on his way to conquer Florida. Although Cartagena had not been attacked, the crown made provision to send an agent with masons and other construction tradesmen to build a fort there, to be paid for by the local royal treasury.[59]

The following year brought more raids and petitions for fortifications, but also some progress in making up the deficiencies resulting from prior neglect of this form of defense. In April and May, corsairs were again active in Cuban and Puerto Rican waters. Reacting to these events, the Cabildo of Santiago de Cuba petitioned for a bulwark and artillery to guard the landing before the town, while San Juan de Puerto Rico asked for permission to use royal funds to build a bulwark on the Morro (the water battery). At Santo Domingo, the building of a similar artillery platform at the junction of the river and the sea was begun under the Audiencia's authority. Permission was soon given to San Juan to follow suit, thus beginning the monumental works of El Morro.[60] Meanwhile work on the main fort at San Juan continued.

Santiago's petitions were answered not by the crown, but by the direct action of Hernándo de Soto. He arrived two months after the attack and quickly began construction of a wood and earth breastwork capable of protecting several pieces of artillery, their crews, and one hundred militiamen. This work went well during de Soto's stay in the city, but after he left the official in charge fell ill and the city's interest and funds were diverted to slave raids against Indians in the interior. Even the subsequent granting of royal funds for the work did not get construction going again.[61]

Moving on to Havana, de Soto held consultations with local residents about the best site for a fort, awarded a contract for it to Juan de Azeituno, and broke ground for the building on Saint John's day, 1538. The site chosen was next to the town, even though de Soto had been told before leaving Spain that La Cabaña hill made any location on the city side of the harbor (the west) unsuitable and that experts at Seville believed he should fortify the Morro. His error in choosing a site, repeated in 1556, eventually cost the crown dearly. But for the moment, the city obtained a *cortijo* for the modest sum of 2,500 pesos de oro (3,000 ducats). The building was a square keep, two stories tall, with a plaza (bailey) and a low curtain wall. Neither the site nor the design were suitable for sixteenth-century warfare, but what contemporaries commented on was the way in which de Soto seized funds from the royal treasury to pay for the construction.[62]

Cartagena and Nombre de Dios were not so fortunate. Despite the crown's orders of the spring of 1538, nothing was done to fortify those ports. When Lope de Saavedra, the crown's agent, reached Cartagena in October and held a meeting to decide where to build the fort, the meeting decided that no fort should be built, giving as its reasons the fact that there was no stone closer than six miles and that to fetch it would run the costs of construction to 30,000 pesos de oro (36,000 ducats), money better spent on other things. The militia and some artillery would be an adequate defense, because there were "men" among the residents of the city. In any case, more than one fort was needed to defend the approaches to the city.[63] Saavedra and his journeymen went their way.

Pascual de Andagoya, ordered to construct a new fort at Nombre de Dios as well as to take weapons to its militia, did not leave court during 1538. The obvious attractions of court life were probably the primary reason he delayed, but another reason may have been controversy within the councils of government resulting from the emphatic opinion of Blasco Núñez Vela that only Santo Domingo was worth further fortification. All the other ports were too thinly populated to be able to defend a fort for more than a few days. To him this suggested that military prudence would dictate leaving the ports without formal defenses so that no enemy would be handed a strong position from which he might be difficult to dislodge.[64]

Núñez Vela's strongly reasoned opinion did not carry the day. The crown remained intent on fortifying Cartagena and Nombre de Dios and willing to receive petitions from other ports for additional defenses, including fortifications. Cartagena was again ordered to build a fort. Andagoya was again told to go to Nombre de Dios; provision was made for four masons and stonecutters to accompany him, and he was formally given the title of warden of the as-yet unbuilt fort. He and the journeymen apparently reached the Isthmus that summer; the men died soon afterwards and Andagoya went off to Peru to seek his fortune.[65] Cartagena ignored the royal will. The Truce of 1538 did the rest. Fortification projects not already underway received no further stimuli from Spain.

The threat implicit in Cartier's preparations in the fall of 1540 changed this situation. By January 1541, the regency government had authorized repairs to the fort at Santo Domingo, the donation of royal funds toward the cost of walling that city, and the construction of forts at La Yaguana and San Germán. Orders were sent to the Audiencia of Santo Domingo to report on the desirability and cost of fortifying Puerto Plata and Azua, to the officials of Cartagena to build a fort of tabby concrete if stone was not available, and to the governor of Santa Marta to fulfill his father's contract as *adelantado* and build a fort at that port as well as another fort wherever it might be needed to control the province. The Casa de Contratación was instructed to make a chain boom for the entrance to Santo Domingo's harbor. The *visitador*, Licenciado Vaca de Castro, was instructed to report on the forts at San Juan de Puerto Rico, Santo Domingo, and Nombre de Dios. A request may have been sent for a report on the fortified wharf of San Juan de Ulúa.[66]

These orders were followed by a general order of April 15, 1542, that all forts previously ordered and all work previously authorized to existing structures be rushed to completion in anticipation of a possible invasion of the Indies by the Cartier-Roberval expedition, which had sailed from France.[67]

Compliance with these orders varied according to place. At Cartagena and Santa Marta nothing was done. Defenseless except for an inadequate militia and a few small pieces of artillery, both towns fell to French forces in 1543. Subsequently, Cartagena obtained permission to impose an excise tax to pay for a wall around the town. Santa Marta rebuilt, unsuccessfully requested royal funding for a fort in 1543 and 1548, and was raided again (1547, 1548). The proposed forts for La Yaguana and Puerto Plata were studied by the authorities at Santo Domingo but not recommended for construction. Studies for Puerto Plata and Azua got lost in bureaucratic red tape and disputes that developed within the Audiencia over other matters. A generation later Puerto Plata was to get its fort, but La Yaguana and Azua were never fortified, although the city council of Santo Domingo asked for this, along with the fortification of Puerto Plata.[68]

Vaca de Castro made his inspection of Nombre de Dios in March 1541 and found that Andagoya had not built the fort. Castro recommended a site, a contractor (Antonio de Arquello, a twenty-five-year resident of Nombre de Dios), and the number of slaves required. The Council of the Indies debated his report and other evidence as part of its on-going consideration of measures to be taken to defend the Indies against the Cartier-Roberval expedition and concluded that nothing could be done in time for that emergency. Nonetheless, Nombre de Dios was included among the ports ordered to finish fortifications by the general letter of April 1542. However, nothing was done in response to this order by officials on the Isthmus, except for the writing of letters in 1544 and the sending of an advocate in 1545, both seeking royal funding for a fort at Nombre de Dios and both stressing the city's importance to the transisthmian trade. The central authorities, now under the direction of Prince Philip, responded by seeking information on the problem from Licenciado La Gasca (1546) and the governor and officials of Tierra Firme (1548).[69]

The fortification of San Germán, Puerto Rico, was actually begun during May 1541 following renewed raids in the area. A certain Juan de Castellanos rented slaves and began to build either an actual fort or some sort of earthworks, but he abandoned the work in December because of financial difficulties and a decision, probably by the Audiencia of Santo Domingo, to suspend the project because of its projected cost. A mild protest was subsequently made by the royal officials of San Juan, who feared that the lack of defenses would cause the residents of San Germán to leave. Raided and burned again in 1543, San Germán was finally moved to its present location in 1546, in a vain effort to escape the corsairs by removing from the seacoast.[70]

The officials at Santiago de Cuba and Havana, like their counterparts at Santa Marta and Cartagena, ignored the royal order of 1542. However, after the arrival of news of the fall of Santa Marta and Cartagena in 1543, Santiago completed the breastworks begun in 1538. Not satisfied with that, the city petitioned for a fort, a request that the crown ignored. At Havana, a new governor repaired the fort and added a battery on the water side. Although he thought that this improved the defense somewhat, he decried the building as "no fort at all except in name."[71] Following up on this indictment, the crown ordered the commanders of naval units passing by Havana to look into the condition and location of the fort. The details of these reports will be discussed below.

At San Juan de Ulúa work was renewed in 1541, under the direction of Pedro Varela using slaves purchased by the royal treasury. The other costs of construction were paid by a port tax, a fact that makes it difficult to follow the progress of construction because those records have not survived.[72]

At San Juan de Puerto Rico, the officials exceeded their instructions and undertook the construction of an enclosed casemate (*cubo*) on the Morro, thereby supplementing the water battery built in 1538 with an enclosed tower reaching to the top of the rock face. The work was incomplete, however, for in 1543/44, when corsairs again threatened the city, the treasury records show construction of a munitions store, embrasures, and a parapet. At the same time, a trench (presumably for matchlockmen) was dug beside the main anchorage and repairs and additions were made to the main fort, La Fortaleza.[73]

By far the costliest response to the royal orders of this period was the resumption of construction of the wall and water battery of the fort at Santo Domingo. Suspended during 1539–1541 pending submission to the crown of a report on their projected costs, work on these projects was resumed over the objections of the city council following Vaca de Castro's inspection.[74] The water battery was finished by 1546.

In informing the crown of the city council's opposition to the water battery, Alvaro Cavallero, the city's advocate, prophetically informed the Council of the Indies that an enemy was unlikely to attempt to enter the river but would prefer to land at *la Playnela*, a beach some one and one-half miles west of the city, or at another beach nine miles to the west. From either he could march against the city. Because of its location, the fort, "even with five bastions," could not prevent such an attack. A wall running from the sea to the river around the western and northern sides of the city, and then along the riverfront, was the solution. Acknowledging an earlier royal grant of 4,000 pesos for this wall and the authorization of an excise tax to pay the city's part of the cost, Cavallero asked for more royal funds. The city received a further grant of one-third of the cattle in the crown's extensive herds. Only later did the crown learn why the wall was going to cost so much: the circuit was laid out well to the west and north of the actual area of housing. Oviedo charged, and no one ever refuted him, that this was done because the *alcaldes* and the judges of the Audiencia owned the land thus brought inside the walls.[75] The result of this real estate speculation was that thirty-five years later, when Drake attacked the city from the west, the wall was still incomplete.

The other major defensive improvement for Santo Domingo ordered by the crown was a chain to close the mouth of the river. It duly arrived at Santo Domingo in 1543, was tested and found to work, and then was put away in the fort, where it remained until 1547 when Oviedo obtained permission to break it up and use the iron in repairing artillery carriages.[76]

With the return of peace in Europe in 1544 and in the Indies by early 1546, the fortification program ordered piecemeal before 1542 and brought together in the order of that year came to an end. Spending for fortifications dropped off, thus ending the first period in the history of fortifications. Its historical significance was greater than contemporaries could have realized. As a percentage of total spending, the construction costs of fortifications were never again to be as great. The pattern of geographic placement established before 1547 was to remain the essential pattern down to 1586. Important mistakes had been made in locating the forts at San Juan de Puerto Rico, Santo Domingo, and Havana, where the main forts had been built next to the towns where they could protect the houses and the ships anchored off the town but could not prevent corsairs from running into the harbors. This weakness had been partially remedied at San Juan by the building of additional fortifications on the Morro and had been largely corrected at Santo Domingo by construction of the water battery at the point where the river entered the sea. None of these structures was secure from attack from behind, from the land, and two (San Juan and Havana) were overshadowed by hills from which long-range artillery in enemy hands easily could have dominated the fort. All these faults were observed at the time, but little was done to correct them before 1548. In the late 1540s,

1535–1547. THE PRECEDENTS TAKE SHAPE 59

it must have still seemed possible that additional forts would be built and that changes in existing structures would be approved.

Artillery

If forts were the crown's greatest expense, artillery was among its smallest. In part this was because some guns were shipped to the Indies from inventories in Spain and hence do not appear as costs in the royal books. But this low cost is also an indication of the degree to which the crown neglected artillery, even though it was the necessary complement to men and fortifications in the defense of towns and cities.

Following the raid of 1528, Santo Domingo and San Juan de Puerto Rico requested additional artillery. Oviedo, for Santo Domingo, and Juan de Castellanos, for Puerto Rico, obtained what they sought by the late summer of 1535. The Casa was ordered to provide Santo Domingo with two culverins and two half-culverins to supplement the two culverins, one old cannon, one falconet, and a half dozen smaller pieces already there. Puerto Rico was to receive two half-cannon (twenty-five-pound shot), three falcons (four-pound shot) and three *ribadoquins* (one-and-one-half-pound shot). A contract for what ultimately proved to be twenty pieces of bronze artillery was let.[77]

Two of the eight "extra" pieces were intended to supply the fort at Cumaná, which had lost its artillery during an Indian attack. Guns sent out in 1534 had been seized by the Cabildo of New Cádiz, which requested replacements. These were authorized by the crown in November 1535, with their casting becoming part of the contract for the Puerto Rican and Santo Domingan guns.[78]

The entire lot of guns seems to have been turned over to the Casa in the spring of 1536, but they were taken for use on the coastal patrol squadron fitted out that summer. As soon as they learned of this development, the officials of Santo Domingo complained. In reply, the crown ordered some of the guns sent with the Núñez Vela fleet. A half-culverin, two culverins, a saker, and five falconets were put aboard the ships, but the two culverins were shipwrecked when the fleet sailed. Salvaged, they were sent with Perea when he went to reinforce Núñez Vela.[79]

In the end, the fort at Santo Domingo obtained most of its artillery from the *Serafín*, one of Núñez Vela's ships which had been forced to put into Santo Domingo in April 1538 in sinking condition. It had four cannon of different calibers, a half-culverin, four falconets, and fifty-two *versos*, along with munitions and tools for all of them. With the addition of these weapons to its earlier holdings, Santo Domingo came to possess the largest and most diverse collection of artillery in the Indies. Neither Puerto Rico nor Cubagua received any artillery, and subsequent orders to the Casa to send guns to both places seem to have been ignored.[80]

Thus equipped, the fort of Santo Domingo soon became the source from which artillery was drawn to equip the patrol fleet sent out by the Audiencia in 1543 and to provide some of the artillery used by Licenciado La Gasca for his expedition to reestablish royal authority in Peru, 1546/47.[81]

Elsewhere in the Indies, other towns acquired a few pieces of artillery before 1547. Note has already been made of New Cádiz' (Cubagua) seizure of guns in 1534. Following the taking of ships by a French corsair, the town of Nombre de Dios purchased ten *versos* and two *pasamuros* by popular subscription (1537). Santiago de Cuba obtained four guns from de Soto and others from some of its own residents. The crown eventually ordered the Casa to send four falconets, apparently the weapons already delivered by de Soto. Santa Marta had some artillery by the summer of 1541, perhaps brought in by the *adelantado* of the Canaries, Alonso Luís de Lugo, who held the contract for the settlement of that area. Some of those pieces may have been taken to Cabo de la Vela and Río de la Hacha. In 1544 the *adelantado* laid claim to those at Cabo de la Vela but was prevented by the town council from removing them. La Gasca took the guns from Río de la Hacha when he went to Peru. Like the guns that he removed from Santo Domingo, which were still on the Isthmus in the 1550s, the guns from Río de la Hacha remained away from the city, at Lima, until the 1550s.[82] A few additional pieces were probably bought for the wharf at San Juan de Ulúa, but no record of them has been found. Only the city of Cartagena, of the ports of the Main, was without artillery.

Havana obtained its artillery late, much as its fortifications were developed later than those in the other Antillian ports. The first order for artillery for the newly finished tower fort seems to have been issued in September 1541, and followed up the next year; but by early 1545, no guns had been delivered. Finally, in May and July of that year, the newly appointed warden, Juan de Lobera, was able to buy two cannon, two half-culverins, and two sakers, with munitions and small arms, from the estate of the duque de Bejar. These weapons arrived at Havana in early 1546, giving it the second best collection of artillery in the Indies at that time.[83]

In the same year that Havana was finally acquiring artillery, Nombre de Dios and Santiago de Cuba petitioned for guns. The crown deferred a decision on Nombre de Dios' request until after a fort should be built to defend that port, while sending Santiago's petition for a dozen small pieces of artillery in a breastwork at the mouth of the harbor back for cost estimates, a move that ultimately killed the project.[84]

Puerto Rico was neither so unfortunate as Santiago and Nombre de Dios nor as fortunate as Havana. Royal orders to the Casa to send the guns authorized in 1535 were ignored in 1538 and again in 1539. The Cartier threat brought the subject back to the crown's attention, but its orders to the Casa for four falconets, a half-saker, and two lombards seems to have produced only another order, delivered at Puerto Rico by Alonso de los Ríos in 1542, that the Audiencia of Santo Domingo surrender a cannon and a culverin. The Casa continued to be short of guns with which to fulfill the many demands made upon its supply. At San Juan, the warning of possible invasion by the French led to renewed calls for artillery, including additional guns for the new tower on the Morro and for the fortifications that had been begun at San Germán. Going beyond words to deeds, the treasury officials took the crown's order to prepare against the French at face value and sent an agent to Santo Domingo with authority to buy any artillery he could find. He obtained two iron *pasamuros* and some stone balls, which were duly installed in the new Morro fortifications. Sent back in 1542 to get the guns authorized by the letter that came with Alonso de los Ríos, the agent had to initiate a suit to try to get them. This was partially successful since three iron guns and four *versos* were delivered to San Juan in December 1542. By early the next year they were installed in the Morro fortifications, which were improved to provide shelter from the elements for them.[85]

Thus did various towns obtain some artillery, although most of it was in the "man-killer" classes. Those towns with royal forts and their caretaker garrisons generally had someone to take care of the guns acquired and royal funds to pay for routine maintenance of the carriages. In the other towns, the weapons probably received minimum attention, if that, and soon fell into states of corrosion for the guns and disrepair for their carriages. This physical decay seems to have been accompanied by the ruination of the munitions, especially powder. The weapons thus became inoperative. Hard pressed, the crown was barely able to supply powder and the materials for refining it to the forts at Santo Domingo, Puerto Rico, and Havana. There is no record that any was sent to the other ports with artillery.[86] In short, the simple fact that a given town had some pieces of artillery did not mean that those weapons were effective parts of its defenses during the 1530s and 1540s.

That the crown was aware of the need for more artillery, and especially of the need for guns of larger calibers, is shown by the orders issued in 1546 and 1547 for a completion of the inventory of the Casa's holdings and for the founding of new weapons at Málaga. The Casa's twenty-three guns were thus supplemented by sixty more. At the same time, several guns were cast from copper sent from Cuba. These experimental pieces were not entirely satisfactory, thus ending efforts to use Cuban copper for a number of years.[87]

Summary

In sum, the first period of the defense of the Indies saw relatively little royal spending for defense because the crown was still trying to legislatively coerce individuals into providing their own defense. Thus provided with ultimate responsibility for the defense of commerce and the provision of manpower in the Indies, private interests showed themselves unwilling to carry out the crown's wishes when individuals thought they lacked, or actually did lack, the resources to defend themselves, or when they thought that they had no reason to put life and property on the line in a battle with corsairs. Down to 1548, the crown did little to augment private resources, aside from providing fortifications, caretaker garrisons, and some stocks of weapons with small amounts of munitions. Frustrated because its interests as a shipper and as sovereign were not being adequately guarded by its subjects, the crown was slowly but surely forced to bear a greater financial burden for defense. The change in attitude becomes evident after 1548. So too do a series of changes in military strategy dictated by the patterns of corsair activity and the various failures of earlier defense efforts.

Chapter III   **1548—1563.**
                      Naval Warfare Creates Its Own Precedents

THE SECOND PERIOD in the history of the defense of the Indies begins not in 1552 when war was resumed in Europe between Charles V and his French opponent, Henry II, but in 1548 when the crown started spending funds for defense as a consequence of the Franco-Portuguese naval war that began that spring. Having been forced by events during the preceding dozen years to reexamine its policy of relying on private persons to defend commerce, especially in the critical zone of the Triangle, the crown now embarked on a program of patrol squadrons paid for from its general tax revenues from the Indies.

The patrols were soon extended to the Antilles as raiders and traders once again appeared in that area, especially after the outbreak of war in 1552. Unlike earlier corsairs, those of the 1550s devoted more of their efforts to raiding commerce than to attacking towns. This development, partially attributable to the defenses developed during the first period, made the war in the Caribbean more clearly a naval war than earlier conflicts had been and thus kept the crown's attention fixed on the system of patrols that it wished to develop for the defense of commerce. That those patrols also served to deter some raids on towns was all to the good and, with the initial decrease in raids on towns, meant that land defenses did not seem to require substantial improvements, at least not until the raid on Havana in 1555 dramatically highlighted the inadequacy of the system developed in the late 1530s and early 1540s.

Even then, little was done during the rest of the war to remedy the weaknesses thus exposed, aside from beginning a new fort at Havana. Having paid for patrols that, with other expenses, had driven costs to levels four times what they were in the first period, the crown was unwilling to pay out more for additional fortifications and garrisons, although both were clearly needed from a local point of view. The return of peace, broken before 1564 only by the need to fit out patrols against North African pirates in the Triangle, allowed the postponing of these changes in the defenses of the Indies.

Those changes had to be made after 1564 because the defense that would have really protected the towns and commerce of the Indies eluded the Spanish, not on the seas or beaches but at the conference tables and in the chanceries of Europe, where diplomats failed once again to resolve the problem of French access to the Indies by resolving the definition of the Indies. This failure came at the same time that the English finally began to sail directly to the Caribbean. In that same year, 1563, the crown took away what little discretionary authority the royal officials in the Indies had had in fiscal matters. Thereafter, all defense spending except under very unusual conditions had to be approved in advance by Madrid. Together with the drop of defense spending to zero, these developments marked the end of an era, and the end of the second period in the defense of the Indies.

The Corsairs

The Franco-Portuguese naval war of 1548–1550 developed from the reversal of French prohibitions of 1545 on sailing for the Indies. Those prohibitions had arisen from the diplomatic effort to resolve the problems of French exploration in the New World and French interest in trading with it, issues first raised in connection with the Cartier-Roberval expedition in 1540–1542. Unresolved then, they reappeared in the negotiations of 1544 and resulted in provisions in the Treaty of Crépy-en-Laonnois (September 18, 1544) conceding trading rights to Frenchmen in exchange for Francis I's promise to leave the Spanish in control of "whatever of the Kingdoms, estates, dominions, countries, and seigneuries" Charles V then held or "possessed."[1] An additional article was prepared that specifically applied these provisions to the Indies, which were extended to include the Portuguese possessions as well as those of Spain. The Spanish thus hoped to guard not only the territories they actually held, but also areas like Florida, which, they were speculating, might be worth having and which they might occupy in the future. In return, they were prepared to concede trading rights to French subjects similar to those enjoyed by the Flemish subjects of the emperor, or by the English. Although the concession appears remarkable, it can be shown that it was in line with the crown's position on its "just titles," as those titles were understood in the years immediately following 1542. In the end, the additional article was rejected by the Spanish councils. In order to close the loophole provided by the language of the treaty, in 1545 the emperor obtained a decree from Francis I prohibiting Frenchmen from sailing to the Indies.[2]

Discussions of French trading privileges within the Iberian empires seem to have been renewed the next year, but without any resolution of the conflicting views of the parties. Then in 1547 Francis I died, and with him the agreement prohibiting Frenchmen from sailing to the Indies. In October, Henry II, Francis' successor, granted his subjects permission to sail to the Portuguese empire.[3] By early the next year, fighting had begun between the French and Portuguese and was soon accompanied by French attacks on Spanish shipping in the Triangle and in the Caribbean. French traders also began to appear in the Indies. These hostilities continued into the 1550s with but a brief interruption during 1551. In 1552 they became part of the new European war between the emperor and the French. Nominally resolved by the Treaty of Cateau-Cambrésis of 1559, the war continued into 1561 as a few Frenchmen ignored or remained ignorant of the return of peace.

The statistical patterns of corsair activities between 1548 and 1563 partially duplicated the patterns of the first period, but with some important changes, many of them the results of Spanish defense measures (Table 11). The geographic zones retained roughly the same order of importance, with the Triangle the most dangerous zone, followed closely by the Antilles. Danger during this period may be measured not only by numbers of ships captured—in that department the Antilles were the undisputed leader—but also in the size of enemy fleets deployed against shipping. By that criterion, the Triangle remained predominant, since nothing like the fleets of ten, fourteen, or sixteen sail passed to the Indies. A comparable Antillian figure of eleven from 1553 included a host of small craft that had been seized by the corsairs. Such small ships were generally not reported in the Triangle figures. The

Table 11   **Spanish Losses to Corsairs, 1548–1563**

Atlantic Triangle		Antilles					The Main					Central America				Totals	
Ships Taken	Largest Corsair Group	Ships Taken	Successful Land Raids	Unsuccessful Land Raids	Illegal Trade Noted	Largest Corsair Group	Ships Taken	Successful Land Raids	Unsuccessful Land Raids	Illegal Trade Noted	Largest Corsair Group	Ships Taken	Successful Land Raids	Unsuccessful Land Raids	Largest Corsair Group	Total Ships Taken	Total Land Raids
1548																	
1	1	4			X	3	4	1			1					9	1
1549																	
4	4	5			X	6	2				1					11	0
1550																	
1	2	3			X	2										4	0
1551																	
																0	0
1552																	
1		3	1			2					1					4	1
1553																	
	14	11	4+			11					1					11	4+
1554																	
1+	16	4+	5		X	4										5+	5
1555																	
4	4	1	3			4+		4			3					5	7
1556																	
	2+	1	1			5										1	1
1557																	
	10	3+				2										3+	0
1558																	
	8+	12	3	1		5				X	1+	1	2		4	13	6
1559																	
		1	2	1		5	5	5	1	X	5	2+	1	1	1	8+	11
1560																	
	6						4	1		X	3					4	1
1561																	
	19	2				4						2	1		1	4	1
1562																	
	9															0	0
1563																	
	12	4	1		X	2					1+					4	1
Totals:																	
12+		54	20	2			15	10	2			5+	4	1		86+	39+

Figures for the 1550s may understate the number of ships lost because of non-reporting of ships captured along with towns.

Main remained in third place in terms of losses, with Central America entering the listing for the first time in 1558–1559.

Within these broad trends of losses, other changes were occurring that are masked by this compilation. Corsair raids on towns were almost entirely confined to nonfortified ports. Only Havana, of the fortified ports, was raided successfully. The areal pattern of shipping losses in the Carribbean changed as well. Havana ceased to be a major point of loss of shipping (although it was occupied twice), while the Mona Passage and, even more, the Windward Passage assumed more importance, particularly in the 1553–1555 period (Table 12). Indeed, as early as 1549 the Audiencia of Santo Domingo noted a shift away from the Mona Passage towards raiding and trading on the northern and western coasts of the island.[4] The apparent importance of corsair activity in these two areas reinforced the impression derived from earlier wars that these were the keys to the Indies and that a patrol squadron should be based at Santo Domingo. But the activities of the squadron served to drive the corsairs further afield in the Caribbean to areas like the western Main and Central America, where they had not been in any numbers before. This push was enhanced by the pull of towns and coastal commerce as yet unraided and still lightly guarded. Together, the push of developing defenses in the Antilles and the pull of easy prey elsewhere in the Caribbean caused corsair activity to spread to the periphery of the area, a development largely unnoticed by contemporaries who focused on the Antilles as the center of the military problem. The continuation of this perception after 1559 was to create major problems during the next period of defense history.

The nonquantifiable aspects of corsair activity assume greater importance during this second phase. Two changes in particular merit close attention: the use of small oared craft by the corsairs and the development of illegal trading. The psychological impact of the raids and the nearly constant threat of corsair attack continued to be factors in defense decision-making, but they were probably less important than during the initial onslaughts of the 1530s and 1540s.

The origins of the French use of small oared boats for attacking shipping are not clear. They could have been imitating early Spanish use of such ships—for example, in a patrol of 1543—but the idea may well have been the inspiration of men who had been in the Indies, becalmed within sight of a tempting prize.

Whatever the origins of the idea, it was first applied with spectacular success in August 1549 when a *patache* of eighteen benches cut a ship loaded with sugar out of a group of six ships beating through the Mona Passage. The *patache* later captured two caravels and a slaver with 120 blacks from São Tomé. Beginning with the next year, reports of corsairs in the Antilles and on the Main frequently state that they had a ship and a *patache de remos*. The *pataches* were even brought out in pieces for assembly at Mona or some other port. This change in tactics had become so notable that in 1553 it was formally reported to the crown,

Table 12   Spanish Losses to Corsairs Around Española, 1548–1560

	Mona Passage		South Coast		North Coast		Windward Passage	
	Ships Taken	Land Raid	Ships Taken	Land Raid	Ships Taken	Land Raid	Ships Taken	Land Raid
1548	2				2		p	
1549	5		p					
1550			1				2	
1551								
1552	+						1	1
1553	2	1	4	1		1	3	1
1554	2	1		1			1	1
1555						1		
1556	1							
1557	3+							
1558			1		6	2	3	
1559								1
1560								

p signifies possible loss to corsair
+ signifies losses not specified as to number

with the observation that once a ship had been spotted by the corsairs, it could not escape, even with favorable winds.[5]

Because of these small, swift craft, the corsairs became masters of the seas once Spanish naval defenses faltered (1552–1557). Writing from Panamá in 1554, one observer assured the king that "the corsairs are as much the lords of this coast as Your Majesty is the river of San Lúcar [the Guadalquivir], because there is not a ship in all the Caribbean which has not been robbed two or three times. The result is that the trade of those islands [the Antilles] is lost." From Española came the observation that the French "are so powerful in these seas that a bird cannot fly without being seen."[6]

The craft in question, the *patache*, was seldom described with precision. The one operating in the Mona Passage in 1549 was variously said to have had eighteen benches (thirty-six oars), thirty oars, or thirty oars to a side (sixty in all). The latter is unlikely since that would have made it a thirty-bench galley, large even by Mediterranean standards. More likely the type was an open boat, shipping from ten to eighteen oars to a side, carrying a crew of forty to seventy men, and having a displacement of 60 to 200 tons. These boats were of shallow draft and carried sails, although what type is not stated. They probably did not carry any artillery other than *versos*, which explains why they did not attack armed—that is, artillery-carrying—ships.[7]

The *patache* gave the corsairs speed under almost any wind and current conditions. It also gave them the ability to flee into shallow water beyond the reach of larger, deeper-draft Spanish ships. This advantage was not at first recognized in the Antilles, but it came to play an important role in corsair activity and Spanish defense actions once the corsairs began to frequent the Main in the 1550s. Finding effective defenses against these shallow-draft, swift raiders as well as their larger consorts—who were often close enough to lend assistance in a fight—proved to be a long process ultimately ending in the use of galleys.

Equally important for the future was the development of the illegal trade. Prior to 1549 only the Portuguese were regularly involved in attempting to break the navigation laws of the Spanish Empire during peacetime. The French had done some bartering in the 1535–1544 period, but no regular trade seems to have arisen from it. But in 1548, after the breakdown of the agreement of 1545 prohibiting Frenchmen from sailing to the Spanish and Portuguese empires for trade, the French entered the Caribbean. That fall three French ships appeared off San Germán, then off Santo Domingo, and finally at La Yaguana. Refused trade at the first two towns, the French obtained it at La Yaguana, whose residents claimed that they had been "forced" to trade by threats of attack.[8]

Details of the development of this illegal trade are not recorded in surviving documents. From a few scraps of evidence and later charges (which will be more fully discussed in considering corsair activity from 1564 to 1577), it seems that the corsairs found ready markets for their wares in the remote ports and ranches of the Antilles and along the eastern end of the Main, from Cabo de la Vela eastwards. These areas were poorly served, if at all, by the legal trade eminating from Seville and the Canary Islands. What goods they did get were expensive, becoming both scarcer and more expensive during the war of the 1550s. In the Antilles the corsairs caused scarcities by virtually cutting communications with Spain, 1553–1554, at a time when price increases on Española and in San Juan were further accentuated by the manipulation of the vellon currency by a few merchants, creditors, and royal officials.[9] The merchants of Seville added to these problems by deliberate manipulations of supply and by refusing to allow ships to sail outside the protection of the convoys because of an almost paranoid fear of losses. They also claimed there were shortages of shipping so that none could be spared for the lesser markets.[10] Under these conditions, illegal trade with the corsairs became necessary for many Spanish subjects who might have obeyed the law had legal goods been available. For others, obeying the law meant exclusion from a lucrative trade.

Among the individuals who figure in the category of those wishing to break the hold of the Seville merchants for their own benefit were no lesser personages than the judges of the Audiencia of Santo Domingo. Ever since the early years of the century, the judges and treasury officials had periodically forgotten their duties and had allowed the Portuguese to trade in the Indies. In 1556, they began to do so again, this time extending the special permission to Portuguese ships making port not only on Española, but also at Puerto Rico, Margarita, and La Burburata (Venezuela). The pretext was that the ships had been blown off course on their ways to Brazil or São Tomé and needed to sell small amounts of wine and merchandise to pay for repairs and supplies which would permit them to continue their trips. It was an old excuse that had not been accepted by less corrupt Audiencias. The crown did not find it any more acceptable because the Portuguese paid taxes on the goods they sold.[11]

This particular instance is the only one to surface in the 1550s. But similar actions were taking place at La Yaguana, the other ports of northern and western Española, and the ports of eastern Cuba. Reading backwards from later accounts of a flourishing trade, it would seem that during the late 1540s and throughout the 1550s the French not only arranged to trade in these ports on a more or less regular basis, but that they also recruited Portuguese and Spanish middlemen to market goods and provide information on the activities of defense forces commanded by men who were not a part of the operation. Many of these Portuguese and Spanish middlemen were leaders of their communities and had relatives and patrons at Santo Domingo. Thanks to this network of interested persons, a trade was built up by degrees despite the misunderstandings and fairly frequent acts of violence that mark the 1550s.

The Pattern of Defense Spending

The pattern of defenses developed during the second period in interaction with this pattern of corsair activities was radically different from that of the first period (Table 13). Royal expenditures rose to a mean yearly level four times what they had been earlier. Aggressive naval patrols became the characteristic defenses of this period, with 55 percent of all monies being spent to support squadrons in the Triangle (79 percent of all coastal patrol costs) and in the Antilles (21 percent of all coastal patrol costs; 59 percent of all monies spent for Caribbean defenses). These squadrons were intended to improve the security of commerce by protecting it in areas where it was most likely to be attacked, thereby allowing the crown to try to rely on ship armament regulations and group sailing orders for the protection of ships in other areas. However, as will appear below, wartime conditions made it possible for the Seville Consulado to turn a temporary reinstitution of the convoy system into a more permanent feature of defense (24 percent of all costs), even though the crown continued to try to abolish it as unnecessary because of the security that the coastal patrols, ship armament rules, and group sailings supposedly provided.

Compared to expenses for the defense of commerce, those for land defenses remained small until after the capture of Havana in 1555. That event led to the fortification of the port with a new, modern style of fort, and to resulting high levels of expense (75 percent of all monies spent for forts were spent for Havana; 22 percent of all funds spent for defenses in the Caribbean were so spent). Almost all other forms of defense were given little royal support. The coastal patrols should have provided the Antilles with security by driving corsairs from the area; additional expenses with land defenses should have been unnecessary. In fact, for a variety of reasons, the coastal patrols did not provide security in the Indies. The way was thus prepared for a future change in royal policy towards additional defenses for some of the towns.

Coastal Patrols and Convoys

If events during the early 1540s had taught the crown that its interests as a shipper and as sovereign would be subject to the vetoes of the merchants of Seville so long as they helped to pay the bill for the defense of commerce, those events seem also to have taught the crown

Table 13 Mean Yearly Costs of Various Types of Defense by Geographic Area, 1548–1563 (in Ducats)

Place	Total		Land Total		Man Power		Fortifications		Artillery	
Empire	67,347		5,580	8/100	770	1/100	3,813	6/100	943	1/100
Triangle	30,664	100/46	0		0		0		0	
Caribbean Total	12,993	100/19	4,955	38/89	770	6/100	3,813	29/100	318	2/34
Antilles Total	11,771	100/17	3,965	34/71	581	5/75	3,027	26/79	314	3/33
Puerto Rico	383	100/1	322	84/6	139	36/18	11	3/<1	160	42/17
Santo Domingo	657	100/1	630	96/11	372	57/48	160	24/4	68	10/7
Cuba	3,017	100/4	3,013	99/54	71	2/9	2,856	95/75	86	3/9
Non-Antilles Total	1,034	100/2	802	78/14	7	1/1	786	76/21	4	1/<1
New Spain	682	100/1	450	66/8	0		450	66/12	0	
The Main, Total	352	100/1	352	100/6	7	2/1	336	96/9	4	1/<1
Tierra Firme	349	100/1	349	100/6	5	1/1	336	96/9	4	1/<1
Santa Marta	2	100/<1	2	100/<1	2	100/<1	0		0	

00/00 should be read: the first number is the percentage of total costs for a given area spent for the type of defense in that column (reads across). The second number is the percentage of the total for that type of defense spent in that place (reads down).

Naval Total	General Purpose	Convoys	Coastal Patrols	Place
57,149 85/100	3,473 5/100	16,462 24/100	36,978 55/100	**Empire**
26,402 86/46	0	250 1/2	26,139 85/71	Triangle
7,681 59/13	0	0	7,681 59/21	Caribbean Total
7,681 65/13	0	0	7,681 65/21	Antilles Total
34 9/<1	0	0	34 9/<1	Puerto Rico
0	0	0	0* /<1	Santo Domingo
0	0	0	0	Cuba
0	0	0	0	Non-Antilles Total
0	0	0	0	New Spain
0	0	0	0* /<1	The Main, Total
0	0	0	0	Tierra Firme
0	0	0	0	Santa Marta

* A patrol sent from Cartagena, cost unknown

that transoceanic convoys and a system of group sailings reinforced by patrols in the Triangle were alternative means of protecting commerce. Moveover, the 1540s had taught the need for patrols in the Antilles to guard commerce there. By early 1548 the crown had drawn one conclusion from these lessons: that it should pay for patrols in the Triangle when it wanted them. It had not as yet resolved the related problem of whether to use group sailings or transatlantic convoys to protect merchantmen, even though it had been considering this question since 1546.

For want of documentation from the highest levels of government, the decisions leading to the system announced in 1552 cannot be completely traced, but it is clear from events from 1548 to 1551 that the crown was moving rapidly toward a decision. As always, the path was not straight because emergencies required ad hoc responses.

The first emergency was the need to bring home some 150,000 ducats in revenues available in New Spain in the spring of 1548. Because of the restriction against shipping more than 10,000 ducats in royal revenues per ship, it appeared unlikely that the crown would get all of that money during the current year, when it was badly needed for the war in Germany and to pay debts. To meet this problem, the crown ordered the fitting out of three ships to go and get whatever monies had not already been sent. In funding and purpose, but not in size, this would have been another treasure fleet like those of 1537 and 1542. But more urgent uses for armed ships appeared when it was learned that three French ships had sailed to intercept shipping in the Triangle. Fearful that some of the New Spain money was already on the high seas, the crown at once ordered the enlargement of the squadron and its dispatch to the Azores. In advance of it, orders were sent that all shipments be held in the Indies and that ships arriving in the Azores either wait there for escorts or land their bullion before coming to Spain.[12]

These responses to two very different needs were consistent with earlier policy and the new decision to fund patrols in the Triangle. Also consistent with past practices were the delays in sending Diego López de las Roelas and his ships to sea. Five months passed before he sailed, and by then it was November. Storms soon drove the fleet into port and resulted in the loss of the two largest ships out of six; quite by accident the fleet captured two English ships and was instrumental in the capture of a French ship forced into San Lúcar by weather.

Following these developments, the squadron was refitted at Seville with the addition of its French and one of its English prizes and sent off to the Azores. Over the winter ships had been gathering there as ordered, so that when Roelas returned to San Lúcar on July 25, 1549, he had a good-sized convoy.[13]

Having disposed of the emergency created by the return of French corsairs to the Triangle, the crown turned back to the larger problems of retrieving its funds from New Spain and of providing security for commerce both in the Triangle and in the Antilles. Over the winter it had received a proposal from Álvaro de Bazán, the Elder, that he be given a monopoly of shipping to the Indies in exchange for the introduction into the trade of twenty galleasses of a new type (*de la nueva invención*) and the carriage of the royal revenues at minimal fees. This solution to the problem of secure, regular transatlantic commerce had been referred to the Consulado of Seville, which had objected to it in the strongest terms. In the Consulado's view, group sailings of heavily armed ships, escorted in times of need by a *capitana* (a merchantman with less than a full cargo and more armament and men than the other ships), were the answer, especially if at least four ships were required to sail as a group from any given port in the Indies. In short, they had wanted to continue the practices then in use, with minor adjustments to improve the security of returning shipping. But the Council of the Indies had been prepared to go along with Bazán, using a financing scheme involving a combination of *averías* and some crown funds. In the end, however, a joint meeting of the Councils of State and the Indies had brought out a number of objections, including the observation that "His Majesty has an obligation to provide security on the seas for his subjects," and that the galleasses were technologically unsuited for the trade.[14]

Because this conclusion coincided with the arrival of the first of what proved to be a number of requests from the Antilles for a patrol squadron to deal with the reappearance of corsairs there, the crown decided to try to kill several birds with one stone. On June 27, it ordered Roelas' squadron split into two so that Don Diego could take a ship and two caravels to the Antilles for a combined treasure, anticorsair, and fact-finding mission, while his brother Pedro remained on duty in the Triangle with the rest of the ships. One of Diego's principal jobs in the Antilles would be to obtain the views of the local authorities on Bazán's proposal and the Consulado's reply. In addition, he was to examine the defenses of Havana, which would be the port of assembly for convoys or groups. The wheels were thus set in motion which ground out a decision to create a two-squadron system of patrols.

The brothers' squadrons got to sea in mid-September. Pedro's Spanish squadron sailed to the Capes, where it met four Indies ships. After escorting them to a point east of Cape Santa María, the squadron returned to the Capes, where it remained until late December. Upon its tying up at San Lúcar, the ships were turned over to the Casa.[15]

Diego reached Puerto Rico about mid-November and entered Santo Domingo's harbor at the end of that month, after vainly seeking corsairs in the Mona Passage. From Santo Domingo he reported that the Audiencia felt that a continuous patrol of the Antilles was the only way to prevent future corsair raids. When quizzed about their views on the Bazán proposal and the Consulado's alternative suggestion that group sailings and convoys be reestablished with Havana as the rendezvous point, the Audiencia and other local officials objected because Española was already feeling a shortage of ships to carry away the bulky hides and sugars that were her sole exports. The local officials felt (correctly as events would show) that the convoy would severely limit the supply of ships available for Española's trades. They did not object to using a patrol squadron in the Triangle, so long as such a squadron did not prevent the sending of a coast guard squadron to the Antilles.[16]

Having completed his mission at Santo Domingo, Roelas sailed to Havana. There he inspected the fort and harbor, apparently concluding that the fort was inadequate. That done, he formed a convoy from his ships and six merchantmen. He arrived off San Lúcar about May 13, 1550.[17]

At almost the same moment that the Audiencia of Santo Domingo was rejecting both Bazán's and the Consulado's schemes for the security of commerce, Bazán was submitting a new proposal to use galleons. A committee of members of the Councils of State and the Indies discussed this, after which the proposal was forwarded to each council for its opinion. Bazán proposed to use six galleons during a two-year trial period and to carry royal revenues at a cheap rate in return for various privileges and honors. The Council of State approved the proposal, but the Council of the Indies had some suggestions. These differences were resolved and Bazán was asked to reply, while the Casa was ordered to obtain the views of interested parties at Seville. That done, a complete report was sent to the emperor.

Following receipt of the emperor's order to conclude the agreement under certain conditions, a new round of consultations was made in late January and early February 1550. The resulting draft contract was signed on February 14, even though a few points remained unsettled and some concessions that the emperor had not authorized had been made to Bazán. In forwarding the documents to Charles, his regents, the Kings of Bohemia, noted that, had a contract been signed with Bazán two years earlier, the costs of the Diego López de las Roelas fleet would have been saved and it would not have been necessary to send the fleet then being prepared.[18]

This treasure fleet, being prepared in the spring of 1550, was intended to go to Panamá to bring back to Spain the loot that Licenciado La Gasca had gathered while suppressing the Pizarro Rebellion (1544–1548) in Peru. Diego López de las Roelas' return sped up the preparations because he brought news that La Gasca had almost a million pesos de oro (1.2 million ducats) in silver on the Isthmus. Sancho de Viedma was named to command the treasure fleet, which sailed in early June under orders to go directly to the Isthmus, with only a wood and water stop at San Germán, Puerto Rico.[19]

Almost at the same time that Viedma put to sea, the emperor finally replied to the proposed Bazán contract. His answer was a flat "No!" on certain points. Negotiations began again amidst complaints by the regents about the attitudes of various councilors, including those of the Indies. In reply, the Council of the Indies stated that of the twenty or twenty-one persons who had been consulted about the contract, only five or six had supported it. The Council and most of its clients (the officials of the Casa, the Consulado, and various persons interested in the Indies) had objected, especially to the provision that would have given Bazán and his agents jurisdiction over all other merchants and shippers in the trade. The agents were, after all, merchants in their own right, or so the Council charged. Moreover, the provision that Bazán was to look first to the security of the royal revenues and had no obligation to fight corsairs, even if he met them, did not serve the interests of the Indies nor meet the emperor's original terms for the contract. And Bazán's ships were too few to guard the Indies, even if he took an aggressive stand. Further, the Council said that he had only two of the new galleons, not the three promised. In short, the Council of the Indies believed that it had acted in the best interests of the crown and of its subjects by refusing to agree to the contract.[20]

Nonetheless, by the end of the year agreement had been reached with Bazán on two of the three points to which the emperor had objected. But the result was not entirely satisfactory, despite much effort. Bazán's interest had already turned to providing galleys for the Mediterranean fleet. In the end, the contract was not concluded and the Indies trade and its defense continued along lines already developed.

Precisely what discussions were held during 1551 is unknown, but it is clear that the views of the Audiencia of Santo Domingo, reinforced by Diego López de las Roelas' reports upon his return, and the crown's interest as a shipper who now needed frequent ship movements rather than one or two crossings a year in a convoy, carried the day. The return of Viedma's squadron with relatively little money but many bills probably further solidified opinion against treasure fleets and their cousins, the convoys. Moreover, groups of ships had been sailing safely since June 1550. Licenciado La Gasca had shown that it was possible to arm merchantmen on the Main for the return, and the crown used that idea during the summer and fall of 1551, sending artillery and gunners to man eight ships that it intended to use to bring back additional sums being shipped from Peru.[21] In effect, La Gasca's fleet and that to be prepared the following year on the Isthmus were simply armed groups of ships, exactly what the law required. Having consulted appropriate authorities and seen the course of events since 1546, the crown was at last ready to decide how it would defend commerce during the next war, which was drawing closer with each passing month.

Apparently unaware that the crown's investigations and considerations of the problems of defending commerce and the Indies were about to bear fruit in a new system involving group sailings and coastal patrols, the Consulado had begun to fit out a squadron to sail to the Azores to meet a number of richly laden ships reported heading into European waters newly buffeted by the storms of war. When the crown offered to take over the squadron, the Consulado rejected the offer, except for some artillery from the royal stores. In reply the crown ordered the Casa to prepare two ships plus supplies for the Consulado's four, which were to be seized for the new royal patrol fleet when they returned from the Azores. In due course, the Consulado's fleet and its commander, Cosmé

Rodríguez Farfán, sailed on a voyage that lasted from March until shortly after the fourth of July.[22] Rodríguez Farfán's sailing followed by a few days the proclamation from the steps of the Cathedral of Seville of the crown's new policy for the protection of commerce.

As announced by the chief crier of Seville on that Saturday, March 5, 1552, the crown's policy would be to maintain patrol squadrons in the Triangle and in the Antilles, while demanding that individual ships be armed according to a revised formula that raised the minimum size to one hundred *toneladas* (from eighty) and increased the calibers and numbers of guns to be carried. Once armed in this way, ships would be free to come and go from Seville and the Indies. Because few shipmasters had the required arms and artillery was unavailable in Spain, the crown provided for a nine-month grace period before the new armament requirements went into effect; meanwhile, the crown set about seeking a contractor in the Low Countries who could supply bronze artillery of the types required by the new rules. During the grace period, all shipping was to travel in escorted groups, with four ships of 250 to 300 *toneladas* and two caravels of 80 to 100 *toneladas* as escorts. In addition, some 360 soldiers were to be added to the crews of the escort vessels. The escorts would leave Seville and sail to Havana, spend three months there seeking out corsairs, and then return to Spain with the ships that had gathered. An *avería* of 2.5 percent would cover the cost.[23]

The new orders required the crown to fit out four ships and two caravels for duty off Spain. A similar squadron of four ships would be fitted out at Santo Domingo, with replacement ships and supplies to be sent from Spain. The Antilles squadron thus provided met the requests of officials at Santo Domingo. Note has already been taken of the early requests and of the Audiencia's view of 1549. Similar views were expressed on various occasions in 1548 in the wake of the appearance of three ships of French traders, in letters both preceding and following Roelas' visit, and on at least two occasions in 1550. The composition of the proposed squadron varied from a maximum of two galleons and a *patache de remos*, as proposed to Roelas, to two *zabras*—the smallest size and number of ships capable of meeting the corsairs on their own terms, which by then included the use of similar small oared boats. Other types of ships were also mentioned, but they generally seem to have been craft of between eighty and one hundred tons, swift under sail and equipped with oars for times when the wind failed or was contrary. All proposals argued for lead sheathing for the hulls to prevent damage from marine borers during the periods when the ships were in Santo Domingo's harbor. Santo Domingo was to be the base because of its manpower pool and supplies and because of the apparent concentration of corsairs in the Windward and Mona passages.[24] Moreover, it was the politically obvious choice.

The new system of 1552 was an ingenious solution to the varied problems connected with the defense of commerce. At a stroke it provided for the crown's interest in cheap, safe, and regular shipment of its bullion, for its obligation to defend commerce and its possessions against the corsairs, and for its need to try to enforce the empire's navigation laws, then coming under attack by traders in remote areas of the Antilles. Private interests were provided with protection in the danger zones where shipping was most likely to be attacked. A minimum of restriction was placed on commerce, because ships could sail when cargo and weather permitted. Merchants had security, and at a very low cost, because the costs of the new armament had to be met by the shipowner, who could recover them, if at all, only through competitively determined freight rates. In short, there was something for everyone except, possibly, the shipowners.

Difficulties in implementing the new system of commercial defense began to appear almost at once and grew in magnitude with the passage of time. Similarly, the adjustments in the rules that these difficulties occasioned were minor at first but by the mid-1550s had become so important as to vitiate the strategy underlying the new orders. As king, Philip II was able to reestablish some parts of the policy but did not succeed in restoring it to its original form, with the result that by 1563 a new policy had developed whose lines became clear during the 1560s.

The first problems with the new system developed because a group of shipmasters wanted permission for twenty ships, armed, they said, according to the ordinances, to sail without awaiting the escorts ordered by the crown during the nine-month period before the new rules would go into full force. The crown's reply was to order the selection of six of these ships for partial loading with merchandise and increases in armament and crews. These "warships" would provide the escorts, and an *avería* of 2.5 percent would pay the cost of lost freight revenues, extra crewmen, and extra weapons. That reply in turn produced grumbling from the Casa, which had already embargoed ships for the escort and claimed it did not like using partially loaded merchantmen. Ordered to carry out the crown's demands, the Casa showed no haste in doing so, nor did the merchants hasten to load ships. The shipowners' voices were not heard again. By the time the convoy got to sea under the command of Bartolomé Carreño, on August 11, 1552, it consisted of about fifty ships. It had an eventful voyage lasting some fourteen months.[25]

Preparation of the patrol squadrons presented no more than the usual difficulties of fitting out a fleet, but the fate of the squadron based on Santo Domingo proved to be the first of a series of problems involving the Antilles squadron, problems not resolved until 1557.

The patrol for the Triangle was placed under the command of Alonso Pexón in late July. It consisted of two ships fitted out by the Casa and the four ships that had composed Cosmé Rodríguez Farfán's squadron. Sailing shortly after the first of August, Pexón went to the Azores to await ships coming from Tierra Firme. Resupplied there from Seville, he returned to San Lúcar towards the end of October with the Tierra Firme ships. Paying the crews and refitting the ships began at once and lasted into December.[26]

The king's orders for the fleet at Santo Domingo were received there in early April with enthusiasm. The Audiencia took charge of selecting two ships and two caravels. Artillery was taken from the fort and money provided from funds accumulated by the treasury from ships putting in under stress of weather. Because men and certain materials were in short supply, the crown was asked to send one hundred men and various supplies on the first available ships. Several writers also suggested that the crown would save money if it sent two or more ships, with full crews and supplies, from Spain. In Spain, at the same time, the crown had accepted the recommendations made by experts called in by the Casa that only supplies be sent.[27]

With flags and pennants snapping in the breeze, the Española Squadron sailed on the Day of St. James, July 25, 1552. Cristóbal Colón, grandson of the Discoverer, was in command of two ships and two caravels ranging in size from the 360-ton *capitana* to a small, 80-ton caravel. The squadron's first objective was to capture two French corsairs reported at Mona. Forewarned, the intruders fled. The squadron continued its patrol of the Mona Passage. Licenciado Alonso de Zorita reported that the ship in which he was sailing to Santo Domingo was chased by the squadron. Each thought the other to be a corsair.[28]

Not long after Zorita was chased, on Monday, August 29, 1552, a hurricane of considerable force hit the coast of Española. The squadron was caught at sea near Saona. The small caravel was driven ashore and wrecked, but without loss of men or artillery. The *capitana* and the other caravel were demasted but were saved from sinking because everything except the bronze artillery was thrown overboard before they too could be driven onto the shore. The fourth ship was separated from the others and presumably sank without a trace, along with all 120 men aboard. Once the remains of the squadron had reassembled in Santo Domingo's harbor, the crews and ships were discharged.

The seriousness of the losses sustained in the wreck of the Colón squadron was not at first apparent. Enough guns and munitions remained so that in September the Audiencia felt able to order the arming of four ships to attack a corsair reported at Saona. However, the treasury officials objected that there was little money and that the expense had not been authorized from Spain. The squadron apparently did not sail and the corsair left the area.[29] The crown's representatives at Santo Domingo then set about trying to get replacement ships, men, and matériel from Spain. This proved to be the first major difficulty that the crown's new system encountered.

Elsewhere in the Caribbean, another group of local officials took up the crown's idea of a patrol squadron and applied it in the time-honored manner by fitting out an ad hoc group of rowing barges (*barcos*). The incident occurred at Nombre de Dios and involved the capture of a French corsair becalmed off that port.[30] This was the first of a number of such ad hoc squadrons fitted out in the 1550s and 1560s. The need for such squadrons suggests that the crown's plan of 1552 was already out of date, a conclusion that the crown did not reach at the time because the pattern of corsair raids still seemed to center on the Antilles.

News of the disastrous end of the Española Squadron did not reach Spain until the spring of 1553. In the intervening months the crown fitted out a number of additional ships to reinforce Pexón's squadron, arranged with merchants to have supplies given to the fleet while on station in the Azores, and refitted the squadron so that Pexón was again at sea in early June.

Following Pexón's departure, the Casa de Contratación turned its attentions to fitting out the two 200-ton ships that the crown had just ordered for the Española Squadron. By late July two ships were on hand, but they did not meet the specifications. Diverted by other matters, the Casa did little about fitting out the squadron for the rest of 1553. It was the first of several delays.

The principal cause of the Casa's failure to prepare ships for the Española Squadron was its involvement in the preparation of a convoy. Had the letter of the rule of 1552 been carried out, there would have been no convoy. Indeed, in late 1552 it appeared that the rule was going to be enforced. Groups of ships sailed to the Indies, apparently armed according to the new rules. This continued to be so in the spring of 1553. Moreover, the crown refused in March and May to allow the Consulado to collect an *avería* on the value of merchandise being shipped in groups of ships, even though the money was supposed to pay for additional patrol ships in the Triangle, the reinforcements for Pexón already noted. Following Pexón's departure for the Azores in June and the receipt of additional reports of corsairs, the Consulado, backed by the Casa, made a frontal assault on the rule of 1552. Some twenty-five merchantmen were ready to sail, but the merchants did not want to pay the extra costs of additional soldiers and artillery for each. Instead, they asked the crown to allow them to equip a warship of 250–300 tons, with a crew of 150 men, to accompany the group. The crown rejected this proposal, ordering that each ship be armed according to the rules of 1552. Nonetheless, because the Consulado had begged permission to fit out two escort ships at the expense of the *avería*, the crown agreed to allow this provided that the convoy sailed by the first of September and provided that all the ships were armed according to the rules. Only if all shippers agreed to delay the departure beyond September 1 could it be delayed. The crown thus sought to uphold the letter of the ordinance while unwittingly destroying its intention: frequent sailings of small groups of merchantmen armed to resist attacks. The Consulado capped its success in Valladolid by securing an order directly from the emperor in Flanders limiting convoys to two per year, each escorted by three warships. One would sail at the end of August, the other at the end of January. The system of 1543 had been reestablished.[31]

Having revived the convoy system, the merchants proceeded to show the ways in which it could be used in their own interests. Already caught up in the early stages of the great depression of trade during the 1550s, the merchants began to drag out the loading of additional ships while they awaited the return of the Carreño convoy. As a result the convoy scheduled for August did not sail until December. That it consisted of some forty ships was less significant than the deliberate delays. Needless to say, no convoy sailed in January 1554.

While this situation was developing, Pexón continued to patrol, and French commerce raiders continued to prepare and sail. The Azores squadron was reinforced in August with one of Álvaro de Bazán's galleasses, just in time to break up a French attempt to intercept the returning convoy. Pexón remained in the Azores until October, when he found preparations underway to send him back to sea to patrol as far as the Capes until March 1554, when he would be sent to the Azores to pick up treasure left by the *almiranta* of the Carreño fleet and escort in any ships that had gathered over the winter. Although ready to sail by the end of the year, bad weather kept him in port until mid-February, when an order was received diverting the squadron to La Coruña to form part of the fleet being assembled to carry Prince Philip to England for his marriage with Mary Tudor.[32] Once again, emergencies had arisen that overrode the crown's plans.

The order diverting Pexón to La Coruña also diverted Fray Juan de Menderichaga and his squadron of four ships from their projected voyage to Española, where they were to become the coastal squadron replacing the ships lost in 1552. A request for them had come during the summer of 1553 and had been acted on quickly. Except for trouble in finding ships acceptable to Menderichaga, preparations had moved ahead rapidly and the squadron was well on the road towards sailing when the order came in February. Thus began the second delay in fitting out the new Española Squadron.[33]

Coincident with the diversion of Menderichaga to La Coruña, the need for that squadron, and another on the Main, was being urged on the crown. Pedro Menéndez de Valdés (later known as Pedro Menéndez de Avilés), a seaman with good connections at court, had been entrusted with documents and oral expressions of the desire of the Audiencia and other officials for a speedy replacement of the first squadron. He arrived at court in early February 1554, where he and the documents he carried argued for a squadron of eight ships, half of them equipped with oars because the corsairs were using rowed craft. In addition, the crown had before it a report from the governor of Cartagena stating that in June 1553, a corsair had been sighted off his town and that the governor wished the crown to supply a three-caravel squadron for the Main. He offered to help finance it with an *avería* on his port's commerce. A similar proposal had been made as early as 1548; the ad hoc squadron fitted out at Nombre de Dios in 1552 had suggested a similar need.[34] Not as yet convinced of the need for a squadron on the Main, the crown archived the request, as it did the proposals carried by Menéndez de Valdés. Provision for the Española Squadron would be made once the more pressing business of getting Prince Philip to England was out of the way. However, that short-sighted attention to the needs of the moment left the Antilles at the mercy of the corsairs, with results to be noted below, and also brought about a situation in Spain that resulted in the crown's backing away from an important part of its plan of 1552. What happened was that there were confrontations with the Consulado over the security of commerce in the Triangle.

Because of the absence of a royal squadron following Pexón's departure for La Coruña on March 21 and then Menderichaga's in early April, the Consulado again decided to fit out its own fleet to go to the Azores to carry out the tasks that Pexón would have accomplished. Four ships and a caravel were prepared and one Antón Camacho given the command, but the crown then took that post from him and bestowed it on Juan Tello de Guzmán. The merchants protested, but in vain; the crown was determined to control the fleet even if it did not pay for it. But that was not the end of the matter, for when the crown ordered the Consulado to help the Casa obtain loans so that Tello de Guzmán could be refitted, the Consulado replied that it had taken out 12,000 ducats in loans for the convoy of 1553 and suggested that the crown seek its own loans. Hitting where it hurt, the crown replied that in that case an *avería* would be collected to pay the cost of Tello de Guzmán's cruise after refitting and noted that it had ordered Menderichaga to sea from La Coruña at its own expense. In short, the crown would only pay for one patrol squadron, although it might order more and pay part of their costs by an *avería* on its own shipments. That the crown intended to dominate the situation was further shown by its refusal to let the Consulado take charge of refitting Tello de Guzmán or to allow the lumping of the costs of his squadron with those of the convoy escorts under Cosmé Rodríguez Farfán, whose convoy he was to meet in the Azores that fall.[35] The merchants were compelled to accept the crown's orders, but they did not like them. Tello de Guzmán sailed and spent the fall waiting in vain for Rodríguez Farfán, whose ships were scattered by a storm.

The disagreement over Tello de Guzmán was soon followed by a conflict over whether to allow a group of eight ships to sail for the Indies without escorts. The Consulado persuaded the Casa not to allow them to sail because there were no "warships" available to escort them. The crown saw this as the excuse it was, saying that "very commonly merchants and private persons ask for the license of our Council of the Indies to go [to the Indies] with single ships without escort or group."[36] If the ships were armed according to the rules of 1552, they would be adequately defended. The ships were so armed and therefore were allowed to sail.

At Seville that fall, Menderichaga tried to get his ships and crews into shape for the Atlantic crossing that he had been ordered to make early in the next year, but his death on November 28 brought the preparations to a halt. Four months passed before new orders were issued for the Española Squadron. In the interim, the crown apparently hoped that the two oared caravels that it had ordered purchased at Santo Domingo for the squadron would be adequate. That they would not be had been shown that summer when the small squadron commanded by the treasurer, Alonso de la Peña, had sailed against corsairs reported in the Mona Passage. Peña had chased them from the Passage—to Santiago de Cuba and Jamaica, where they stole over 50,000 pesos worth of goods! In the aftermath, the crown received a number of petitions for a larger squadron.[37]

Aside from the lack of a squadron for Española, the year 1554 closed on what appeared to be a note of the crown's resolution to continue the system ordered in 1552 in spite of the emperor's approval of convoys. In particular, the crown allowed four slavers to sail for Cabo Verde over the protests of the Consulado, which said that it objected to any license that would allow anyone the advantage of getting to the Indies with his goods before the other mechants could do so. The crown also announced to the Casa that it had made arrangements with Álvaro de Bazán, the Younger (later the marqués de Santa Cruz) to use a squadron of two galleasses and two *zabras* as a royal patrol force in the Triangle. Until Bazán could sail, Luís de Carvajal, who already had six ships at sea, was being ordered south from the Cantabrian coast to the coast of Andalusia.[38]

While thus making arrangements to continue the patrol system and seeming to uphold the intent of the 1552 rules, the crown deviated from those rules by allowing the Casa and the Consulado to agree to refit Tello de Guzmán for a return trip to the Azores and, more significant, by changing its mind on convoys to the extent of ordering the Casa to prepare a convoy for April! Perhaps the only way to reconcile these conflicts with the crown's other actions is to accept them as expedients resorted to in wartime—in this case because of the numbers of French corsairs sighted on the Capes during December 1554 and January 1555 and those reported arming to join their fellows in the spring.

These same reports caused the crown to take advantage of delays in the sailing of Tello de Guzmán's twelve-ship squadron to order that four of them be prepared for duty in the Antilles. Tello de Guzmán was to command them if he returned from the Azores by the time they were ready to sail.[39] However, it soon became evident that the squadron's departure would be further delayed.

First, Tello de Guzmán decided that he wanted two new ships, in addition to three older ones that he would take from the coastal squadron, because of the marine borers in the river at Santo Domingo. The crown approved this request, again stating its desire to have everything in readiness so that Tello de Guzmán, some of the crewmen, the artillery, and some other supplies could be transferred from his Triangle squadron to the ships of the Antilles squadron immediately upon his return to San Lúcar. However, a subsequent royal order approved the use of two ships from the Azores squadron if two new ships could not be found. That provided the Casa with an excuse to put off preparations for the squadron. No new ships of suitable size could be found, so the problem was left to await Tello de Guzmán's return from the Azores.[40] By that time, August 11, the Casa was under orders to prepare Bazán's ships for a voyage to Flanders. Having just sent three of Carvajal's ships to Puerto Rico for cargoes left there by three of Rodríguez Farfán's convoy ships and being engaged in trying to get the convoy going in the face of merchant resistance, the Casa saw no reason to hasten the departure of the Española Squadron, especially because suitable ships were not at hand. The ship problem was referred back to court.

While patrols off Española were thus being delayed yet another year, patrols in the Triangle continued. Carvajal and Bazán had, between them, provided security during the summer of 1555 by coming down to the Capes in the spring, with Bazán then taking his squadron to the Canaries to guard them against a French attack that did not materialize. Carvajal eventually returned to the Cantabrian coast, while Bazán sailed to the Azores, then to San Lúcar, and thence, after refitting, to the Capes. Brought back to Seville to prepare for the Flanders voyage,

Bazán found that his orders for the following spring took him to the Capes, where illness caused him to remain. Receipt of the news of the Truce of Vaucelles made his projected trip to the Canaries unnecessary and allowed the crown to order his ships prepared to go to the relief of Oran.[41]

The coming of the truce was the signal not only to disband the patrol in the Triangle, but also to cease convoys. That summer the Casa allowed six, then four ships to sail as a group, provided they were armed as required by the rules of 1552.[42] Disbanded too were active preparations for the Española Squadron. Under orders issued in December 1555, the Casa had eventually found one small ship (ca. 150–180 *toneladas*) of the five that it was supposed to supply. This ship had been under embargo until April, when it was released because the crown decided to buy the ships in Vizcaya; but that plan in turn was abandoned, and by May the Casa was again seeking ships. At this point, the crown, undoubtedly motivated by the truce and its financial problems, decided to postpone fitting out the squadron until after the wheat harvest (August) when flour, and hence biscuit, would be cheaper. Nonetheless, it authorized the Casa to purchase *La Gineta* (135 tons), one of Bazán's French prizes. During September the *Santiago* (200 tons) and the *San Juan* (80 tons) were added to the list. The former was described as a "galleass" and the latter as a very small galley (*galeaceta pequeña*). All the ships were sent to the dockyards to have lead sheathing attached to their bottoms. The final two ships were acquired that fall, one from Vizcaya, the other in Andalusia.[43]

The truce of 1555 was short lived. Even as Bazán was being prepared for the relief of Oran, the crown learned that French corsairs were continuing to sail. Moreover, a large amount of money was being shipped from New Spain, and there were reports that the Tierra Firme convoy had been hit by a storm that had heavily damaged many of its ships. For all of these reasons, a patrol force was urgently needed in the Azores to meet the returning ships. Resorting to a pre-1552 practice, the crown ordered the Consulado to fit out a squadron, with payment to be made by an *avería*. Shipmasters in the incoming fleet were sent an order to gather at the Azores and wait for the escort. Seeing the danger, the Consulado agreed to fit out two ships and nominated a commander; however, the siege of Oran was lifted and Bazán's squadron became available, thus shifting the burden of patrols to the crown's purse. By then it was September. Bazán's six-week cruise took him to the Capes and resulted in the capture of a French ship.[44]

In anticipation of the complete breakdown of the truce, which came in the late spring of 1557, the balance of 1556 and the first six months of 1557 were spent in the preparation of the Española Squadron, the Bazán patrol squadron, and a convoy. Tello de Guzmán was assigned the job of escorting the convoy, which accounts for much of the delay in the sailing of his squadron for Española. Bazán's squadron seems to have been delayed by the Casa's inability to efficiently handle so many chores at once.[45]

Tello de Guzmán finally took the Española Squadron to sea on July 20, 1557, just five days short of five years after the original squadron had sailed from Santo Domingo on its ill-fated maiden voyage. In the interim, the corsairs had had almost free reign in the Antilles as well as elsewhere in the Caribbean. Understandably, residents of the Antilles had been disappointed by the continual delays in sending the squadron from Spain, especially after the convoy of 1555, which passed Puerto Rico in January 1556, left word that the squadron was on its way and would arrive in March 1556. This news had been greeted with expressions of great pleasure, but also with a reminder that the squadron was needed earlier and could have done service against French corsairs.[46] But Tello de Guzmán did not appear, although French corsairs continued to do so, even after the truce.

So desperate did the situation in the Antilles become that during Holy Week of 1556, the governor of Puerto Rico and a wealthy resident of that city sent a caravel against a *patache* of Frenchmen who were raiding in the Mona Passage. At Santo Domingo, a little later that spring, a newly purchased brigantine and two ships being maintained pending the arrival of a squadron from Spain were sent out under the command of Captain Juan de Montejo, apparently to counter a corsair threat. The same ships were sent out again in January 1557 under the joint command of Juan de Guzmán and García de Escalante.[47]

Neither Tello de Guzmán nor Bazán got to sea until after the truce had broken down in the spring of 1557. For present purposes it is enough to note that Bazán remained on patrol with varying numbers of ships until the fall of 1559, when the return of peace caused the crown to discharge his ships after six cruises, including two to the Azores, two battles with the French, the capture of four French ships (1557), two battles with "Turkish" corsairs off Andalusia (1558, 1559), and the loss of two ships to them (1559).[48] Although his effectiveness in driving corsairs from the seas was no greater than that of earlier squadrons, Bazán did carry out the crown's general policy of patrolling in the Triangle and prevented, with the help of the convoy system, the loss of any important Spanish cargoes returning from the Indies. The same could not be said of Tello de Guzmán's squadron, to whose history we now turn in some detail because the problems he encountered were to remain for later squadrons to try to solve.

After leaving Spain in July 1557, Tello de Guzmán spent some two months in the crossing, arriving at Santo Domingo on October 9. Six weeks were spent gathering supplies and preparing the fleet for patrols. At the same time, the treasury officials forwarded an order to Tierra Firme for payment of 20,000 ducats in silver as a subsidy for the fleet. This was the first subsidy for defenses for the Indies. That it was needed is shown by the discontent and desertions among crewmen paid in the vellon currency of the island.[49]

The squadron put to sea on November 25 on a voyage no details of which have been preserved except that the ships returned to port on December 28. Resupplied, the squadron sailed for the Mona Passage on January 5, 1558, as the escort for two merchantmen bound for Spain. One of these ships got ahead of the group and was captured by a French corsair based on Mona without the squadron being able to do anything about it, if indeed Tello de Guzmán even tried to do anything. The ships next entered San Juan de Puerto Rico (February 22). Resupplied in twelve days, they sailed to San Germán, where they remained until Palm Sunday (late March). Again short on supplies, the squadron sailed to Santo Domingo, narrowly missing another corsair at Guadianilla, where it had captured a Portuguese slaver from São Tomé. The squadron reentered Santo Domingo's harbor on April 14.[50]

Continuing desertions of the crew led the squadron's officers to take a number of steps to keep the squadron effective. In consultation with the Audiencia and the local treasury officials, they agreed to pay the crewmen two ducats worth of vellon quartos for each ducat of salary they were entitled to, although it was recognized that even with this improvement such a wage was still inadequate because of local prices. It was also agreed to sell one of the ships for which there was no crew. This was the second ship to be sold. The first had been sold the preceding October and replaced by a caravel.

Resupplied again, the squadron set out for San Germán in early May. An intermediate objective was a French ship reported at Soco. It escaped. Apparently learning that corsairs frequented the Windward Passage during the summer months, Tello de Guzmán decided to split his squadron. The *almiranta* and a *patache* were left on duty off Saona while Tello de Guzmán took two other ships and went first to Ocoa and then to La Yaguana, leaving orders with the squadron's treasury officials to send supplies to him at the latter port. He arrived at La Yaguana at about the same date that his admiral entered Santo Domingo (ca. May 15), thinking that his ship would be put into the dockyard for a badly needed careening. Instead, it was loaded with the supplies the general had requested and sent to La Yaguana. The *almiranta* was sent instead of the *patache*, which was in better condition, because of a report that some French ships had robbed Puerto Plata and were planning to attack La Yaguana.[51]

At La Yaguana, Tello de Guzmán had also heard of the attack on Puerto Plata. About mid-June he grew tired of waiting for the French to come to him and decided to sail to Santo Domingo by way of the northern coast. He attempted to get to sea a number of times but failed because of adverse winds. He then decided to wait out the hurricane season at La Yaguana and sent orders to Santo Domingo for more supplies and ship tackle to be forwarded. The *Francesa*, which had just been sold, was rented from her new owner to carry those supplies and the squadron's officials to La Yaguana. Meanwhile, corsairs had raided San Germán and attempted to attack San Juan, thus causing some residents of Puerto Rico to write to the crown requesting that the squadron be based on their island, which was to windward of all the places the corsairs visited, and complaining that the squadron was a joke among the corsairs. They charged that the people at Santo Domingo only wanted the squadron to protect themselves, not the Antilles in general. That was a perceptive observation, but Puerto Rico lacked the political power to have its view—correct on strategic grounds—prevail.[52]

Tello de Guzmán and his ships remained at La Yaguana until September 29, 1558. They got as far as Monte Cristi on the return voyage before adverse weather again created problems. The squadron twice attempted to sail from that harbor and was twice forced back. Finally, because of a critical shortage of supplies, the sick were put ashore and told to make their ways overland to Santo Domingo as best they could. The ships finally made it back to Santo Domingo at the end of December. They were immediately careened, and supplies were gathered for another patrol the next spring. It had been a disappointing cruise that had served only to keep the French from some parts of the island's coast, which meant that they raided other areas. The contrast of this performance with the fortuitous capture of two French ships off Havana by escorts of the Roelas convoy must have convinced the crown of the rightness of ending the Tello de Guzmán squadron, an action already ordered before the news of the fall of 1558 could have been known in Spain.[53]

The disbanding of the squadron was ordered on December 19, 1558, in response to the letters written by Tello de Guzmán and his officers in July. Even that early (July), the ineffectiveness of the squadron against the French was obvious. Its supply and crew problems, which both came down to money, were also telling arguments against its continued existence. Accordingly, the crown ordered the crews paid off and all but the two best ships sold. They were to remain at Santo Domingo for use in fitting out ad hoc squadrons.[54] Initiative would thus be returned to the local authorities who had shown in the years between 1552 and 1557 that they could equip and dispatch squadrons.

While these orders were on their way to Santo Domingo, the squadron's ships, less the unseaworthy *capitana*, which had been sold, prepared for a voyage as escorts for a group of merchantmen going through the Mona Passage. By April 5, all was in readiness. The voyage followed the same pattern as the first voyage in 1558. The squadron escorted the merchantmen through the Mona Passage and then put into San Juan, almost as if it were answering the complaints of its absence that the Puerto Ricans continued to send to Spain. It remained there from May 17 until June 11, leaving only when word came that a French ship was at San Germán attempting to extort food from the residents. After failing to intercept the corsair, the squadron returned to Santo Domingo, arriving on June 21.[55] The next day it received the order to disband.

The squadron's performance was, to say the least, equivocal, neither demonstrating that a windward squadron could drive the corsairs from the Antilles nor proving that it could not. All that was demonstrated were the high cost, the need for subsidies (recognized as early as 1552), the logistic problems of maintaining a fleet based on the Antilles, and the difficulties of capturing corsairs who had allies at every ranch along the coasts. These were important problems, some of whose solutions would be incorporated into subsequent attempts to patrol the Antilles.

The problem of means (costs) versus ends (defense) had thus been posed in the form that it was to have for the rest of the colonial period. The answer to the problem had not been worked out as a policy; politics and a general sense of royal obligation to subjects would provide the answer in later years.

That such an answer would have to involve more than just a squadron in the Antilles was demonstrated anew by the patrol that the governor of Cartagena had occasion to fit out that spring in a vain search for corsairs who had taken most of the ships in the coastal traffic along the Main.[56] By patrolling in the Antilles, the Spanish had made the undefended Main more attractive. Nonetheless, the patrols in the Antilles were a step in the right direction. War in the Caribbean after 1563 was to be a naval war, which would be best dealt with by aggressive patrol squadrons rather than by passive land and sea defenses.

But after the establishment of peace with France in 1559, such problems receded into the background. The system of defenses for commerce ordered in 1552 and modified in 1554 by the addition of the convoys was brought to an end. As has been noted, Bazán's ships were dismissed from the royal payroll in the fall of 1559. At Santo Domingo, the two ships left from the Tello de Guzmán squadron were removed from the royal accounts, the one by sale, the other by gift to a Franciscan who wanted to use her in a pacification project. At Seville, the last convoy had sailed that spring. A subsequent order to fit out a warship to escort ships going to Tierra Firme that fall should be viewed as the crown's effort to provide the new viceroy of Peru with passage befitting his station rather than as a royal interest in continuing the convoy system as such.[57]

Except for the failure to get a squadron operating in the Antilles until late in the war, the system of defenses had worked well. Commerce moving in the Triangle had suffered minimal losses to the corsairs, although whether that was because of the convoy system, the new rules of armament, the work of the patrol squadrons, or even some failure by the corsairs to develop a coordinated plan of attack was not clear. The various methods of defense had worked as a package. On the transoceanic run the results were equally hard to evaluate. On the surface, the convoy seemed to have been completely successful in preventing losses to corsairs, but such a judgment needed to be offset by a consideration of the danger from them. Groups of ships armed according to the rules of 1552 had moved just as unharmed through the Atlantic,

Caribbean, and Gulf of Mexico, and they continued to do so in late 1559 and into the early 1560s. Thus the methods that might be used when commerce was again threatened, or seemed to be threatened, would not be a function of some demonstrated superiority of a set of weapons or techniques, but rather a function of the balance of political forces involved in making that decision. Events during the war suggested that the balance had changed between 1551/52 and 1559. Developments in 1560/61 confirm that observation.

Beginning in the spring of 1560, "Turkish" corsairs—probably North Africans like those of 1558 and 1559—again struck at Spanish coastal shipping. Because there was no patrol squadron, they enjoyed success and continued their raids during the next two years. So serious did the situation become that the crown arranged for the Consulado to hire Bazán to operate a squadron of eight galleys along the coast, to be paid for by an *avería* because the crown was broke. However, this patrol squadron did little because its creation coincided with the reestablishment of the convoy system, which soon absorbed what little money the merchants were willing to put up for the defense of commerce. Bazán's other commitments and the crown's growing disinterest in a squadron that seemed to be unnecessary finished off the patrol squadron in 1565.[58] Other means were found in later years to deal with the threat that these North African raiders presented; those means will be noted in the following chapter.

What is of moment here is the resumption of the convoy system, a decision inspired by a series of corsair attacks on a group of seven ships that sailed from Santo Domingo in March 1561. Improperly armed (under the rules of 1552), four of the ships were captured by four small French ships while beating around Saona. The remaining three ships escaped but were attacked by other French ships off the Azores and again off the Capes. This news caused the Consulado and the Casa to air their pet grievances about the way the trade was being conducted. They claimed that under the group sailing and ship armament rules, shipping ran great risks from the corsairs; and they went on to attack the trade between the Canaries and the Antilles, claiming that improperly armed ships entered the *carrera* via that route. The remedies they sought were resumption of the twice-yearly convoys and severe restriction on the Canaries-Antilles trade.[59]

The case for the resumption of the convoy made in Seville that summer bordered on the absurd. The convoy had never tried to protect shipping sailing from the Antilles, that is, from Santo Domingo. Those ships came in their own group or singly, but never in convoy from Havana. The trade with the Canaries did allow improperly armed ships to enter the trade, but that was not the real reason for the Consulado's objections to it. But absurd or not, the Council of the Indies agreed with the proposal. The convoy system was reestablished by an order of July 16, 1561. The rules were further elaborated in 1562 and 1564 and modified thereafter as need arose.[60] The merchants had been provided with the device they were to use so successfully to control the trade. Significantly, 1561 was a time of economic difficulties for the Indies merchants.

The power that the merchants demonstrated in this situation was both financial and political. Financially they were about to start providing most of the money for Bazán's patrol squadron as well as offering to take on the defense of commerce in a way that was clearly cheaper for the crown than the system of patrols ordered in 1552. Yet the fact that they had their way was due to political rather than economic facts. The crown had been just as short of money in 1552 as it was in 1562. What had changed was the relationship between the crown and this important group of clients. The merchants had won a series of political victories on this issue in the 1550s and had probably strengthened their political position at court in numerous other ways that await their historian. Moreover, it could be argued that their system of defense—the convoy—had seemed to work better than the crown's and had, with a few exceptions, provided the same regular, secure, and cheap shipment of the royal revenues that the crown had wanted to obtain via its system of 1552. That the exceptions to regularity had occurred precisely in those years when the trade was depressed passed unnoticed even though that fact foretold similar breaks in the convoy system should similar economic conditions develop. In the absence of any organized opposition from shipowners or powerful interests in the Indies or the royal *fiscal*, the merchants had their way. The patrimonial assumptions behind royal policy-making allowed no other outcome.

Particularly important in the political equation was the change in the crown's perception of its own interest. In 1552, it had believed that convoys were not in its interest as a shipper, and had thus acted to provide another system of defenses for commerce, one that also agreed with the interests articulated by the Audiencia of Santo Domingo, then still relatively powerful but a decade later a shadow of its former self so far as court politics were concerned. No one considered the general public welfare, as we are accustomed to define that term in this post-Utilitarian age, in either decision (it was pure coincidence that the crown's system of 1552 would have been beneficial to almost everyone in the empire). A numerically small juridical group was thus allowed to seize advantages that were to prove detrimental to the interests of the crown and of other groups in the body politic. On the surface, it was simply a military decision decided on technical grounds in response to a petition from those most immediately concerned.

In the Indies, a similar absence of any clear royal policy to the contrary allowed the subjects to have their ways when the need seemed to arise to use royal money to fit out patrol squadrons to chase the few corsairs who seemed to be in ignorance of the peace made in Europe. Thus in August 1560, merchantmen were used to patrol the coast near Cartagena. On its second voyage, the squadron sailed east to Santa Marta and tried to reach Río de la Hacha to pick up royal funds to protect them from English corsairs reported on the coast. Three years later the officials of Santo Domingo sent out a patrol squadron to escort merchantmen past Saona, a response to the debacle of 1561.[61] These were the first of several such squadrons fitted out at Santo Domingo or on the Main, mostly at Cartagena, in response to the resumption of corsair activity after 1559. They form part of the history of events leading to the creation of the Indies Fleet in 1567.

In sum, by 1563, when royal spending again dropped to near zero and when the last hope of a diplomatic defense of the empire was dying, the system of defenses for commerce developed during the 1550s had been resurrected in its essential elements, although only the convoy and the patrol squadron in the Triangle had taken on forms that were more than ad hoc responses to passing threats. Precedent, patrimonialism, and royal parsimony (really poverty) thus set the stage for a new period of defense spending when undeclared naval war again engulfed the Indies.

Land Defenses: Fortifications

By comparison to the coastal patrols and convoys, land defenses of all types did not receive much royal money before 1557, and even after the new fort at Havana was begun in that year, the total spent on land defenses from 1548 to 1563 was quite low (89,278 ducats of a total defense bill of 1,077,553 ducats). This situation arose because prior to the mid-1550s the crown was able to assume that the system of small forts, a few pieces of artillery, caretaker garrisons, if any, and the militia would do the job of protecting the towns from raids.

The crown and its agents in the Indies did see to the maintenance of existing forts and tried to bring to completion the system of forts envisioned in the order of 1542. In particular, the crown tried to get a fort built at Nombre de Dios (orders of 1549, 1550, 1551, 1555), but the only result was the construction of a bulwark on the beach in 1552. Like the fortification of La Yaguana and additions to the fortifications at Puerto Rico and Havana, this bulwark at Nombre de Dios was as much the result of community effort as of royal funding.[62]

For other areas, the crown received requests for funds for fortifications and ordered investigations, but little was accomplished, probably because the apparent decline in corsair raids on towns and the decision to send the patrol squadron to Santo Domingo seemed to negate the need for additional fortifications. Examples are the requests for funds from Río de la Hacha (1550), which led to an investigation; the requests of Cartagena and Santa Marta (1553), which were not even replied to; and the efforts of the Audiencia of Santo Domingo to follow up on earlier royal orders for forts at La Yaguana, Puerto Plata, and Azua. Corsair raids from 1550 onwards had convinced the judges that La Yaguana needed a *tapia* "strong house" consisting of a central tower and a curtain wall around a courtyard, the wall provided with loopholes for artillery. The successful flanking of the town's bulwark on the beach in 1553 reinforced the Audiencia's conviction, but the crown did not authorize a fort for La Yaguana. Similarly, the Audiencia's projects for keep and bailey forts at Puerto Plata, Puerto Real, and Azua met with no reply. The corsairs were able to stop Spanish trade with those ports and begin their own, because without defenses the residents soon gave up the uneven struggle.[63]

Havana was a different case from those just noted. From the mid-1540s its fort, which was nothing more than a keep and bailey, had been criticized as inadequate for guarding what was by then the assembly port for much of the shipping returning to Spain. This shift in the navigation pattern of the Caribbean, coupled with criticisms made in 1545 and the renewal of the undeclared naval war in 1548 resulted in a series of royally directed inquiries and reports on the port and its fort. In 1550 and 1551, the captains-general of the royal treasure fleets, Diego López de las Roelas and Sancho de Viedma, inspected the town and fort. The new warden, Juan de Lobera, sent the crown a detailed description of the existing structure and a request for workmen, funds, and a plan for enlarging the fort.[64] The town council seconded Lobera's request. The crown apparently did order New Spain to send some money, but nothing came of the order. Visitors to the city continued to warn of its inadequate defenses, one even going so far as to say that "if it is taken, in my judgment Your Majesty will not have any Indies."[65] Efforts of the city to remedy this weakness of its defenses by completing a bulwark on the beach to the west of the entrance of the port, by purchasing artillery, and by posting guards did not materially change the tactical realities.

Jacques de Sores captured Havana on July 10, 1555, forced the surrender of the fort after a brief fire fight, and occupied the town for almost a month (until August 5). When he left, he finished burning the fort's doors and other combustibles in the tower. Defenseless except for the dispirited militia, the town was taken again in September.

As soon as news of this disaster reached Spain, plans for a new fort for Havana, apparently already drawn but not sent, were brought out and approved and funds were ordered from New Spain. But it required almost seven years to get construction into high gear. Two years were taken up hiring an engineer, stonecutters, and masons, and gathering tools, which then took eight months to reach Havana. The result was that excavation of the foundation trenches only began on December 1, 1558. The pace continued at that slow rate, even though the crown infused funds from New Spain (Table 14). Exasperated, the crown fired Bartolomé Sánchez, the engineer, in August 1560. His replacement, Francisco Calona, did not arrive in Havana until June 1562, a month before the first group of slaves owned by the crown came to begin work.

Calona found that Sánchez had completed the expropriation of land, had finished the foundation trenches, had quarried and cut stone, and had lime at hand for mortar. Also at hand were most of the problems that were to plague the construction of the fort in the future. Money was in short supply despite the crown's drafts on New Spain. Conflict between the governor and other local officials and the engineer in charge was rife, a condition to which Calona was to contribute his share. Labor, then being supplied largely by slaves furnished by the city's resi-

Table 14   **New Spain Subsidy for Havana Fort Construction, 1558–1578**

Date	Amount	Source and Notes
1. January 15, 1558	12,000 *pesos OM*	Royal Order, December 9, 1556. AGI, Contaduría 666, "Data de los pesos ... que el y los dichos oficiales ... enviaron a la Habana ... ," sin folio, fol. [3–4]. Cited hereafter as "Data a Havana."
2. March 13, 1561	6,000 *pesos OM*	AGI, Contaduría 666, "Data a Havana," fols. [5–6]. See also AGI, Contaduría 667A, No. 2, R. 1, no folio.
3. April 4, 1562	12,000 *pesos OM*	AGI, Contaduría 666, "Data a Havana," fol. [7–9], and AGI, Contaduría 667A, No. 2, R. 2, no folio.
4. April 5, 1566	6,666 *p.* 5 *t.* 7 *g. OM*	AGI, Contaduría 671A, No. 2, R. 1, no folio. The balance of 1,333 *p.* 2 *t.* 5 *g. OM* needed to make 8,000 *pesos OM* was to be paid by the treasury in Vera Cruz. See entry 5.
5. April 15, 1567	2,265 *pesos OC*	AGI, Contaduría 877, No. 3 (1563–1569), 214:3–4.
6. 1572	4,000 ducats	Royal order of May 24, 1571, AGI, Santo Domingo 99, R. 2, No. 46. Discharge from the Mexican accounts has not been found, but see the receipt of this money in Havana in AGI, Contaduría 1174, No. 3, R. 2, fol. 127vto, under date of May 17, 1573.
7. 1573	22,000 reales	Charged to the Havana treasury, May 28, 1574, AGI, Contaduría 1174, No. 3, R. 2, fol. 156vto.
8. 1574	52,872 reales	Royal Order, May 12, 1574, for 4,000 *pesos OM*, in AGI, Santo Domingo 112, bk 5, fol. 17. Charged at Havana as this amount, AGI, Contaduría 1174, No. 3, R. 3, fol. 10vto.
9. 1578	22,000 reales	Royal Order, June 7, 1576, copy in AGI, Santo Domingo 118, R. 2, No. 139, *anejo*. Charged to Havana accounts on May 14, 1578. AGI, Contaduría 1088, No. 1, fol. 26vto.
Total	58,426 ducats	

Mexico City and Vera Cruz paid other drafts connected with this construction totaling at least another 4,056 ducats. *OM* indicates *oro de minas*, a unit of account in which the peso is valued at 450 maravedís. *OC* indicates *oro común*, a unit of account in which the peso is valued at 300 maravedís prior to 1572. The real is the silver coin worth 34 maravedís.

dents and supplemented by an assortment of wage laborers and vagabonds, was dilatory and often used for other purposes—a situation little changed by the subsequent use of the royal slaves. Calona also found that the design of the fort was under attack, in this case an attack centering on the one-hundred-foot height that Sánchez had projected for the walls. In short, the new fort was a liability against the royal purse that was not to be lessened in the near future. Indeed, three-quarters of the entire cost of fortifications between 1548 and 1563 was due to the Havana fort.[66]

Artillery

The history of artillery duplicates that of fortifications. Even though the crown's Iberian inventories of guns, especially bronze cannon, increased markedly between 1548 and 1563, the Indies continued to be undersupplied with this vital weapon, and even more so with the munitions needed to use it.[67] The only important addition to artillery holdings in the Indies came in 1555 when the officials of Puerto Rico seized nine bronze and two iron cannon from ships in the Farfán convoy forced into San Juan by bad weather. These weapons were placed on the Morro and in La Fortaleza. Pleas for munitions and payment for the pieces were sent to Spain, where both received favorable royal responses.[68]

Set against this gain were the losses of guns in the wreck of the Colón Española Squadron (1552) and the sack of Havana (1555). The elements also took their toll of the iron guns that some towns had acquired earlier.[69]

In view of these facts, it is not surprising to find continued requests for artillery, even from Puerto Rico, which felt it needed several more large-caliber, long-range guns. From Havana, both before and after the Sores raid, came pleas for artillery to supplement the guns already there. So great was the need that in 1552/53 the town bought a number of small pieces to place on either side of the entrance to the bay. Nombre de Dios also felt the need for artillery, particularly after the capture of Havana. So too did Santiago de Cuba, although its needs were partially met by purchases in 1557 following an inspection by the new governor, Diego de Mazariegos. Only Santo Domingo did not ask for more artillery, although it did try to get its guns back from Panamá, where they had been taken by Licenciado La Gasca, and did point out the losses sustained in the wreck of the Colón squadron. Of more concern to Santo Domingo was powder so that the guns could be fired. It received only a part of what it requested.[70]

In short, the Indies emerged from the wars of the 1550s with little more, and probably less, artillery than they had had at the end of the wars of the 1540s. The major forts at San Juan de Puerto Rico and Santo Domingo were a bit stronger, but Havana was weak, with only four pieces, while the other ports that would service the convoy system were without important holdings of artillery. Only the ships plying the trade routes of the Atlantic and Caribbean were better equipped with guns than they had been earlier. The documentation offers no explanation for these facts aside from the obvious shortage of weapons for uses other than on shipboard, and even ship artillery was scarce. Perhaps shortage was the explanation.

Soldiery: Experimentation With Garrisons

A similar pattern of growing, or at least more evident, inadequacy was to be seen in the area of manpower, one of the few defenses for which the crown spent less than it had in the previous period (measured as a mean yearly figure).[71] Attention has already been called to the crown's plan of 1542 to send out garrisons should Cartier try to invade the Indies and the basis for that plan in the inadequate population of many of the ports and to Núñez Vela's insight that a successful invasion of a port could be countered by sending forces from elsewhere in the empire. An example of the Núñez Vela strategy was the suppression of the Pizarro Rebellion in Peru in the late 1540s. Troops from all over the Caribbean and from Spain rallied to Licenciado La Gasca's standard, eventually giving him overwhelming numbers.

The need for a similar rallying of forces beyond those locally available seemed to have arrived in the spring of 1553 when the Audiencia of Santo Domingo learned that some 800 Frenchmen were supposed to be sailing to attack the Indies. Fearful of an invasion of their city, which was the richest in the Antilles and still had a reputation for wealth that outdistanced its economic reality, the judges ordered the hiring of transients to form a garrison in the fort. One hundred ten men were hired with royal money to serve for three months, beginning on the first of May. By mid-August, when the corsair season was nearly over and it was evident that the French would not appear, the garrison was reduced by fifty men. The remaining sixty were let go at the end of the month.[72]

The following November receipt of the crown's warning of a new French force sailing for the Antilles caused the hiring of another 100 soldiers, this time paid for by a special *avería* imposed on merchandise passing through the port. But the crown disapproved of the *avería* and ordered the soldiers dismissed.[73] The need for these men had been self-evident at Santo Domingo but was not at Valladolid.

This conflict between local perspectives and the crown's perspective was not the case at Havana in the fall of 1555. Arriving just after the last of that summer's raiders had departed, Captain-General Pedro Menéndez de Valdés lent the governor twenty matchlockmen from the soldiers in the convoy's escorts. They seem to have remained on duty until news of the truce in Europe arrived at Havana. The crown approved Menéndez de Valdés' action.[74]

No other garrisons were placed in the Indies prior to 1565 even though the need for additional men throughout the Caribbean was established by the events leading to the placement of the temporary garrisons at Havana and Santo Domingo and by events during 1559. In that year, the militias of Santa Marta and Cartagena gave way before concerted attacks by the French. Smaller towns had been overwhelmed earlier; La Yaguana fell in 1553 and Santiago de Cuba in 1554. In every case the French had attacked in unexpectedly large numbers. Outnumbered, ill equipped, and ill led, the militias suffered defeats. At the same time, the beginnings of illegal trade between corsairs and residents was further increasing the disinclination of the residents of the smaller towns to fight. When the French also beat the militias of the larger towns, among which Cartagena and Havana are the best examples, they were effecting the final collapse of the militia-caretaker garrison system.

The Balance Sheet

The balance sheet for the warfare of the years 1548–1560 is not easily struck. The corsairs did well, in part because of some notable changes in tactics and in the areas and types of targets attacked. As has been shown, these changes also indicated the success of some of the Spanish defenses. In the Triangle, losses were almost null if nonwestindiamen are excluded. Convoying, sailing instructions, accurate intelligence data quickly disseminated, and the patrol squadrons all helped to cut Spanish losses. In the Antilles, fortifications generally discouraged raids on towns that had them. The coast guard squadrons were briefly effective but failed to prevent shipping losses because the patrols were neither numerous enough nor kept at sea. Similarly, on the Main and in Central America the absence of defenses made the ports tempting targets, especially once the Tello de Guzmán squadron made activity near Española risky (1558–1559).

Effective as these defenses were in minimizing Spanish losses, they did not inflict very many losses on the French. The greatest French losses undoubtedly occurred among the backers of unsuccessful expeditions, particularly those in the Triangle where several large fleets (ten or more ships) operated for months without any results.[75] Actual losses of men and ships before 1557 probably amounted to less than 100 men and a dozen ships.[76] The Spanish exacted a higher toll, but still a very light one, during the last years of the war. In one patrol down the Portuguese coast in May 1557, Bazán captured four French ships and inflicted over two dozen casualties. A year later he fought two more corsairs in the Azores.[77] In the Indies, the convoy escort commanded by Pedro de las Roelas captured a French corsair near Havana, killing some crewmen and capturing 130 others. This was the most spectacular success against the corsairs that the Indies would see for almost a decade. That same fall of 1558 also saw the residents of Trujillo successfully capture a small French ship and its crew. Yet the next year the French met little resistance when they raided the towns on the Main. A few were killed at Cartagena, but that was all.[78]

These scant results from Spain's defense efforts point up two characteristics of corsair activity: that they tended to avoid fights in which they did not have a demonstrable advantage and that when they attacked in force they were seldom resisted. The first characteristic explains why they avoided the Mona Passage when it was being patrolled. The second suggests the weakness of those towns and ships that were attacked. The combination of these two phenomena meant that the Spanish defenders achieved little beyond preventing losses and driving the corsairs to seek undefended targets. That was not a very satisfying way to fight a war.

Diplomacy Also Fails

Spain's indifferent success in battle was complemented by a failure in diplomacy, a failure from which sprang the unofficial but very real war on commerce that began about 1563. Accompanying that war was an illegal French, Portuguese, and later English commerce with those parts of the Spanish empire that were inadequately defended and inadequately served by a commercial system straitjacketed by the apparent military necessity to use convoys to protect shipping. This was essentially the same situation that had existed in the 1550s, which the Spanish tried to solve by negotiations. Their first steps in the direction of a negotiated end to French raiding and illegal trading were made in the 1555/56 negoiations; bolder action was attempted in 1559–1561.

The negotiations leading to the Truce of Vaucelles of February 5, 1556, mark the beginning of a new phase in Spain's diplomatic defense of her empire in America. Because these discussions are not well documented it is not possible to state to what extent, if at all, the territorial definition of the Indies was discussed. What does stand out from the terms of the treaty is the shift in Spanish interest away from defending the speculative territorial claim of 1494 (the Tordesillas line) to a pragmatic interest in defending trade and obtaining French recognition of the navigation laws. To that end, the French agreed that "the subjects of the said Lord King of France, or others at their instigation, may not navigate, traffic, or trade with the Indies belonging to the said King of England [Philip], without his express knowledge and license."[79] Anyone who violated this agreement could be the object of Spanish *hostilité* without that act being a violation of the truce.

As an interim settlement, the Truce of Vaucelles could avoid definition of "the Indies belonging to the King of England," but as the negotiators prepared for the peace conferences of 1558/59, they realized that a more specific definition was required. French raiding and trading had continued during the ill-kept truce. The usual French excuse for such activity had been that their ships were sailing peacefully to Brazil or some unoccupied part of the New World when they had been attacked, or forced to trade in order to obtain food, or had been blown off course and forced to put in at Spanish ports. In short, they claimed valid destinations in the New World, under cover of which they set out to raid the Spanish Indies.

The most practical way to stop this commerce raiding in peacetime by supposedly peaceful French ships was to define the Indies so that the French could not claim a valid destination in America near any Spanish trade routes or ports. In his initial instructions, Philip II ordered his diplomats to try to get the French to accept the Tordesillas line and to reject distinctions between Spanish-occupied lands (*las tierras que possemos*) and those merely claimed (*que avemos*) and discovered (*y tenemos descubiertas*). The delegates responded later in March that no agreement would be possible on the terms suggested and asked that the question be settled separately. Philip and his Council of State in Brussels approved this suggestion.[80] Accordingly, the matter of the Indies was not mentioned in the final text of the Treaty of Cateau-Cambrésis, signed on April 3, 1559.

The treaty did contain, however, a modified version of the affirmation made in the Treaty of Crépy-en-Laonnois (1544) that the subjects of the parties "whosoever they may be, may, *guarding the laws and customs of the countries*, go to, come from, dwell in, frequent, commune with, and return to the lands of the one and the other in mercantile fashion and as shall seem to their benefit, whether by the sea or by the land" (italics added).[81] The modification consisted of the addition of the phrase "guarding the laws and customs of the countries."

This provision of the treaty granted the French commercial access to the Indies under the express condition that they abide by the navigation laws.[82] Important as this agreement was, it still avoided the basic issue—the definition of the Indies. In early May, the Spanish negotiators returned to that problem.

Abandoning their initial definition, the Spanish negotiators suggested that the French accept a latitude and a longitude as the limits of the Spanish Indies. South and west of these lines Frenchmen violating the navigation laws would be subject to punishment. No specific lines were mentioned. The French rejected this proposal in July, ostensibly because it would have exposed to capture any ships accidentally blown off course while engaged in legitimate trade.[83]

Taking a different tack, the Spanish next restated their position in terms of specific provinces and "any other lands, whichsoever they may be, discovered by the Kings of Castile and Portugal, their subjects and servants."[84] Frenchmen caught in or off these lands without licenses would be subject to summary punishment by the Spanish, Portuguese, or French crowns. Those claiming injury because of such action would not receive redress from the French crown. Frenchmen already (illegally) in the Indies were to leave. A draft article embodying these demands was given to the French in mid-August (?) and a reply was received in early September.

Once again the French refused to accept the Spanish proposal. Instead, they said they wanted the right to sail the seas except for Spanish territorial waters, narrowly defined, where they would require a license. They also wanted the right to establish colonies in any unoccupied part of America, regardless of prior Spanish or Portuguese discoveries. This position probably reflected French ignorance of the fate of the Huguenot colony at Guanabara Bay, Brazil. It was, in any case, a restatement of the Vaucelles terms of 1556, with explicit definition of the Indies in terms of effective occupation.

Philip's reply was delayed until December by his trip to Spain. He rejected unregulated French navigation because it would open the way for the very peacetime piracy that the Spanish wanted to prevent. Nor would he accept colonization of unoccupied areas since "all" of the Americas had been discovered and "possessed" by the Spanish and Portuguese.[85]

While thus holding to his position that discovered as well as occupied lands were his, Philip moved to see that the latter included the strategic southeastern coast of North America. Two years earlier he had approved a royally funded effort to establish colonies on the Gulf Coast and at Santa Elena. Now, in December 1559, he sent orders to the viceroy of Mexico to see that Santa Elena was occupied without further delay to forestall French designs on that area.[86] He thus tacitly accepted French demands for effective occupation as the basis for defining the Indies.

Upon receipt of Philip's letter, his ambassador to France, Tomás Perrenot, sieur de Chantone, again pressed the French to accept Spanish demands and also discussed the naval preparations of Jacques de Sores with Admiral Gaspard de Coligny. Coligny assured him that Sores was not going to the Spanish Indies and did not have piracy in mind. To this Chantone replied that "to remove these problems a demarcation by parallels and latitudes would be good."[87] His suggestion did not please Coligny nor other Frenchmen.

As of February 2, 1560, the French had not taken any action on the Spanish proposal, although Chantone assured Philip that the cardinal of Lorraine and the duc de Guise, leaders of the pro-Spanish Catholic League, had copies of the papers dealing with the matter and would see that the King's Council dealt with it.[88] There the discussions ended. The French refused to accept Spanish demands, and the Spanish rejected those of the French.

1548–1563. NAVAL WARFARE CREATES ITS OWN PRECEDENTS   107

Twenty-three months passed before the Spanish brought the problem up again. In the interim, Spanish efforts to colonize Santa Elena had failed and Admiral Coligny had organized a company that was planning to send Jean Ribault and six ships to a point on the North American coast which the French claimed to have discovered in 1539. Ribault's scheduled departure in February 1562 led Chantone to protest the plan as an infringement of Spanish interests. The French reassured him that the voyage and colony would not be prejudicial to the interests of the Spanish crown.[89] The stage was thus set for the confrontation of 1565 over possession of Florida (*i.e.*, North America south of the Chesapeake Bay). Diplomacy had failed. With the benefit of historical perspective it can be seen that 1563 marked the end of any possibility during the sixteenth century of a negotiated settlement of the conflicts of the French and Spanish crowns over territorial possessions in the New World and between Frenchmen and Spaniards over trade there.

The End of An Era

The year 1563 marks not only a new low point in royal spending for the defense of the Indies and the failure of Hispano-French diplomacy, but also the end of an era in the history of the crown's control over its revenues in the New World. Down to 1539 it was understood, but apparently never formally stated, that major expenditures of royal funds would have to be approved in Spain. Audiencias, however, had power to approve expenditures in any amount. This fluid situation seemed to change in November 1539 when Charles ordered that no bills were to be drawn on any of the treasuries, including the Casa's, except to repay funds seized between 1535 and 1538.[90] If this order was published in the Indies, and it is doubtful that it was, it soon became a dead letter. The outbreak of war in 1542 brought royal orders to complete projects approved earlier with a carte blanche for the use of royal funds for those purposes. This continued to be the situation until 1563, despite royal orders of 1554 that the accounts of all treasuries be audited on a yearly basis and that no new projects be undertaken without prior approval.[91] All that was required to avoid problems with the auditors was a vague royal order for or approval of some action; with that, the local officials could justify spending the crown's money, even from other treasuries, as they did in 1555 at San Juan de Puerto Rico, when they bought artillery, most of whose cost was to be paid by the Casa.

The crown finally made its fiscal controls effective during the 1560s. The legal instrument for this was an order of 1563 to all audiencias, and by implication to the treasury officials as well, prohibiting all loaning or spending of royal funds for any reason without prior, express royal approval of the purpose and amount. The only exception allowed was when an audiencia felt that "irreparable damage" would be done by the delay involved in asking for prior approval from Spain. Under those circumstances, an audiencia and the local treasury officials could jointly authorize the use of the crown's funds. Failure to abide by this rule would lead to the authorizing parties having to pay the entire amount from their own pockets. This prohibition was followed up by the implementation over the next decade of the yearly auditing of the local books.[92]

Thus from 1563 defense expenditures were more carefully controlled. The second period of the history of defense had contributed a number of important precedents and decisions and had revealed problems with the then-current combinations of means. During the third period the crown was forced to deal with these problems as well as to continue to act on those decisions and precedents.

Chapter IV   **1564–1577.**
          A System Takes Shape

FRENCH DETERMINATION to proceed with the Ribault voyage and colony in 1562 and English attempts to change the then-current interpretation of their trading rights within the Spanish empire produced a breakdown in what little law and order had existed in the Caribbean prior to 1563. Diplomacy proved unable to patch up these differences over access to the Indies, with the results that corsairs again began to appear there, that there was a major confrontation of French and Spanish power in Florida, and that the defense of the Indies entered a period of crisis from which it did not emerge until the mid-1570s. This crisis was a catalyst that precipitated a new combination of defenses from among the various methods used during earlier troubles.

The new combination of means used after 1563 incorporated most of the precedents of earlier periods into what almost became a comprehensive system of defenses. Because of the decision of 1561, the main body of commercial shipping was already protected by convoys. With the growth of raiding after 1563, the crown was forced to recreate a fleet to patrol the Antilles, while employing a squadron of galleys based on Gibraltar as its patrol force off the Iberian coast. In effect, the crown recreated the system that had emerged during the 1550s. However, the spread of corsair raids to the Main soon forced the splitting of the Indies Fleet into squadrons, one to patrol the Main and another to patrol the

Antilles to defend the local coastal trades and to try to interrupt the smuggling trade carried on by the corsairs in addition to their raiding. Had these ships been maintained on station, a system might have existed defending commerce in its major and more important minor branches. That the squadrons of the Indies Fleet were not maintained on station prevented the system from taking final form. Local protests against this state of affairs led to locally supported patrols and to the decision to send out galleys for coastal patrol duty. Their deployment in 1578 marks the beginning of a new period, one in which the system of naval defenses was fully established, with patrols on the Main and later in the Antilles that could not leave station because the ships were unsuitable for transoceanic navigation.

Land defenses show less evidence of a system during the years 1563–1577, but the historian's eye can discern in the decision to create garrisons for key areas along the convoy route (Florida, Havana, San Juan de Ulúa) and at San Juan de Puerto Rico, the first steps toward the system developed after 1586. Prior to 1578, however, these steps were hesitant and advances were frequently withdrawn, as was the case with Puerto Rico's garrison. Continued fortification followed the precedents of the 1540s, with a resulting neglect of the Main's ports, a neglect only partially made up by local initiatives, the sending of artillery from Spain, and the stationing of a squadron from the Indies Fleet at Cartagena.

In sum, a system of land and naval defenses was taking shape during the years 1563–1577 but had not yet obtained its classic, seventeenth-century form. That such a system would be expensive and involve use of royal resources over the entire area of the Caribbean was already clear in the pattern of defense spending, which saw an increase in mean yearly spending to a level double that of the previous period and having a very different areal and topical distribution.

Diplomacy

As has been shown above, the failure of Franco-Spanish diplomacy to resolve differences over the French crown's desires for colonies and French subjects' desires for trade in the New World had already developed by 1563. Thus it is not surprising that the Spanish did nothing diplomatically about Ribault's colony once he had sailed, but did send ships from Cuba to expel it from North America. Nor is it surprising that Spain remained silent about Laudonnière's colony until after it had been destroyed by Pedro Menéndez de Avilés. When the subject did come up, it produced a series of angry confrontations in Paris in which the French refused to consider the partition of North America and ominously protested as tyrannical the Spanish demands that French ships be prohibited from trading (directly) with possessions of the Iberian monarchies. Thereafter, the French crown made no effort to restrain those among its subjects who wished to attack the Spanish empire and rebuffed the few diplomatic protests that the Spanish lodged.[1]

The collapse of Anglo-Spanish accord concerning English access to the Indies developed at the same time but did not come to a head diplomatically until 1569–1574. The essential problem was religion. Englishmen trading through Andalusian ports, and thus within the legal Spanish system, had to be Catholic or face the loss of their goods to the Inquisition. But to be residents of England, they had to swear an oath of allegiance that named Elizabeth as head of the Church of England—a heretical position so far as the Spanish were concerned. A few English merchants were permanently resident in Spain, but most seemed to prefer the itinerant life, tramping about Europe with their own ships. In the climate of heightened religious awareness that developed after 1533, these merchants could no longer safely visit Spain and hence could not legally enter the trade with America.[2]

As Williamson long ago demonstrated, John Hawkins was one of those itinerant merchants. In concert with Pedro de Ponte of Tenerife he attempted to try the same trick that the Portuguese had used in the 1550s: sail directly to the Caribbean and there obtain licenses, pay taxes, and conduct a peaceful trade. The Spanish navigation laws would thus be upheld except for the detail of obtaining a license in Seville *before* sailing westward. As is well known, the crown did not accept that arrangement.[3]

Following Hawkins' first voyage, the Spanish applied diplomatic pressure to England to prevent others, but failed. What brought the issue to a head was the expulsion of the English ambassador at Madrid for allowing Anglican services in his home and Elizabeth's seizure of monies destined for the duque de Alba's army in the Low Countries. In the negotiations that followed, the English stated their demands regarding the Indies trade: (1) that the Spanish confirm earlier treaties, including the original trade treaty of Medina del Campo (1490), which granted the English access to *all* of the Spanish crown's domains; (2) that Englishmen in Spain be allowed to practice their religion freely; (3) that they be allowed to trade with the Indies on the pattern of Hawkins' first voyage; and (4) that Hawkins' property taken at Seville after the first voyage and at San Juan de Ulúa on the third be restored or its value applied to Spanish claims against Englishmen. Philip dismissed these demands as "nothing but tricks and subterfuges" intended to prevent the restitution of the money. Nothing was done about them except to issue a law that separated religion and property when the goods of a third party were involved.[4] From about 1570 onwards, the English did what they wished, and the Spanish had to deal with that fact militarily and administratively.

Freed of restraints by their own governments, French and English and, later, Dutch subjects sailed for the Indies in increasing numbers. Because few Frenchmen showed the restraint and peacefulness of the first English corsairs, open war was soon a fact of life in the Caribbean. In number and severity the raids grew until the mid-1570s. Accompanying them was a vigorous development of the illegal trade of the Antilles and the eastern end of the Main (roughly the area of modern Venezuela). Because these topics form an essential background for the history of defense, they will be examined before the details of Spanish responses to them.

The Corsairs: Raiders, Traders, and Invaders

The statistical pattern of corsair raids shows a number of changes from previous patterns (Table 15). The Triangle ceased to be the scene of important losses of West Indiamen, because an effective intelligence system and the refinement of convoying after 1562 prevented the large squadrons of corsairs that frequently patrolled there from capturing more than an occasional straggler from the convoys. Indeed, the highest loss, that of a dozen sail in 1572, consisted mostly of coastal and non-West Indies shipping captured by the corsairs.[5] This Spanish success in defending commerce in the Triangle may have been a cause for the increasing frequency with which large squadrons of corsairs began to appear in the Caribbean during the 1570s.

In the Indies, the corsairs spread their attentions more equally than ever before among the various coastal areas. The Antilles continued to

Table 15 Spanish Losses to Corsairs, 1564–1577

Year	Atlantic Triangle		Antilles						The Main						Central America			Fla.	Total Ships Taken	Total Land Raids
	Ships Taken	Largest Corsair Group	Ships Taken	Successful Land Raids	Unsuccessful Land Raids	Illegal Trade Reported	Estimated Yearly Total	Largest Group	Ships Taken	Successful Land Raids	Unsuccessful Land Raids	Illegal Trade Reported	Estimated Yearly Total	Largest Group	Ships Taken	Total Land Raids	Largest Corsair Group	Raids of All Types		
1564		17	3		+			3											3	+
1565	2	6	2					6		1				4				A	2	1
1566		18	11			X		2+		1		X							13	1
1567		8	7	1				2+		4	2	X	30	8				1	7	7
1568	2	12	1					4	8	1	2	X	60	10	1	1	5		12	5
1569		25	7					1+	5+	2	2	X		6					12+	4
1570	4+	14	4	1				1+	3		2	X		12			+		11+	3
1571	1+	6	8	2				14	4	2				2					13+	2
1572	12	14							+	2		X		1+				1	12+	3
1573	2	18	3			X		3	4	1		X		1+					9	1
1574						X		3	15+	2				2+			1+		15+	3
1575			6			X		10			1			2	1	1	2		7	1
1576		13	1	1		X	20	8	2	1	1		20	5+	1	1	+		4	3
1577	2	14	3	1	1	X		5	1+					4	6	1	2		12+	3
Totals	25+		56	6	1+				42+	15	10				9	3		2	132+	37+

+ designates a generalized report without specific numbers or my inference of incidents from incomplete documentation.

be the most dangerous place in the empire for Spanish shipping and towns. Close behind the islands in numbers of attacks suffered came the western end of the Main. At a more distant third came Central America. Detailed examination of the attacks over a slightly longer time (1561–1578) shows that they occurred in such remote spots as Campeche (1561), San Juan de Ulúa (1568), and the Gulfo Dulce (1578), as well as the more accessible waters off Trujillo and Puerto Caballos. These Central American figures, when read with those for the Main and Florida, are the statistical evidence of the spread of corsair activity to the periphery of the Caribbean.

Other evidence of this generalizing of corsair raids is found in the figures for successful and unsuccessful land attacks. The gross totals show that more raids (20) were attempted on the Main than in the Antilles (6).[6] The early raids along the Main were mostly against the eastern ports (Margarita, Burburata, Río de la Hacha), whereas the later ones (post-1570) were against the towns of the western Main (Nombre de Dios, Veragua). This shift in the locus of raids on the Main, while further underlining the idea of a generalization of corsair activity, also indicates that the towns of the eastern Main were coming to terms with the corsairs, terms that usually amounted to allowing them to trade and obtain provisions as they wished. On the western Main, by contrast, royal authority was strong and the commercial motives for illegal trade weak, with the result that there was continued resistance to the raiders.

The distribution of raids over time was unequal. The heaviest raiding occurred during the years 1566–1571 in the Antilles and during the years 1568–1574 on the Main. In the Antilles, the number of raids begins to increase again in 1576, a phenomenon that happened in Central America as well. The drop-off in raids in the Antilles from 1571 to 1576, and along the Main after 1574, resulted, as we shall see, from increased Spanish naval activity in those areas during those periods. The effect of that activity on illegal trade cannot be determined. It is known that during the 1560s and 1570s illegal trade by the corsairs became highly organized. By the end of the seventies, the crown's officials had a detailed working knowledge of the system.

Illegal trade and the Caribbean's cattle economy were virtually synonymous during the late sixteenth century.[7] Wherever that economy was strong or the only form of economic activity, as along the Main from Margarita and Cumaná to Río de la Hacha and in the Antilles outside of the cities and the few sugar plantations (largely ruined by 1560 because of storms and earlier corsair raids), illegal trade flourished. It did so because the Spanish could not or would not provide the market for hides and the terms of exchange—barter—that Portuguese, French, and eventually English merchants offered. The failure of Spanish ship captains to arm and defend their vessels and the failure of the Spanish crown to provide effective defenses against the French and English traders—who were able and willing to drive their competitors from the markets with violence—left residents of the hide-producing areas little choice but to trade with the only available market. That this market was also one that offered the highest real purchasing power and probably the widest range of products was but further incentive for individuals as diverse as Treasurer Miguel de Castellanos of Río de la Hacha and nameless black, mestizo, and poor white cowhands of Venezuela and the Antilles.

Along the Main east of Río de la Hacha, an indirect trade with the gold fields of Colombia and a direct trade with black pearl divers at Margarita provided additional incentives for the corsairs and helped to maintain the illegal trade in areas where hides were not as abundant as in the Antilles. West of Río de la Hacha, the gold trade, coupled with other trades involving Peruvian silver making the Isthmanian transit, offered inducements to the corsairs. But at least one informed contemporary specifically states that traders did not prefer money and specie, because they only made one profit on the transaction in contrast to the two they made when purchasing hides in exchange for merchandise.[8] Moreover, the Main from Santa Marta to Veragua was an area of vigorous royal administration, fairly large Spanish populations, and increasingly better-organized defenses. Consequently, only raiders like John Hawkins (1568) went west to Río de la Hacha during the period under consideration. In Central America north of Veragua, there was nothing of value to be had except in Honduras. There the major form of economic exploitation seems to have been Indian tribute based on agriculture and traditional handicrafts. Although cattle existed along the Yucatán, Campeche, and Mexican coasts, those areas were too remote to attract most traders. The only lucrative enterprise for corsairs in those waters was raiding.

Because of this zoning of the cattle economy, the Caribbean was divided fairly sharply into areas where illegal trade flourished, with an occasional raid to punctuate and disguise its course, and those where the corsairs were exclusively raiders. Illustration 5 shows this zoning. Note that even within the zone of illegal trade, the areas immediately around the administrative centers of Puerto Rico, Española, and Cuba were apparently free from this trade. There the same combination of administrative vigor (or at least a desire to keep up its appearance), Spanish population, and defense operated to make trading too dangerous, just as the same combination did on the western end of the Main.

Contemporaries distinguished two types of traders. The Portuguese were always peaceful and probably seldom armed. The French and English, by contrast, were heavily armed and would frequently turn to raiding to supplement cargoes obtained through trade or to drive competitors—whether Spanish, Portuguese, or their fellow nationals—from the seas. This contrast in national styles is illustrated by the half dozen unarmed Portuguese trading ships captured by Menéndez de Avilés and his lieutenants in 1565–1566 and the heavily armed, pugnacious character of John Hawkins when he visited the Main in 1565. Another example of the violent tendencies of the non-Portuguese is Jean Bontemps, a well-known French trader along the Main in the 1560s. He was killed in October 1570 while attempting to force the Barbudo brothers (virtual owners of Curaçao and Bonaire) to trade.[9] There are no records of Portuguese attacking Spaniards who refused to trade with them.

This alternation of trading and raiding as occasion offered was one of the things that the crown had hoped to prevent by diplomatic means. Having failed to do so, the crown then ran up against the fact that, although local residents would probably have been happy to receive protection from the crown against the raiders, they were not willing to allow their trade to be disrupted. They therefore frustrated most efforts to provide effective naval defenses by keeping traders informed of the movements of patrol squadrons. This was done at the price of an occasional raid, but residents appear to have accepted that as a necessary risk. For the crown, this attitude meant expenditures of large amounts of money and increasing frustration as its most able commanders proved unable to prevent raids or stop illegal trade, and indeed sometimes joined in the latter. Eventually the crown resorted to extreme measures, such as depopulating the northwestern part of Española even though it had been warned that removing the population but leaving the cattle would solve nothing and might make the situation worse by permitting unhindered French occupation of the area.[10]

Illustration 5 **Corsair Routes and Cattle**

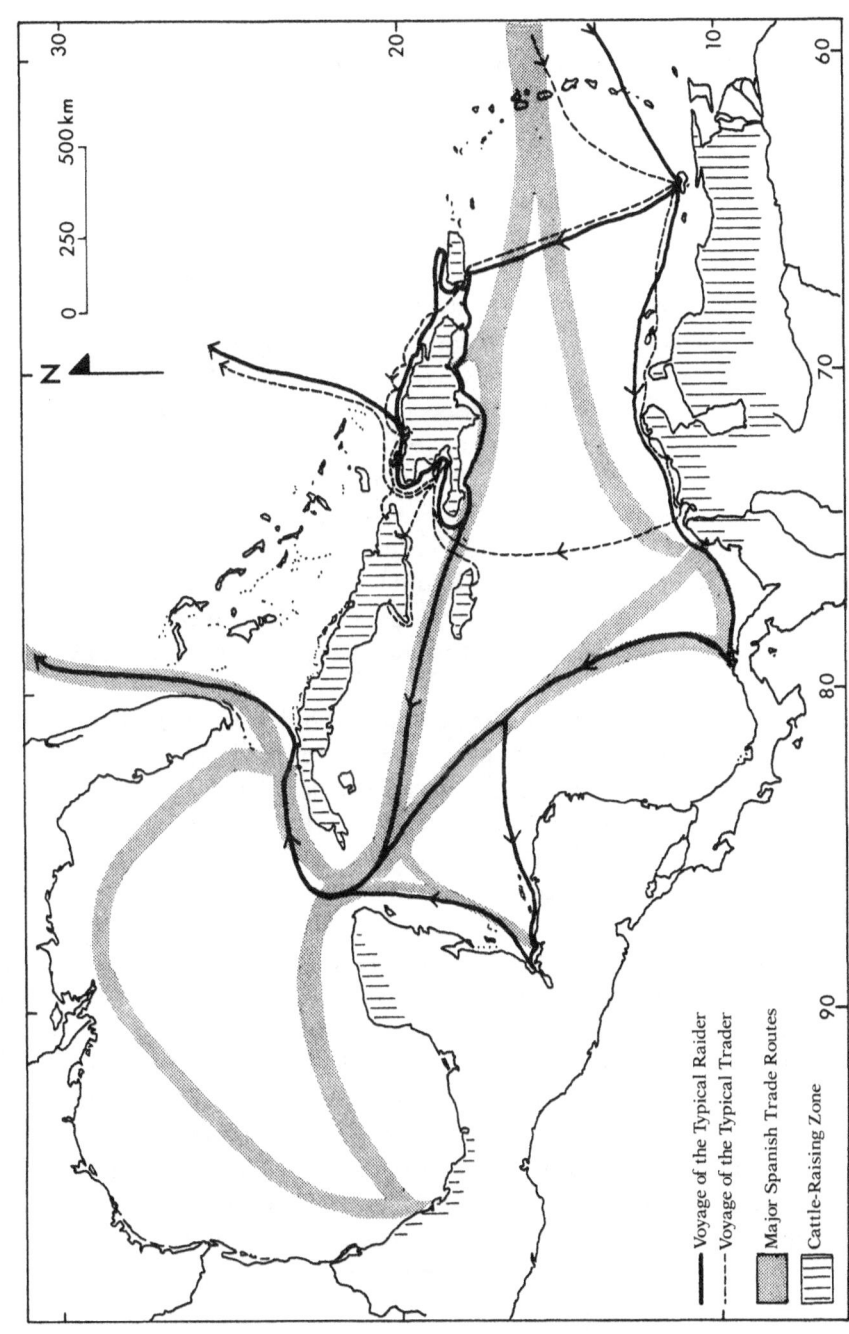

Contemporary evidence tells much about the ports used for trade and the dissemination of intelligence on Spanish naval movements. The ports of the eastern Main (Cubagua, Cumaná, Margarita, Cabo de la Vela, and Río de la Hacha) were visited, if at all, but briefly. They offered fewer hides and tropical products than the Antilles and were generally not very secure from storms, nor at times from Spanish warships. Margarita in particular provided basic information on trade and military conditions elsewhere in the Caribbean. The normal trader would leave the eastern Main for the southwest coast of Puerto Rico (in particular for old San Germán, Guadianilla, or New San Germán) where he would learn about the prospects for trade in the Antilles, any news of sailings from Santo Domingo (which might be worth attacking), and of the presence of warships. This stop was brief because the governor of San Juan frequently sent forces against landing parties and because there were few products for trade. Once informed about the situation in the Antilles, peaceful traders would sail for the northern ports of Española, unless a Spanish squadron was known to be there. In that case, or in the event the corsair wished to raid, he would head west to Mona and Saona.

West of Saona most traders could find hides and information at the various ranches along the coast. Local ships could be found at the Macorís and Coco rivers and at Azua and Ocoa. The last two were favored by slavers whose wares found a ready market among the sugar mills of the area. No more than a week would be spent at Azua, for example, because of the danger of attack from Santo Domingo.

The next stop on the south coast was Yáquimo (Jacmel), a mere eight leagues (about twenty-five miles) by land from La Yaguana, which lay just across the mountains. This port was used primarily for intelligence purposes. Few hides could be brought overland to it due to the terrain. During May, October, and November of most years, it was possible to bring hides from La Yaguana to Yáquimo by sea because the winds slackened or reversed their customary direction, but normally the trade went to the west, around Cape Tiburón. If a hurricane was expected, the corsairs would put into Yabaque (Île-à-Vache), the island lying off the coast. Its port offered protected anchorages and its ranches—belonging to Yaguaneros—had some hides as well as foodstuffs to offer.

If Spanish warships were reported at La Yaguana, the corsairs would wait at Yáquimo or at Yacabo or Sabana (Les Cayes) until the Spanish squadron had left La Yaguana. During the wait, the local residents could gather materials for the trade. The ranch at Yáquimo, like those of Yabaque, was the property of a resident of La Yaguana, which suggests how close the alliance of corsairs and local residents was. Once all was clear at La Yaguana, the corsairs would round Cape Tiburón and enter that port.

After a brief stay at La Yaguana, most traders went north to Guanalisbez (Gonaïves?). This port offered ideal military security because of its reef-guarded harbor entrance, and near-ideal trading conditions because it was connected by roads with most of the cattle-raising areas of the north coast.

Along the northern coast of Española the inhabited ports of Monte Cristi and Puerto Real were open for trade. Puerto Plata, which had a fort, was theoretically closed, but in fact it was open to trade. In addition, the uninhabited ports of Isabela, Manzanillo, Bayahá (prior to 1578), Puerto Francés, Guarico, and La Tortuga offered shelter, trade with nearby ranches, and news. Royal squadrons cruising the coast frequently learned of corsairs at these ports while at La Yaguana and just as regularly found them gone by several days when they rounded Cape St. Nicolas.

In eastern Cuba all ports were used by the interloping traders. Santiago de Cuba became noted for the fact that the lieutenant-governor of Cuba, resident there, was usually a participant in the trade. The sad fate of Captain Francisco de Godoy, commander of a garrison of fifty men put into the port in late 1566, is evidence of the strength of the trading group. Godoy was eventually executed by the local authorities on trumped-up charges because he dared to try to prevent trade in the very port of Santiago. By the end of the century, it could be charged that the local clergy and justices of the peace (*alcaldes*) were the leaders of the trade.[11] That charge probably applied equally to the entire area, and on Española, in the period considered here.

Western Cuba seems to have been freer of the trade except for the area around Havana. There corsairs refitted and gathered final cargoes before setting out through the Bahama or Florida Channel for Europe.

Jamaica's ports were frequented by corsairs, but to what extent is not known because it was not under royal administration. Columbus' heirs (known in Spanish as the Colóns), to whom the island belonged, prevented any investigation of its affairs.

The involvement of residents of the Caribbean in this trade was very extensive, reaching from the most humble slave cowboy to individuals as highly placed as members of the Colón family and the judges of the Audiencia of Santo Domingo. The type of involvement varied with the individual and his social status. The cowboys provided the eyes and ears of the corsairs and more influential persons in exchange for clothing and some simple luxuries given them for the information supplied or in trade for hides taken from the herds. After the crown cracked down on important officials because they had openly traded with Hawkins in 1563 and 1565, those individuals began to employ intermediaries, a practice probably predating the Hawkins voyages. Usually bachelors and often non-Spanish, these men took orders for merchandise and gathered the hides. White, black, or colored, they made a good commission on the transactions. In return, they had to be prepared to flee their residences to avoid inspecting officials and to face legal penalties should they be so unlucky as to get caught.[12]

Next on the social scale came the Portuguese who were resident in the Indies. Precisely when they began to drive the illegal trade is not clear. As early as 1514 Portuguese slavers put into Santo Domingo seeking to sell their goods under cover of distress occasioned by storms. The incident of 1553–1556 when they were freely permitted to trade in islands under the jurisdiction of the Audiencia has been noted above. By the mid-1560s they were well established at La Yaguana, Puerto Real, Monte Cristi, and perhaps at Puerto Plata. The governor of Puerto Rico reported that their ships were more in evidence in the Antilles than the ships of Castillians and that they went from port to port offering their goods. He also told how a resident of Puerto Real had defended the Portuguese ship on which he had come from Lisbon against his (the governor's) efforts to capture it. He had even heard, he said, that departures for the Indies were cried in the streets of Lisbon and that the ships were cleared by the Portuguese customs officials! From the Main came reports that the Portuguese supplied the pilots of the raiders there. Subsequently the crown ordered their expulsion, but without effect.[13] By the time Portugal became another of Philip II's kingdoms, the Portuguese were well entrenched throughout the Caribbean. Many had become naturalized, had married Spanish women, and were growing old, sometimes claiming to do the king's service.

An example of a Portuguese who was also an important figure and thus occupied two classifications at the same time is Captain Francisco Luís of Española. He was appointed "Captain of the Northern Coast" in 1568, having already established his residence at Monte Cristi, where he had extensive ranches. In 1574 he was selected to inspect the new fort being built at Puerto Plata. One critic charged that the inspector and the fort's warden, Pedro Rengifo de Angulo, were business partners. In 1578, Luís rose higher and secured the contract to settle Bayahá, intended as an antidote to the trading propensities of the Españolans. Thus did a wolf get to guard the sheep.[14]

At the top of the social scale among alleged participants in the trade were such distinguished persons as Don Luís de Colón, Doña Aldonça Manrique, and the judges of the Audiencia of Santo Domingo. The first two were accused of using their private jurisdictions on Jamaica and Margarita to cover illegal trade. Don Luís, who was the grandson of the Discoverer, was able to block an investigation of these charges in 1568 with regards to his island of Jamaica, but Doña Aldonça was forced to allow an inspection of Margarita. The judges, it was charged, engaged in the trade indirectly through the collection of salaries levied on the local residents when on circuit to the west coast of Española to investigate trade that had already been completed and by an occasional fine levied against some minor figure in the trade.[15]

Trade at the level that the ranches of a Colón could support seems to have been intended to supply not only local needs poorly supplied via the legal Spanish trade, but also a growing reexport trade from the Antilles to the Main. It is not clear on what scale this was done, because the seas were not safe for Spanish shipping whatever it carried, but it is certain that the illegal trade at its various levels provided the slaves and goods of consumption that were in short supply everywhere in the Antilles and even along parts of the Main.[16]

Another aspect of the history of the corsairs that does not show up in the table are the reports of real or projected invasions of the Caribbean by large French or English expeditions intent on capturing and colonizing some part of the area. Because of the invasions that did occur in 1562 and 1565, the Spanish gave credence to the reports of plans for invasions in 1566, 1567–1568, 1570, and 1571–1573. But after the "invasion" of 1572 failed to materialize, the Spanish seem to have been less credulous. They hardly reacted to reports of planned invasions in 1573 or 1576.

122 THE SPANISH CROWN AND THE DEFENSE OF THE CARIBBEAN

Still another aspect of the corsairs' activity that is imperfectly reflected in the quantitative data is the number of ships the corsairs used. There is no clear numerical pattern. Impressionistic estimates suggest that they brought many ships with them, but at least one witness said that they came out with a few ships (no more than five) and then added their prizes to their squadrons in order to overawe the Spanish.[17] The English certainly employed groups of five or more ships, and some French captains may have done so as well, especially a trader like Jean Bontemps.

The preferred ship in coastal waters continued to be the light launch or *patache*, used first in the Antilles but employed on the Main with great success in the late 1560s. The numerous shallow bays, inlets, and river mouths offered such ships interior lines of communication along the Isthmian coast and sanctuary from larger Spanish craft that could not enter the shallows. These oared, swift-sailing craft allowed the corsairs to attack the trade route from Venta de Cruces on the Chagres River to Nombre de Dios. Their work there devastated that trade until the Spanish began to meet them on their own terms with frigates and small galleys.

The Overall Pattern of Defenses

As the corsairs began reappearing on the shipping lanes and in the coastal waters of the Caribbean, and as their activities spread to include all parts of the basin and illegal trade as well as raiding, the Spanish were forced again to defend themselves and in doing so to extend the areal coverage of their defenses well beyond the limits of earlier periods. The results were a different pattern of spending for various types of defense and a different areal distribution of defense costs.

Table 16 indicates that a new general-purpose naval fleet, the Indies Fleet (*Armada Real de la Guardia de las Costas, Islas, y Carrera de las Indias*), absorbed 41 percent of the crown's spending. Although precise figures cannot be worked out (see Introduction), about a third of this money probably went for patrols by the Fleet in coastal waters, meaning that as much as 25 percent of total defense spending was spent for coastal patrols, not just the 11 percent given in the table. Perhaps a fourth of the Fleet's expenses ought to be allocated to the Fleet's duty as a convoy escort, raising that category of defense costs to about 40 percent, not the 28 percent that could be identified without question and that appears in the table. Approximately 16 percent of total defense costs would thus remain for the general expenses of the Indies Fleet. This distribution of naval defense costs is closer to that which attained after 1578 than it is to the distribution of the 1548–1563 period, during which coastal patrols accounted for 55 percent while convoys cost only 24 percent of total defense costs.

Another major change from all previous periods is to be found in the figures for various types of land defenses. They cost a full 42 percent of total spending, more than ever before. Manpower costs rose to 33 percent, their relative high point prior to 1586, because of the permanent and temporary garrisons the crown supported during these years. This change in defense costs had been prefigured in the failures of the militias during the 1550s and by the decision to build a large fort at Havana, a fort requiring more than a caretaker and a few slaves for its effective manning in the face of constant enemy activity off the port. But the basic cause of this dramatic change in the costs of garrisons was the crown's support of troops based in Florida.

The same crises that compelled the crown to place first temporary then permanent garrisons at various ports in the Antilles and in Florida also led to a resumption of the building of fortifications at other towns besides Havana. In combination with the costs of the new fort at Havana, these new programs boosted fortifications to a higher absolute mean yearly figure than ever before and to a relatively high 7 percent of total defense costs. Artillery costs, on the other hand, continued at minimal levels.

In general, the land defenses used in this period may be characterized as passive; and when their costs are added to the costs of convoys the result is that passive defenses were once again, as in the first period, receiving more royal money than aggressive defenses (about 75 percent of the total). However, unlike that of the first period, the imbalance between passive and active defenses in this third period is not so great, and aggressive naval patrols were active for much of the period and over much of the area where corsairs were active.

This reordering of the crown's tactical approach to defense brought with it a change in the geographic distribution of defense costs. The Triangle, so important in earlier periods, sinks to but 4 percent of allocated costs. By contrast, the Caribbean's defenses cost at least 54 percent of the total, and probably closer to 60 or even 70 percent, if

Table 16 Mean Yearly Costs of Various Types of Defense by Geographic Area, 1564–1577 (in Ducats)

Place	Total	Land Total	Manpower	Fortifications	Artillery
Empire	130,722	54,483 42/100	42,846 33/100	8,876 7/100	409 1/100
Triangle	5,439 100/4	81 1/<1	81 1/<1	0	0
Caribbean Total	70,296 100/54	54,402 77/>99	42,764 61/>99	8,876 13/100	409 <1/100
Antilles Total	17,492 100/13	9,716 56/18	3,825 22/9	5,600 32/63	242 1/59
Puerto Rico	618 100/<1	584 95/1	481 78/1	53 9/1	21 3/5
Santo Domingo	1,265 100/1	1,131 89/2	347 27/1	670 53/8	103 8/25
Cuba	10,539 100/8	7,999 76/15	2,998 28/7	4,875 46/55	118 1/29
Non-Antilles Total	43,398 100/33	38,675 89/71	32,929 76/77	3,276 8/37	167 <1/41
Florida	27,443 100/21	27,221 99/50	24,481 89/57	637 2/7	17 <1/4
New Spain	4,018 100/3	3,654 91/7	770 19/2	2,640 66/30	121 3/30
Central America	122 100/<1	116 95/<1	25 21/<1	0	9 7/2
The Main, Total	11,814 100/9	7,685 65/14	7,653 65/18	0	20 <1/5
Tierra Firme	7,606 100/6	7,606 100/14	7,606 100/18	0	0
Cartagena	90 100/<1	57 63/<1	25 28/<1	0	20 23/5
Santa Marta	22 100/<1	22 100/<1	22 100/<1	0	0

00/00 should be read: The first number is the percentage of total costs for a given area spent for the type of defense in that column (reads across). The second number is the percentage of the total for that type of defense spent in that place (reads down).

Naval Total	General Purpose	Convoys	Coastal Patrols	Place
72,433 55/100	53,451 41/100	36,885 28/100	14,382 11/100	**Empire**
4,871 90/7	1,478 27/3	1,407 26/4	3,203 59/22	Triangle
12,574 18/17	11,369 16/21	0	10,647 15/74	Caribbean Total
5,084 29/7	4,996 29/9	0	5,084 29/35	Antilles Total
0	0	0	0	Puerto Rico
0	0	0	0	Santo Domingo
15 <1/<1	0	0	15 1/1	Cuba
4,096 9/6	2,980 7/6	0	3,223 7/22	Non-Antilles Total
0	0	0	0	Florida
0	0	0	0	New Spain
0	0	0	0	Central America
4,096 35/6	2,980 25/6	0	3,223 27/22	The Main, Total
0	0	0	0	Tierra Firme
0	0	0	0	Cartagena
0	0	0	0	Santa Marta

allowance is made for the costs of the Indies Fleet that could not be allocated. Within the Caribbean, areas other than the Antilles were the major drains on the royal purse. Florida alone accounted for 21 percent of all defense costs. New Spain, Central America, and the Main together accounted for 12 percent, as compared to almost nothing in earlier periods. That the Antilles still accounted for 13 percent of defense costs (exclusive of coastal patrols) is due primarily to the fort and garrison at Havana. The geographic pattern of defense spending thus parallels the geographic pattern of corsair activity. Corsairs, and defenses against them, had become Caribbean-wide problems by 1577.

Convoys and Galleons: A System for the Defense of Commerce

By the time the third period in the history of the defense of the Indies began in 1564, the merchants of Seville had already persuaded the crown to reinstitute the convoy system. Rules for the convoy were issued in 1562 and again in 1564, providing that institution with the basic legal definition it was to retain for a century. But the convoys, even supplemented by a few ad hoc patrols in the Antilles and off Spain, where galleys were used, did not provide adequate protection for commerce, especially the coastal commerce of the Antilles. By 1567 the crown was forced to face the issues of how to defend that commerce and its associated ports and of how to break up the illegal trade that was beginning to flourish in the Antilles and along the eastern end of the Main. The Indies Fleet was the result. With its creation, the crown completed the revival of the system of defenses for commerce that evolved in the 1550s. Patrol fleets swept the coasts of Spain and the Antilles, while convoys provided security on the high seas and in the danger areas of the northeast Caribbean and the Triangle. But that system of defenses was soon modified by royal decisions to use the Indies Fleet to escort convoys and by pressures from residents of the Main for patrols by the Fleet in their coastal waters. The result, after 1574, was a truly empire-wide system of maritime defenses, with patrol squadrons on the Main and in the Antilles and off Spain, and convoys between the areas where these squadrons worked.

The history of the convoy is outside the scope of this study except as the histories of the convoys, of the Indies Fleet, and of the patrol squadrons off Spain are intertwined. For the moment, it is enough to say that the convoy provided excellent security for the majority of ships moving across the Atlantic and that, like any shipper, the crown contributed to the *avería* that paid for the escorts—payments that account for most of the 28 percent of defense costs allocated to convoys in Table 16. The studies of Haring, Artinaño, and the Chaunus, cited above, can supply the details not found here.

The precise reasons for the decision to build a new fleet for the Indies are lost with the documentation containing them, but from the title of office (*titulo*) of the first captain-general, Pedro Menéndez de Avilés, it is clear that the crown was moved by a combination of motives including the religious—the corsairs were "Lutherans"—and the pragmatic— the need to defend commerce and the interests of the king's subjects, as well as the king's own interests. The fleet was to guard the coasts and ports of the Antilles, the Main, and Florida. It was thus one of the crown's responses to the French challenges of the 1560s.

Further evidence of the purpose of the fleet when built is found in the design of the ships. Menéndez de Avilés chose the galleyed galleon. In theory, these ships were suitable for patrol work in the shallow waters and often adverse wind conditions of the Antilles and, to a lesser extent, on the coasts of the Main. These ships were not large enough (ten of the twelve were of 250 *toneladas*, the other two of 350 *toneladas*) to carry a full crew of about 130 men and supplies for prolonged voyages such as those necessitated by convoy duty.[18] In effect, the Indies Fleet was the Española Squadron under another name and with larger, oared ships to meet the changed conditions of naval war in the Caribbean.

The twelve ships were built at Bilbao during the winter of 1567–1568. Upon launching, they were given the names of the twelve apostles. They were also given a payroll (subsidy of some 11,480 ducats per ship per year for crew salaries and rations, with 1,000 ducats more for repairs). This money was to be drawn in equal amounts on the treasuries of Tierra Firme and New Spain.

The maiden voyage revealed that the ships were fast and good handlers, but also revealed that they heeled over under sail, making it necessary to close the lee gun ports and rendering the windward ones useless as well. It was also found that the rowers lacked leverage between decks because the first deck was at the waterline when the ship was loaded. But even worse developments occurred off the Arenas Gordas west of San Lúcar. There North African pirates attacked the squadron with their *fustas*. Apparently because of cowardice by their crews, three of the galleons were run aground and burned.[19] The remaining ships put into Cádiz for supplies.

The need for a patrol fleet in the Indies reached a critical stage at the very moment the new Indies Fleet was preparing to sail. This is shown by the number of patrol squadrons fitted out locally between 1567 and 1568. As has been noted, officials at Santo Domingo fitted out a number of ships to escort merchantmen around Saona and through the dangerous Mona Passage in 1563. The danger from French corsairs again became intense in May and November 1567, causing those same officials to fit out escorts again. The May squadron was funded on a fifty-fifty basis between the crown and local interests; but in the November case, the crown paid all of the costs except for the donated use of ships. Both squadrons seem to have escorted their charges to the relative safety of the Atlantic.[20]

On the Main, the governor of Cartagena felt compelled to fit out squadrons in March and May 1568 in an effort to deal with the increasing numbers of corsairs off the Isthmus. The May squadron recaptured some prizes from the corsairs off Tolú, but the March squadron, like the squadron sent out by Nombre de Dios in May, returned to port empty-handed. The crown eventually forced private persons to pay for all of these squadrons, even though the governor and treasury officials of Cartagena had tried to use royal money, arguing that they were doing the crown's job for it, even if they lacked prior authorization from Madrid.[21]

Yet other evidence of the need for the Fleet is to be found in the patrols performed by the convoy escorts off Cuba in 1561, 1565, and 1566, and at Nombre de Dios in 1567. The first chased but did not catch a corsair who had chased a Spanish ship into Havana. The second captured a corsair off Mariel, killing fifteen of its crewmen and capturing another fifty. The third resulted in the capture of a Portuguese trader. The action at Nombre de Dios served mostly to deter corsairs from attacking shipping entering that harbor. It formed the background for the patrols fitted out at Cartagena and Nombre de Dios in the spring of 1568, before the Indies Fleet sailed on its first patrol.[22]

The voyages of the Indies Fleet, 1568–1577, fall into two broad periods: 1568–1574 and 1574–1577. During the first period the Fleet patrolled in the Antilles and served as a convoy escort from Havana (1569, 1570, 1571), as a patrol in the Triangle (1573), and in place of the regular Tierra Firme convoys of 1572 and 1574, in both cases because the merchants refused to send ships from Spain because of market conditions on the Isthmus of Panamá and in Peru (Illustration 6). Two major developments during this period affected the subsequent history of the Fleet and other forms of maritime defense in the Caribbean. These developments were (1) abandonment of the Indies Fleet's role as a patrol force based in the Antilles, and (2) the failure of the Fleet to provide adequate protection for coastal shipping on the western Main. The second development in particular caused not only a change in the Fleet's role after 1574 but also pointed in the direction of locally based patrol squadrons, a development that would occur after 1578.

As has been noted, the design of the galleyed galleons built in 1567 clearly indicates that they were intended for use in the Antilles as a patrol force based on its major ports. For want of documentation, it is not clear whether Menéndez de Avilés had already formulated his grand strategy at that time; but it is clear that by early 1570 he had done so and had, moreover, drawn the lesson from the Fleet's patrol of 1568–1569 that the galleons needed escort ships of the frigate type to scout out corsairs and to engage them when they entered areas too shallow for the galleons. That spring he signed a contract for the construction of eight frigates, which would enter service with the galleons. His grand design was to "close up the passages" on the corsairs by having patrol squadrons stationed in the Mona and Windward passages and in the Straits of Florida. He reasoned that preventing the traders and raiders from returning to Europe with their booty would eventually discourage their backers and so bring corsair activity to an end.

The need for some form of action to drive the corsairs from the Caribbean, not just small areas of it, was already before the king. Santo Domingo's need for a patrol squadron, even while the Fleet was on the north coast, was shown in 1569. From Panamá came a request for ships able to patrol the Main, then the scene of unprecedented corsair activity and Spanish losses.[23] Menéndez' scheme promised to solve the problem for all areas of the Caribbean by concentrating the crown's naval forces in the critical narrow water passages of the northeastern Caribbean. That such a plan also suited his interest in the hide trade, in taking prizes from which he would get a share, in maintaining the Florida colony, and in shipbuilding in the Antilles was all to the good. Yet that very multiplicity of his own interests, and the crown's continual need to employ its ships as escorts for, or even substitutes for, the

Illustration 6. Voyages of the Indies Fleet, 1568–1574

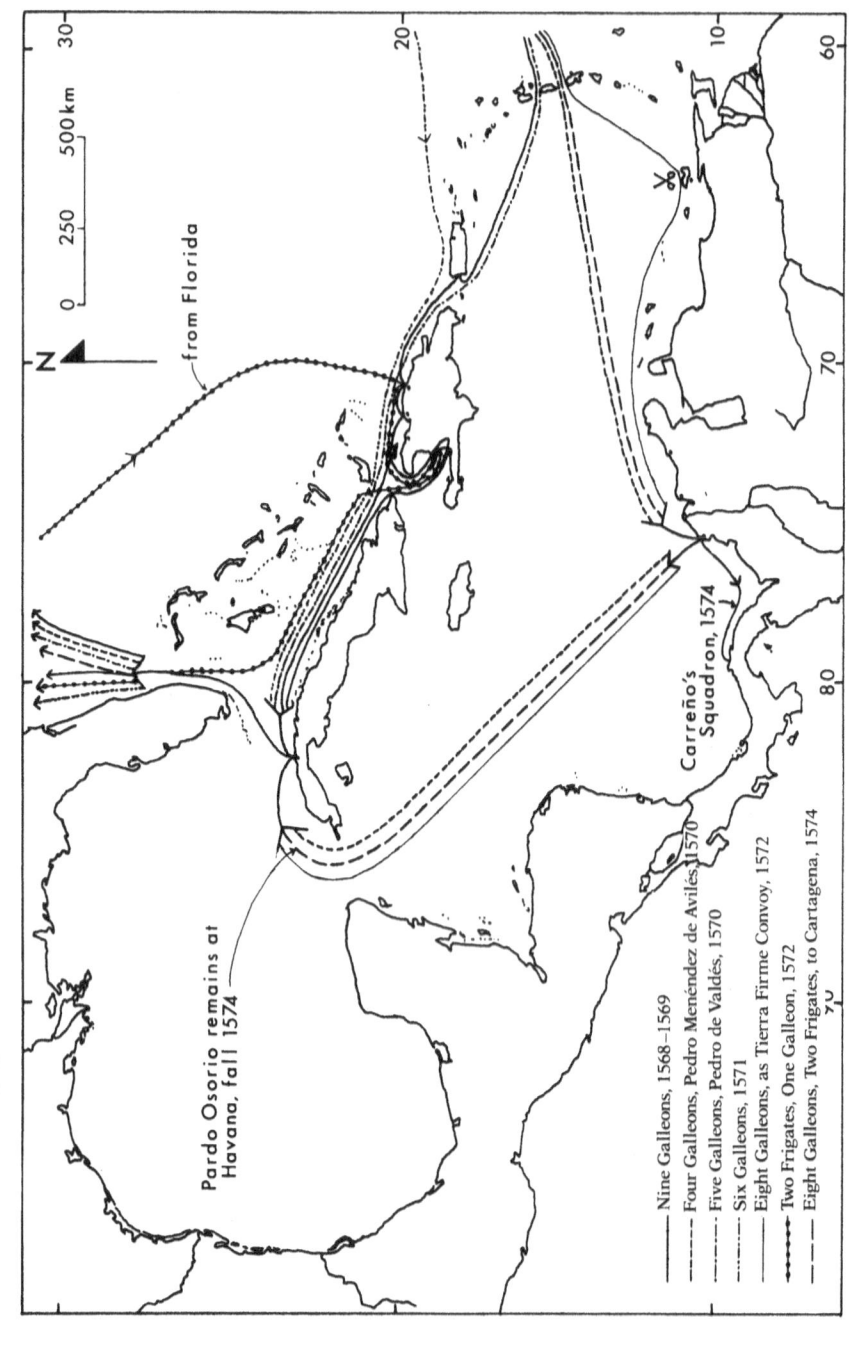

convoys, doomed the scheme before it was ever tried. For it to have been successful, it would not only have required the crown and Menéndez to devote two to five years of single-minded attention to it, but would also have required the development of a logistics system surpassing anything previously known in the Indies. Success would also have depended on the corsairs not upping the ante by sailing in larger squadrons of larger, more heavily armed ships. None of these conditions attained, and the Indies Fleet continued to patrol and escort as the circumstances seemed to dictate.

Because of its duties as a convoy escort, the Fleet was unable to protect coastal shipping, even in the Antilles—the area through which it passed most frequently prior to 1574. Consequently, local officials were forced to fit out ad hoc squadrons, beginning in 1571. Reporting their actions, they intensified the pressures in Spain for changes in the pattern of the Fleet's patrols.

The first of the local patrols was sent out from Nombre de Dios in January by the captain-general of the Tierra Firme convoy, Diego Flores de Valdés. Using two galleons and a shallop, he sought the corsairs who had taken a bark from the Chagres trade and its cargo valued at 50,000 *pesos de oro*. The corsairs, who were using a thirty-oar galliot and a fifteen-oar pinnace, escaped into shallower water than the galleons could enter, losing three prizes in their flight. Enlightened by the experience, Flores de Valdés and the city of Nombre de Dios fitted out three frigates, all having oars as well as sails, for the purpose of escorting fifteen barks to the Venta de Chagres. The ships were then sent on three cruises in a vain effort to capture the corsairs. This qualified success led local authorities to call for the establishment of a permanent squadron of oared ships to convoy coastal shipping on the Main and to chase corsairs.[24]

At Margarita, the need for a patrol force to control corsairs around the pearl fisheries led to the signing of a contract between Antonio Luís de Cabrera, captain-general of Margarita, and the Audiencia of Santo Domingo. Luís de Cabrera failed to carry out the agreement, but it suggests the seriousness of the problem at that time and, like the call for a squadron of oared ships on the western Main, is one of the origins of the plans to send galleys to the Tierra Firme coast.[25]

In the Antilles, the presence of corsairs and the absence of the Indies Fleet, except for the brief visits of Admiral Nicolás de Cardona in the summer of 1571, caused the Audiencia to equip a squadron under Treasurer Diego Jiménez de Peralta (fall of 1571, exact dates unknown). The corsair escaped.[26]

Because of the need to ship its revenues from the Main to Spain during 1572 in the face of what was expected to be an attack by the numerous ships gathering under the command of Count Louis of Nassau, the crown could make only a limited response to the news of the patrol squadrons of 1571 and the demands for local squadrons or more aggressive patrolling by the Indies Fleet. The Fleet's orders were changed to the extent of having it sail along the Main from Margarita. The result was the capture of two French ships. It was one of the few sea battles the fleet was to record and, like almost every action involving a prize, resulted in litigation.[27] The Fleet was at Cartagena by early April.

Because of its orders and the lack of suitable shallow-draft ships, the Fleet spent its time fitting out for the return to Spain rather than patrolling. Searching out the corsair reported east of Nombre de Dios thus once again fell to local residents. The governor of Cartagena persuaded various shipmasters to sail to Tolú in search of the corsair (who was Francis Drake). Because of weak leadership, the patrol did not find the enemy, nor did a second patrol. The ships' masters refused to allow their craft to be used for further voyages. Drake was thus left free to plan and execute his raid on Nombre de Dios.[28]

The change in the sailing orders of the Indies Fleet for its voyage of 1572 was followed up by other, more direct ways of dealing with the corsair problem on the Main. That fall, the Tierra Firme convoy took along two knocked-down brigantines to escort shipping from the Chagres River to Nombre de Dios.[29] At the same time, the crown began seeking bids for a contract to run a galley fleet on the Main. Pressure from local officials, as well as the crown's own needs and the *Adelantado's* lack of single-mindedness, thus joined the forces moving the defense of the Indies away from the grand design that Menéndez had formulated in the late 1560s. Fittingly enough, the *Adelantado* was removed from the command of the Indies Fleet in late 1573.

When the Fleet sailed in 1574, it was in place of the convoy of Tierra Firme that the merchants had refused to send, just as they had refused in 1572. Upon arrival at Cartagena, the main body of the Fleet was joined by a new galleon, a *zabra*, and two new frigates. Under new orders, the Fleet was split into three squadrons. One, consisting of those ships most in need of careening and other repairs, was left to patrol the Main under Admiral Francisco Carreño, while the others were sent to Havana. There three galleons were set to Spain with the convoy, while the other ships were refitted for a patrol in the Antilles.[30] Thus began the second period of the Fleet's history before 1578.

During the period from 1574 to 1577, the Indies Fleet carried out a series of patrols in the Caribbean that seem to have been intended to disrupt the illegal trade of Española on the one hand, while on the other trying to provide protection for the coastal trade servicing the convoys on the Main (Illustration 7). In general it may be said that the Fleet spent more time in the Antilles than on the Main, with the result that the officials of the latter continued to press for a squadron that would be based in their ports.

There were several reasons for the Fleet's failure to patrol the Main as extensively as the Antilles during this period. For one thing, the squadron left at Cartagena in 1574 was destroyed in a December storm at Nombre de Dios. Replacement ships, including a twenty-two-oar galliot, *Nuestra Señora de Candelária*, had barely been readied when the entire fleet was pulled off the Main by its officers in what proved to be a successful effort to prevent an investigation at Cartagena of alleged illegal trading. The following year, the Fleet was ordered to pick up the ships that had wintered on the Main and to return with them to Spain. Only vigorous protests by the local officials and the taking of prizes by corsairs while the Fleet was at Nombre de Dios and Cartagena caused the captain-general to allow a brief patrol by some of his frigates. That failing, he took the fleet to the Antilles for the winter, to return again in the spring of 1577 to escort the assembled merchantmen to Spain. On that occasion, because John Oxenham was still at large, he left his son with a small squadron on the Main.[31] In short, whether by fiat of its officers or on royal order, the Indies Fleet spent most of its time in the Antilles, ostensibly trying to break up the illegal trade of the Windward Passage area, a task it accomplished by wintering at La Yaguana, one of the centers of that trade.

Because of the Fleet's inability to be everywhere at once, local squadrons were fitted out, notably at Nombre de Dios in 1575 and 1576 and at Havana in 1576. The first succeeded (in 1576) in finding John Oxenham's ships at Acla and burning his fort. The Havana patrol helped a dispatch boat escape from its two French pursuers.[32] These squadrons

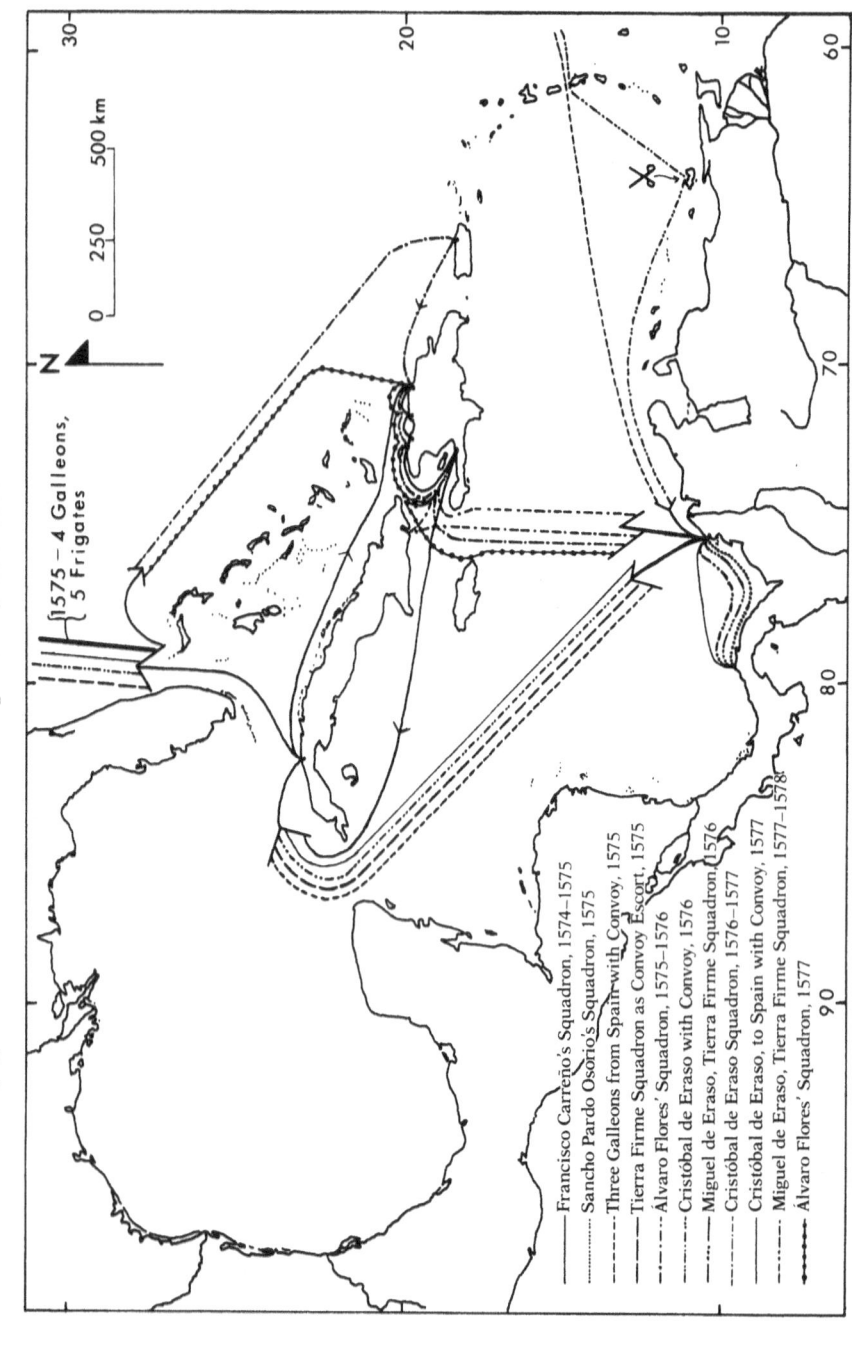

Illustration 7   Voyages of the Indies Fleet and Its Squadrons, 1574–1577

1564–1577. A SYSTEM TAKES SHAPE 135

again showed the timeliness of the discussions then going on in Spain about using galleys for local squadrons based on Cartagena, Santo Domingo, and even Havana.

The return of the Fleet and its chief officers to Spain in the fall of 1577 was the signal for discussion and resolution of four problems connected with the Fleet's future. There were numerous outstanding debts to be paid and little money to meet them, even after the *avería* had been tapped for part of the costs of escorting the convoy of 1577. The old galleons and the newer ships (*naos*) needed to be replaced, the first because they had reached a point of service where repairs cost half or more what a new hull would cost, the second because they were unsuited for use as warships and were poor sailers. Connected with this matter was the question of using galleys in place of or to supplement the Indies Fleet. And finally, there was the problem of finding the money to pay the crewmen a ration and some of their past-due wages so that they would remain in service. The first three questions were immediately addressed by the returning officials, the fourth only became serious late in the fall when funds in the Fleet's treasury were exhausted.

By combining what little money (12,260 ducats) was left from the subsidy collected on the Isthmus before the Fleet had sailed that spring with the 48,000 ducats collected from the *avería*, the Fleet's officials were able to pay many of the debts they owed to merchants who had supplied them on credit in previous years.[33] But that left only enough money to pay a ration to the crews during the fall. The following spring's dispatch would present grave financial problems, as will be noted in Chapter V.

The need to replace the aging galleyed galleons and the poor-sailing ships purchased in 1575 and 1576 tied in with consideration of the galley experiment. By mid-October 1577, when Captain General Cristóbal de Eraso arrived at court to press for the replacement of the ships, the crown had at hand a considerable file of information and opinion on whether galleys should be deployed in the Caribbean, where, and what resources they might find there (see below for more details). It had been agreed as early as the spring of 1576 that at least two galleys would be sent. The meeting of the special committee (formed in 1575 to consider the matter) on October 21, 1577, took that for granted. Debate centered on the number of galleys, their financing, and the actual source of the ships. Recommendations were sent to the king that two galleys taken from the Mediterranean squadron under the marqués de Santa Cruz be sent to the Main, with financing to come from the Indies Fleet's subsidy. It was agreed that for the time being the Fleet would be renewed and used for patrolling other parts of the Caribbean.[34]

The recommendation of the galley committee that the Fleet be renewed reflected not only prudence in the face of the uncertainties of using a new weapon (the galley), but also the investigation into the form that new galleons might take in view of the varied uses to which they could be put. The outcome of that investigation and the committee's recommendations were orders to Cristóbal de Barros to build two large (500 *toneladas*) oarless galleasses to be followed by four smaller galleons (350 *toneladas*) when the larger ships were done. Some 38,000 ducats were allocated for the project.[35] It was hoped that the galleasses would be finished in time for the spring sailing to the Indies Fleet, thus obviating the need to buy or lease other ships to replace the galleons on hand.

Coastal Patrols in the Triangle

Another aspect of the maritime history of the empire during the third phase of its military history needs to be discussed—the coastal patrols in the Triangle. Their recorded costs were due almost entirely to the expenses of the Indies Fleet in 1569 and 1572. But the crown supported other patrols as well, beginning with Álvaro de Bazán's ineffective galley squadron of 1562–1565 (see Chapter III). Because of Bazán's failure to patrol off Andalusia and the Algarve, the crown ordered the fitting out of a four-ship squadron under the command of Pedro López de las Roelas in 1562 and of fifteen *chalupas* under the command of Martín de las Alas in 1564. Roelas' squadron made a trip to the Azores to meet an incoming convoy and spent time off the Capes. Alas' *chalupas* were diverted to an attack on Tetuán, North Africa. The protection thus provided to shipping in the Triangle was slight.[36]

Bazán's contract was allowed to expire in 1565, unmourned by anyone, although the *avería* of three-quarters of 1 percent to support his squadron lingered on into 1566, at royal order and over the protests of the merchants. It provided the funds that sent three galleons from Málaga to the Azores to meet the returning convoys during the summer of 1566.[37]

The variety of stop-gap fleets fitted out between 1562 and 1566 gave way from 1567 onwards to a policy of using Mediterranean galleys to patrol as far as the Capes, while relying on the strength of the convoys (often reinforced by escorts from the Indies Fleet) and the cooperation of the Portuguese royal fleet to provide security in the Azores. Of equal if not greater importance to the security of the convoys as they entered the Triangle from the west was the system of dispatch boats (*avisos*) that provided the commanders with the latest intelligence reports on corsairs, allowing course changes to avoid squadrons such as those the English regularly sent to the Azores. The combination of these defenses was exceptionally effective. Losses to the corsairs were almost nil, despite the occasional presence in all parts of the Triangle of large squadrons of French and English corsairs and the almost yearly raids by North African pirates along the southern coasts of Spain and Portugal.

The galleys were ordered to the Capes in 1567, 1568, 1572, and 1574 to confront threats posed by northern Europeans. North African pirates were the objects of the cruises of 1569, 1570, a second cruise of 1572, and those of 1575–1578. However, the galleys were not always on hand when needed. For example, in late August 1568 the New Spain convoy was attacked by the Barbary pirates off Andalusia, after the galleys had retired from the Capes. Nor did the galleys sail as planned in 1572, 1574, and 1575.[38] In short, like their predecessors under the Bazán contract and the substitutions made for Bazán's ships, the galleys used off Andalusia and the Algarve between 1567 and 1578 accomplished little, aside from deterring corsairs and reassuring anxious merchants. Perhaps their greatest role, largely unintentional, was to provide a Spanish *quid* for the Portuguese *quo* of sending squadrons of warships to the Azores, squadrons intended to provide security for the Indiamen returning from the east, but also providing protection for Spanish convoys passing that way on their voyage home from the Americas.

As has already been noted, formal and informal Spanish cooperation with the Portuguese in a common defense of the Triangle against corsairs had existed for some time by the 1560s. In some cases, as in 1563 and 1567, commanders simply worked together on their own initiative when their squadrons came into contact. At other times the Spanish formally sought cooperation through diplomatic channels; for example, during the winter of 1570–1571. At that time an agreement was reached under which the Portuguese were to send a squadron to the Azores while the Spanish provided one off the Algarve. The Portuguese sent their ships to sea in July, but the Spanish delayed their action too long. On the 28th of July they abandoned their part of the agreement, although resolving on a show of preparations to appease the Portuguese. The failure of the Indies convoys to arrive on time in August led to further negotiations during which the Portuguese agreed to keep their fleet in the Azores until mid-September, at the expense of the *avería*. At least one Portuguese warship was off the Capes at the same time.[39]

The Luso-Spanish cooperation of 1571 was not revived in a formal way until 1576, but informal cooperation and perhaps an understanding as to spheres of naval responsibility did continue. The Portuguese fleet was in the Azores in 1572, 1574, 1576, and 1577. In 1576, the Portuguese fitted out a second squadron in addition to the one in the Azores to patrol the Algarve's coasts. This squadron seems to have been sent to the Azores to reinforce the squadron there. The Spanish sought and seem to have obtained the cooperation of that combined squadron with the escorts of their own convoys. This aid—and luck—prevented the French and English corsairs from capturing any of the ships in the convoys.[40]

The Portuguese naval units were not active in 1578 because of preparations for the ill-fated expedition to Morocco. The Spanish had to fend for themselves. Once again alarmed by reports that the French and English hoped to intercept the returning Tierra Firme convoy, which was known to be weakly armed but richly laden, the crown ordered galleys to the Capes and sent the *capitana* and *almiranta* of the New Spain convoy back to the Azores to await the Tierra Firme fleet.[41] Despite the danger, the reinforced Tierra Firme convoy arrived safely at San Lúcar. The system for the defense of commerce evolved during the years after 1521, and especially since 1564, was working to insure the safe movement of private and royal cargoes in the Indies trade.

As has already been indicated, the actions that the crown and its officials took to defend the towns of the Caribbean area pointed towards the system of forts, garrisons, and reformed militias that came into being after the military disasters of 1586. To the eyes of contemporaries, however, these actions were ad hoc responses to a series of crises involving the corsairs, which began with the discovery of the new French colony in Florida in 1564. Moreover, the same pattern of patrimonial decision-making, with some important differences in terms of who got what, continued to function. The result is a patchwork of events best considered in terms of the type of defense involved, beginning with garrisons and proceeding to militia supplies, fortifications, and artillery.

Garrisons

The dramatic increase in spending for garrisons arose from the French attempt to colonize peninsular Florida and from what the Spanish thought were their larger intentions in the Antilles, and in particular at Havana, the key port in the then newly reestablished convoy system. Initially the crown did not intend to support permanent garrisons at either location, but events worked out otherwise. At the same time, other towns in the Caribbean were employing new garrisons, either of the caretaker type or temporarily because of some emergency. For almost all, the crown paid the bill.

News of the Laudonnière colony in Florida was received at the end of March 1565. The crown immediately rewrote the contract for the colonization of Florida that it had signed ten days earlier with Pedro Menéndez de Avilés. It now provided him with 300 soldiers to be paid from the royal treasury and a bonus of 15,000 ducats if he got to sea by the end of May. Orders were also sent to Santo Domingo to raise 250 men and to provide horses and supplies for them at royal expense. Havana was ordered to provide 50 men. In addition, provision was made for the *capitana* of the New Spain convoy to go to Havana to be at Menéndez' disposition should he feel the need for her guns and crewmen.[42]

Menéndez de Avilés' voyage to Florida and his acts there of founding St. Augustine, attacking the French at Fort Caroline, and then killing Ribault's men at the Matanzas River are well known. Lyon has recently shown how the funding and supply operations actually worked, a point that earlier writers had ignored.[43] For present purposes it is enough to note that Santo Domingo sent a few men, many supplies, and horses, while Havana did not send anything, but rather received the crew from the *capitana* of the New Spain fleet as the nucleus for a garrison. The two major pieces in the new structure of royally supported garrisons were thus fashioned, although at the time the crown had no intention of building a new edifice. Events were to change that intention.

Even as Menéndez de Avilés and his expedition were still at sea in the summer of 1565, the crown received new reports of additional

French forces assembling for Florida. Orders were sent to the Casa to raise up to 1,800 more men and to the Audiencia of Santo Domingo to begin to prepare food for that force for nine months. Sancho de Archiniega was named to command the fleet. By the end of March 1566 the troops were ready to be embarked, but bad weather delayed them for a week. At the same time, early in April, the Casa received a memo of items to be purchased in addition to those already bought and loaded on the fleet. The *urca*, *Pantecras*, was hired to take these supplies later that summer. Between the 6th and the 13th of April the ships got to sea. The preparations had cost almost 130,000 ducats.[44]

The apparent wisdom of these preparations was underlined by information that Menéndez sent to the crown after he had interrogated the prisoners taken at Fort Caroline and Matanzas Inlet. They told of a French grand design to use Florida as a base from which to attack the Antilles. They planned to promise freedom to the black slaves in exchange for support against the Spanish. With reinforcements expected in 1566–1567 and the help of these slaves, the French had expected to capture the strategic keys to the Caribbean and thereby cut Spain off from her American empire.[45] Archiniega's fleet thus assumed even greater importance.

The fleet made an uneventful crossing, arriving off St. Augustine on the evening of June 29, 1566. Within days of arriving, most of the men had been landed and put to work on a new fort. The *Adelantado's* return two and one-half weeks later set in motion the landing of (inadequate amounts of) supplies and a series of discussions about what to do with the men. By mid-September, several ships had been unloaded and released from service. Men had been enlisted to replace those lost to death, desertion, and the Indians. Seven hundred and fifty soldiers were to be left in Florida when the rest were taken to the Antilles. St. Augustine was in a reasonable state of defense; Santa Elena and San Mateo were garrisoned, although short on supplies. A number of other posts had been or were to be established along the peninsula's coast (Table 17). Supplies were short everywhere, but there was nothing to do about it pending the arrival of the *Pantecras* and such supplies as could be sent from the Antilles. Accordingly, Menéndez turned his attention to his orders to place garrisons in the Antilles.[46]

Menéndez sailed from St. Augustine on October 20, 1566, with six ships and six smaller vessels. During the next two months, he established the temporary garrisons noted in Table 18.

Besides establishing the garrisons that he and the Audiencia of Santo Domingo felt were necessary to protect the Antilles against the French "grand design," Menéndez took the opportunity to extend his supply arrangements for Florida, which already included the Canary Islands and Puerto Rico, to Santo Domingo, Puerto Plata, and eastern Cuba.[47] He thus remedied one of the problems that had defeated Luna and Villafañe. However, he was only able to supply the Antilles garrisons with money, food, and saleable items adequate to supply their needs for three months. Beyond that time, the crown would have to send additional funds or supplies. Menéndez reminded the king of this in December 1566, February 1567, and upon his return to Spain that fall. Other individuals also requested this aid as the initial supplies ran out.[48]

Pending receipt of royal funds or supplies, each community that had a garrison was obliged to make what arrangements it could. At San Juan, the troops were billeted on the town at first, but the householders preferred to pay them a ration from their own pockets rather than have them live in their homes. At Puerto Plata and Santo Domingo the troops were sustained by loans after the original supplies ran out. The Havana garrison was sustained by loans from Menéndez and the residents of the city. At Santiago de Cuba, the garrison seems to have broken up after its supplies ran out and its commander was executed.[49]

Subsequent efforts by the cities of Santo Domingo and San Juan to recover their residents' costs in supplying these troops were rebuffed by the crown with the observation that each city had failed to provide foods for the garrisons in Florida as ordered in February 1566. Their penalty for that failure to "carefully guard and fulfill our orders" was to absorb the cost of the support they had given the garrisons.[50]

Aside from their deterrent value, which cannot be measured, the Antilles garrisons did little to further the defense of the area. At Puerto Plata, Santiago de Cuba, and Havana the soldiers were to be employed in the building of fortifications. They do not seem to have done very much because of disinterest in the job and because of quarrels between their commanders and the local authorities that prevented carrying out the work Menéndez had ordered. At Santiago the troops were briefly used to interrupt illegal trading, while at Havana they participated in various displays to discourage corsairs hanging off the port. Nowhere were they put to the test in combat.

The passing of the threat of a French invasion and the mounting evidence of the cost of the Antilles garrisons at a time when the crown's

Table 17 Florida Military-Mission Posts Established and Abandoned, 1565–1574

Place	Date Established	Size of Party at Founding	Date Abandoned	Remarks
San Mateo	September 20, 1565	?	April 25, 1568	Garrison fled French-Indian attack. AGI, Justicia 1000, No. 2, R. 5
Aís	November 2 or 3, 1565	200 Spanish 50 French	December, 1565	Garrison mutinies. Part march down coast to near Sta. Lucía, others set out for Havana in ship. Garrison reestablished near Sta. Lucía. AGI, Justicia 894, No. 8.
Santa Lucía (Jupiter Inlet)	December 13, 1565	Over 100 men	March 18, 1566?	Survivors escape in supply boat after mutiny. AGI, Justicia 894, No. 8.
Guale	August 17, 1566	20 men	November 18?, 1566	AGI, Contaduría 941, Listas de gente de guerra ... 1566–1567. Lyon, *Enterprise*, 154. Note: a mission was active in Guale in 1568–1569, involving a few Jesuits.
Santa Elena	April 15?, 1566		August 16, 1587	
Inland from Santa Elena (in order, from the coast)				First Pardo expedition, December 1, 1566, to March, 1567.
Orista	after September 1, 1567	?	By April, 1568	Ruidíaz, *La Florida*, II, 484–86. AGI, Contaduría 941, Listas de gente de guerra ...1566–1567. These posts were abandoned or overwhelmed by Indians. Some men may have escaped to Santa Elena or Chiahá.
Canos	"	?	"	
Guatari	"	?	"	
Joara (Juada)	"	18 men	"	
Cavehi (Cawchi)	"	31 men	"	

Chiahá	January 1, 1567(?)	39 men	Sargent Moyano and some of the men fought their way to Santa Elena, bringing at least six Indian women with them.
"Carlos" (San Antonio de Padua)	post-October 15, 1566	23 men and friars 50 men added March, 1567	Survivors evacuated by Pedro Menéndez Marques. AGI, Justicia 1001, No. 2, R. 2. Lyon, *Enterprise*, 170, 177–78.
Tocabaga (Safety Harbor)	March, 1567	30 soldiers	All were killed by Indians. Lyon, *Enterprise*, 177, 202–3.
Tequesta (Near Miami, Fla)	April, 1567	30 soldiers 1 Jesuit	19 survivors rescued by Pedro Menéndez Marques and taken to Carlos. Lyon, *Enterprise*, 179, 203.
San Pedro de Tacatacuru (Cumberland Island, Ga)	?–1569	50 men as of August, 1570	Abandoned. AGI, Justicia 906, No. 6.

Table 18 Temporary Antilles Garrisons Installed by Menéndez de Avilés, 1566–1568

Place	Date Installed	Size	Commander	Notes
1. Santo Domingo	December 3–15, 1566	150	Capt. Rodrigo Troche[1]	Agreement, Santo Domingo, November 28, 1566, AGI, Patronato 173, R. 18.
2. San Juan de Puerto Rico	December 16, 1566	100	Capt. Juan de Zorita	Agreement, San Juan, December 16, 1566, AGI, Santo Domingo 164, R. 2, No. 53.
3. Puerto Plata	December 24, 1566	50	Capt. Juan de Garibay	AGI, Justicia 1001, No. 4, R. 3; AGI, Justicia 900, No. 5, question 8.
4. Santiago de Cuba	January 16–18, 1567	50	Capt. Francisco Godoy[2]	Agreement, January 16–18, 1567, AGI, Indiferente General 1219.
5. Havana	January 20, 1567	200	Capt. Baltasar de Barreda	

1. Found guilty of violating the monastery of Sta. Clara (OFM), December 24, 1568. AGI, Justicia 21, No. 2, R. 2.
2. Executed by Martín de Mendoza, Teniente of Governor García Osorio, April 12, 1568. AGI, Justicia 21, No. 2, R. 1. In addition to the sources indicated, this table is based on: Pedro de Valdés to Crown, Havana, January 29, 1567, AGI, Santo Domingo 155, No. 187 (Stetson); Pedro Menéndez de Avilés to Crown, Santo Domingo, December 3, 1566, AGI, Santo Domingo 71, bk I, fols. 341–344vto; Wright, *Early History*, 278–79.

resources were being stretched by wars in Granada, the Low Countries, and the Mediterranean, caused the crown to order those garrisons withdrawn. The disbandings were carried out by the newly formed Indies Fleet during the late fall of 1568, The men were given the choice of enlisting in the fleet or receiving certificates of service that they could present when and if they got home to Spain. Most chose the former alternative, although a few remained in the Antilles. For those who returned home, the process of obtaining payment proved long and expensive because royal penury, Menéndez de Avilés' claims against their pay, and the need to seek legal help drew out the process of payment until as late as 1582.[51]

In Florida, the contribution of the royal garrison was greater in the sense that it helped to establish a permanent Spanish presence and in the sense that the royal soldiers were slightly less ruthless than the *Adelantado's* private soldiers in trying to extract natural products of value and salvaged gold and silver from the Indians because, unlike the private soldiers, they had a promise of pay for their services. However, soldiers were soldiers and the presence of the colony continually provoked hostilities with the Indians. Officially, the blame for what soon became continuous Hispano-Indian hostility was laid to the presence of Frenchmen among the Indians.

Failure to keep the peace with the Indians and to incorporate them into the Spanish economy as providers of food through tribute and labor made it almost impossible to develop agriculture that might have made the Spanish population self-sufficient. It also meant that the crown's apparent intent to keep a garrison in Florida for a few months or a year at most was frustrated. By the fall of 1567, when Menéndez was again at court, it was clear to him that he could not carry out his contract by June of the next year, when its three-year term expired. Accordingly, the crown had to decide to renew it with additional benefits to him and costs to itself or to revoke it. For reasons of state and patronage, the Menéndez contract was renewed, but with the beginnings of rationalized support for the crown's garrison. The newly created Indies Fleet was to pay 150 men from its subsidy, with Menéndez and his appointees and associates both in the Fleet and in Florida continuing to run the supply operation.[52] In addition, the crown ordered supplies sent to Florida and payment made on many of Menéndez' claims for the 1565-1567 period. The temporary royal garrison thus took one step towards becoming a permanent charge on the royal purse.

The final step in putting the Florida garrisons on a permanent basis was the creation of a subsidy or payroll for the troops, to be paid from Tierra Firme. Royal orders of November 15, 1570, provided approximately 23,400 ducats each year for 150 men. Most of the money was to be spent for food and salaries, but 1,500 ducats were set aside for bonuses for those performing special offices or enjoying the *Adelantado's* favor, and another 1,800 ducats were allocated for powder and munitions.[53] With the subsidy as its guarantee, a trade in supplies of all types gradually grew, to be complemented in the 1570s by agricultural activities around St. Augustine and Santa Elena. The Florida settlements became permanent, thanks to this growth of their economy, the absence of a prolonged external threat (an uneasy peace was made with the Indians), and occasional examples of bold leadership that pulled the settlements back from the brink of disaster.

At Havana, the removal during early 1569 of the 200-man garrison created in 1567 forced the town to resume the series of rotating watches at the entrance to the bay and at various points within the town. All able-bodied residents were confined to the town unless they had the governor's permission to leave. Counterrounds on horseback were also established. During the two years of the garrison's presence, the residents had been free of these duties, which interfered with business. The acting governor, Diego de la Rivera, asked for a return of the 200 men to defend the town until the new fort was completed. The town council asked for 50 men. Rivera buttressed his appeal by noting that half of the 200 militiamen had to be outside of Havana most of the time, thus placing an unfair burden on the men who remained.[54]

Because of the strategic importance of Havana and the historically demonstrated inadequacy of its militia, again underlined by Rivera's letter, these appeals produced immediate results. On November 15, 1570, the crown ordered Menéndez de Avilés, who was governor of Cuba as well as *adelantado* of Florida, to raise six artillerymen and forty-four soldiers as a garrison for Havana. A subsidy of 6,158 ducats was to be paid by the treasury of Tierra Firme and administered by the treasury officials of Havana.[55]

During the same years that the Florida garrisons were taking on their air of permanency, 1566–1570, other towns in the Caribbean, besides those in the Antilles, began to move in the direction of royally paid garrisons. Caretakers of various types were employed at Santa Marta,

Trujillo, and Cartagena (Table 8 and 9, above). Cartagena had sought a dozen artillerymen, but the crown only authorized one, and he was paid by the city.[56] San Juan de Ulúa, still only a roadstead, faired better with the beginnings of its permanent garrison. Nombre de Dios, like San Juan de Ulúa a key port in the commercial system, received its first temporary garrisons.

On the Main, the emergency created by the sudden increase in the number of corsairs in the late 1560s and early 1570s caused the Audiencia of Panamá to order the recruitment of a series of companies, which served for varying lengths of time. The first was a group of one hundred men sent to Nombre de Dios in May 1569. That fall, during the visit of Viceroy Francisco de Toledo to the Isthmus on his way to Peru, he and the Audiencia agreed to send an expedition against Vallamo (or Ballamo), the chief settlement of escaped slaves whose raids against the trans-Isthmian road traffic were becoming too dangerous to ignore.[57] The long war that followed from this decision was essentially a police action and thus falls outside the boundaries of this study, except for the 1577–1579 period, when John Oxenham was active on the Isthmus as an ally of the Cimarrons.

Two years after the first temporary garrison was sent to Nombre de Dios, another group of fifty men was sent to protect the town during the summer. One hundred men were sent in October 1572, following Drake's raid, because of reports that eight large ships were off the town. These men remained on duty until the convoy arrived in January 1573. The convoy's departure led to the creation of another garrison, this time of sixty, then eighty soldiers, and finally of ninety soldiers. The troops were discharged at the end of November 1573.[58] Four years passed before another garrison was sent to Nombre de Dios.

Creation of the subsidies for Florida and Havana, together with approval of the garrison of San Juan de Ulúa, brought the crown into a new era. Because of the inadequacy of private resources for the defense of each place (at San Juan de Ulúa there were almost no permanent residents at this time), the crown itself had to create and support garrisons of regular troops.

This new policy did not mean an end to consideration of sending temporary garrisons to meet specific emergencies. In the summer of 1571, for example, the Spanish learned that Count Louis of Nassau had assembled a squadron of twenty-five ships. Other groups of ships, usually smaller, were rumored to be at sea or being prepared in France. The objective of these squadrons remained unclear, but when it was reported that one group of seven ships was to sail in the spring of 1572 to attack one or more ports in the Indies, the crown ordered the Casa to send 150 soldiers to Menéndez de Avilés, to be placed in fifty-man garrisons at Havana (in addition to the fifty men already there), San Juan de Puerto Rico, and Cartagena or another port on the Main. Once the danger had passed, the men were to be absorbed into the crews of the Indies Fleet.[59] The report turned out to be false and the men were not sent.

No further changes were made in the garrisons before 1578. From the perspective of Madrid, the manpower problem of the 1570s turned not on numbers, but on how to supply the garrisons, caretaker garrisons, and above all the militias with adequate numbers of arms and amounts of munitions. For convenience, consideration of these related themes—arms and munitions—will cover the period to 1585.

War Matériel for the Militias

The supply of weapons and munitions for the militias continued to be inadequate down to 1586. The crown did manage to send out matchlocks and some pikes to a few ports in 1566–1568 in an apparent effort to replace weapons taken for the enterprise in Florida or needed to bring local defenses up to the challenges they seemed to face in that period.[60] In 1577 it sent out 400 *mosquetes* (a larger-bore, heavier version of the matchlock) to the port towns and an additional 200 to the Casa de Munición in Mexico City. In 1572 and 1582 it sent a few weapons to Puerto Rico and Havana (Table 19). However, many other requests, such as those of Puerto Plata and Yucatán, went unanswered, as did most requests made after 1577.[61] And even when requests were answered by either the 1566–1568 or 1577 shipments, many of them had been on the books for years. Most militias continued to be without adequate numbers of weapons.

Even more serious for the military effectiveness of the militias was the failure to keep an adequate supply of munitions available in the Indies. Once again the complaint was heard that there was not enough powder for regular drills and that the men could not afford to pay for what little was given to them.[62]

The traditional remedy for such shortages was again applied. Letter

Table 19 Crown Shipments of Arms Primarily for Use by Militias, 1563–1585

Year	Puerto Rico	Santo Domingo	Havana*	Honduras	Santa Marta	Cartagena	Isthmus
1566			36 matchlocks (1565)		100 matchlocks 100 pikes	100 matchlocks 200 pikes	
1567		150 matchlocks 200 pikes					
1569	84 matchlocks 63 pikes		12 matchlocks (1570)				
1572	100 matchlocks 100 pikes		36 matchlocks			(50 matchlocks)[1]	
1577	50 mosquetes	50 mosquetes	50 mosquetes 100 matchlocks	50 mosquetes	50 mosquetes	50 mosquetes	20 mosquetes
1583	40 matchlocks,* 16 mosquetes, 40 pikes		50 matchlocks, 16 mosquetes, 50 pikes				

*Indicates that most weapons were probably placed in the fort rather than given to militiamen.
1. These weapons were captured by a corsair before they arrived at Cartagena.

after letter went to Spain asking for munitions and bespeaking the dangers that would follow if they were not supplied. Responses before 1585 were infrequent, although the crown issued more orders for munitions than the Casa was able to fill. At its best, petitioning was a slow method increasingly unsuited to the continual state of war that had developed in the Caribbean after 1563.

The crown took few initiatives in sending munitions to all the major ports. The general resupply of 1566–1568 was one. Another occurred in 1572 because of the threat posed by Count Louis of Nassau's fleet.[63] Other munitions were sent out with the *mosquetes* of 1577. These were steps in the right direction, but they did not go far enough.

The solution to the needs of the militias and the forts was first suggested by the crown itself when it ordered the Casa to see that Puerto Rico received fifty ducats worth of munitions each year. That order of 1573 seems to have become known in the Indies and sparked requests from other towns for a similar arrangement. Havana (1577), Santiago de Cuba (1579), and Santo Domingo (1580) all asked for yearly shipments of munitions. They do not seem to have been deterred from their requests by the fact that the Casa had failed to send all but the first of the yearly supplies to Puerto Rico, despite repetition of the order in 1577.[64]

The crown finally became aware of the inadequacy of this sort of hit-and-miss supply operation in 1583. It initiated an investigation into the Casa's failure to supply Puerto Rico and to send the entire amount of powder ordered for Santo Domingo in 1569. What it found were claims in Seville that there had been shortages of funds and of supplies of powder and other munitions.[65] No solution for the problem was found before 1586, although supplies continued to be sent where the need seemed great and the local authorities had been insistent enough, as they had at Havana and Puerto Rico.

Table 20 summarizes the evidence on when and where munitions were sent between 1564 and 1585. It is evident that munitions were in short supply in the Indies in early 1586. Indeed, the need was so great at Cartagena that General Pedro Vique, commander of the galleys, seized the munitions that a dispatchboat (*aviso*) was carrying for Havana. He and his captains claimed that they had less than 400 pounds of powder of all types, and almost no lead or matchcord.[66] In short, because of failures in the supply of munitions and weapons, the militias

Table 20   **Munitions Shipments from Spain to the Indies, 1563–1585**

	Puerto Rico	Santo Domingo	Havana-Cuba	Honduras	Santa Marta	Cartagena
1563	1500 lbs. P.					
1565	1268.5 lbs. SP 103 lbs. S		400 lbs. L 3000 lbs. CP 300 lbs. AP 200 lbs. SP		500 lbs. AP 200 CBall 400 lbs. L	
1566						470 lbs. AP 400 lbs. L
1567		995 lbs. AP 400 lbs. M 800 lbs. L				3+ lbs. L* ? lbs. P (AP)* (1568)
1569	325 lbs. AP ? lbs. L					
1570		2000 lbs. AP 2948 lbs. SP				1136 CBall
1571		1200 lbs. AP 1609 lbs. CP		? lbs. AP*		
1572	275 lbs. CP 850 lbs. AP 300 lbs. M 500 lbs. L	700? lbs. AP 300 lbs. M 500 lbs. L	700 lbs. AP 300 lbs. M 500 lbs. L	234 lbs. AP* 350 lbs. CP* 200 lbs. L*		674 lbs. AP 300 lbs. M 500 lbs. L (lost to Corsair)
1573	100 lbs. AP				AP,M,L* (1575)	
1576			490.5 lbs. AP			
1577			2000 lbs. AP 1000 lbs. M 1000 lbs. L			
1578	539 lbs. AP					
1582	1800 lbs. AP 800 lbs. M 800 lbs. L		1400 lbs. AP 1000 lbs. M 1000 lbs. L 2000 lbs. AP**			

AP=Matchlock Powder
CBall=Cannon Balls
L=Lead
M=Match Cord
S=Sulfur
SP=Saltpeter
P=Powder
CP=Cannon Powder
*=Purchased locally, not shipped by the Casa de Contratación.
**=Sent from New Spain

and even most garrisons were ill equipped to deal with attacks throughout the 1570s and the early 1580s.

Fortifications

The various programs of fortifications proposed or undertaken during the third period found their inspirations in some combination of concern over local defenses because of the fall of Havana in 1555, local incidents that brought home the need for more defenses, or on-going plans for fortifications not fully realized during the previous periods of war. As in the past, whatever the local officials thought was needed constituted the project sent to the crown, which would either accept it or reject it. Having abandoned the grand scheme of 1542 to fortify all the ports of the Caribbean, the crown had no overall plan for fortifications, nor did it send inspectors to gather data that might have been used to formulate such a general plan. Indeed, only one inspection of a group of forts was made, that by Pedro Menéndez de Avilés in the Antilles in 1566–1567, and it resulted in the confirmation of local views rather than a thoroughgoing critique of plans and existing structures.

If the crown had no general plan regarding fortifications, on what basis did it make its decisions? A detailed examination of the history of fortifications, such as appears below, shows that, with the exception of Havana, strategic importance alone, as we might measure that value, was not enough to ensure the crown's support for fortifications. Besides being in a key military location, a port also needed local supplies of building materials, money, and construction personnel. But most importantly, it needed the right political connections with a nearby Audiencia and in Spain. Those connections could provide subsidies to make up deficits in money and construction personnel. This political factor explains why a minor port like Trujillo, Honduras, could eventually obtain (limited) funding, while strategically important ports like San Juan de Puerto Rico and Cartagena went begging. Trujillo benefited from the grudging interest of the Audiencia of Guatemala, just as Santo Domingo and Puerto Plata did from the interest of the Audiencia of Santo Domingo. Where such a local power center was not interested in fortifications, as was the case with San Juan de Puerto Rico, the town got only crumbs or was forced to use locally generated resources. In short, patrimonialism, often influenced by precedent and parsimony, was the determining factor in royal decisions about fortification projects during this period.

The effects of precedent, patrimonialism, and parsimony are evident from the figures for the crown's expenditures, which were relatively little (8,876 ducats, mean yearly cost) in absolute terms as well as in relative terms (7 percent of total defense costs). As was true in the second period, Havana's new fort accounts for most of the expense (55 percent), although the additions to the forts at San Juan de Ulúa in the 1570s occupy second place (30 percent).[67] Notable amounts were spent for a fort at Puerto Plata, Española (8 percent of total costs for forts) and at Florida, the two new projects undertaken during these years.

Where royal money was not made available and the need for improved defenses seemed urgent, local officials and residents frequently pitched in to make temporary improvements in their fortifications. A notable example is San Juan de Puerto Rico, where the residents built a wall from La Fortaleza to the Morro (1556). Cartagena, which would seem to be the extreme case because of its support of the costs of building a tower and two gun platforms (completed ca. 1574), remains a unique case because its construction of defenses arose from a continuing, if weakening, determination to go it alone, without royal help.

Aside from the role of patrimonialism, precedent, and parsimony in the making of decisions, a detailed survey also shows that, with the exceptions of the fort at Havana and the additions made to San Juan de Ulúa in the 1570s, the structures built during this period were of the old style, being essentially keeps and baileys with attached gun platforms, as at Puerto Plata and the Boquerón at Cartagena, or additions to existing works that either extended walls or added more artillery emplacements, as at San Juan de Puerto Rico and Santo Domingo. Except for Menéndez de Avilés' survey in the Antilles in 1566 and discussions at Cartagena (1560s) and Havana (1577–1579), no one examined the towns with an eye to developing a system of fortifications that would aid defenders in holding off attacks. Even these inquiries were limited in their assessment of the tactical use of local geography. The closest thing to a system of defenses was the use of town walls—an anachronism employed with little or no thought to the advantageous use of terrain. Technically, then, the fortifications built during the second round continued to be aligned with earlier assumptions about their role in defense, a defense that still rested on the militias and was limited by what they could, or would, defend. The basic strategy outlined by Núñez Vela in 1538 thus continued to be the rule of the empire, even as a few more ports were added to the list of places with fortifications.

154 THE SPANISH CROWN AND THE DEFENSE OF THE CARIBBEAN

There follows an examination of the history of fortifications at each of the ports for which there are data, beginning with San Juan de Puerto Rico and proceeding counterclockwise around the Caribbean to Cartagena. For the sake of completeness, these mini-histories begin with the responses to the fall of Havana in 1555 and continue into the 1580s, when those limits are appropriate.

San Juan de Puerto Rico

Upon learning of the fall of Havana, the Puerto Ricans contributed the labor of their slaves to the building of a wall from La Fortaleza to the Morro bastion, along the main landing beaches on the bay-side of the town. A new *cubo* or water battery was built on the Morro below the old bastion, and a request was made for royal funds to pay for a more extensive remodeling of the old bastion atop the Morro. Some work was undertaken at royal expense in 1557, although it was not extensive. The result of this was that only the landward end of the island was undefended. The danger from that quarter was perceived in 1558, and a request was made for slaves and an excise tax to build defenses along that side of the island. The following year, during another emergency caused by the fear of a French attack, the governor again got the residents to contribute the labor of their slaves to build fortifications, in this case breastworks on the beach before the town.[68]

The crown did not respond immediately to the requests for funds for either an extensive remodeling of the Morro or for a wall across the landward end of the island, but it did not object when local officials used royal funds to repair La Fortaleza, 1564–1567 and 1570, and to make small changes in the Morro, 1570. Direct royal responses to the petitions of San Juan came in 1566, when Menéndez de Avilés inspected the city's defenses and made recommendations agreeing with the earlier local observations, and in 1573, when slaves were sent from Havana to work on repairing the rocks below La Fortaleza, which were being undermined by wave action.[69]

Once in possession of a labor force, the governor and officials of San Juan decided to build a wall with two cavaliers along the city side of La Fortaleza. The slaves were put to work gathering the materials, and plans and cost estimates were sent to Madrid for study. There the matter rested for years. Meanwhile, the slaves began to cost the treasury money—although they were being rented to private persons and used for a variety of purposes useful to the city but not connected with fortifications—and the rock face below La Fortaleza's battery fell down, carrying part of the battery wall with it. The king's response to the first problem was to order the slaves sold![70] The second was left for later discussion.

Santo Domingo

At Santo Domingo, storm damage and the continued threat of corsair attacks motivated the enlargement and rebuilding of the water battery with royal funds. The city wall continued to present problems into the early 1560s, but references to it disappear from the documents thereafter. The difficulty with the wall arose from a recommendation that it be run through the plaza on the waterfront along the river. Opposition to this location was eventually silenced and the work went ahead. The wall was eventually completed and remains today, right in the middle of the old plaza.

The storm damage to the fort seems to have been noticed only in 1564. Within a year the crown had authorized repairs, but they were blocked until early 1566 by a power struggle within the Audiencia. When Menéndez de Avilés inspected the fort while in the city in 1566, he endorsed the repairs and a new covered battery that was being built on the seaside. In addition, he recommended that the wall on the cityside of the fort be rebuilt, because men using crowbars could have torn it down, and that the fort wall be completed all the way around the grounds. He made no mention of reinforcing the stone below the water battery to correct the undermining. Nor was anything done about this undermining when the new covered battery was built at that location. The new battery was finished in the summer of 1571.[71]

News that Count Louis of Nassau's pirates had sailed from their bases in the English Channel caused local officials to look to their defenses and find that the wall along the river had not been completed. A dispute ensued over whether the excise tax could be appropriated again for this purpose. That dispute was compounded by the Audiencia's attempt to charge the residents for work at the beach of Guivia, a mile to the west of the city.[72] No further work, aside from routine maintenance in 1572–1573 and 1575, was done on the fortifications at Santo Domingo until 1578 (Illustration 8).

Illustration 8 **Santo Domingo under attack by Sir Francis Drake's forces, 1586.**
British Library, London.

Northern Española

Fortification of the towns on the northern and western coasts of Española had been discussed during the 1540s, but no action was taken until 1563 when the crown ordered the fort at Puerto Plata built. By that time it was clear that the western and northern coasts of the island had become the bases for illegal trade with Portuguese and French merchants. It was apparently thought that a fort which offered protection to the Spanish would serve not only to remind Spaniard and foreigner alike of the royal laws forbidding trade but might also give the locals enough courage to resist the threats which they claimed the corsairs used to force trade. Whether intentionally or not, the Audiencia of Santo Domingo neatly turned aside the thrust of the crown's will by contracting the work to Francisco de Caballos, a prosperous sugar planter and rancher with extensive property near the port, where he also served as deputy royal treasurer.[73] The royal intent was further weakened by the decision to pay for the work from the collection of debts due to the crown. Money from that source dribbled in all during the 1560s, prolonging the work, although not at any great cost to the crown. When Caballos finally died in 1571(?), he left a bulwark with some artillery, the trenches and some of the walls for the tower fort, and little else.

Caballos' successor at Puerto Plata was Pedro Rengifo de Angulo. Possessed of more energy and better connections at Santo Domingo and in Spain, he began to push the work on the fort. By early 1578, he could report that he had completed the tower of the fort and was at work on its curtain walls and barbican, both of which had already been criticized as too costly compared to the importance of the town. This criticism may have been motivated by consideration of the new settlement at Bayahá, then underway and shortly to result in the construction of a stone and earth rampart guarding the entrance to that bay.[74] Like the fort at Puerto Plata, that at Bayahá was supposed to provide security for the Spanish population and so encourage them to stop their illegal trade with the corsairs. And like Puerto Plata, the work was largely in the hands of residents of the north coast. Both efforts to thwart the corsair trade were undermined by the failure of the regular Spanish merchants to provide alternative markets and sources of goods at competitive prices. That, rather than military security, was the real reason for the trade by the late 1570s.

Construction at Puerto Plata continued. By the fall of 1580 the wall was about nine feet high around its circumference. The fort was completed by August 7, 1584, twenty years after it was begun.[75]

Santiago de Cuba

Santiago de Cuba was important militarily because it lay near one of the corsairs' main trading areas, the Windward Passage. Requests made in the 1540s for aid in fortifying the port had been answered by granting an excise tax for that purpose, but those funds were diverted to wars with the Indians and other uses of importance in the eyes of the town council's members. Consequently the city's only defenses were its bulwark, artillery, and militia. Because these were not enough, the city was raided a number of times during the 1550s. To provide more protection, Menéndez de Avilés placed a fifty-man garrison in the port in early 1567 and put the men to work building a battery at the entrance to the port. This work soon ceased because the residents were antagonistic to the project and the workmen.[76] The corsairs again became regular visitors, and Santiago became notorious as one of the ports where illegal trade occurred.

Knowledge of these facts as well as concern that the corsairs might seize the port as a permanent base for use against the New Spain convoy prompted its inspection in 1575. The recommendation that followed was referred to the Audiencia of Santo Domingo for study. Although witnesses called during the inquiry had supported extensive fortification, the Audiencia recommended no action because proper fortification would be expensive, require a garrison, and not provide security for trade because other nearby ports could be used by the corsairs. Continued suggestions by the governor of Cuba and the petition of the advocate of the city were required to obtain a royal order that a dozen of the slaves working on the Havana fort be sent to Santiago to repair its defenses when the fort at Havana was finished.[77] There the matter rested. Santiago made no improvements in its fortifications prior to 1586.

Havana

The beginning of the new fort at Havana was discussed in Chapter III. What is of interest here is the work carried out after 1563, when the new engineer, Francisco Calona, and the first group of slaves arrived. Under this combined stimulus, the work went ahead briskly until early 1565, when shortages of money and labor produced the first of a new series of delays. Fresh infusions of money allowed construction of the walls to ground level by 1567, but four more years were required to complete the casemate closest to the port (the so-called Northeast Cavalier) and to raise the walls of the remaining three casemates to the level of the gunports and loopholes. All four casemates were complete, except for the parapets, by January 1574. By that date, too, the curtain walls were well along, and much of the stone for the vaulting behind them had been cut. But again, the money ran out and work almost stopped. During the next three years, the white journeymen frequently struck in demand of their back pay. Slaves were rented out to raise at least some revenue to feed their fellows and to make token payments against the salaries of the white workers. Finally in April 1577 the last vault was closed and the fort was certified as ready for occupancy. Final finishing took an additional two years, and some aspects of the work, notably the cisterns, were not finished until the mid-1580s (Illustration 9).

At completion, a number of inspectors found faults with the new building. To begin with, it was very small, with a central courtyard only twenty feet (*pies*, about eleven inches) on a side. The rooms off this courtyard were dank and unsuited for habitation or for the preservation of stores. The arches of the vaults in the casemates were found to be too thin to support the recoil of the pieces placed inside the casemates and on top of them. The moat was dry and only partially as large as planned. But worst of all, the fort was open to fire from La Cabaña, which overshadowed the upper deck and gave some view of the courtyard.[78]

In time, remedies were found to all of these problems. The courtyard was eventually destroyed in remodelings after the terminal date of this study. During the late 1570s and the early 1580s the wardens and governors built wooden sheds on the upper deck of the fort for the garrison to live in. These sheds were freer from the dampness and mosquitoes of the lower rooms. The vaults were eventually thickened; the moat was deepened and given access to the bay and tidal waters. The problem of La Cabaña remained for later generations to solve by fortifying that hill.

The structural problems of the new fort are partially attributable to its being one of the early examples of the design, and hence not quite up to the rapidly changing standards imposed by changes in artillery. The construction delays and problems reflected the crown's continuing difficulties with getting its servants to do its bidding promptly and with

Illustration 9 Havana, showing fort and projects for fort and boom at entrance to the harbor, post-1580. Archivo General de Indias, Seville.

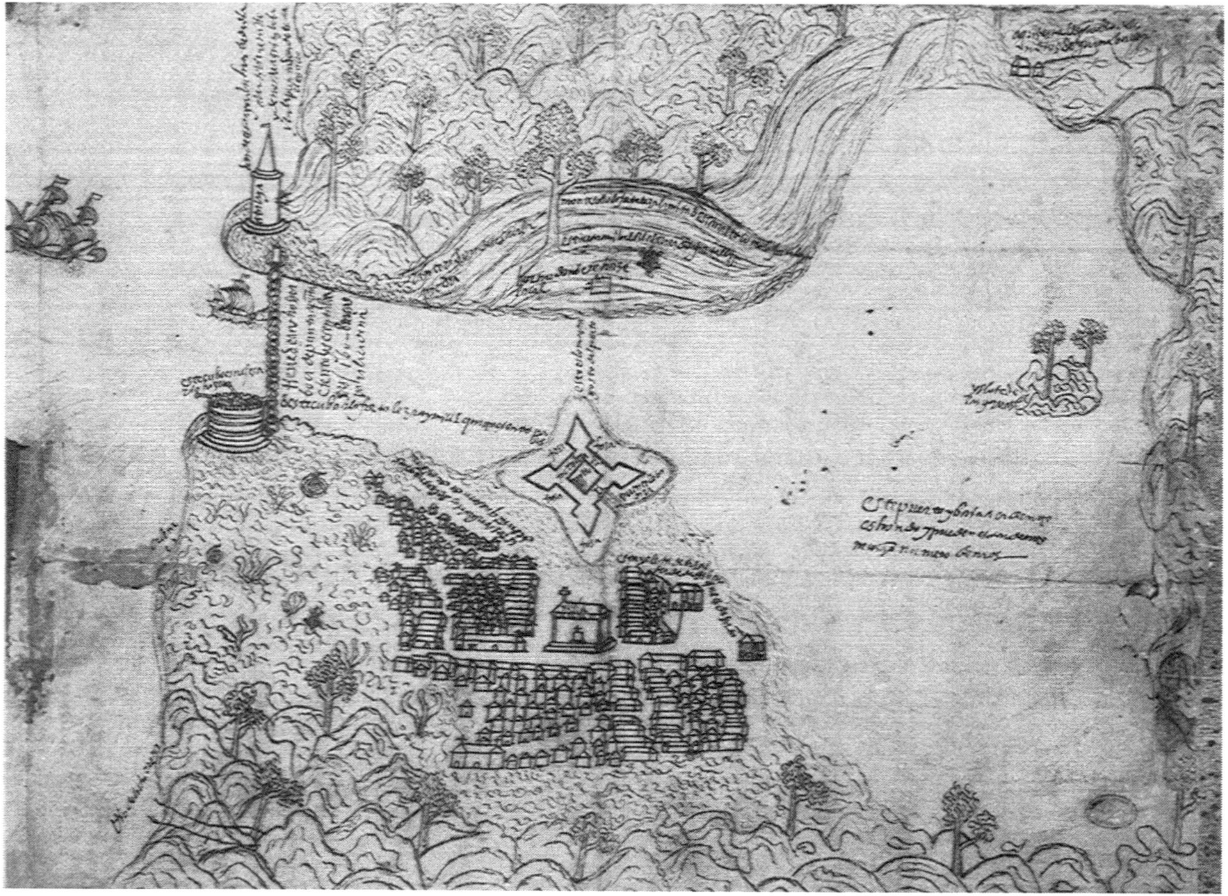

some efficiency, and the on-going financial problems of the empire. The shortage of money from 1574 to 1577 cannot be directly tied to the royal bankruptcy of 1575, but it clearly was part of that period of depression that accompanied the renunciation. The location of La Fuerza seems to have resulted from unthinking imitation of the original mistake in placement, and like it, harked back to the medieval stronghold situated on the edge of town rather than ahead to the positional fortifications that became the rule in the sixteenth and later centuries as engineers attempted to cover all possible lines of approach and angles of fire.

Some appreciation of the positional problem was already present, as demonstrated by the critiques of the new fort's location. Other evidence of this appreciation at Havana are the efforts to construct something on the Morro that might prevent an enemy from boldly sailing into the bay. As early as the 1550s the town council had ordered trenches and watch sheds set up, often with small pieces of artillery, on either side of the mouth of the bay. In 1563, Governor Diego Mazariegos proposed to build a permanent tower on the Morro. The king approved but ordered a new port tax to pay for it. That apparently killed the project, for in 1566 the town council decided to build a shed or *bojío* on the beach opposite the Morro to shelter the watchmen and their munitions. The next year, Pedro de Valdés inspected the west side of the entrance and proposed to build a tower there using his troops as laborers, if the city would also contribute to the project. The city refused and a dispute ensued; nothing was done.[79] The Morro remained unfortified.

Florida

The fortification of Florida accompanied the attempt to colonize under Menéndez de Avilés. By his contract he was obligated to build two fortified settlements. His first fort was built around the longhouse of an Indian chief near the site of modern St. Augustine. It consisted of little more than earthworks to protect the artillery and soldiers. A temporary structure built because of fear that Ribault's forces might attack the new Spanish colony, it was soon replaced by two wood and earth structures about which very little is known. These were followed in 1570–1571 by a two-story fort on the mainland, built with casemates to the northwest and southeast of the central part of the building and a gun platform on the east, facing the bay. This structure was built of wood, roofed with lime cement. It and a successor lasted until 1586, the objects of derision from critics who referred to them as "houses of boards" and "warehouses for mice."[80] Gutierre de Miranda and Pedro Menéndez Marques replaced this fort in 1586 with a wood and earth structure on an island in the bay, San Juan de Pinillo, more in keeping with the emerging geometric style of design. Both buildings were burned by Drake on June 8, 1586.[81]

At Santa Elena (modern Parris Island, South Carolina), the forts that existed prior to the Indian revolt of 1576 are not well documented. The structure existing at that time was destroyed and replaced in 1577–1578 by a building that duplicated the fort at St. Augustine in every detail except that the gun platform was triangular rather than rectangular. This structure remained in existence, with repairs, until the late 1580s—in this instance surviving the attacks of 1586 because Drake could not find the entrance to the bay.[82]

None of the forts of Florida were large or costly, although the costs must remain inexact because the soldiers worked on them without extra pay. Except for the first fort at St. Augustine, each fort seems to have had the largely incompatible purposes of providing defense for the town, residence for most of the garrison, and storehouse for its foods. By the time the fort of 1570–1571 was built at St. Augustine, it is evident that the Spanish were more concerned about the Indians and the weather than about a European attack. The building that resulted was suited to defense against Indian attacks but useless against Europeans. Only in 1585 did a man with a wider experience (Gutierre de Miranda) begin to bring the Florida forts back into line with developments in the on-going war against Europeans in the Caribbean. For that war, renaissance style (*i.e.*, geometrical) forts were essential. Fortified warehouses were as useless as the keeps that still constituted the main forts at Santo Domingo and San Juan de Puerto Rico.

San Juan de Ulúa

Realization of the changing scale and type of warfare came somewhat earlier at San Juan de Ulúa than in Florida. As early as 1555 the crown had authorized the reimposing of a port tax to pay for the repair of the wharf and its guard forts following a damaging hurricane. It is not clear that any changes were made in the forts (really just towers), although the crown instructed the viceroy to look into criticisms that the main tower was improperly placed for defense. These repairs seem to have been substantially completed sometime prior to 1568 and the encounter between the new viceroy, Don Martín Enriquez, and John Hawkins.[83]

The Hawkins affair seemed to demonstrate a need to enlarge the defenses of San Juan de Ulúa. Accordingly, proposals first made in 1552 were dusted off and work was begun to extend and widen the wharf (the so-called *"muro de argollas"*) and to complete the tower that became known as the "old tower." At the same time, a proposal was made and eventually accepted to add another, larger tower on the eastern end of the wall. This was to become the bastion of San Crispin. A more extensive proposal for squaring off the island and building a small city behind walls was advanced but died under study.[84]

The new work can be only partially documented from treasury records (to 1574) and letters. It seems to have been completed by 1580, when Captain-General Bartolomé de Villavicéncio inspected the fort in detail, finding the old tower, the wall, and a new bastion[85] (Illustration 10).

Honduras

Attempts to fortify the ports of Honduras began in 1559 after corsairs sacked both Trujillo and Puerto Caballos. The Audiencia of Guatemala requested royal funds, while its president, who had arrived at Trujillo during the attack, took more direct action. He helped the residents build what later writers describe as a wall of *tapía* around the city, and he recommended that Puerto Caballos be moved to a similar hilltop site and be fortified by putting a wall around it. His recommendations were not acted upon, although he continued to urge it. Funding for the defense of Trujillo, including additions to its fortifications, was authorized in 1559, with the tributes of the island of Guanaza being given for that purpose. However, no payments were made from this fund. There the matter rested until in 1572 the crown authorized 1,000 ducats per year from vacant encomienda revenues for the building of a bulwark before Trujillo, equipping it with artillery, and keeping it supplied with munitions. This order was opposed by the Audiencia on the ground that the encomiendas supported the men who in effect constituted the garrison of the town, and that using the money for the fortification would weaken rather than strengthen defense by forcing these men to leave the city. Nonetheless, Trujillo's officials continued to ask for funding for

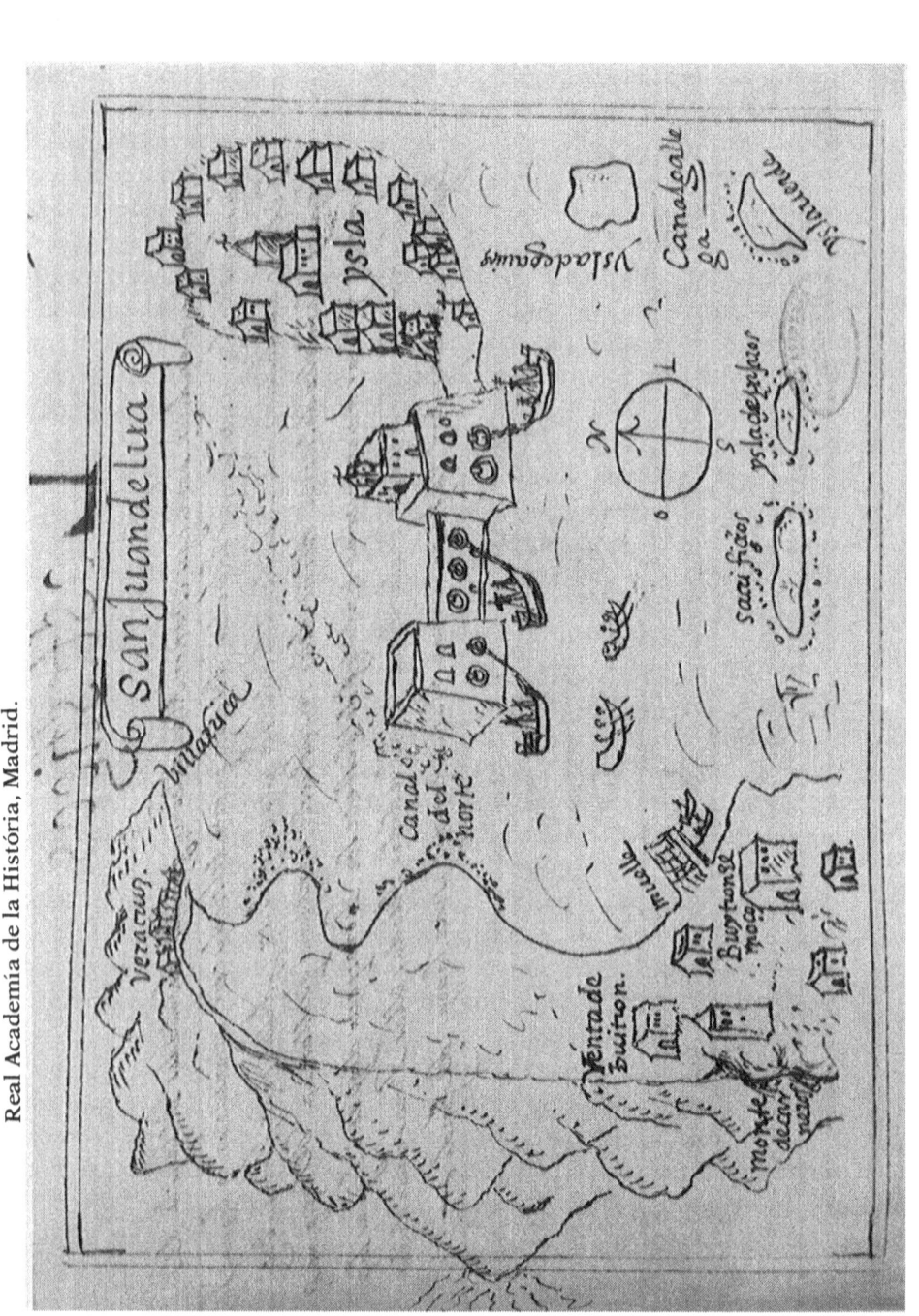

Illustration 10 **San Juan de Ulúa,** *ca.* **1580.**
Real Academia de la História, Madrid.

a fort from vacant encomiendas. The crown answered with an order that 1,000 *pesos de minas* (each worth 272 maravedís as compared to the 375 maravedís of the ducat) be dedicated to the work, and in 1578 the Audiencia of Guatemala reluctantly assigned revenues from various encomiendas and villages to that purpose.[86] The defense of Trujillo continued to depend on its militia and the remains of the *tapía* wall built in 1559. Puerto Caballos remained unfortified.

Nombre de Dios

The story of the fort at Nombre de Dios is simply told. In 1556 the crown issued orders for its construction, but work began only in 1561 with the purchase of a few slaves and tools and the cutting of 545 blocks of stone. However, there was no mason to begin the delicate job of setting the first courses on the reef. The work was ordered or requested again the next year and in 1568, 1569, and 1574, but nothing came of it.[87] This failure to complete the project was in part the result of the physical problem of building a fort, compounded by the openness of the bay, which seriously weakened the ability of one fort to control access (a point noted in 1540), the competing claim of Panamá for a fort, and the apparent confusion in Madrid over what had been ordered and who was responsible for it. Not even Drake's raid of 1572 and the subsequent problems with the Cimarrons produced energetic actions. Nombre de Dios continued to be defended by earthworks and troops from Panamá. Her long-term defense was entrusted to mosquitoes and to the ability of the empire to gather and send reinforcements or a reconquering expedition.

Cartagena

Royal indifference toward Santiago de Cuba is understandable, given its lack of importance in every area except that of illegal trade, but Cartagena de Indias was far from being unimportant, and in fact became more important as the years rolled by. Yet the crown did little to aid in its fortification despite some requests from its residents and the obvious need. Again, as at San Juan de Puerto Rico and Nombre de Dios, a political failure seems to underlie the inability of the town to obtain royal funding for defenses. In this case, the cause of that failure is somewhat clearer than that of the other two: Cartagena had early rejected royal help offered during the governments of Philip's boyhood, and when it did apply for aid at the beginning of his reign, it sought permission to wall the city using an excise tax rather than royal revenues. The city thus seemed to say that it could and would provide for itself, a position that the finances of the empire prior to 1580 probably made particularly appealing in Madrid.

Cartagena's request for a wall came four years after the sacking of 1559. The town council reasoned that a wall would allow the city to hold off an attacking force for at least a week, by which time the effects of the climate would begin to decimate the attackers. This idea was eventually presented to the court by the city's advocate and elicited enough interest to cause the crown to order a full report on the existing defenses and the prospects for improving them. The inquiry revealed that work had already been begun on a cavalier at the Boquerón and that the royal revenues at Cartagena were inadequate even to support the treasury officials. An excise tax was proposed to meet the projected costs of 30,000 pesos for a wall and 20,000 pesos for two forts. The following spring the acting governor began a fort or cavalier at La Caleta, in response to the news of possible French invasion of the New World. By that fall (1567), the work had stopped and an accounting of the 2,000 pesos spent had been exacted from the agent in charge. A new governor inspected the city and not only endorsed the work already begun, but also recommended additional fortifications and a partial wall. These papers were duly forwarded to Madrid with an advocate who obtained an order for the collection of a tax on tavern wines until 4,000 pesos had been accumulated, the amount thought needed to finish the two forts, and the subsequent order to Viceroy Francisco de Toledo to inspect the city and report on its defense needs when he passed that way on his way to Peru.[88]

Toledo's visit provided the occasion to present a variety of proposals for fortifying the city, some of them dating from several years earlier. In 1567 Governor Martín de las Alas had proposed building a large cavalier next to the Santo Domingo convent, behind the fort of La Caleta, and another at the Bojío de la Vela. These two batteries, with the Caleta fort, would cover the approach to the city up the beach along its northern side. This view was seconded in 1569 by Captain Vallejera, an experienced officer traveling with the viceroy. Alas had also proposed building a large fort at Jaqueves, opposite the proposed battery at the Bojío de la Vela, and a drawbridge into the city, but nothing was said of this in 1569.[89]

The basic soundness of the Alas proposal was to be demonstrated in 1586, but in the interim the objections of Governors Pedro Fernández de Busto and Francisco Bahamond de Lugo buried it. Busto in particular bears responsibility for sidetracking the plan. As early as 1571 he charged that the money put into the two then unfinished forts had been misspent. Subsequently, during his long tenure as governor (1574–1586), he did nothing to develop them and nothing at all about the additional forts proposed in 1567–1569. Lugo, who served only one year as governor, 1573–1574, made some improvements in the design of the Boquerón fort and may have seen it finished during his brief term, but his proposed changes in the Caleta fort apparently were used by Busto as an excuse to do nothing about fortification.[90]

Busto's ideas on fortifications were demonstrated in 1571 when he wrote to the crown that the two forts at the Boquerón and La Caleta were completed, by which he apparently meant that they had reached a state that justified abandoning them and working on a project of his own—a fortified wharf that he felt would better defend the town and would not divide her militia, as manning the outer forts would. Lugo later (1574) agreed that the *"fuertecillo"* of the Boquerón—which consisted of a stone tower with a battery before it—was in good condition and needed only artillery. The battery at La Caleta had already ceased to exist. Yet as late as 1576 the crown was authorizing more money to complete the "towers" at the Boquerón and La Caleta, while demanding a report on what had been achieved—a report it apparently never received.[91]

Funding for the new wharf and for a wall, both authorized by 1578, came from taxes on the wine drunk in taverns and, after 1578, also from meat sales. Labor for the projects was provided by slaves seized on behalf of the Treasury and sent to the city. The work proceeded slowly because of the delays in collecting funds in amounts large enough to make action worthwhile and because the slaves were employed for many other purposes. On the day that Drake appeared to test the forts and the wall, they were still incomplete (Illustration 11).

Other Towns

A few other ports requested fortifications at the crown's expense during the second round of fort building; none received the coveted gift of funds. Veragua and Santa Marta sought this support, and at Santa

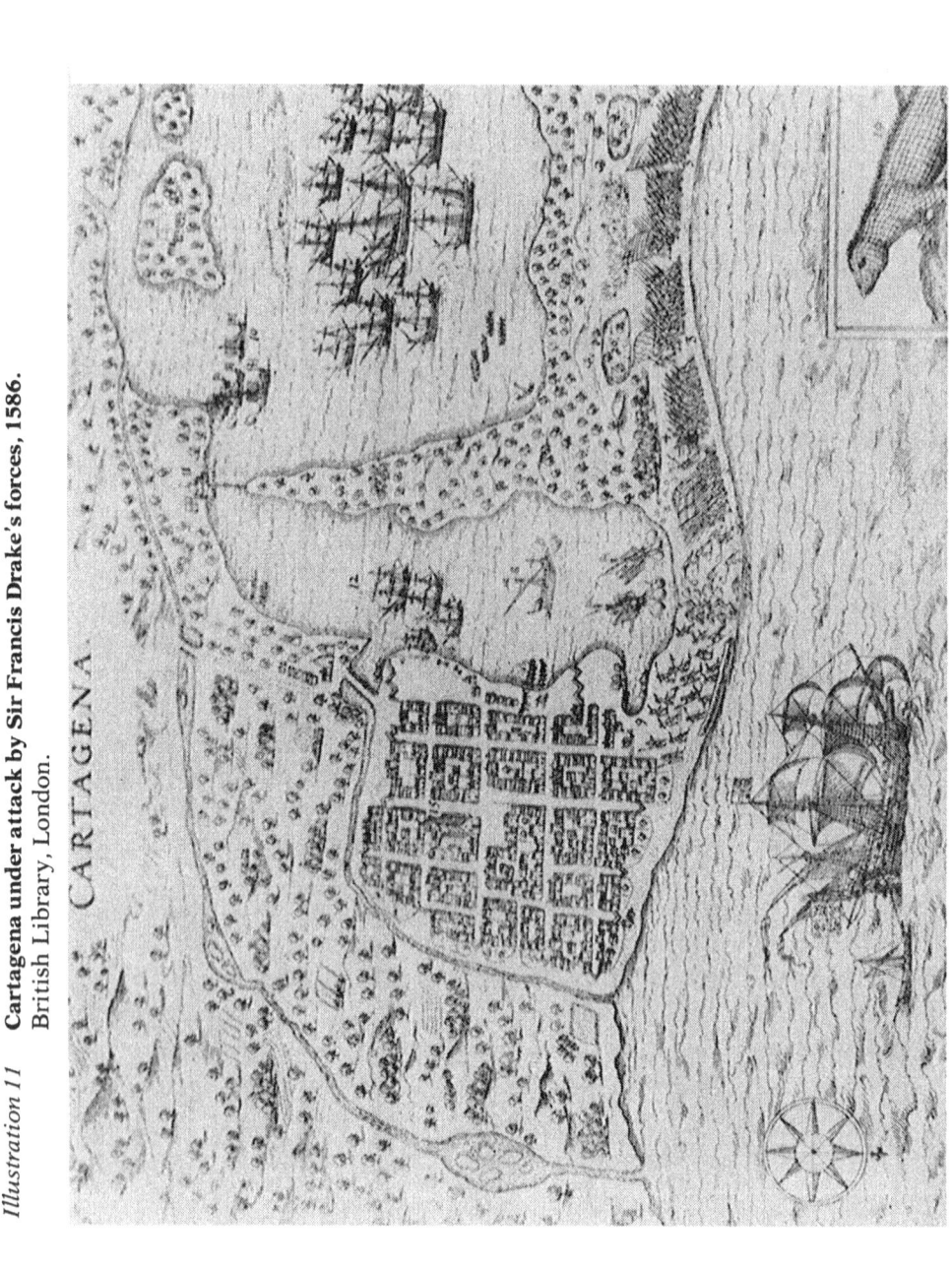

Illustration 11   Cartagena under attack by Sir Francis Drake's forces, 1586. British Library, London.

Marta an arrangement for the building of a fort was actually entered into but never fulfilled. At Margarita and Río de la Hacha the residents built what passed for fortifications. At the first, the "fort" was nothing more than the jail; at the second, a series of earthworks was thrown up to defend the town during the 1560s. Margarita's governors occasionally noted that the island needed more formal defenses, but they did nothing and resorted to hiding the royal strong box in the woods whenever corsairs were expected in the area.[92]

Artillery

The crown's distribution of artillery during this period followed a pattern similar to its support of fortifications, with the exception of Cartagena. As in previous periods, costs do not fully reflect this activity because of the use of guns held in inventory in Spain whose shipment produced minimal expenses in the treasury books.

Thanks to the large inventory of artillery that the Casa had built up during the late 1550s and to which it added by salvage during the 1560s, there was a radical improvement in artillery holdings at many Caribbean towns during the late 1560s. The key events affecting this improvement have already been identified as the crises of 1565–1572. In response to this crisis period, in 1565 the Casa supplied pieces to the *Adelantado* of Florida for his conquest, and to the governor of Cuba for Havana. The next year a large number of pieces were sent with the Archiniega fleet. From among them four guns went to San Juan de Puerto Rico, which had not received the artillery ordered from the Casa in 1563, four went to Santiago de Cuba, two may have been left in Havana, and over three dozen pieces ended up in Florida. Offsetting these gains were the loss of seven pieces, one from Puerto Rico and six from Santo Domingo, which were sent to Florida for the conquest but were lost at sea or not returned to their points of origin. Three years later (1569), the Casa sent three guns to San Juan de Ulúa, where they joined and eventually replaced guns mounted from among those taken from John Hawkins' ships. And finally in 1570, the Casa sent Cartagena twelve pieces, although only four were bronze.[93]

The result of this effort and of the resumption of the convoy system was that the Casa's inventory was unable to meet demands for guns during most of the 1570s. Many means were used to try to rebuild the store, including salvage, refounding, purchase, and attempts to obtain a large group of guns from the Low Countries. The merchants seem to have temporarily solved their need for ship artillery by establishing a special levy on top of the *avería* to provide a fund to purchase 120 pieces of artillery to add to their store of 80 pieces.[94] For nonmerchants, the Casa had no spare guns. Requests from the Indies went unfilled, even though the crown ordered guns almost yearly.

The number of requests for artillery and munitions rose during the early 1570s in response to the French threat and the spread of corsair raids to areas previously untouched or infrequently raided. Margarita sought artillery without success. Trujillo's petitions for weapons were not granted until 1574, and then the Casa failed to send the guns. Santiago de Cuba's needs were noted in 1575, although no particular stress was placed on them. Puerto Plata petitioned in vain for artillery from Spain and finally had to arm its new fort with two small "man-killers" obtained at Santo Domingo. Corsair raids on the Isthmus during 1572–1574 provoked a number of requests from the Main for artillery at the same time that the crown was ordering the Casa to send artillery previously ordered for Santo Domingo, Havana, and Cartagena so that they would be prepared should Count Louis of Nassau actually carry out his rumored plan to invade the Caribbean. Examples of the requests from the Main are a request by the officials of the province of Tierra Firme for field guns for use against the Cimarrons and for permission to keep two guns that had been removed from Santo Domingo. Concepción de Veragua asked for bronze artillery, munitions, and an artilleryman to supplement the three iron cannon and assorted smaller pieces that it had used in fighting corsairs in 1574, while Santa Marta renewed its requests for munitions.[95]

The Casa was unable to meet these requests, and the more urgent and long-standing ones for long-range artillery of the culverin class that it had received from Havana, Puerto Rico, and Cartagena, until the late 1570s. Indeed, prior to 1578 Havana received no artillery except the four guns sent in 1565 and two others added to the inventory between 1566 and 1577. Not surprisingly, the new warden, Francisco Carreño, asked for eight heavy guns for the casemates and three or four long-range pieces for the Morro even before he left Spain, upping the request to a minimum of twenty-seven guns once at Havana, but saying at the same time that forty pieces were needed. Puerto Rico fared little better.

1564–1577. A SYSTEM TAKES SHAPE   171

The Casa failed to provide two culverins ordered for the Morro in 1568, despite repeated orders. It did no better with additional pieces requested in the 1570s, though it did send a small quantity of munitions.[96] Cartagena's request fared better and merits a more detailed examination as an example of the problems of getting artillery from Spain.

The construction of the fort at the Boquerón and the battery at La Caleta, together with visits by John Hawkins and raids off the city by other corsairs, led Cartagena to petition for artillery to be paid for one-third by the crown and two-thirds by the city. In response, Viceroy Toledo inspected the city's defenses and approved the purchase of twenty-four pieces to supplement the six on hand. Sixteen were purchased by the city and a request made for the rest and several additional pieces for use as replacements. At the crown's order, the Casa supplied them, sending eight iron and four bronze guns, with munitions, in 1572. Both because the guns were iron and because they were of the wrong types—it having been observed that longer-range guns were needed—the city spent five years petitioning the crown to replace them with bronze pieces of the culverin class.[97] These guns were finally sent in 1578.

In sum, after the initial supply of artillery at the Casa was exhausted by the shipments of the mid-1560s, no further artillery could be sent except for the guns for Cartagena. In the area of artillery, too, the defenses of the Indies continued to lag behind European practice with all that this lag portended for the outcome of future conflicts.

Few contemporaries would have agreed that one period or phase in the history of the defense of the Indies was ending in the last months of 1577. Some programs of fortification were continuing; the garrisons were established and were suffering the same sorts of problems with money, morale, and numbers of men that had characterized them from the beginning; the convoy system was working; a squadron from the Indies Fleet was prowling the Antilles and the Main as similar squadrons had done in the past. Local petitions for various additions to existing defenses were still being formulated, or were awaiting the king's pleasure, or were being fulfilled, as the political and strategic facts of the time might dictate. In short, nothing seemed to be changing. In fact, however, defense spending was about to peak at a pre-1586 yearly high of 391,342 ducats (1578), and the introduction of galleys was about to work a major change in the balance among the various forms of defense. Within two years contemporaries were acknowledging that a new phase in the history of the defense of the Indies had begun, one that carried with it a marked decline in the number of corsair incidents. In modern terms, the defenses of the empire were finally equal to, and a bit ahead of, the offense as represented by the corsairs.

The Balance Sheet

What had the crown gotten for all the money it spent during the third period? It had obtained two important victories, the chief of which was the expulsion of the French from Florida. The crown's claim of sovereignty was thereby vindicated, and more extensive troubles in the Antilles were apparently headed off. The other victory had occurred at San Juan de Ulúa, where John Hawkins had finally suffered for his open violation of the empire's navigation laws. Yet both were pyrrhic victories, for they marked (although they did not cause) the collapse of any hopes that diplomacy could resolve the growing conflicts between Spaniards and Frenchmen and Englishmen.

The other losses suffered by the corsairs were the consequences of the steady improvement in the empire's defenses to meet the challenge of unofficial but quite real war in the Caribbean and the Atlantic. About a dozen illegal traders were captured in widely scattered incidents. In another dozen cases, mostly during the years 1570 to 1572, corsairs suffered casualties when attacking on land. Among the more notable of these incidents were the deaths of fourteen Frenchmen at Baracoa, Cuba, in 1563; the death of Jean Bontemps at Curaçao in October 1570; the losses suffered by invaders of the Canaries (1571–1572); and the elimination of Oxenham's men on the Isthmus (1577). The corsairs lost about a dozen ships to the Spanish in open combat. The first such Spanish success was off Havana in the fall of 1565, followed by other incidents off Margarita in 1572 and 1576, off Veragua in 1574, and at La Yaguana in 1575. On at least seven other occasions corsairs were either driven off in pitched battles at sea or suffered losses before they could capture Spanish merchantmen. Shipwreck also took its toll, especially on the Main in 1569 and 1574. Yet measured by the amount of money spent and the number of corsairs operating in the Caribbean during these years (ca. 40 or fewer sail per year), these results were not terribly impressive. The war with the corsairs continued to be a frustrating, expensive, almost quixotic venture notable for what Spanish defenders seemed to be preventing, rather than for their success in battle.

That the Spanish had so few battles in which to be successful was largely due to their failure to pursue a policy of aggressive defense—that is, a policy that relied on naval patrols in all parts of the Caribbean and during all seasons of the year. Only Menéndez de Avilés seems to have been able to envision the problem for what it was: a naval war in which victory would go to him who sought out the enemy. His inability to have his view accepted, if indeed he even wanted to act on it in a serious way, is indicative of the political and technological realities that would have prevented such a plan from being implemented if implementation would have meant no new construction of forts, no garrisons, and no supplies for the militias. In a political system in which the king was the principal patron and responded paternally to the petitions of his subjects, the demands of local interests took precedence over larger strategies, indeed impeded the formulation of such strategies. The technical problems of supply and funding, while not beyond the ability of the empire's accomplished bureaucrats to solve, were nonetheless formidable by contemporary standards and would in any case have demanded a proliferation of offices and expenditures that was not in the crown's interest. In short, politics and short-term interests, whether local or the crown's, demanded the shift back to passive defenses that took place during the third period. Therein lay the weakness of the defense of the Indies. Such defenses were not the solution to the larger problem. They were bandages applied where stitches were needed.

From an historical vantage point, it is clear that despite the ad hoc nature of many of the decisions made regarding defense during the thirteen years between 1564 and 1577, a system of sorts was emerging. Building on the precedents of the wars of the 1540s and 1550s, the crown had abandoned any attempt to rely on private interests alone, although it had not completely replaced militias with garrisons nor merchant-controlled convoy escorts and ship armament rules with the Indies Fleet. The defense of commerce had taken on a degree of system and permanence with the regularization of the convoy system under the rules of 1564, with the creation of the Indies Fleet to patrol in the Caribbean and to provide escorts for the convoys as necessary, and with the fairly regular coordination of convoy movements with those of the Portuguese royal fleet in the Azores and with galley patrols along the coasts of Andalusia and the Algarve. The main lines of commerce were well protected by 1577 even if the lesser trades of the Caribbean were still largely at the mercy of the corsairs. Yet even on that front progress was being made because the Indies Fleet had begun to patrol regularly on the Main as well as in the Antilles.

Land defenses, while benefiting from the Indies Fleet's harassment of the corsairs in the Caribbean, remained largely inchoate, though the historian's eye can perceive the beginnings of the system that developed after Drake's great raid and the onset of the Anglo-Spanish war of 1585–1603. The geographic distribution of fortifications remained much as it had been in the late 1540s, but Cartagena had begun to build, even if it used its own rather than royal money. Improvements in the fortifications at San Juan de Ulúa and San Juan de Puerto Rico, the completion of the fort at Havana, and the installation of forts and garrisons in Florida all pointed in the direction of a system of fortified termini for the convoy system. The placement of permanent garrisons in Florida, Havana, and San Juan de Ulúa also pointed in that direction. The temporary garrisons of Nombre de Dios pointed, however faintly, towards a greater royal involvement in the defense of the Main. The crown's concession of money for artillery for Cartagena was a straw in the wind of history blowing in the same direction.

But for all these hints at the beginning of a system of land defenses, those defenses remained the stepchildren of policy makers. Patrimonial politics and local interests still counted for more than any clear strategic design. Unlike the defense of commerce, which was early analyzed and which had clear, natural priorities defined by the volume and movement of shipping, the defense of land areas in the Caribbean did not have any clear priorities before 1577 beyond defending Havana and preventing French occupation of Florida. And even there, both the new fort at Havana and its garrison and the garrisons of Florida were largely reactions to French action, much as the new defenses at San Juan de Ulúa were reactions to John Hawkins' visit to that port. A similar pattern of response, as influenced by precedent, patrimonialism, and parsimony, governed decisions on petitions from the various towns and cities of the Caribbean. In short, while a system was beginning to take shape around the galleons and garrisons, it was far from being well defined by 1577.

Chapter V   **1578-1585.**
The System Refined and Neglected

To the eyes of contemporaries, the distinguishing characteristic of the history of defense during the eight years that preceded Drake's raid of 1586 was the use of galleys as coastal patrols, first along the Main and then in the Antilles. In both areas the results of their introduction were dramatic, with sudden drops in the number of corsair raids and some decrease in illegal trading activities (Table 23). Their effect on royal spending was also dramatic, although contemporaries may not have been as able as the modern scholar to appreciate the change in the pattern of royal spending brought about by their use. Coastal patrols, which included some patrols by the "highside" ships of the Indies Fleet in 1578–1581, cost the crown as much as four times more in the fourth period than they had in the third period (a mean yearly figure of 60,138 ducats compared to 14,382 ducats)—a greater increase than that registered in any other category of expenditure. On the Main the increase was even more startling: sixteen times more was spent for coastal patrols than during the previous period (Table 21).

The sharp rise in expenditures for local coastal patrols was part of a general rise of naval costs in both absolute and relative terms. These costs more than doubled (2.5 times as much) in ducat amounts (from 72,433 ducats to 185,043 ducats, mean yearly figures) and rose by twenty percentage points, from 55 percent to 75 percent of total expenditures. These increases reflected not only the fourfold increase in

Table 21 Mean Yearly Costs of Various Types of Defense by Geographic Area, 1578–1585 (in Ducats)

Place	Total		Land Total		Man Power		Fortifications		Artillery	
Empire	245,558		57,132	23/100	35,622	15/100	4,630	2/100	1,229	1/100
Triangle	34,300	100/14	37	<1/<1	0		0		37	<1/3
Caribbean Total	117,226	100/48	57,096	49/100	35,622	30/100	4,630	4/100	1,192	1/97
Antilles Total	21,557	100/9	18,296	85/32	13,948	65/39	3,901	18/84	271	1/22
Puerto Rico	317	100/<1	305	96/1	284	89/1	9	3/<1	13	4/1
Santo Domingo	1,501	100/1	1,469	98/3	489	33/1	651	43/14	180	12/15
Cuba	16,198	100/7	16,102	99/28	12,756	79/36	3,241	20/70	77	1/6
Non-Antilles Total	92,258	100/38	38,303	42/67	21,178	23/59	729	1/16	922	1/75
Florida	26,147	100/11	26,147	100/46	10,442	40/29	258	1/6	1	<1/<1
New Spain	2,511	100/1	461	18/1	0		461	18/10	0	
Central America	183	100/<1	144	79/<1	88	48/<1	10	5/<1	46	25/4
The Main, Total	63,389	100/26	11,522	18/20	10,647	17/30	0		875	1/71
Tierra Firme	10,647	100/4	10,647	100/19	10,647	100/30	0		0	
Tolú	8	100/<1	8	100/<1	0		0		8	100/<1
Cartagena	867	100/<1	867	100/2	0		0		867	100/71
"Venezuela"	29	100/<1	29	100/<1	0		0		0	

00/00 should be read: The first number is the percentage of total costs for a given area spent for the type of defense in that column (reads across). The second number is the percentage of the total for that type of defense spent in that place (reads down).

Naval Total	General Purpose	Convoys	Coastal Patrols	Place
185,043 75/100	107,698 44/100	60,674 25/100	60,138 24/100	**Empire**
34,243 100/19	30,645 89/28	0	4,332 13/7	Triangle
57,903 49/31	19,676 17/18	0	55,539 47/92	Caribbean Total
3,120 14/2	1,973 9/2	0	3,117 14/5	Antilles Total
0	0	0	0	Puerto Rico
0	0	0	0	Santo Domingo
0	0	0	0	Cuba
51,867 56/28	14,966 16/14	0	50,230 54/84	Non-Antilles Total
0	0	0	0	Florida
0	0	0	0	New Spain
0	0	0	0	Central America
51,867 82/28	14,966 24/14	0	50,230 79/84	The Main, Total
0	0	0	0	Tierra Firme
0	0	0	0	Tolú
0	0	0	0	Cartagena
0	0	0	0	"Venezuela"

spending for coastal patrols but also a 64 percent increase in the crown's cost for convoy escorts (from a yearly mean of 36,885 ducats to a yearly mean of 60,674 ducats), and a doubling of the monies spent for the Indies Fleet (including costs of the galleys) from a mean of 53,451 ducats per year to 107,693 ducats. However, the benefit in terms of the defense of the Indies was not proportionate to the increased costs because the Indies Fleet performed mostly convoy duty after 1579 and ceased to cruise the Caribbean after 1581. Convoy escorts were, by definition, of limited military value, although they continued to prevent losses in the Triangle and at some points in the Caribbean.

The corollary to the relative cost of naval defenses was a decrease in the relative cost of land defenses, from 42 percent to 23 percent of total costs. In absolute figures, land defenses cost slightly more: a mean of 57,132 ducats per year compared to a mean of 54,483 ducats per year for the third period. This increase was due largely to increased spending for artillery and to additions to the list of places receiving small amounts of crown money for land defenses. Translated into categories, the land defense costs show a decline of 17 percent for manpower expenses (to 35,622 ducats from a high of 42,846 ducats, mean yearly figures), a 48 percent decline in expenditures for fortifications (to 4,630 ducats compared to 8,876 ducats), and a rise of 300 percent for artillery (from 409 ducats to 1,229 ducats). Only the decline in spending for fortifications was significant because it indicates that the crown did not continue to improve fortifications after the plans approved in the 1560s had been carried out. Manpower costs remained essentially the same,[1] with some decrease because the men who had served from 1566 to 1568 had finally been paid off by the Casa, thus placing spending for manpower on a more current basis reflecting the troops in the field and the supplies sent to the militias. Manpower costs should have been higher because of the new garrison at San Juan de Puerto Rico and increases in the strengths of the garrisons at Havana, the Floridas, and San Juan de Ulúa, but the crown did not pay these men their full salaries and rations. By 1586 it owed its soldiers money, although the records do not show just how much.

This sharp shift back to a system of defenses centered around naval means was accomplished primarily by increasing the amounts spent for coastal patrols and in the construction of the new galleons of the Indies Fleet while reducing expenses for land defenses only in the area of fortifications. Those changes aside, the pattern of spending remained much as it had been during the third period (taken as a whole). The garrisons were all in the northeastern part of the Caribbean, as were most of the royal forts and artillery, and except for the new garrison at San Juan de Puerto Rico, all the major additions to these passive defenses were built on what already existed. In other words, the passive defenses of the area changed little, even though the crown had their weak spots pinpointed by reports of what invading enemy forces planned to do and by inspectors it sent out. All these reports noted the vulnerability of San Juan de Puerto Rico, Santo Domingo, and Cartagena to seizure because each town lacked adequate passive defenses. The crown could have remedied those inadequacies to the degree that they were not deficiencies in basic manpower, and even then it could have done something, as it did at San Juan de Puerto Rico. Its failure to do so is one of the most significant facts about the fourth period. That it did not do more than put a garrison at San Juan is probably accounted for by the fact that the galleys, which answered another defense need of greater immediate priority, also may have seemed to provide small core garrisons around which the militias of Santo Domingo and Cartagena—which had two of the largest populations in the Caribbean—could rally. Deeply involved in the Netherlands and with the acquisition of Portugal, the crown allowed the defenses of the Indies to continue according to the precedents of the time, making only such changes as were dictated by particular emergencies or overwhelming pressures from its subjects. The results were that the system of defenses that began to appear in the third period was refined and improved, but not brought to perfection or maintained at the level of the early years (1578–1582) of the fourth period.

Galleys, Galleons, and Patrol Squadrons

The brief account of coastal patrolling by the various squadrons of the Indies Fleet given in the last chapter showed that they did not offer continuous patrols in any part of the Caribbean. Initially this was because the Fleet was intended to patrol just the Antilles, but even after that policy was abandoned in 1574, various causes, including the demands of the crown for convoy escorts, prevented the squadron from being active along the Main and in the Antilles with enough frequency to drive off corsairs. Moreover, the squadron commanders patrolling the Main had found that the galleons were unsuited for those shallow waters and had ended up relying on frigates, rowing boats, brigantines, and galliots—all shallow-draft, oared, swift sailers similar to the ships the corsairs were using in their raids. These developments early suggested the need for patrol squadrons composed of oared ships of some type different from the "galleyed galleons" that Menéndez de Avilés had designed for the Fleet. Galleys were the obvious answer and, once deployed, provided the sort of continuous local coastal patrols required to stop the raiding and trading.

The decisions of 1577, 1582, and 1585 to send galleys to the Caribbean to replace the patrol squadrons of the Indies Fleet had a background dating from at least 1567, if not earlier. As ships, the galleys were the next step upward in size, speed, and firepower from the galliots, brigantines, *pataches*, and oared frigates that Spaniards and corsairs had been using in the coastal waters of the Caribbean since the 1550s. Indeed, in 1567 galleys were proposed instead of the "galleyed galleons" of Menéndez de Avilés' design, but the proposal failed to stop the preparation of the new Indies Fleet.[2] Once suggested, the galley alternative to the galleons of the Fleet remained a favorite of the critics of the Fleet's performance as a coastal patrol force.

The supporters of galleys began to receive serious attention during 1568–1569. Fleeing from the Antilles because of the patrols of the Fleet, corsairs appeared on the Main in record numbers and inflicted unprecedented losses on the Spanish. The corsairs' weapon was the small, shallow-draft, oared ship of the frigate or *patache* type. A few residents of the Main asked for patrols by the Fleet, but even they agreed with the supporters of galleys that the Fleet was unlikely to provide the sort of continuous patrol that their coastal commerce required for protection. Generally speaking, these advocates of the Fleet favored a permanent patrol by galleys if the Fleet could not be made to stay on the Main. They thus differed from the residents and town councils of Nombre de Dios and Cartagena, who wanted galley patrols until their ports were fortified, but not afterwards.[3] Exactly how forts were supposed to protect coastal shipping was not stated.

These proposals resulted in an order of December 11, 1569, that various officials in the Indies give their own and local experts' views on galleys. Replies exist from Santo Domingo, the viceroy of México, the town council of Nombre de Dios, the Audiencia of Panamá, and the governor of Cartagena. All except the viceroy approved the proposal and provided varying amounts of information on such matters as supplies and local resources for the support of the galleys.[4]

These opinions and a second report from the Audiencia of Panamá[5] were gathered into a file in the fall of 1572. In the interim, Menéndez de Avilés had come up with his strategy for driving the corsairs from the Caribbean by intercepting them when they attempted to leave it by the various passages and channels between the Antilles and Florida, and had begun work on the frigates that would be able to meet the corsairs and their swift oared ships on equal terms. The success of the Nombre de Dios brigantine in 1572 had led the crown to order *pataches* sent out with the convoy of 1573 to patrol the Chagres-Nombre de Dios route while the convoy was loading. These events, Menéndez de Avilés' undoubted political influence, and the lack of local resources for funding the operation of the galleys seem to have resulted in the matter being shelved.

However, requests for galleys continued to arrive from the Indies. In 1572 Cartagena continued its calls, which were joined in 1573 by others from the town council of Panamá and from a friar in Santo Domingo. Cartagena even began to construct its own eighteen-bench galliot, but the effort got no further than the cutting of the wood. The cost of completing the boat was too much for the limited resources of the town council. Other requests were made in 1574, primarily from the Main.[6]

The crown replied to these numerous petitions by ordering the Indies Fleet to patrol the Main, an order that placed Admiral Carreño and a patrol force on that coast in the fall of 1574. At the same time, the crown replied that if the city or governor of Cartagena could find someone to run galleys on a contract, the Council of the Indies would consider the contract.[7] These responses temporarily stilled the outcry.

Despite the crown's evident efforts not to send galleys to the Main, by 1575 enough requests for them and enough evidence that they were needed existed to justify the Council of the Indies in beginning inquiries into how galleys might be sent from Spain and in pressing the king for a trial run. The Council had even located three men who were willing to contract for the experiment. The Council claimed that disbanding the Indies Fleet and replacing it with the more effective galleys, under terms of the proposed contract, would save the crown some 120,000 ducats per year.[8]

Attractive as such savings must have been to a monarch then going bankrupt, the king did not rush to a decision. Instead, he formed a committee, which normally consisted of two members of the Council of the Indies; two members of the Council of War; the secretary of the latter, Juan Delgado; and other individuals who might be invited to attend. Meeting for the first time on July 31, 1575, the committee considered the Council of the Indies' opinion (*consulta*) and decided that galleys should be tried as an alternative to building more ships of the type of the aging "galleyed galleons." Advised of this, Philip replied with a list of questions about how the galleys might be acquired and sent to the Indies. After further consideration of some of these matters, the committee called for opinions from the crown's galley commanders in the Mediterranean.[9]

While the Mediterranean galley commanders were being sounded out on the feasibility of sending galleys to the Caribbean, a variety of developments occurred. The Casa unsuccessfully sought a contractor for a galley squadron on the Main. A new set of opinions on galleys was received from Tierra Firme. Admiral Carreño, whose galleon squadron had been on patrol until it was destroyed in a December 1574 storm, along with Alonso Criado de Castillo, president of the Audiencia of Panamá, various witnesses called to testify at an inquiry held at Nombre de Dios, and the bishop of Cartagena joined in supporting the galley as the preferred naval weapon. Carreño's experiences had conclusively proved that the deep-draft galleons were unsuited for patrol work against the shallow-draft oared ships of the corsairs. The opinion of men in the Indies was thus solidly in favor of the galleys, although some recognized that getting them there and using them would present unusual problems.[10] As news of the crown's interest in galleys for the Main got out, other parts of the Caribbean began seeking them. In October 1575 the advocate of Santo Domingo and the islands requested four for duty in the Antilles. About the same time, the governor of Havana asked for some, and his request was endorsed by the Council of the Indies. And finally, the Council of the Indies advised the king, on his request, that fifteen million of the Indies Fleet's annual subsidy of sixty million maravedís could be diverted for the galleys because the Fleet was smaller due to losses of ships.[11] These events added more weight to the arguments in favor of the galley experiment.

In contrast, the Mediterranean commanders stated unanimously that ordinary Mediterranean galleys could not be sent across the Atlantic. This view was seconded by Diego Flores de Valdés, sometime commander of the Indies Fleet, who thought that sea conditions off the Main would prevent the galleys from operating. Thus the galleys being released from duty off Italy by the abatement of the Turkish naval offensive west of the Straits of Messina would not be suitable. On the other hand, one of the commanders suggested that a new type of galley, more like a galleon in design, might do. But inquiries revealed that the royal shipyards at Barcelona could not build such ships until 1577.[12]

When the committee met again in the spring of 1577 to consider all these developments and opinions, it divided between a majority who still favored using traditional Mediterranean galleys and a minority, the members of the Council of War, who upheld the views of the Mediterranean commanders in opposing the project. Continuing doubts that the galleys could cross the Atlantic resulted in a subsequent order that persons in the Indies be asked to state whether it would be possible to build galleys there and at what cost. A suggestion that a *saetía* might be a suitable type of ship instead of the galley led to inquiries at Seville into the usefulness of that type of ship, long used as an escort and scout for galleys in the Mediterranean.

The investigation at Seville and further committee deliberations yielded the opinion that *saetías* would be suitable escorts for the galleys. Opposing views, which proved correct, were discounted. Orders were given to Valencian shipwrights to build a *saetía*.[13]

Completion of the hull of the *saetía* and calls for funds for its rigging coincided with the arrival in Spain of replies to the order of July 1577 requesting opinions on the galleys. They were again endorsed by the Audiencia of Santo Domingo, the captain-general of the Indies Fleet, the Audiencia of Panamá, the governor of Cartagena, and the advocate of Nombre de Dios. Only the town councils of Havana and Santo Domingo opposed the galleys, mostly for financial reasons. Hernán Manrique de Rojas, a rich resident of Havana, had also sent the crown a proposal for fifteen galleys deployed about the Caribbean, for some of which he offered to serve as contractor.[14] Once again, opinion in the Indies supported the use of galleys.

Advised of these developments, the King ordered the committee to meet in October 1577. Cristóbal de Eraso, the captain-general of the Indies Fleet, was invited to present his views. After hearing him, the committee resolved to send two galleys and the *saetía* to the Main.

Funding was to come from the Fleet's funds and shipwrights were to be sent to see if galleys could in fact be built in the Indies. A number of administrative details were raised and became the subject of most of the committee's subsequent deliberations during 1577. At later meetings, the committee ratified the king's suggestion that galleys be taken from those at Puerto Santa María and provided suggestions for the solutions of other problems.[15] By mid-November the only outstanding problem was the naming of the officers.

For the next four years, 1578–1581, the history of the galleys was bound up with the history of the Indies Fleet, both because the galleys were administratively subordinate to the Fleet and because their patrols along the Main were part of the Fleet's general activity of patrolling and escorting convoys. This relationship begins with the outfitting of the ships in 1578.

The decision to send galleys to the Main was followed by a decision to build six new, larger galleons for the Fleet. The largest two of the six (500 *toneladas* capacity each) were supposed to be ready to use in the spring of 1578. When they were not, the crown was forced to buy two ships and lease two more to replace the ship *San Salvador* and the galleons *San Pedro*, *Santiago Mayor*, and *Santiago Menor*, all of which were found to be unseaworthy and too rotten to be repaired. At the same time, the Casa had to meet the costs of the rations for the Fleet's crews and some of the wages due to them. Money was scarce and a series of loans had to be arranged, followed in turn by other loans as costs continued to rise beyond the early estimates.[16] The galleys added their share to these rising costs. But in the end, the galleys and the ships of the Fleet were prepared. Cristóbal de Eraso continued to be captain-general, and Don Pedro Vique y Manrrique was named to command the galleys.

The renewed Indies Fleet sailed from San Lúcar on July 5, 1578. The galleys, *Santiago* and *Ocasión*, were only partially loaded; most of their supplies and crews were in the *saetía*, *Santa Clara*, and the frigate, *Santa Catalina*. Thus made buoyant and favored by good weather until midpassage, the galleys gave the lie to skeptics by showing that they could make the voyage. Indeed, a midpassage storm gave Vique the opportunity to sail ahead in an attempt to reach the Main before the rest of the Fleet and so win the glory—and spoils—of taking any corsairs that might be there. Eraso sent the *saetía* and the frigate in pursuit, while the Fleet continued westward at a slower pace. The *Santa Clara* and

Santa Catalina did not catch up with Vique until Curaçao, where the galleys had put in for water. Unable to enter that shallow harbor, the ships went on to Santa Marta. The Fleet, meanwhile, made for Dominica, where the scattered ships were reassembled. Two ships taking men and supplies to Florida were dispatched for Havana under escort of the frigate, *Nuestra Señora de Guadalupe*, which was on her way to New Spain for the thirty million maravedís of subsidy due from that treasury. The other ships turned south, coasting along the Main from Margarita, touching at Santa Marta to join the *Santa Clara* and *Santa Catalina*, and then entering Cartagena on September 16. Vique had arrived six days earlier, without finding any corsairs. The arrival of the galleys "gave great happiness to all [the residents] of this coast of Tierra Firme, it being understood that they would be of great effect."[17]

While these events were occurring in Spain and the Atlantic, at Cartagena Miguel de Eraso, son of the captain-general, had undertaken at least three trips to Nombre de Dios, primarily in an attempt to collect the subsidy, but secondarily to seek out corsairs, including the survivors of Oxenham's force. Eraso had also built and launched a fifteen-bench galliot or *fusta*, *Nuestra Señora de Candelária* (the second of that name), and had another under construction.[18] He was at Nombre de Dios on the third of his trips when the galleys and the Fleet arrived at Cartagena.

During the six weeks following the Fleet's arrival, an attempt was made to send ships to Nombre de Dios with passengers, soldiers, and the bulls of the Crusade, but weather prevented it. The galleys were rigged and investigations made that resulted in the decisions not to try to build replacements at Cartagena (they would be too expensive), to use Miguel de Eraso's second galliot in place of the *saetía* as an escort for the galleys, and to send the galleys to Nombre de Dios with the people and goods undelivered in September.[19] That trip proved short (18 days), thanks to a marked improvement in the weather.

Upon the return of the galleys to Cartagena, a council of war agreed to sell the galleon *San Andrés* and use the money to fit out a squadron to patrol the Windward Passage over the winter under the command of another of Don Cristóbal's sons, Alonso de Eraso. Arrangements were also made to obtain supplies from Jamaica. However, storms turned back two attempts to send the squadron, so that it was not until early February 1579 that it cleared for the Windward Passage. By then the squadron had been enlarged because of reports that there were numerous corsairs and that the New Spain convoy had been struck by a storm and might need assistance. The course of the voyage is shown in Illustration 12.

Christóbal de Eraso and the rest of the Fleet remained inactive at Cartagena until mid-March, when the subsidy arrived from Nombre de Dios. With that money in hand, the ships and the galleys were prepared for the spring sailing, the first to Spain with the convoy, the second to patrol the coast.

News of Drake's raid in the Pacific broke in on these preparations on April 10, setting the galleys in motion for the first time since their cruise to Nombre de Dios the previous November. Accompanied by the galliot, they sailed for Tolú for supplies and a detailed six-week-long inspection of the coast as far as Nombre de Dios, while Don Christóbal took the galleons direct to Nombre de Dios to provide men and matériel should Drake attempt to cross the Isthmus and return to England. Vique subsequently was sent to patrol off the Chagres River to prevent Drake from using it as an escape route. That done, the galleys returned to Cartagena at the end of July. In the interim, Don Christóbal had returned to Cartagena and had, with considerable difficulty, gotten a convoy together. He sailed for Havana on August 4.[20]

At Havana he received word that the Triangle was more dangerous than usual. Accordingly, he took the three additional ships and all five of the Fleet's frigates with him to Spain, rather than leaving any as a patrol squadron. The storm-wracked crossing cost him one ship, but not her bullion cargo, which was transferred before she disappeared. At Seville the squadron was searched for contraband and then split up so that a galleon and three frigates could sail to Cartagena to join the merchantmen who had wintered there during 1579–1580. Delayed by funding and supply problems at Seville and then by other difficulties at Cartagena, the convoy returned to Spain only in September 1580.[21]

That fall the decision was being made to send a colonizing expedition to the Straits of Magellan for the purpose of fortifying the Atlantic entrances, if possible, to prevent a repetition of the Drake raid of 1579–1580. At the same time, the Council of the Indies returned to a consideration of the long-range status of the Indies Fleet. By March 1581 it had been decided to send the galleass *San Cristóbal* and four of the Fleet's frigates to the Straits and to retain a galleon squadron to patrol the Caribbean and provide the extra escorts that the convoys might

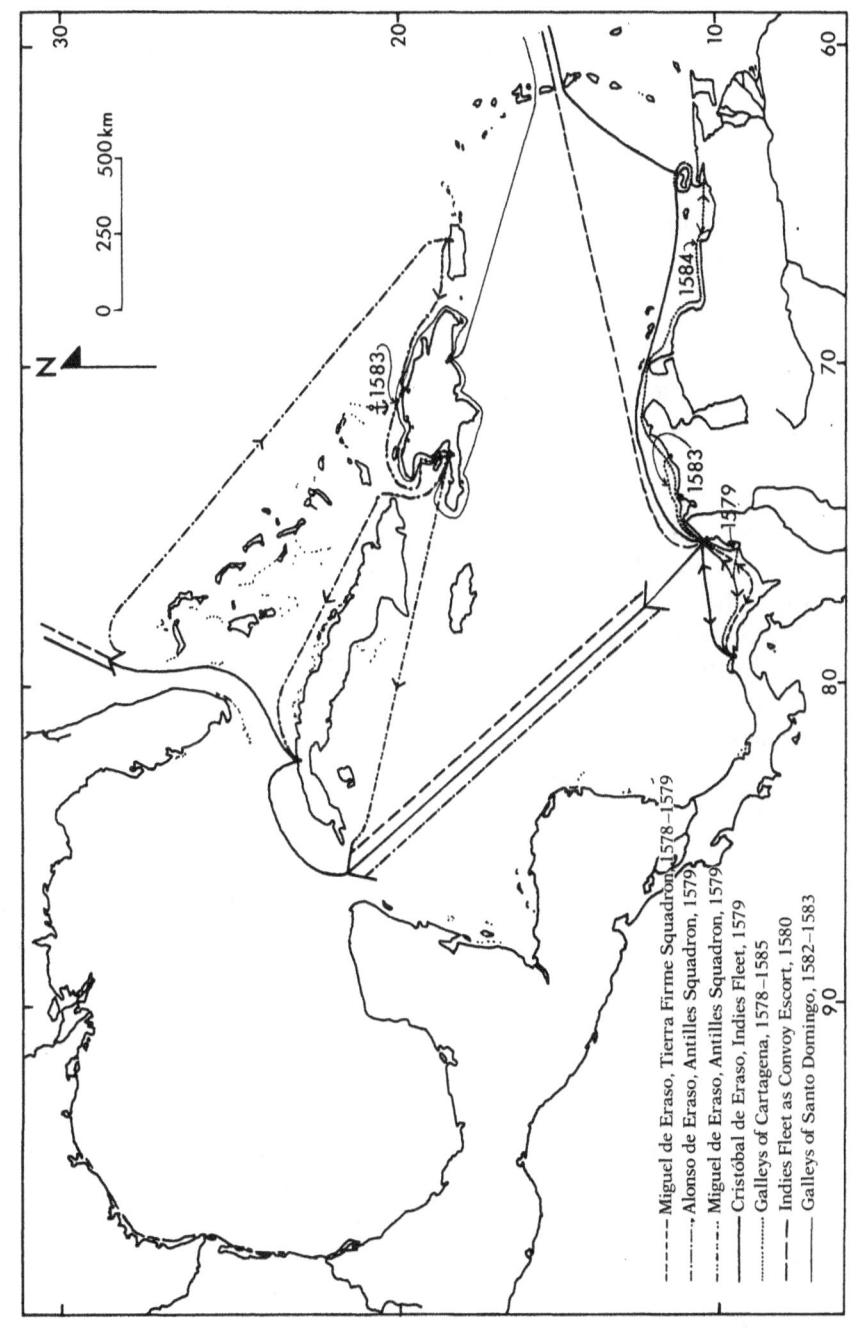

Illustration 12 Voyages of the Indies Fleet and Its Squadrons, 1578–1585

need in times of heightened danger from corsairs in the Triangle. Because nothing had been done about building the four small galleons authorized in 1577, the Council of the Indies advised the king to construct a new fleet of nine ships. Philip agreed and added that he was not inclined to send any more galleys to the Caribbean, although he did approve replacing those at Tierra Firme with new ones.[22] He thus sought to dispose of the proponents of sending galleys to Santo Domingo, Margarita, and Havana. The Main was a special case requiring special weapons; for the rest of the empire a multipurpose fleet provided a better long-term defense.

The corollary to consigning the remaining ships of the original Indies Fleet to their fates at the Straits was the ending of the administrative dependence of the galleys on the rest of the Fleet. Vique had tried to obtain independent command almost from the beginning of his service. In May 1578 he sent letters to Spain that probably asked for independent command and complained about Don Cristóbal, although exactly what they said cannot be known since Alonso de Eraso intercepted them at Havana and apparently destroyed them. Undaunted, Vique continued to complain about Don Cristóbal's leadership and to demand independent command. The result was the revision of Vique's instructions during the summer of 1580. Vique responded by sending an advocate to court to represent his views on designating part of the Fleet's subsidy for the galleys and to argue for an independent command for Vique. That campaign bore fruit during 1581 when Vique was given virtually independent command, with control over the galley's subsidy.[23]

Vique's success in persuasion was not matched by victories over corsairs between 1579 and 1583 nor by success in obtaining the numbers of men and types of supplies he felt were needed for the continued operations of the galleys.

According to later witnesses, Vique's pattern of operations during these years was to remain at Cartagena until the spring of each year, when the galleys would sail to Nombre de Dios for the ten million maravedís of subsidy paid by that treasury (Cartagena paid another five million). Until 1583 he did not engage a single corsair, apparently because the presence of the galleys deterred them, sending them off to the eastern Main and the Antilles. His manpower problems grew steadily worse during this period. He received as many as 57 convicts to serve on his galleys, but found that by the spring of 1581 over 100 of the 170 rowers had finished their terms and refused to stay aboard unless he compelled them to do so. Within two years, he had only enough rowers to man one galley. By then, he was also missing key skilled free crewmen, primarily because the wage they received was completely inadequate, given the cost of living at Cartagena.[24] In short supply too were critical items of matériel, although the Casa had sent him stores in 1580 and 1581.[25] For all of these reasons, he could use only the galley *Ocasión* and looked forward to receiving the replacements that the crown had authorized.

Replacement of Vique's aged galleys had been foreseen when they were sent out in 1578 and was agreed to in 1581. However, as the crown tried to implement that decision, it found that a number of areas other than Tierra Firme also wanted galleys and that the Casa and the shipyards of Barcelona again claimed to have more work than they could handle. The new hulls were due for delivery in April 1582, but April came and went without completion of the galleys. They were finally finished towards the end of the year but did not arrive at Cádiz until June 1583.[26] By then, the crown had replied to requests for galleys from other areas of the Caribbean.

Persons interested in Margarita had been arguing for several years that because of its small population but strategic location and rich pearl beds Margarita should receive protection from at least one galley.[27] In 1581–1582 the crown took no action on this proposal, just as it had not in 1575–1577. Margarita lacked the fiscal resources to support a patrol squadron, and the crown probably realized that one galley would not provide enough strength against corsairs freshly arrived from Europe.

Santo Domingo's request for galleys was another matter. Oared ships had been used there against corsairs since the 1540s. The "galleyed galleons" of the Indies Fleet and the frigates built later had both been intended to use oars to supplement sails during patrols in the Antilles. In 1576 and 1577 galleys were proposed for use against the trading corsairs. The initial success of the galleys of Tierra Firme led to another proposal for use of galleys in the Antilles to stop raiders as well as traders. That proposal reached Spain at the same time that there was renewed discussion of the grand design for the use of galleys, a design that would have placed them in pairs in the Pacific, off the coast of Florida, and on the northern and southern coasts of the Antilles (two squadrons), while leading to the abandonment of much of Florida and the nonrenewal of the Indies Fleet. Objections by the marqués de Santa Cruz, Álvaro de Bazán, and the king killed the general plan, but the matter did not die.[28]

By October 7, 1581, the Council of the Indies had received further requests for galleys for the Antilles, including one from the *visitador*, Licenciado Rivera, in which he noted that the city of Santo Domingo was willing to supply meat and *cacabi* bread for the crews of two galleys if the crown would supply the hulls and pay other costs. The Council, which had been advocating galleys for every part of the Caribbean, at once brought this offer to the king's attention. Philip accepted the city's offer and ordered preparations of a galley and an escort ship. Both he and the Council of the Indies chose to ignore a warning from one resident of Santo Domingo that the city did not understand the size of the responsibility it had so willingly offered to assume.[29]

Changes in the plan began to appear almost at once. A group of experts called by the Casa suggested minor changes in the scheme, mostly in connection with the ship that was to escort the galley. Santo Domingo's advocate got into the act in January 1582, getting the crown to order a "light galley" in place of the frigate originally planned as an escort for a standard Mediterranean galley. Inquiries by the Casa eventually determined that such "light galleys" did not exist, so a second Mediterranean galley, somewhat smaller than normal, was authorized. By then the crown was having second thoughts about the cost and ordered the Council of the Indies to try to get the city's advocate to agree to the city's paying part of the salaries for the galleys' crews. This problem remained unresolved when the ships were finally ready to sail in mid-July 1582.[30]

Within days of arriving at their new base, the galleys set out on a patrol. This sweep yielded one prize west of Santo Domingo, two small French ships and about twenty-five Frenchmen and fifteen black slaves near La Yaguana, and engagements with other corsairs. By early January the squadron was back at Santo Domingo. Again refitting, the galleys sailed west in search of a French slaver that had also taken one of two dispatch boats from Spain. By the 26th of January the galleys were again at La Yaguana. On the 5th of February they took a ship (*navío*), frigate, and launch of Frenchmen at Puerto de Mosquitos and captured part of the crews. The galleys then passed on to the north coast and returned to Santo Domingo. Ruidíaz de Mendoza, the commander, later said that he made another trip around the island that spring, but there is no other evidence of it.[31]

This vigorous activity was both a source of comfort to the local residents and the focus of criticism. None of the surviving letters from Santo Domingo comment favorably on Ruidíaz de Mendoza's vigor, probably because the fiscal disadvantages of the galleys, and his temper, loomed larger than the benefits. But the governor of Puerto Rico could report that at least one French corsair had taken a hasty departure from his island upon learning that galleys were based at Santo Domingo. On the other hand, that same official complained a few days later that the galleys' work on the western and northern coasts of Española had driven the corsairs to the Mona Passage, which they had effectively closed to Spanish traffic in the seven months since the galleys' arrival.[32]

Paying for the galleys also proved to be a problem. A 1-percent *avería* had been instituted at San Juan and Santo Domingo shortly after they arrived, but within a year the merchants were unwilling to pay it and the city of Santo Domingo was writing demanding either privileges such as trade with Galicia or full royal support via a subsidy. Puerto Ricans also expected privileges if they were to continue to pay the *avería*, demanding that the base of the squadron be transferred to San Juan. But of more direct importance to the galley crews was the failure of the Españolans to supply the meat and *cacabi* bread promised in 1581. The crews had been forced to endure half-rations over the winter in the hope of more in the spring, but the supplies did not appear. As discontent among the crewmen rose, the Audiencia ordered a series of farms created along the coasts to raise provisions for the galley crews.[33]

The tragic outcome of these difficulties occurred on the next cruise. Sailing from Santo Domingo on May 29, 1583, the galleys escorted ships bound for Havana to Cape Tiburón and then proceeded by stages around the island to the north and east in an attempt to make the circuit before mid-July and the beginning of the hurricane season. West of Puerto Plata, the *Santiago*, the smaller of the two galleys, ran onto a reef. Doubled up on the remaining galley, the rowers organized a rebellion in which they killed three of the crew, fatally wounded Ruidíaz de Mendoza, and less seriously wounded eleven others. Putting all ashore who would not join them, they sailed off to the west coast. There Diego

Osorio, formerly commander of the *Santiago*, was able to recover the hull, stripped of artillery, tackle, and other essential items.[34] Returned to Santo Domingo in early 1584, the galley saw only limited service against French raiders off Saona and finally deteriorated to the point that it had to be beached for careening in the fall of 1585.[35]

The replacement of the lost galley and supplies for the remaining hull failed to arrive before Drake, even though the Council of the Indies and the galley committee moved with unusual speed to authorize them once they knew of the mutiny. As seemed to be increasingly the case during the 1580s, delays began to develop as soon as the orders left Madrid.[36] The spectacular career of the galleys of Santo Domingo was over less than eighteen months after it began. Illegal traders all over Española must have offered quiet prayers of thanksgiving!

While the career of the galleys of Santo Domingo was thus drawing to its untimely end, new galleys for Tierra Firme were sent across the Atlantic, arriving separately at Cartagena on November 3 and 9.[37] Vique did not meet the new ships at Cartagena. In May he had sailed the *Ocasión* to Río de la Hacha to protect the pearl fishery from the corsairs and to attack coastal Indian tribes who were alleged to have attacked parties of Spaniards. Vique's campaign occupied him until November and the arrival of reports that the new galleys were at Cartagena. He captured at least forty Indians and enslaved them, first on the galleys and then on his own plantation near Cartagena. Returning to Cartagena on November 15, Vique at once began to complain that Captain Rodrigo de Junco, who had brought the ships from Spain, had sold most of the supplies, leaving Vique with little food, and more men to feed in the bargain.[38] Whatever the truth of his allegations about Junco's misuse of the supplies, Vique managed to find enough food to feed his crews and enough spare parts to keep his ships in good repair until late 1584.

Once provided with supplies and men, Vique spent ten months consolidating his forces and preparing for what he announced would be a six-month cruise to Margarita, an answer to demands for galleys there. Sailing in September, Vique required two months to reach the island. He spent three months cruising about it without encountering a single corsair. Having made his demonstration that galleys could work in those waters, Vique gathered up the royal fifth (*quinto*) from the pearl fishery and sailed back to Cartagena, arriving in early March 1585.[39]

Toward the end of March, the galleys sailed to Nombre de Dios to pick up their subsidy and to protect coastal shipping during the loading of the convoy. Vique claimed that during this patrol he was able to aid three overloaded, nearly sinking frigates carrying materials to the convoy. That done, he returned to Cartagena in June.[40] As was the custom, the galleys lay idle for the rest of the year.

Vique had every reason to try to impress upon the crown how active he had been. When he returned from Margarita he found an order "allowing" him to go to Spain to face a growing list of charges against him, including charges of smuggling aboard the galleys. He would have been well advised to have gone with the convoy when it sailed that spring. His poor performance against Drake in 1586 was the last straw, ensuring his trial and condemnation to death.[41]

The successes of the galleys of Tierra Firme and Santo Domingo weakened the crown's resistance to a further expansion of the system, especially after the duque de Medina Sidonia and the Casa put their prestige behind the renewed efforts of Havana to obtain galleys to patrol its coastal waters and the area off Cape San Antonio. Corsairs had become more numerous in both areas during the late 1570s and especially after 1581, when the convoys from Santo Domingo to Spain were ordered to go to Havana to join the other convoys rather than sail east around Saona. By early 1585 orders had been drawn to send two galleys to Havana, but they did not arrive until 1587.[42]

Although the galleys occupied the center of the stage after 1581, the crown did not lose interest in, nor its need for, a fleet of ocean-going warships. In the spring of 1581 it ordered galleons from Lisbon to meet the returning convoy. Warned in late 1581 that corsairs were going to raid the Indies the next spring, Philip again ordered galleons from Lisbon to the Azores and sent instructions to change the sailing orders of the Straits Fleet so that it would return via the Antilles if the corsairs carried out their plan. He also sent two privately owned galleons to Madeira to recover monies left there by convoy ships. In short, during 1581 and 1582 the king and his councils had more than enough evidence at hand to convince them that a fleet of galleons was still needed.[43]

Being convinced of the need and actually getting a fleet to sea were, as always, very different things. To begin with, the Council of the Indies had second thoughts about the design because of a proposal by the joint commanders of the Straits Fleet, but in the end the original plans of

1578 were used. In reviewing the file, Philip commented that the Indies Fleet was to be composed of nine ships of 300 tons (except for the *capitana* and *almiranta*, which were to be larger) because he thought that was enough for normal levels of corsair violence. If a larger threat developed, like an invasion, preparations to deal with it could be made when it arose.⁴⁴ Blasco Núñez Vela, then forty years in his grave, would have approved the king's continued adherence to the principle Núñez Vela had first advanced in the late 1530s.

Throughout 1581, 1582, and early 1583 the construction of the new galleons was complicated and delayed by a lack of money and by preparations for the expedition to Tercera (early 1582). Finally, in May 1583 one or two of the hulls were close enough to completion that there was some discussion of sending two of them to Seville for use as the escorts of the Tierra Firme convoy of that year; however, this plan fell through because of a lack of artillery, masts, and crewmen, and because the ships could not be completed and sent to Seville by the end of July.⁴⁵ Work continued.

The two larger galleons and one of the smaller arrived in San Lúcar on November 15, 1583. For the moment there was nothing for them to do. Tercera had fallen some months before, and the rumors of corsair expeditions to the Indies for the following spring did not require immediate action. Consequently, arrangements were made to fit the hulls with new pine masts, replacing the beechwood ones installed at Santander.⁴⁶

Discussion of whether to send a fleet to the Indies to counter reported French plans to invade and capture major cities (San Juan de Puerto Rico, Santo Domingo, and Cartagena) continued from the fall of 1583 into the early months of 1584. As originally discussed, the Spanish force was to consist of ten ships taken from among merchantmen available at Seville and 1,500 men, but by the next year consideration had turned to what it would cost to send the galleons for seven months. By then it seemed clear that the remaining six galleons would be ready to sail sometime that spring. Money continued to be a problem.⁴⁷ However, the French force was not assembled and so the Spanish discontinued consideration of how to deal with it.

Juan Martínez de Recalde was commander of the remaining six galleons when they sailed from Santander on June 21, 1584. Short of artillery, equipped with beechwood masts that broke, and subject to heeling over under sail to such an extent that some of the gunports were unusable, the galleons nonetheless were good ships that promised to be a match for their enemies.[48]

The king soon had a use for them: sailing to the Azores to meet returning convoys. They performed this role in 1584 and 1585, returning after each cruise to Andalusia for refitting. They were in port when news of Drake's intentions finally reached Seville in late October 1585. After a debate over the best course of action, the Casa dismissed the crews for the winter and went ahead with the careening that the ships required. A few small arms and some munitions were taken from the fleet and sent to the Indies on the dispatch boats that carried the warning of Drake's design, but the Indies Fleet itself remained in Spain.

The Indies Fleet thus passed the winter in port while Drake crossed the Atlantic. Because they had not learned what Drake intended earlier in the year, the Spanish were caught repairing their fleet at the very time when it should have been in the Indies. And as it turned out, the refitting took until April, by which date the Fleet had lost any hope of catching Drake in the Caribbean. When it arrived, it found only the ruins of Santo Domingo, Cartagena, and St. Augustine. Sunk off the coasts of the first two towns were the charred hulks of the galleys. Never intended to deal with fleets the size of Drake's, they had been of minimal use in the defense of their home ports. After taking both towns, Drake had stripped the galleys and burned them at sea. But that was not to be the end of them, for replacements were already being prepared in response to needs stated before 1586. At least for a time longer, galleys would seem to be the ideal patrol craft for the coastal waters of the Caribbean—so long, that is, as they were backed by a squadron of galleons able to move in reinforcements against attacks involving more than the handfuls of small ships that the corsairs would continue to use for many years.

The history of land defenses during the fourth period is not as tidy as that of galleys or other coastal patrols. Prior to 1579 decisions on garrisons, supplies for the militias, new fortifications, and artillery were made in the old way, in response to petitions from local authorities who had faced some particular threat or conceived a desire for some particular addition to their local defenses. With Drake's raid in the Pacific, that situation began to change ever so slowly as the Council of the Indies undertook a study of the state of fortifications throughout the Caribbean. Then, during 1581–1583, Don Antonio, the Portuguese pretender, seemed about to lead an invasion of the area, intent on seizing such key ports as San Juan de Puerto Rico, Santo Domingo, Havana, and Cartagena. That plan caused the Spanish to look more closely at the strategic geography of the Caribbean and at the manpower pools in those key cities, and in consequence to decide to send a garrison to Puerto Rico and to increase the size of that at Havana. By then, the reports on fortifications had revealed the need for projects to provide them where they were missing or had not been properly developed. But nothing was done about this matter, aside from some minor improvements at San Juan de Puerto Rico, because the threat of invasion, against which forts were a remedy, was not quite strong enough. Moreover, the process of making any important decision was lengthy. The result was that only a few of the deficiencies in land defenses inherited from earlier periods were made up during these years, although what those deficiencies were was learned in a systematic way for the first time.

Garrisons and Militias

With the exception of the garrison sent to San Juan de Puerto Rico in 1582 and the gathering of troops to fight Oxenham and his Cimarron allies on the Isthmus, 1577–1579, all of the changes in garrisons during these years arose from manpower needs generated by events during the third period. Thus the sending of 55 men to Florida in 1577 with Pedro Menéndez Marqués and then 150 men in 1578 were both responses to the abandonment of Santa Elena in 1576 in the face of an Indian uprising and the subsequent flight from Florida of Menéndez de Avilés' successor as *adelantado*, Hernándo de Miranda, and a significant segment of the pre-1576 garrisons of both Santa Elena and St. Augustine. The appearance of an apparent French threat to the province in 1577 only served to support those who had argued for a reinforcement of its pre-1576 garrison of 150 men. And naturally the new men had to be paid, with the result that by late 1580 the subsidy for Florida had been raised to 47,670 ducats a year from its previous figure of 23,400 ducats.[49]

Completion of fortifications at San Juan de Ulúa and Havana brought about a need for more soldiers to man them. San Juan de Ulúa had had a few artillerymen and a warden for some years, but after 1580 it also had at least six soldiers in a garrison that fluctuated from twenty-four men to as many as seventy men when the fleet was in—the most vulnerable time, as Hawkins had shown in 1568. Havana also needed more men after its fort was built, but the crown delayed an increase until 1582, spending the intervening years deciding whether to raise the governor to the rank of captain-general (it did) and ironing out some of the conflicts of jurisdiction and responsibility that had arisen between the governors and the wardens of the fort.[50] Only when it appeared that Don Antonio might attack the city did the crown order a reinforcement of 800 men, a development we shall examine in more detail below.

On the Isthmus, the last years of the 1570s saw the winding up of the war on the Cimarrons as allies of Oxenham, although the fighting continued with those rebellious blacks for many years into the future. Because of reports of corsairs, the Audiencia of Panamá had placed temporary garrisons at Nombre de Dios and Panamá in the spring of 1577. Therefore, when Oxenham struck the Pearl Islands in the Pacific, the Spanish were able to send thirty men to Acla by land while others were immediately sent by ship to track him down in the Pacific. As news of Oxenham's raid spread, volunteers were sent to Panamá from Peru and units of seamen and soldiers were detached from the Indies Fleet.[51] Following Oxenham's capture, these soldiers, all on the crown's payroll, spent their time seeking out the few Englishmen who had escaped to the Cimarrons.

In Spain, receipt of the news of the Oxenham raid brought the decision to make full war on the Cimarrons. Four captains, 120 men, and various munitions were authorized and eventually sent. Additional supplies were ordered from Peru. The arrival of these forces on the Isthmus in the summer of 1578 soon brought about a change, and by June of 1579 the Cimarrons of Puerto Belo were suing for peace and those of Vallamo had been driven from their homes.[52] The war went on and was attended by various scandals and conflicts between soldiers and officials, but its essentially defensive phase—the effort to remove Oxenham and his men from the area—was over by the end of 1579.

The men thus raised for the Vallamo war were also put to use against Drake when he sailed up the Pacific coast in 1579. As is well known, the ships sent from Panamá did not find the elusive corsair and he chose not to attack that city. No further posting of temporary garrisons, except in the villages of the pacified Cimarrons, occurred until 1582 and the threat of invasion by Don Antonio of Portugal. At that time forty men were placed at Nombre de Dios for four months.[53] After that, no troops guarded the Isthmus through 1585.

Rumors of the Pretender's plan to invade San Juan de Puerto Rico, Santo Domingo, Cartagena, and possibly Havana first reached the crown at Lisbon in late 1581. This came on the heels of an apparently garbled version of Oxenham's objectives reported from Santo Domingo in 1578 and reports of a possible invasion by Don Antonio's partisans in 1580. Reacting to these reports in ways similar to its reactions to the French threat of 1566–1567, the crown ordered a garrison sent to San Juan de Puerto Rico, and a captain and 800 men to Havana. The captain was to inspect its defenses and "bring them to the state of perfection they should have once and for all" and then inspect the other ports, beginning with Puerto Rico and continuing through the Antilles to the Main. At each point he was to give instructions to local authorities on how to bring defenses into a state of readiness.[54] However, that grand plan was not carried out, probably because of the need for men for the expedition to conquer Tercera (1583), Don Antonio's last stronghold on Portuguese territory. Instead of a captain and 800 men, the crown sent a new warden, Diego Fernández de Quiñones, and seventy men. One hundred men, and their supplies for seven months, were ordered from New Spain.

Fernández de Quiñones and his men arrived at Havana in July 1582, followed in January 1583 by the men from New Spain. Thus enlarged, the garrison was ready when the crown sent a warning that spring that Don Antonio had been chased from Tercera and had disappeared to sea with several ships and a large number of men. That invasion threat, important in another connection for the history of the garrisoning of the Indies, did not materialize, allowing the discharge of the men from New Spain in the fall. The garrison of Havana was then able to settle down to trying to get its payroll from Nombre de Dios and to backing its warden in his fight with the governor over control of the men.[55]

At San Juan de Puerto Rico, the garrison of fifty men ordered out in 1582 under the command of Diego Menéndez de Valdés experienced similar problems. The jurisdictional and ceremonial quarrels with the governor were solved in 1584 by appointing Menéndez de Valdés to that office. Paying the garrison proved to be another matter. It was supposed to have been paid a subsidy of 7,163 ducats (2,686,275 maravedís) from the treasury at Santo Domingo, but the royal officials there refused to send the money, forcing Menéndez de Valdés to use other means to try at least to feed his men.[56] By 1586, the crown owed the men for most of four years' wages and rations.

Don Antonio's threatened invasion of 1583 had one further effect on the history of garrisons in the Indies. The Council of the Indies, consistent with the experience of 1566–1568, urged the crown to garrison Santo Domingo with fifty men and Puerto Plata with twenty-seven men. They were the only ports with royal forts that lacked garrisons (other than a caretaker force), but the threat passed and in any case the crown had already sent galleys to Santo Domingo. Their crews could, in an emergency, serve as a garrison. Moreover, the president of Santo Domingo wrote assuring the crown that the militia could defeat "eight ships" of corsairs.[57]

A similar calculus that the militia and the crews of the galleys would be an adequate garrison must account for the omission of Cartagena from all discussions of garrisons during this period. Given the fact that it was one of the Pretender's objectives, this omission is curious and shows again the lack of a systematic consideration of the empire's defense needs.

No further action was taken on improving the garrisoning of the Indies, even though William Hawkins' reconnaissance in 1583 and reports of Grenville's and Drake's preparations in 1584 and 1585 indicated that the threat of invasion by large numbers of men and ships had not diminished.[58] Thus for Santo Domingo and Cartagena, as well as a host of smaller towns, the militia remained the chief source of manpower to defend the beaches and such fortifications as existed. In considering the militias' states of preparedness for the events of 1586, it is helpful to go back to 1564.

Because the militias continued to be small in numbers (Table 7) and poorly armed, their record after 1564 is not very different from what it was prior to that year. Somewhat more stress seems to have been put on drills, especially during the 1570s when invasions seemed to threaten, but, as has been noted, lack of powder prevented really effective training and target practice. Moreover, the mustering routine prescribed by law could be interrupted by official neglect or even, as at Santo Domingo in 1570, by a feud over who had the right to call the muster. On the other hand, keeping watch seems to have become almost a normal part of life for the residents of most coastal towns whenever there was a warning of possible corsair attack. Paid watchmen were used more frequently, especially to man remote posts, but the basic burden of watches by night and day during time of danger fell on the residents.[59]

In the field, the militias continued to be successful only in small engagements, usually where they and their opponents combined numbered less than one hundred men. Actions on a larger scale did not occur, making it impossible to formulate a judgment on the quality of the militias in larger towns before 1586. The corsairs did attempt raids on Nombre de Dios (1569, 1572), Havana (1568), and Cartagena (1568). Of these raids, the attempts on Havana in 1568 and Nombre de Dios in 1569 did not result in any landings, the first because the corsairs did not want to risk a battle with an obviously well-armed militia and the second because a storm and the difficulties of entering the harbor over its protecting reefs forced the French to break off their attack. It is doubtful that Hawkins intended to land troops at Cartagena in 1568, although he did bombard the town and probably had enough men to present a serious threat to it. Drake's raid on Nombre de Dios in 1572 was carried out with a small force.[60] In short, the corsairs never tried or at least never succeeded in carrying out a raid on a major town with a large number of men. Accordingly, Spanish victories over corsairs on land were limited to small skirmishes involving few men and causing few casualties among the corsairs (Table 22).

There does seem to have been some stiffening of resistance in the 1570s, particularly in the Antilles (especially at Puerto Rico and Puerto Plata), but this must be considered in the light of higher Spanish losses of ships and clear evidence of increasing trade between residents and French, English, and Portuguese smugglers. Although no quantification is possible, the documentation suggests that the number of armed encounters between corsairs and residents of the Caribbean was a continually decreasing percentage of all corsair-resident encounters. Moreover, a number of clashes may have been staged either to establish a case for trade under duress (as at Río de la Hacha in 1568) or to build a case for a later claim of meritorious service (as may have been the case with several of the "raids" on Puerto Plata).[61]

In short, the militias continued to be short of men, short of arms, short of munitions, ill trained, and generally lacking battle experience.

1578–1585. THE SYSTEM REFINED AND NEGLECTED

Table 22. **Corsair Attacks, Militia Initiatives, and Militia Successes in Battles With Corsairs, 1564–1585**

	Antilles			Main			Central America			
	Corsair Attacks on Land	Militia-initiated Actions	Militia Successes	Corsair Attacks on Land	Militia-initiated Actions	Militia Successes	Corsair Attacks on Land	Militia-initiated Actions	Militia Successes	
1564										1564
1565				2						1565
1566	1			1						1566
1567	1		.5	6		1.5[a]				1567
1568				3		1.5[a]	1			1568
1569				2	1	2				1569
1570	1			2		2				1570
1571	2									1571
1572				2		.5				1572
1573				1				1	.5	1573
1574				3		1				1574
1575							1		1	1575
1576	1		.5	2		1(?)		1	1	1576
1577	2		1	1[b]		.5[b]	1	1	.5	1577
1578	2		1				1		.5	1578
1579	1	1	.5							1579
1580										1580
1581		2	1							1581
1582	1		1							1582
1583		1	1	1		1	1			1583
1584	1		1	1		1				1584
1585										1585

[a] 1567–1568 actions against the English at Río de la Hacha are questionable victories. Hawkins' attack on Cartagena in 1568 did not involve any attempt at landing.
[b] Oxenham's raids in the Pacific.

In the years after 1563 the crown did make some effort to overcome the arms and munitions problems (see above), and some local officials took drilling to heart when they had the munitions. These efforts were not enough, nor were they continuous. Nor did they deal with the basic weaknesses: numbers of men and lack of combat experience. Drake revealed just how weak the militias were, although there could have been little doubt about that in the mind of anyone informed about the record prior to 1586. Had garrisons been provided in 1582 and 1583 when the threat of a large-scale invasion of Santo Domingo and Cartagena was first clearly visible, Drake's raid of 1586 might have had a different history. The same thing could be said about the crown's failure to act on the need for fortifications revealed in the aftermath of Drake's epochal raid in the Pacific.

Fortifications

Beginning in the fall following receipt of news of Drake's raid in the Pacific, the Council of the Indies apparently instructed various individuals to report on the status of fortifications at key points in the Caribbean. From this came reports on San Juan de Ulúa and Havana by Captain-General Bartolomé de Villavicéncio of the New Spain convoy of 1579, by Viceroy Diego Velasco on San Juan de Ulúa, by the *visitador*, Licenciado Rivera, on Santo Domingo, and by Admiral Antonio Navarro de Prado on Nombre de Dios.

The reports on San Juan de Ulúa showed that the additions projected about 1570 were nearing completion but that work still remained to be done. The viceroy said that he was exerting every effort to get the work finished. The record suggests that by 1584 he had achieved that objective. The report on Havana showed that the fort was complete, although it raised a number of matters such as the state of the moat—issues that shortly became the subjects of controversy to be examined below. Visitador Rivero found that the replacement of the covered gun platform at Santo Domingo was proceeding slowly and at a cost that he felt was excessive. He did not like the vaults of brick that the Audiencia had begun, thinking them unsafe, and recommended instead that a cavalier with small artillery be built on the river-side of the fort, where the guns could prevent ships from entering the port. The big battery facing the sea served only to keep ships at a distance. He also recommended destruction of a nine-foot wall that ran across the fort grounds between the bastion (water battery) and the tower. In spite of these views, work on the water battery was resumed in 1584. Admiral Navarro de Prado's report was generally critical of Nombre de Dios as a port. It forms part of a larger study then underway as to whether or not the trans-Isthmian

1578–1585. THE SYSTEM REFINED AND NEGLECTED   203

route should be removed from Panamá to Honduras.⁶² That discussion was not directly concerned with fortifications but did reflect the fact that Nombre de Dios had not been and probably could not have been fortified.

Cartagena de Indias does not seem to have figured in the various reports made during 1580–1582. Her omission is curious in light of an anonymous memo, probably dating from the late 1570s but no later than 1584, that specifically points to the weakness of that city. The omission is only explicable either by a loss of documentation in the archives or by the crown's belief that with galleys successfully installed there no further defense was needed.

This memo provides the only nearly complete review of the state of fortifications in this period. Port by port, it examines the fortifications within the Caribbean, leaving only San Juan de Ulúa and Florida outside of its purview. Its author recommends forts at Margarita, Cubagua if it was not depopulated, Río de la Hacha, Santa Marta, Cartagena, Nombre de Dios, Veragua, Puerto de Caballos, Santiago de Cuba, and Guadianilla, Puerto Rico. At Cartagena he recommends fortifying the sea and bay sides of the city and building a new fort at the Boquerón. At Nombre de Dios, he proposes to have a fort built on the reef, as originally planned in 1540. At Santiago de Cuba, he would have a watchtower at the entrance to the port replaced by a small fort with artillery. Also recommended are enlargement of the Morro fort at San Juan de Puerto Rico and the construction of a Morro fort at Havana. At Santo Domingo, he recommends that a battery be built on the east side of the river because the one on the west side was ill placed for preventing ships from forcing the river mouth. La Yaguana should be depopulated or moved inland; the first was the preferred action. Bayahá and Puerto Plata were commended as being excellent ports and, in the latter case, well fortified.⁶³

Unlike earlier recommendations for fortifications, which tended to view the forts as ends in themselves, this report couples the extensive fortification recommendation with support for galleys to control local corsair problems much as was the custom in the Mediterranean. Really large invasion forces—at one point it is stated that an attack by 1,000 men could overwhelm Cartagena as then defended—would still have to be met in some other way, just as Núñez Vela had argued in 1538. The forts and galleys were intended to provide day-to-day security against corsairs with small numbers of men in a few ships. In two instances, Cartagena and perhaps Havana (the document is not clear), the author apparently thought that building the fortifications he recommended would prevent capture of the city by even a thousand men. The proposal was thus a summary of the overall posture of the empire and of the policy that local interests wanted pursued, as well as a partial preview of the plans that were to be put into effect after Drake's raid of 1586. It is tempting to speculate that the raid might not have been so successful had this plan been given serious study and its recommendations acted upon.

The general drift of royal defense policy was, however, in a different direction. Naval matters, in particular the galley experiment, absorbed the attentions of Peninsular authorities. Requests for fortifications, such as those from Panamá and Santiago de Cuba, were still handled in routine ways, which in the bureaucratic style of the time was tantamount to assigning them to lingering death by inattention.[64] Only the fortification of the Straits of Magellan, of San Juan de Puerto Rico, and of Havana received more than routine treatment before 1586. Of these, the Straits forts are outside the geographic scope of this study.

Routine treatment was even the initial fate of San Juan de Puerto Rico's defense needs. Writing in 1579, Juan Ponce de León, the grandson of the island's conqueror, raised three issues: the need for a water battery opposite the Morro, for a watchtower at the Boquerón, and for a stone wall across the mainland side of the island to replace the existing wood and earth rampart, which was topped by tuna cactus. Ordered to report, the local authorities inspected the entrance to the bay and sent a negative report on the proposed water battery. By the time this report was on its way to Spain, Menéndez de Valdés had arrived in San Juan. His initial report made it clear that the undermining of the main fort's battery had gone on unchecked, that the Morro was still open on the land side, and that the city's request for a stone wall opposite the mainland had not as yet been met. Subsequently asked to report on the latter item, he tartly replied that he had already recommended it three times and that "anyone without military experience would see its utility."[65] That letter in turn caused the calling of a committee in the fall of 1583, which tossed the matter into the lap of Don Francés de Alava, the captain-general of artillery and an important military adviser of the period. He duly reported with recommendations that a house belonging to Ponce de León (Casa Blanca?) be fortified because of its strategic position between the Morro and the main fort. He supported construction of a drawbridge between the island and the mainland but was only mildly enthusiastic about the proposed wall. The Boquerón fort he claimed was not needed because an old ship sunk in that channel could effectively close that entrance to the bay. Given these changes and proper watches, Alava concluded that San Juan would be impregnable. These recommendations formed the basis for action—a two-year-long attempt to find a contractor to supply the 100 slaves needed for the wall construction.[66]

Events did not wait for the slow consultative process. In the summer of 1583, an English fleet spent some time near San Juan. Menéndez de Valdés immediately organized the residents and their slaves and was able to report that he had put a strong door on the bridge from the mainland, had dug a trench commanding the door and the road into town, and had provided a series of trenches to command the road at other points. He had also built two drawbridges across these trenches to carry the road and to cut it if necessary. Other trenches were dug on the beach of Cabrón and on a point of land overlooking a baylet between the main and Morro forts on the site of the later battery of Santa Elena. Menéndez de Valdés proposed to complete the defenses of the city by putting a raised gun platform on the city side of the main fort, by constructing a new battery behind the Morro and facing the city (the later hornwork), and by completing the wall across the end of the island, as recommended earlier.[67] Approved in principal, these defenses had to wait for construction until after Drake's raid.

Discussion of the need to fortify the point of land opposite the Morro of Havana had a history similar to that of the additional fortifications of San Juan de Puerto Rico, except that it died a proper bureaucratic death within a few years. As early as 1577, the governor suggested that when the new fort was completed, a battery would have to be built on the point because the fort's guns could not control access to the mouth of the port. The anonymous proposal noted above made the same point with regard to the Morro, adding that a battery there could control access to the city from the beaches on the west, which were the likely landing place for corsairs. In 1580, the new governor, Gabriel de Luxan, strongly recommended such a defense and, after investigating the financing of its construction, concluded that the slaves employed in construction would have to be retained at Havana rather than sold and that the crown would have to find money elsewhere for the project. In Spain this proposal was referred to the king, who said that it would have to wait.[68]

Again, events in the form of additional corsair threats and the initiative of the local governor intervened. During the summer of 1582 Luxan began to construct an enclosed guardpost or battery (it is not clear which) on the point, with a trench cutting across the road from the beaches to Havana. He envisioned a wall with loopholes and doors that would effectively seal off that side of the city. To close other parts of it, he had the ends of the streets walled, although doors were placed in the walls. This work soon stopped because the warden of the fort intervened and took the construction slaves for work on the moat and the clearing of the parade ground before the fort. Work on the defenses at the point was resumed in 1583, apparently after Luxan and Fernández de Quiñones, the warden, had patched up their differences. The new works were completed to the point that artillery and a squad of soldiers could be posted there.[69] Thanks to these local initiatives, Havana was ready when Drake stood off the bay in the summer of 1586.

These improvements in the fortifications of San Juan and Havana, like others made during the third period at other places, were but small steps along the road to positional defenses. San Juan, because of its unique local geography, was furthest along in fortifying the key points of attack; Havana was still at the stage of trying to defend its harbor mouth with an artillery emplacement although in this case one that also served to cover the principal landing beach. The absence of similar positional defenses at the landing beaches of Santo Domingo and Cartagena was to work to Drake's advantage in 1586. The need for them had been pointed out by 1584, both by the plans of Don Antonio's partisans and by Spanish investigators, but the orderly shuffling of papers had not as yet produced a plan of action or recommendations for how to pay for such new defenses.

Artillery and Munitions

The same orderly bureaucratic process that postponed action on the clearly perceived need for improved fortifications also worked with shortages of matériel to prevent action on requests for artillery, despite what seemed at first to be a new phase in the history of that type of weapon. In 1578, the crown replied to a number of previously unanswered petitions by sending orders to the Casa for artillery for Santa Marta, Cartagena, Tolú, and Havana, another order to send the yearly supply of munitions to Puerto Rico, and an order to the Audiencia of Santo Domingo to inspect the fort there to confirm the need for guns and balls requested by the warden in 1573. The Casa complied to the extent of purchasing the metal from which to cast eight bronze guns.[70] This single expenditure accounts for Cartagena's dominance of the cost figures for this period (71 percent of all artillery costs, Table 21).

However, this promising beginning was not followed up. The Casa did not send most of the guns or munitions. The four guns cast for Cartagena were shipwrecked in the convoy of 1579; salvaged the next year, they only reached Cartagena in 1581. The Audiencia of Santo Domingo did not inspect the fort until May 1581, perhaps because of the visitation of 1579–1580. This report, which recommended the addition of four culverin-class weapons, as well as the supplying of balls and other munitions for the guns on hand, was forwarded through various hands during the next two years. The Council of the Indies wrote an opinion (*consulta*) supporting it in the fall of 1583, but a year later the weapons and munitions had not appeared at Santo Domingo, nor did they arrive before Drake.[71]

New or renewed petitions from the Indies did not fair any better after 1578, even though the crown was taking a hard look at its defenses because of Drake's Pacific raid and Don Antonio's threats. The warden of Puerto Plata continued to petition for artillery and even sent two of his pieces to Spain for refounding to repair their blown vents. Desperate for munitions and convinced because of an incident in 1577 that artillery would improve the defense of the port, he was able to scrounge up only a little powder and a few balls in Santo Domingo.[72] Lacking the means to defend his fort, he had little choice but to try to maintain a fairly friendly relationship with the corsairs who frequented the northern coast of Española. Similarly, Trujillo reiterated its petitions throughout the early 1580s, to no avail except for a rather laconic marginal note in 1583 to "send another *cédula* to the Casa." Santiago de Cuba's request for a yearly supply of munitions and Margarita's request for artillery did not even merit an ineffective *cédula* to the Casa.[73]

A somewhat similar experience befell the requests for munitions and four pieces of long-range artillery (culverins) sent from Puerto Rico or made by the new warden, Menéndez de Valdés, both before and after his departure from Spain. As early as 1580, the governor asked for twelve long-range guns, although within two years this was scaled down to four. The crown approved the smaller number and sent orders to the Casa. Menéndez de Valdés was unable to get the guns, even though he pestered the Casa with these orders and his own observations about the needs of San Juan. Advised of the Casa's noncompliance with the orders, the crown's marginal note said "there is nothing to reply." Once on the ground, Menéndez de Valdés found he needed munitions and more artillery for the new bastion of Santa Elena, for the expanded works on the Morro, and for the defense of the hill that overlooked the entire island. His want list eventually reached fourteen pieces. He received nothing but a little powder.[74] All of his letters were marked for referral to the newly formed Junta de Puerto Rico.

Havana fared no better at the hands of the Casa; but in this case, as in the earlier case at Cartagena, the local officials were able to make good some of their needs. Four iron guns were acquired in 1579 and four more in 1582. The viceroy of Mexico sent powder in those same years, but the Casa was only able to supply 1,400 pounds of matchlock powder. Santo Domingo followed the same route, taking two bronze guns from a Portuguese slaver in 1583. The Casa managed to send some powder and other munitions, but by November 1583 the fort at Santo Domingo had less than 600 pounds of powder.[75]

Requests from the Isthmus and from San Juan de Ulúa were consulted to a standstill before 1586, although the way this was done was different in each case. For San Juan de Ulúa the request for additional artillery for the new fortifications on the wharf was sent to the viceroy for his opinion—even though he had written supporting the requests! For the Isthmus the request from the city of Panamá, which was just recovering from the shocks of Oxenham's and Drake's raids, was sent back to the Audiencia and to the commander of the Indies Fleet for opinions. This was followed by a demand for a list of artillery said to be on the coast of Tierra Firme. Those guns were to be put on carriages and placed under someone's care. Apparently nothing further happened until 1584, when the city of Nombre de Dios sued the city of Panamá to get back four guns taken in 1580.[76] It was a timely suit since the galleys, which had provided most of the area's defense since 1578, were inactive, with the result that corsairs were once again cruising off the Isthmus.

Why had this situation in which the Casa failed to comply with repeated orders for munitions and artillery developed? No final answer can be given without a more intensive investigation, but partial explanation in the form of shortages of both commodities can be found.

The crown's desire to control the production of munitions, so that none could be sold to its enemies in North Africa, resulted in its making decisions whose cumulative effect was that any extraordinary demand for gunpowder quickly exhausted the small stock on hand at Seville. Nor could such a demand be quickly met by the local producers. A key event in this history is the controversy of 1576, which began with a royal order that no native of Spain could make more than 40 *quintales* (4,000 pounds) of powder per year or buy more saltpeter than was required for that purpose. Remón Martín protested, saying that because of a large capitalization, he was able to turn out as much as 1,000 *quintales* of powder per year, or as much as 300 *quintales* on demand. Other powdermakers could turn out only 20 *quintales* on demand. The need for powder at Seville was estimated by Martín to be at least 1,000 *quintales* per year, exclusive of extraordinary demands. He therefore requested licenses from the Council of War to continue to produce at the same rate and to continue to run his saltpeter mine in Almería. A foreigner who was driving the small producers of Seville out of the market, Martín lost his special situation when the crown upheld its order. His eventual fate is not known. What is known is that the Council of War, through Don Francés de Alava, captain-general of artillery, came to exercise nearly complete control over munitions manufacturing. Extraordinary needs had to be referred to Alava.[77] This proved to be an unworkable system, even though Spain had some of the most extensive deposits of saltpeter in Europe. It was an extraordinary example of the failure of central planning and control, but it seems typical of the bureaucratization that plagued the later years of Philip's reign and prevented the Indies from acquiring all of the defenses they needed.

A related problem was the supply of artillery. A preliminary reading of the situation suggests that the expansion of the Dutch Rebellion was the primary reason for this problem. Copper and tin or finished artillery pieces could not be imported as easily as had been true under Charles. The Málaga foundry seems to have virtually ceased operation except for 1576–1579. Founders at Seville could not take up the slack. Searching for alternatives, the crown considered removing all "surplus" guns in the Indies (the origin of the order to Panamá and later orders to Cartagena to report on artillery not in use at those ports) and actually borrowed guns from the pool that the *avería* had built up during the early 1570s. The crown also approved an order that all ships returning from Havana bring Cuban copper as ballast. The impracticality of this arrangement eventually led to the establishment of an artillery foundry at Havana.[78] No solution to the shortage of artillery was found before 1586. The needs of the towns and forts in the Indies went begging in the face of more imperative demands for artillery for the fleets (largely supplied by the *avería*), for the conquest of Portugal, and for other European uses.

Evaluation: The Corsairs

The effect of these changes in the defense of the Indies on the pattern of corsair raiding and trading has already been suggested. On the western Main during 1579–1582, the corsairs disappeared for fear of the galleys, although they recovered their boldness after 1583. In the Antilles, the corsairs fleeing the galleys of Cartagena caused increased losses until galleys were stationed at Santo Domingo (Table 23). They captured at least four prizes from the corsairs within the first year of their operation and resulted in a notable drop in the number of reported raids. Yet the effect was short-lived because of the mutiny of 1583, which effectively ended the galleys' career until after Drake. The corsairs fleeing the galleys of Santo Domingo either went back to the Main or moved their operations westward to Cape San Antonio, thereby decreasing their risk of capture and increasing the chances of picking off intra-Caribbean shipping making for Havana, which from 1581 was the mandatory rendezvous for all ships going to Spain, including those from Santo Domingo.

These eight years witnessed a drop in the number of raids against land targets, partially because of improved Spanish fortifications in the larger towns and vigorous coastal patrolling, especially on the western Main. Elsewhere, the decline in numbers of raids against ranches and small towns was probably due to the working out of trading arrangements between local residents and the corsairs.

Coastal patrols, whether by the ships of the Indies Fleet, ad hoc squadrons fitted out with local resources, or the galleys, did not have more than a temporary impact on illegal trade. Three traders were taken at Guanaïbes in 1579, others were caught near Puerto Plata and

Table 23   **Spanish Losses to Corsairs, 1578-1585**

	Atlantic Triangle		Antilles					The Main					Central America			Fla.		
	Ships Taken	Largest Fleet	Ships Taken	Successful Land Attacks	Unsuccessful Land Attacks	Estimated Yearly Total	Largest Group	Ships Taken	Successful Land Attacks	Unsuccessful Land Attacks	Estimated Yearly Total	Largest Group	Ships Taken	Land Attacks, Total	Largest Group	Attacks of All Types	Total Ships Lost	Total Land Attacks
1578	1	5	5+	1	1	14							1	2			6+	3
1579	1	4	8	1		7		1									10	1
1580			6			9							2			1	6	1
1581	7?[a]	18	6+		20+	3?		1			6						14?[a]	0
1582	1	5	3	1	20+	4											4	1
1583	2	9	4			7+		2	1		8		1	7			8	2
1584			1+		1	3+		2	1		7						3+	2
1585	21[a]		2			5+											23[a]	0
Totals	33[a]		35+	3	2			6	2				2			1	74[a]	10

[a]. The number of ships taken in the Triangle includes many coastal ships not in the Indies trade.

Ocoa in 1581, and three more by the galleys of Santo Domingo on their first cruise (fall of 1582). A few traders were captured at other points in the Caribbean from time to time, but the trade was not permanently disrupted and continued at the level of fifteen to twenty ships each year, which continued to follow the routes described in the early 1570s from Margarita and Venezuela to Puerto Rico and the northern coast of Española and the ports of the Windward Passage.

Investigations such as those of the visitador, Licenciado Rivera, did not make any long-term differences. Rivera could report that the *alcaldes mayores* of the northern coast were involved, that Rodrigo de Bastides, Bernardino de Ovando, Pedro Rengifo de Angulo, Juan Sánchez Quesada, and a certain Machado were implicated as partners of the traders, but his information did not result in judicial actions against any of these prominent persons. Nor was action taken against the *provisor* of the bishop of Cuba, Diego de Vívero, for allegedly organizing the trade at Bayamo in eastern Cuba and leading the resistance to the agent sent by the governor of Cuba to investigate the trade.[79]

The founding of Bayahá in 1578 did not solve the problem, either. Founded on a deep-water port that could be easily defended by some rudimentary fortifications and artillery, it was intended to be a secure settlement for all the residents of towns west of Puerto Plata. Safe under the guns of the king's fort, they were supposed to feel no need to cooperate with the corsairs, who had always used force when other forms of persuasion failed. But as has already been suggested, the plan reckoned without their economic motives for the trade and without the fact that the Spanish merchants could not, or would not, provide the shipping and markets for hides that the corsairs offered. The trade went on.

In sum, several improvements were made during the fourth period in the empire's passive defenses, most notably the garrisoning of San Juan de Puerto Rico, improved fortifications there and at Havana, and the addition of bronze, long-range artillery pieces to the stock defending Cartagena de Indias. In addition, a mechanism was developed for reinforcing Havana from New Spain. Aggressive defenses initially took a step forward with the deployment of galleys, first at Cartagena and then at Santo Domingo. However, for a variety of reasons those patrol squadrons became less effective after 1583. Imbalances still existed, with Cartagena inadequately fortified and Havana with too small a garrison, while Santo Domingo lacked one altogether. Artillery and munitions were in very short supply everywhere. Patrols in the other zones of high corsair activity, such as eastern Venezuela, were few and irregular, with the result that the corsairs driven from the areas of the galley patrols found safe havens nearby. Royal spending was higher than it had ever been, but the money did not serve to plug holes in the empire's defenses that had been revealed during the third period and suggested by enemy plans and Spanish inspections during the fourth. In large part, those holes were not being plugged because they existed only in the event of an invasion—a special case for defense since the 1530s that required extraordinary measures for which the defenses evolved by 1586 through precedents, patrimonialism, and royal parsimony were not adequate and were not intended to be adequate.

Chapter VI

Summary and Conclusions

From the "Cape of Surprises" in 1521 to the beaches of Santo Domingo and Cartagena in 1586 was a fairly direct course for the corsairs, but one marked by many important turnings for the Spanish as they sought to restrain or prevent the expansion of the corsair problem both in area and scale. In the beginning it was assumed that raids on shipping and against the towns in the Caribbean were part of war, to be dealt with on the bases of private resources or localized defenses paid for by the crown. Thus coastal patrols in the Triangle, ship armament and group sailings, reliance on militias, minimal fortifications, and even more minimal numbers of artillery pieces constituted the sum of the defense of the Indies. The crown spent little more for these defenses during an average year before 1548 than it spent for mail service in Castile in 1536.[1] Indeed, if the costs of the treasure fleets of 1537–1538 and 1542 are deducted, the defense of the Indies cost less per year than almost any category of Castile's budget during the late 1530s. The main burden of defense fell on private shoulders.

The general strategy used during the first period of the history of the defense of the Indies was to defend population centers with forts, artillery, and militias, while ensuring the safety of shipping through legislation and the use of a patrol fleet in the one area where the corsairs were too numerous for even well-armed groups of ships—the Triangle. By the end of the period this strategy had been refined to include the

Table 24 **Relative Importance of Defenses as Measured by Mean Yearly Expenditures in Ducats**

Empire-Wide Figures

Period	Total	Land Defenses		Manpower		Fortifications		Artillery	
1535–1547	15,234	3,253	21%	654	4%	1,914	13%	276	2%
1548–1563	67,347	5,580	8%	770	1%	3,813	6%	943	1%
1564–1577	130,722	54,483	42%	42,846	33%	8,876	7%	409	<1%
1578–1585	245,558	57,132	23%	35,622	15%	4,630	2%	1,229	<1%

Caribbean Total Figures

Period	Total	Land Defenses		Manpower		Fortifications		Artillery	
1535–1547	3,405	3,234	95%	654	19%	1,914	56%	257	8%
1548–1563	12,993	4,955	38%	770	6%	3,813	29%	318	2%
1564–1577	70,296	54,402	77%	42,764	61%	8,876	13%	409	<1%
1578–1585	117,226	57,096	49%	35,622	30%	4,630	4%	1,192	1%

Empire-Wide Figures

Naval Defenses		Coastal Patrol		General Purpose		Convoy		Not Allocated	
11,829	78%	250	2%	435	3%	11,140	73%	152	1%
57,149	85%	36,978	55%	3,473	5%	16,462	24%	4,618	7%
72,433	55%	14,382	11%	53,451	41%	36,885	28%	3,806	3%
185,043	75%	60,138	24%	107,693	44%	60,674	25%	3,383	1%

Caribbean Total Figures

Naval Defenses		Coastal Patrol		General Purpose		Convoy		Not Allocated	
97	3%	97	3%	0	0%	0	0%	74	2%
7,681	59%	7,681	59%	0	0%	0	0%	357	3%
12,574	18%	10,657	15%	11,369	16%	0	0%	3,320	5%
57,903	49%	55,539	47%	19,676	17%	0	0%	2,227	2%

The categories of Coastal Patrol, General Purpose, and Convoy overlap during the third and fourth periods because the Indies Fleet's service in coastal patrols and convoy duty is counted under those headings as well as under its own, General Purpose. See text for explanation.

Table 25 Relative Geographic Distribution of Defenses as Measured by Average Yearly Cost. Amounts in Ducats

Period	Total	Triangle		Caribbean[1]		Antilles[2]		Non-Antilles[3]	
1535–1547	15,234	336	2%	3,405	22%	3,139	21%	265	2%
1548–1563	67,347	30,664	46%	12,993	19%	11,771	17%	1,034	2%
1564–1577	130,722	5,439	4%	70,296	54%[6]	17,492	13%	43,398	33%
1578–1585	245,558	34,300	14%	117,226	48%[6]	21,557	9%	92,258	38%

1. Includes coastal patrols within the Caribbean to the extent that their costs could be determined.
2. Puerto Rico, Española, Cuba.
3. Florida, New Spain, Central America, Tierra Firme, Tolú, Cartagena, Santa Marta, Río de la Hacha, Cabo de la Vela, "Venezuela."

The Main[4]		Florida		New Spain[5]		Tierra Firme		Cartagena		Not Allocated
101	1%	0	0%	0	0%	0	0%	1	<1%	11,493
352	1%	0	0%	682	1%	349	1%	0	0%	23,690
11,814	9%	27,443	21%	4,018	3%	7,606	6%	90	<1%	54,987
63,389	26%	26,147	11%	2,511	1%	10,647	4%	867	<1%	94,032

4. Tierra Firme, Tolú, Cartagena, Santa Marta, Río de la Hacha, Cabo de la Vela.
5. Expenses for the defense of San Juan de Ulúa and Vera Cruz only.
6. Total of Antilles and Non-Antilles for these periods is less than Caribbean total because of expenses for patrol fleets roving from the Main to the Antilles and back.

use of convoys moving merchantmen from port to port under escort. Only one effort was made to carry the war to the enemy in the Caribbean; the rest of the area's defenses were passive (Tables 24, 25).

Somewhat more aggressive in tone was the diplomatic effort to defend the Indies either by getting the French to agree to leave them alone (1538) or by opening the trade to French merchants—who provided the backing for most corsairs—while excluding the French crown from any part of the potential riches of the New World (1544). In the end this diplomatic effort failed because the French crown did not want to be excluded from finding its own bonanza in some underexplored corner of North or South America and because the Castilians, whose empire was just forming in the Indies, would not accept the French as trading partners in areas won by Castilian blood, sweat, and treasure.

A consequence of the diplomatic failure was the beginning of naval war in peacetime, first in the Triangle because of Franco-Portuguese and Franco-English disagreements and then in the Antilles because there were no restraints in France to prevent Frenchmen from sailing where they wished and doing what they could. The French were also pursuing their Portuguese enemies, who were already engaged in a quiet, illegal trade in some parts of the Antilles and along the eastern Main.

This new circumstance, apparent from 1548 onwards, soon gave rise to a new understanding of the military problem that the Spanish faced in dealing with their European enemies. Officials in the Antilles seem to have been the first to realize that their defense needs were essentially naval needs, not needs for forts or garrisons or artillery, although they sought those as well. By 1552 the crown had accepted that conclusion and had combined it with its own conclusion about how best to defend transatlantic commerce while ensuring regular, frequent shipments of its revenues. As a result, the second period, 1548–1563, is characterized by a marked shift of royal resources into the funding of coastal patrol squadrons. Fifty-five percent of all defense monies were spent on these squadrons, although a series of accidents produced the result that most of the money was spent in the Triangle and relatively little (7,681 ducats out of 36,978 ducats [mean yearly figures], or 21 percent) in the Caribbean.

As had been true before 1548, so from 1548 to 1563 the corsairs concentrated their efforts on the Antilles, then still relatively rich in coastal shipping, sugar, hides, and minor tropical products. In this area their main activity became trading, backed for most of the 1550s with the threat of force. Elsewhere in the Caribbean, raiders followed up on earlier (1543–1544) raids and attacked the Main and even the remote ports of Honduras. Following the commercial routes of the Spanish empire, the French became a menace in the Caribbean wherever the Spanish had anything of value within reach of seaborne raiders.

Had the crown's new strategy of 1552 been carried out, it is likely that the corsairs would have had to flee the Antilles for the Main or other parts of the Caribbean in greater numbers than they did, or might even have been partially driven from the Caribbean altogether. The patrol fleets did sail in the Triangle, although many ships were sent to La Coruña in 1554 for Prince Philip's voyage to England. In the Antilles, however, nature and the crown's European priorities prevented the scheme from being carried out until 1557. The squadron fitted out at Santo Domingo in 1552 was destroyed by a hurricane within six weeks of its sailing. Replacement squadrons prepared at Seville were diverted for patrols in the Triangle and then for the voyage to La Coruña and beyond. Overburdened with work, short on vital supplies such as artillery and money, and involved in other projects, the Casa de Contratación did not move energetically to replace the ships. By the time the squadron was finally sent out in 1557 under Tello de Guzmán, the corsairs had done their damage in the Antilles, had established their trades, and had unknowingly persuaded the merchants of Seville—and through them the Casa and the crown—to abandon the Antilles to their economic fates by restricting Atlantic commerce to the convoys.

The long-term consequences of the wartime reorientation of much of the trade of the Antilles into French and Portuguese hands at first does not seem to have been apparent to contemporaries. Still operating on the assumption that a diplomatic peace treaty in Europe would mean the end of the war and the consequent withdrawal of the corsairs from the Caribbean, contemporaries took comfort in the thought that the problem was temporary and that in any case the improved defenses of Santo Domingo and San Juan de Puerto Rico discouraged attacks on those cities, just as the new fort at Havana could be expected to discourage attacks there in some future war. They seem to have been relatively unconcerned that corsairs, finally faced with a Spanish naval squadron in the Antilles after 1557, chose to move their operations to the Main. In short, they did not see that naval defenses for the Antilles came too late and had the consequences of forcing the corsairs to explore and exploit an area they had not frequented before and which was less supplied with defenses of all types than the Antilles.

When this situation was topped off by the failure of diplomacy to resolve the outstanding differences between the French and Spanish crowns as well as between French and Spanish subjects over the Americas, the future could not have seemed anything but bleak to residents of the Indies and to shippers. Initially the French agreed to respect the peace of Spanish shipping and settlements but refused to accept the Spanish definition of the limits of their territory. Spain tried to obtain a type of defense for the Caribbean by suggesting a line of demarcation in North America and the Atlantic Ocean that would keep the French sufficiently far from the Caribbean so that if a French ship should appear there it could be assumed to be a breaker of the peace and its crew treated as pirates. The French crown refused this offer because of the interests of its subjects in trade with Brazil and the Antilles and because of its own interest in schemes to colonize North America and Brazil.

Commerce raiding was the first symptom of the breakdown in the diplomatic effort, an effort which went on for a year after the formal peace treaty was signed. Frenchmen were again in the Antilles by 1563–1564. More important, however, was the colony established at Santa Elena in 1562 and then renewed at Fort Caroline in 1564. Deserters from the latter colony appeared as commerce raiders in the Antilles late that year. Still trying to found a Spanish settlement in the area that it claimed as "La Florida," the Spanish crown seized upon this piracy as the pretext for driving out a colony authorized by the French crown. Militarily, this decision carried with it a shift in resources as sharp as the earlier shift to naval defenses. Florida was for a few years (1565–1567) the crown's greatest military liability, although its costs did not come home until after 1570, when regular means of supporting the crown's garrisons—and by indirection the other settlers as well—were developed. Largely because of Florida and the temporary garrisons placed in the Antilles in 1566–1568 to counter the French grand design of which the occupation of Florida was thought to be the first step, expenditures for manpower jumped from a yearly average of 1 percent of all royal defense expenditures to a yearly average of 33 percent, while Florida took up over a fifth (21 percent) of the royal resources devoted to defense during the third period. For the first time, an area outside the Antilles claimed a major part of the crown's funds for defense. Defenses, like the corsairs, had finally begun to shift to the periphery of the Caribbean. The old centers of defense spending, Santo Domingo and Puerto Rico, were left behind and neglected.

The decision to combat the French crown's attempt to establish its sovereignty over the southern part of North America was accompanied not only by the shifts in funding just noted, but also by a renewal of open, if undeclared, war in the Indies. After 1565 the French crown made no effort to restrain the investors, sea captains, and religious fanatics who saw opportunity in trading and raiding in the Caribbean. The addition of Englishmen to the list of enemies at about the same

SUMMARY AND CONCLUSIONS 219

time simply complicated the problem because of its diplomatic ramifications down to 1574 and the added numbers of ships and men the English contributed to corsair activity in the Caribbean. It must also be said that the English contributed Francis Drake, whose daring implementation of the ideas of others, and his own desperation in 1572, added new dimensions to the corsair problem, particularly at the Isthmus.

Because the corsair problem of the 1560s and the 1570s seemed at first to be similar to the problem that had existed in the 1550s, the crown employed a similar strategy against it. Despite local cries about the need for fortifications, the crown did not approve any major fortification programs except for the rebuilding of San Juan de Ulúa, where Hawkins' encounter with Viceroy Enriquez showed the need for such defenses. A number of minor programs were approved, however. Orders for powder and weapons for the militias and for artillery to back them up or supply the changing needs of the established forts were issued but generally not fulfilled by the Casa de Contratación. The crown's intent was quite clear: to provide the means for a well-armed, well-drilled militia. In a departure from earlier policy, which had expected the militiamen to provide for themselves, the crown tried to establish regular (usually, yearly) shipments of powder and the periodic distribution of weapons. The first were at the expense of the royal treasury, the latter at that of the militiamen.

The garrisons of Florida, Havana, and San Juan de Ulúa were the only major departure from the crown's general policy of continuing to use naval defenses. The Florida garrisons followed from the decision to contest French occupation of North America. The Havana garrison was a necessary complement to the new fort as well as a recognition of the greatly increased strategic and commercial importance of that port. San Juan de Ulúa's garrison was required by the expanded fortifications. Curiously enough, those same criteria did not apply to Cartagena, whose need for land defenses against raiders was just as great but was met for most of the third period from the city's own resources.

The naval instrument that the crown revived and then put to a variety of uses was the Española Squadron, now renamed the Indies Fleet (*Armada Real de la Guardia de las Costas y Islas y Carrera de las Indias*). The merchants had already revived the convoy. Command of the new fleet was given to Pedro Menéndez de Avilés, *adelantado* of Florida and a man connected with the idea of the Española Squadron since the 1550s. He had a dozen galleyed galleons built according to specifications that he apparently believed would suit them for warfare in the Antilles, where the corsairs had taken to using small rowing craft to pursue coastal shipping or to make amphibious raids on sugar plantations and ranches. This type of ship allowed them to overcome the problems of frequent calms and the trade winds. However, the design of the galleyed galleons was faulty, and Menéndez de Avilés soon contracted for frigates to serve as the patrol squadrons in the shallow waters of the Antilles.

Taking up where others had left off, Menéndez de Avilés realized that the naval problem in the Antilles was but a part of a larger problem afflicting the entire Caribbean. He also realized that the corsairs no less than the Spanish, had to respect the prevailing winds and currents when sailing in the area. He therefore proposed a strategy that he believed would slowly but surely drive the corsairs from the area: prevent them from sailing home to Europe with their cargoes by blockading the channels and passages among the Antilles and between them and Florida through which all shipping normally left the Caribbean. Without the sale of loot and trade items in Europe there was no profit—and hence no incentive to fit out ships for cruising. It was a grand design that would have depended for success on his ability to keep the squadrons on station over a period of years, if not decades. It also required the construction of frigates, which was only begun during the winter of 1570–1571.

Neither Menéndez de Avilés nor the crown was sufficiently single-minded to implement such a scheme. Menéndez de Avilés had to look after his interests in Florida and its extensive trade arrangments. The crown had another use for its ships: convoy duty. In addition, the few patrols in the Antilles made by the Fleet in 1568–1571 sent the corsairs to the Main in record numbers. That led to cries for naval protection there, a need met at first (1572) by sending out or buying locally *pataches* or small frigates, but in time by stationing some of the Indies Fleet's galleons and frigates at Cartagena (1574). Another squadron was given the job of patrolling the Antilles. For three years, 1575–1577, the Fleet patrolled both the Main and the Antilles, but with mixed success against the corsairs. Knowledgeable local residents soon charged that the Fleet's officers engaged in illegal trade. Thus did politics and the personal interests of the king and the Fleet's officers prevent a fair trial of Menéndez de Avilés' plan.

For reasons that have been explained in the Introduction, the costs of these patrols could not be fully determined. Consequently the coastal patrol figures of 11 percent of mean yearly spending on all defenses and 15 percent of Caribbean defense costs do not reflect what really happened. The real cost of Caribbean coastal patrols was at least 25 percent of total defense costs. In relative terms this was still less than had been spent in the 1550s for coastal patrols, but in absolute terms it was between two and eight times more for patrols in the Caribbean, and up to one and four-tenths more for patrols in all areas of the Atlantic.

These increases in the mean yearly cost of coastal patrols did not produce a proportionate increase in the numbers of corsairs captured. On that score the Fleet did no better, and possibly worse, than the Española Squadron under Tello de Guzmán (1557–1569). The few corsairs it captured were either surprised by the sudden appearance of the squadrons under circumstances that made advance warning by local residents impossible, or else were betrayed by local residents for some reason. All told, the Indies Fleet's ships captured twenty-one corsair ships (1568–1579).

The effectiveness of the Fleet's patrols seems to have been in their deterrent value. News of the Fleet's being or intending to be in a given area was enough to cause the corsairs to pack up and leave. During the late 1560s and the early 1570s the result was a kind of ballet in which a sweep by the Fleet in the Antilles would result in reports of increased numbers of corsairs on the Main. When the Fleet was then sent to the Main, the corsairs would reappear in the Antilles. The system of two squadrons, one on the Main and one in the Antilles, did not entirely solve this problem because weather and sailing conditions, the size of the areas to be patrolled, and the corsair's information system made it possible for the latter to keep out of the reach of the former without necessarily leaving the Antilles or the Main completely.

The value of this deterrent was appreciated by contemporaries, whose major complaints about the Indies Fleet were that it did not stay in their areas long enough. Their complaints, and the aging of the ships, brought about a change in the means by which patrols were carried out. Galleys replaced the galleon and frigate squadrons on the Main on an experimental basis in 1578. They struck terror in the hearts of corsairs. For two years the western Main was free of raiders, and possibly also of traders.

The success of the Tierra Firme galleys caused the Santo Domingans to pressure the crown for galleys also. Aware of the cost, the crown refused until the Audiencia promised that the city would supply the ships with food, thus cutting an important part of the expense. Sent out in 1582, the galleys had a brilliant career, which was cut short by shipwreck and mutiny. They offered an advantage that none of the other types of ship employed up to that time had to the same degree: they could go in any direction at will, whatever the prevailing winds. Their chief disadvantage, in the Antilles and on the Main, was their need for special equipment and specialized personnel not available in the Indies. Although the Casa de Contratación complied fairly promptly with specific requests, the galleys soon fell into disrepair at Cartagena and could not be gotten into fighting trim at Santo Domingo after the mutiny for want of equipment and skilled crewmen. Another disadvantage apparent only later was the fact that the galleys were smaller than many of the sailing ships that the corsairs were using by the 1580s. Thus although the galleys had successful records against the smaller rowing craft (*pataches* and frigates), they would have been outgunned and probably defeated had they attempted to fight some of the 300- to 500-ton ships in which the corsairs crossed the Atlantic. Technologically a step ahead of the ship used by most corsairs in the 1570s for raiding and trading, the galleys would soon be left behind by the escalation in size of the corsairs' ships.

While the galleys were being welcomed in the Indies, in Spain the last of the original galleyed galleons were sold or sent to the Straits of Magellan. Their replacements were ordered from Bilbao. A new design was used that took account of the increased size of corsair ships and of the errors of the earlier design. While these ships were being built, no squadron was available to patrol in the Caribbean. Naval defenses for most of the fourth period consisted of the galleys and the convoy escorts.

Land defenses continued much as before, except that by 1578 most of the fortifications ordered during the 1550s and early 1560s were done. Consequently expenditures for fortifications dropped sharply. San Juan de Puerto Rico used local, not royal resources to improve its forts. Artillery for the forts was sought but not sent, with the notable exception of the guns for Cartagena, finally delivered in 1581—a decade after the crown had agreed to supply them. A new garrison at San Juan de Puerto Rico and increases in the garrisons at Havana, in Florida, and at San Juan de Ulúa did not make any major changes in the geographic pattern of royal spending.[2] They do suggest that the crown was muddling toward a system of garrisons and forts for the strategic ports, although that drift did not extend to the Main because the naval defenses there seemed adequate for the situation and because Cartagena's and Panamá's populations continued to grow, providing a militia of increasing strength—at least on paper.

The balance of this system in terms of distribution of funds between types of defense is evident in Table 24. Land defenses, coastal patrols, and the convoy all claimed approximately equal amounts of the crown's military spending (about 25 percent each). The naval costs for the entire empire returned to the high levels (75 percent) they had in the first two periods, before the conquest of Florida shifted so much of the crown's money to land defenses. Within the Caribbean, land and localized naval defenses cost about the same (49 percent of total, each). In geographic terms (Table 25), the shift of resources to the defense of areas other than the Antilles continued, with the Main taking first place in spending because of the galleys and the war on the Cimarrons and the English (1577–1579). Significantly, however, the higher levels of spending for the Main were for types of defense of little use against a landing party. There were no permanent garrisons and no extensive fortifications equipped with long-range artillery. The Main lay open to an invasion in force, just as it had since 1535.

By 1586 the defenses of the Indies were in poorer condition than they had been in 1578–1580. The galleys were almost inoperable due to deterioration and supply problems. The fleet of high-sided ships to patrol the deeper waters or engage similar ships in open combat or to ferry troops to a port in need of reinforcements to drive off or drive out an invasion or raiding party had just been reestablished and was still in Spain. A series of forts in the Antilles, Florida, and New Spain were completed, but had defects in design and lacked the artillery and munitions needed to make them effective defenses able to hold off an attacker or drive him away. The garrisons were few and understrength, and located in the same towns as the forts. Militias were still ill equipped and undersupplied with munitions and leaders. The need for supplies of weapons and munitions was notable almost everywhere, but the Casa de Contratación continued to be unable or unwilling to supply what was needed. Studies of these problems and ways to remedy them were underway but had not reached any conclusions. In short, the defenses of the Indies were suffering from recent neglect and were in a kind of transition period, awaiting determination of what the changing military situation would require. Drake struck at precisely this moment and at the weakest of the larger port towns.

Conclusions

The system of defenses existing in 1585 was the product of history and politics far more than it was the result of any systematic approach to the defense problem. This is not surprising in view of the fact that the full extent of the problem was not obvious until amost forty years after it began. Only by about 1575 was it clear that corsairs would go wherever there was loot or trade to be had and wherever there were no Spanish defenses adequate to deter them or drive them off if it came to a shooting match. By then too it was clear that the corsairs would operate in the Caribbean regardless of what the diplomatic situation was in Europe and regardless of the formal policies of their sovereigns. And finally, by the mid-1570s it was clear that the normal level of corsair activity was about thirty to forty ships per year, divided about equally into traders and raiders. These ships operated singly or in small groups with crews numbering about one hundred or fewer men. They thus presented one level of threat, a level quite different from that of the invasion forces that the Spanish had feared in 1566 and 1570–1572, or were to fear again in later years.

By the time the areal extent, numerical size, and magnitude of the problem had become obvious, the empire already had a variety of defenses. In spirit, though not in detail, these defenses followed Núñez Vela's dictum of the 1530s—that defenses should be adequate to deal with the occasional raider and trader who operated with small forces, but that the reply to any force larger than could be handled by local resources would have to come from ad hoc arrangements and a gathering of resources from elsewhere in the empire. The forts, militias, and artillery of the Antilles (and to a lesser degree on the Main) and the Indies Fleet provided the sort of low-level forces-in-being adequate to deter attacks on the larger cities or even aggressively seek out the enemy. The breaking up of the Fleet into squadrons to patrol the Main and the Antilles further strengthened this system of defenses by extending its areal coverage. The use of galleys in place of the galleons and frigates of the Fleet in turn served to remedy weaknesses in the patrol system that the Fleet had developed. In short, it was a good system of defenses for the normal military problem of the time, but it rested on a number of assumptions that were subject to turning false and it contained a number of weaknesses because the details of the system had not been reformed to bring them into line with a master plan consistent within itself and with the best of contemporary military practice.

The most important assumption behind the system was that the crown and its agents would have timely information about enemy plans. This assumption operated at various levels. In the Caribbean, timely warnings of corsair raids allowed the removal of families and goods from exposed coastal towns to the countryside and the arming and mustering of the militias. Knowledge of enemy plans was also vital to the success of the naval patrols, and it was precisely the unwillingness of many persons in the Antilles and on the eastern Main to inform the crown's naval units of the movements of corsairs that made the patrols so ineffective and exposed remote areas to raids by the very corsairs protected by the silence of knowledgeable local residents. On the other hand, the crown's consistent success in keeping abreast of corsair sailings for the Triangle allowed it to order the convoys to change course or to take other actions that resulted in a frustration of the corsairs' design and the safe return of the ships. Finally, the system of defenses rested on the assumption that any invasion aiming at seizing a port in the Caribbean would be known about from European sources far enough in advance to allow the preparation of countermeasures of an extraordinary nature.

The importance of knowing about invasion plans in advance was critical to the continuation of the sorts of small-scale defenses developed before 1586. Adequate for the "normal" corsair, they were not adequate for dealing with invasions. If, therefore, there was a failure to learn far enough in advance what an enemy planned, the entire system could be called into question. That is precisely what happened in 1586. The Spanish, for want of a resident ambassador and his spy network in England, did not find out about Drake's destination until so late in the fall of 1585 that he had already cleared the Iberian peninsula after raiding in Galicia. The ships and men that could have been held in readiness to deal with him were scattered for the winter, the former in dockyards repairing the wear and tear of the summer's sailing to the Azores. Thus Santo Domingo and Cartagena were warned but not reinforced or resupplied.[3] Havana, on the other hand, had enough time, thanks to the warning and Drake's activities elsewhere, to gather militiamen from all over the island and to receive troops from New Spain. The force thus assembled would probably have defeated Drake's weakened forces, and at least would have put up a better fight than he got at Santo Domingo and Cartagena. Havana's defenses thus showed that the system could work on the old assumptions. Nonetheless, in the aftermath of Drake's raid the whole system of defenses was revised and many of its cost-saving features were discarded. For want of a spy, the treasury was lost!

Another assumption behind the system evolved by 1586 was that the militias, forts, and ships were adequately supplied with matériel. The money for it was available over the long run, so far as the crown was concerned, but time and again the Casa de Contratación failed to fill orders promptly or at all. In some instances the weapons and munitions were not immediately available because of problems in the Spanish armaments and munitions industries, but generally the problem lay with the administration of the Casa. Sometimes its officials claimed to be overworked, but at other times it is clear that they were more interested in fitting out convoys than in sending small amounts of munitions or shipments of weapons. In the absence of studies about how the Casa worked and of the influences that affected its performance, no final answer to why it failed to supply the weapons and munitions vital to the success of the system can be advanced. What is certain is that there were continual shortages. The Casa was a weak link in the chain of defense.

The consequences of this lack of matériel were most notable during the 1550s, before the crown began to take an active role in supplying weapons and munitions. Underarmed and ill supplied (and also outnumbered and ill led), the militias collapsed in the face of corsair attacks. This might not have happened had the crown moved earlier to supply them or had it adopted a more liberal policy on the trade in weapons, rather than assuming that somehow, in spite of the laws restricting that trade, the militias would acquire the weapons they needed, and the munitions as well.

Once the collapse of the militia system had occurred, the lack of supplies did not again have important consequences beyond local incidents until Drake's attack. By then, the failure of the supply system had left Santo Domingo and Cartagena, to name but his two victims, with so little powder and shot that the militias could not have conducted a prolonged defense even if they had wanted to do so.

Turning from the assumptions of the system to its structure, we find a number of weaknesses that were known at the time and that could and should have been remedied, because it was clear that the crown's enemies would eventually take advantage of those weaknesses to try to seize the major ports of the Caribbean. The most obvious of these weaknesses was the lack of adequate passive defenses for Cartagena. A single fort at the Boquerón, about two dozen pieces of artillery widely scattered about the edge of the city and at the Boquerón, and the beginnings of a wall were not enough. Because of a decision by local authorities in the 1540s and another in the 1560s, the city had not received royal funds for defenses, and thus had only the slender defenses its own money had built, largely after the raid of 1559. It did get a coat of arms (1574), but that was no protection in time of attack.[4]

Cartagena's weak passive defenses point to another general weakness in the system: the failure to coordinate fortifications into a system of positional defenses that would give the defenders maximum advantages by using terrain and strategically placed artillery batteries to partially substitute for numbers of men. Without exception, forts and artillery batteries were placed to protect ships at anchor off a town or to defend harbor entrances. Landing beaches and lines of approach were not covered by batteries. Only Santo Domingo and San Juan de Puerto Rico, and to a lesser extent Cartagena, used walls to provide land-side defenses for themselves. The militias thus lacked the aids that might have enabled them to stand up to an attack by superior forces such as Drake's. But it need not have been so. The lines of approach were known both from inspections by competent military officials and often from bitter experience. That nothing was done seems due to the control that local authorities had over the planning and execution of fortification projects prior to 1586 and to the crown's failure to move quickly once the full extent of the weaknesses of fortifications and artillery holdings were revealed by the reports of the early 1580s. In all likelihood, the crown did not act because of the slow pace of making decisions, the cost, and the realization that extensive, positional fortifications would produce a demand for paid garrisons, even in towns with large militias. Furthermore, as Núñez Vela had observed, one did not want to create defenses so strong that an enemy, once in them, would be hard to dislodge. His test for determining how strong fortifications should be was whether or not the local militia could hold them against a determined attack; in most places it could not if the fortification was anything more than a keep and bailey structure, or even, in the smaller towns, a breastworks. Similar criteria seem to have been applied down to 1586 except where strategic importance, as at San Juan de Ulúa, Havana, and San Juan de Puerto Rico, called for other arrangements.

Another weakness in the system was the crown's overcommitment of resources to the Florida garrisons. The reasons for this commitment made sense in view of the crown's desire to make good its claim to Florida as a matter of dynastic prestige and in view of the failure of private means to colonize the area successfully. But the cost of the colony was out of all proportion to the military benefits gained. A few contemporaries saw this and argued for the use of the money to meet other needs, even going so far as to point out that if the Spanish had trouble keeping a colony going there with the benefit of the royal payroll and a supply system based on the Antilles, then surely an enemy, who would lack those resources, would find it impossible to hold on to it— and in any event he could be attacked by a special expedition.[5] There seems little doubt that this critique was at least partially right or that the 25,000 or more ducats spent for Florida each year invested in forts and garrisons elsewhere in the Caribbean, or even better in more patrol craft, would have resulted in a sounder set of defenses. But the crown's prestige was committed, and no other consideration could outweigh it.

Arguing from the point of view of an acknowledged outsider looking in, Kenneth R. Andrews has recently suggested that another weakness of the system of defenses evolved by 1586 and continued beyond that date was the concentration on the defense of the convoy routes to the neglect of the eastern Caribbean, by which he means the lesser ports of the Greater Antilles and the Venezuelan coast. The thrust of this book is that this concentration dates from the years after Drake's great raid— despite steps before 1586 that contributed to that development—and that the system of defenses existing in 1586 made sense given the assumptions of the time and the facts of corsair activity. Moreover, the neglect of the eastern Caribbean was only relative during the years before 1586. If, as Menéndez de Avilés once argued, the illegal trade and accompanying raids cost Castilians about a million ducats a year, and if no single area of the eastern Caribbean accounted for more than 10 percent of that loss, then it is not surprising that the crown did not expend very much money trying to drive out corsairs and provide local defenses against raids. The investment, particularly for forts and garrisons, would have been many times the loss (Florida is an example of the cost) and would have had to have been made by the crown, not the people who sustained the loss. Nor could the crown have hoped to recover anything like the costs of defenses in the form of taxes on goods otherwise sold to corsairs or stolen by them. In short, the corsair problem in the eastern Caribbean was a minor irritant before 1586 best dealt with by occasional sweeps of patrol fleets and by trying to stiffen the resistance of militias and local royal officials to raids and trade carried on under varying degrees of intimidation. Spain's loss of control in that area in the seventeenth century was not, in my view, the result of long-term evolutionary forces but of the enormous difficulties of the Dutch War of 1621–1648 during which the monarchy's ability to fight on multiple fronts collapsed in the face of an overwhelming coalition of enemy forces.

From the point of view of the theory of naval war, the most serious weakness of all in the system of defenses that developed before 1586 was its failure to deal with the problem where it was most capable of solution. The military problem was essentially a naval one, whatever local land manifestations it might have had. As Mahan might have observed, what the Spanish needed to do was to drive the corsairs from the Caribbean. Doing that would have eliminated the need for passive local defenses. Menéndez de Avilés perceived this in 1570–1571 and suggested the only practical way to do it: intercept corsairs as they tried to sail home to Europe through the narrow water passages of the northeastern Caribbean. Aggressive patrols in areas other than these, while helpful to local shipping and occasionally able to take prizes and prevent raids on towns and shipping and even break up smuggling, did not get at the root of the problem in the theoretical sense, and so failed to be more than palliatives. From that failure arose the need to continue to build localized passive defenses. From it also arose the failure to break up the smuggling trade that slowly converted the Spanish empire into the milch cow of northwestern Europe's merchants, to the detriment of the Spanish.

Much has already been said about why Menéndez de Avilés' scheme was never tried and why it probably could not have been carried to a successful conclusion. It is enough to reiterate here that besides the technical problems, which were not so slight as they might at first seem, there was the political problem. Decisions were made, after all, in the real world of politics, not in the theoretical world of model builders. Whatever the merits of the model in pointing out why a system of defenses was not very effective (and the sea power model is useful for that in this case), it remains a model of ideal behavior, not a description of historical events.

It may be suggested that the sea power model, à la Mahan, may not be the right one for this case. The mental model the Spanish were using may in fact have been derived from land warfare, which was characterized by the use of strong points and the "convoying" of commerce and travelers between them in time of war, with armies (that is, naval patrols) serving to carry the war beyond the frontiers or in limited actions against raiders within them, in the immediate vicinity of the strong points. In this model, the key geographic and demographic localities receive passive defenses, just as they did in the real historical case studied here, and most of the money spent for defense *within* the frontiers is spent for passive defenses because the enemy raids but seldom and then in small forces, his main forces being engaged against one's own main forces beyond the frontiers, in his territory. Whether such a model was in fact in use among Spanish planners cannot be known, but the possibility should not be dismissed. It should also be noted that this type of mental model would be consistent with the political system of the Spanish empire, which placed a premium on localized benefits.

An alternative to the land-warfare model that may have influenced some of the king's councilors was the system of defenses used in the Mediterranean. John Guilmartin's recent study of the use of galleys and fortified ports in the Mediterranean has forcefully made the point that the Mahanian model of "sea power" does not apply to galleys, which operated effectively only when relatively close to their fortified bases. Commerce moved between those bases, and the patrol zones stretching around them, in convoys.[6] Except for some differences in distance, the use of ocean-going sailing ships to escort the convoys, and very real

SUMMARY AND CONCLUSIONS 231

differences in scale and degree of completeness in details such as fortifications, the system of defenses evolved in the Caribbean by 1585 was very similar, even to the use of galleys to control coastal waters around the major ports. It is evident that after 1586 the defenses of the Indies evolved to a system even closer to that of the Mediterranean, but whether that was due to the influence of ideas derived from the Mediterranean or to a desperate need to ensure the safety of the convoys in a time when money was scarce cannot be stated at this time. In any event, the Mediterranean naval tradition was available and with the norms of land warfare may well have influenced the thinking of those who acted on the petitions from Caribbean interests.

It has been suggested that the Spanish failed to master the naval problem because they failed to employ privateers, who presumedly would have cost the crown little and would have aggressively driven the corsairs from the Caribbean. This suggestion fails to take account of the crown's intention to keep the Indies under control and to institute there a rule of law such as was not normally possible in Europe. The crown did license privateers in Spain and had legal mechanisms for ship captains to claim part of any prizes they took, but it did not encourage private cruising. Privateers were, after all, instruments of war, and Spain was officially at peace with both France and England after 1559. By the time Count Louis of Nassau began issuing letters of marque in the 1570s, the crown already had naval forces in the Caribbean adequate to deal with the few holders of those documents who showed up looking for the Dons' treasures. Moreover, to have issued letters of marque against Count Louis' "subjects" would have been to recognize him as head of a state, something the Spanish would not do. But the final argument against privateers was that they too often turned pirate, attacking any ship, friend or foe, to make a living. Precisely this sort of illegal activity characterized the corsairs. The crown could hardly be expected to allow its own subjects to do what it tried to get other sovereigns to prevent theirs from doing!

In sum, it is clear that the *history* of the defenses of the Indies was the most important determinant of the system of defenses that evolved by 1586. General plans hardly exist, and a theoretical understanding of the situation as a naval problem to be dealt with accordingly seems to have been so rare that only one man had it. In the absence of such general plans or theories to inform action, decisions were made in numerous individual cases more or less on the merits of the particular case. Little by little these decisions resulted in the formation of a system of defenses adequate for the normal level of corsair activity, but not consistent within itself nor with the best of contemporary military practice. All of which raises the question of why decisions should normally have been made on a case-by-case basis and why in some cases the crown gave of its resources while in others it did not. In short, it raises the question of patrimonialism.

In a patrimonial polity such as the Spanish empire was during the sixteenth century, the crown was viewed as a source of benefits (*mercedes*) by its subjects. From the crown flowed justice (however one defined that in his own case), special privileges of a legal nature, and economic benefits. The "good" king would always act so as to benefit his subjects, even when imposing taxes and other burdens, for which the subjects usually expected a reward in some other aspect of life. Because the subjects generally derived their status from the various juridical and quasi-juridical groups to which they belonged within the hierarchy of society, the political process was essentially one of articulating, reconciling (if possible), and fulfilling group rather than individual interests. For model-building purposes it is well to consider the king as one of these groups, for he too had a distinct juridical position in the society (which extended to his servants in the state bureaucracy) and he too had particular interests (which might not be the same as those of his bureaucrats).[7] The only way that this sort of political system could give rise to a coordinated policy, rather than individual decisions informed only by specific merits and general values, was for the crown (the king and his immediate advisers) to try to impose a policy by fiat, or for a bureaucratic force such as the Council of the Indies to draw all of the competing group or local interest claims into some larger, general, coordinated plan. The Council performed this function for defense petitions only in 1540–1542 (regarding forts and the creation of a militia system), in 1575 (galleys), and ca. 1582 (fortifications). The Council's failure to coordinate defenses explains many of the weaknesses in the system that evolved by 1586. In place of coordination, the Council abdicated its role to the natural mechanisms within the system; that is, to the particular petition acted on according to the merits of the case and the merits of the petitioner(s). The king, so far as can be determined for either Charles I or Philip II, did not attempt to impose a general system, although he had various general interests that guided decisions into a pattern of sorts.

Given that most decisions were made on an ad hoc basis and in some degree of isolation from earlier decisions, what else can be said about how petitions were acted on? In the law, every subject and every group of subjects, however humble, enjoyed access to the king, but in fact successful access was a function of a complex system of patron-client ties both to and within the official bureaucracy and also outside of it to the court. The complexity of this system grew with time. In the case studied here, it is clear that down to ca. 1560 the Audiencia of Santo Domingo and certain citizens of that city enjoyed unusually good patronage ties to the court, and so were able to get numerous defenses for their town and area at a time when their demographic and economic importance were declining (Santo Domingo had only moderate strategic importance). By contrast, places like Margarita, San Juan de Puerto Rico, and Río de la Hacha had little patronage power either in relation to the Audiencia of Santo Domingo or to the court, and their petitions for defenses generally ended up in the archives. As Governor (of Puerto Rico) Francisco de Solís commented in 1572 when again asking for the king's attention to his request for artillery pieces, "They have not been received nor will they be because this island is so poor that it does not have the possibility of sending an advocate [*procurador*] and because there is no one to solicit at the [Casa de] Contratación nor remind [everyone] of it, everything ceases."[8] He went on to add that the city had asked Santo Domingo to have its advocate speak for this request. In short, differing degrees of patronage ties to the bureaucracy and within it and to the court seem to be one factor accounting for the unequal distribution of royal funds for defense. The importance of this factor has been pointed out in the Introduction. The events studied seem to prove its importance beyond any doubt.

But patronage, while allowing access to the final stages of decision-making and often aiding in the outcome of that process, was not the only factor at work. Equally important in the political process was the articulation of group interests, in particular those of the crown. To get the benefit sought, a group had to be able to convince the crown that granting that benefit would be to the crown's advantage and would not harm the interests of third parties, if those parties raised objection. That was not always an easy process, especially when the crown had a clear conception of its own interests. The struggle between the Consulado of Seville and the crown over the convoy in the 1550s is the best example presented here of such a struggle.

What were the crown's interests? They were both specific and general. In the specific case involving the convoys and the defense of commerce, the crown was primarily concerned about the security of its own funds making the Atlantic crossing, but it also wanted a cheap form of security and, above all, frequent deliveries. Florida ensnared the crown because it touched its dynastic claims to territory.

On the general level, the crown's interests are harder to define. It clearly wished to put on at least a show of enforcing its laws and hence was willing to spend money for the hit-and-run patrolling of the Indies Fleet that showed that the laws ought to be obeyed and that the king was not entirely indifferent to disobedience. Once the crown became convinced that it was obligated to do for its subjects what they were unable, or unwilling, to do for themselves, it began to move to take on the defense burden. However, that sense of obligation was weak and always subject to being overridden by a greater general interest: the careful, even parsimonious use of the crown's funds. Its very position as a patrimonial sovereign, disregarding all sense of obligation in the area of defense, also influenced the crown's decisions, for it could hardly turn down every petition from its subjects, though it might let the routines of the bureaucracy effectively stifle action. *Obedezco pero no cumplo* (I obey but do not carry out) could work for, as well as against, the crown! The failures of the Casa de Contratación to send expensive supplies are the examples of this. Also at a general level of royal "interests" was the fact that the crown was most likely to grant a benefit to petitioners with good patronage ties at court. Purely strategic military considerations seem to have been less important when they existed in isolation, unsupported by other royal interests. Thus Puerto Rico was long neglected despite its clear strategic importance, whereas Havana, which was equally unimportant in the patronage system of the 1550s and 1560s, obtained royal funds because it was not only strategically located relative to natural sailing routes, but also was a key part of the convoy system and hence of interest to the crown as a shipper and to the Consulado, whose voice at court probably supplied the political push needed to get a fort and then a garrison established there.

But of all the general interests that might cause the crown to make up its mind for or against a given petition for defenses, the most important over the long term was the crown's desire (often necessity) to use its funds carefully. Prior to the 1560s, when a greater sense of strategic importance, the threat of invasion, and the crown's prestige came into play, the crown followed a general policy of not authorizing projects that could not be met from local revenues and were not consistent with local militia strengths. Because numbers of residents and volume of trade—and hence of tax revenues—tended to go together, the result was a tendency for the more important towns, like Santo Domingo, to get the lion's share of royal defense spending, unless unusual factors intervened, as they did at Havana and Cartagena. After the 1560s the crown did not entirely abandon the earlier policy. It continued to approve new expenditures slowly and generally only along the lines laid down by the precedents of the pre-1563 period or their logical extensions, such as garrisoning Havana after its new fort was finished or supporting galleys as partial substitutes for the patrol squadrons of the Indies Fleet. It took Drake to break this pattern of parsimony.

In sum, the pattern of defenses built up by individual decisions resulted from the interplay of the crown's general interests, especially its parsimony with its funds, some of its specific interests, and the advocacy of particular projects by interested local groups enjoying differing types of access to the bureaucracy and to the court because of varying patron-client ties to both. The result was an adequate system, provided that its assumptions remained true and given the absence of any major threat that might pick on the weaknesses that had developed for want of a coordinated plan or consistently pursued military strategy.

Because of its parsimony and the small scale of military operations before 1586 (excluding those from 1566–1568), the defense of the Indies was a real bargain for the crown. Even at its most expensive during the fourth period, the average yearly costs of defending the Indies and their commerce were less than the crown had paid to maintain the royal household in Spain in 1536 or the Mediterranean galleys in 1561 and only about a tenth of the average yearly cost of the Dutch Wars in the same period.[9] Even the total of some five million ducats for defense between 1535 and 1585 was but a small part of what the crown ordinarily spent in maintaining its household, the garrisons in Spain, and other costs. The wartime expenses of the Dutch Wars frequently reached at least half that figure for just one year.

In light of the comparative figures, it is apparent that even a doubling of royal expenses for the defense of the Indies would have made a great difference, provided that the money could have been used. However, in view of the Casa's poor record in maintaining naval squadrons in the Caribbean by remote supply or in equipping militias and forts, it seems likely that either the money could not have been used at all or would not have bought a proportionate increase in defenses due to the higher costs of supplies in the Caribbean. This is an interesting counterfactual problem, some of whose solutions may well be found by studying what the crown did after 1586, when it spent many times the quarter of a million ducats per year that were its average between 1578 and 1586.

Having said all of the above about the weaknesses and irrationalities (as we might view them) of the defenses of the Indies, it must be said that the defenses that evolved by 1586 on the bases of precedent, patrimonialism, and parsimony were not without their rational order. They agreed with the resources of the area in men and finances and with the crown's willingness to spend its resources. Taken together, the defenses present in 1586 (however imperfectly executed) constituted a fairly balanced set of defenses that provided security to the major towns, to some coastal shipping, and to all trans-Atlantic shipping under what were, from the 1560s onwards, considered to be "normal" conditions. Moreover, those defenses provided at least a nominal policing of the empire's navigation laws and upheld the crown's claims to sovereignty. From twenty to forty sail of corsairs were in the Caribbean each year, but they did not operate in large squadrons and seldom were more than one hundred men under one command. The defenses met that challenge well enough.

By 1585, the defense had drawn even with, if not slightly ahead of the offense as then constituted. Drake made the obvious response: he took advantage of the relative weaknesses of the system, and he raised the level of violence by a factor of at least ten, putting over 1,000 men ashore at Santo Domingo. Drake's raid was, paradoxically, the mark of the success of the defenders of the Spanish Indies before 1586.

Appendix I
Methodology

THE TIME SERIES DATA used as the bases for the mean yearly figures given in Tables 1, 3, 6, 13, 16, 21, 24, and 25 were generated from entries in the treasury accounts of the Spanish empire using hierarchically arranged program-budget and geographic categories. This appendix discusses the treasury accounts as sources and the methods used to generate the time series data.

As used in this study, quantitative data serve two purposes. First, they are of interest for themselves, there being no published study of military expenditures for the Spanish empire in America during the sixteenth century. Second, the time series, based on the calendar year and organized along topical and geographic lines, supply the data for statistical and graphic presentation of basic trends and changes in the imperial defense posture. These purposes determined the information that was extracted from the treasury accounts, coded, keypunched, and fed through computers that produced the basic tables and the statistics of mean yearly cost used in the text.

The Accounts

The Spanish colonial treasury accounts are of the "charge-discharge" type. An ancient form of bookkeeping, it remained dominant until well into the sixteenth century, despite the introduction into business use of the double-entry system during the preceding one hundred years. Even after double-entry bookkeeping became common, many governments continued to use the charge-discharge system because it emphasized the liability of the person "charged" with the care of items and because the double-entry system offered no special advantages to governments concerned solely with cash flows through one or at most a dozen accounts.[1]

Charge-discharge bookkeeping utilized a book divided into the "charge" or, in Spanish, *cargo* section, and the "discharge" or *data*, also listed as *descargo* in some examples. Typically, entries have the same form as journal entries in the double-entry system. In surviving examples of the Casa de Contratación's books, for example, the entry begins with a copy of the royal order(s) (*cédula*) producing the expenditure; briefly records the authorization of the purchase, often by an agreement (*acuerdo*) of the Casa's officials; notes the substance of the bill drawn against the treasurer—including date, vendor, types and quantities of goods or services rendered, receiver of the items and other minor details; notes the payment; and finally records the documentation of the transaction—the draft (*libranza*) and notarized receipt (*carta de pago*) used to verify the entry. The amount of the transaction was entered in the right-hand margin of the page in roman numerals until quite late in the century.[2]

Multiple accounts were carried by using a corresponding number of books. Loose-leaf records also performed the function of books, particularly with factors' accounts involving items in inventory. In such cases, the discharge was usually entered on the bottom of the sheet rather than on a separate sheet. When fully assembled, these books—whether for the empire as a whole or for a given agency such as the Casa de Contratación—form a set of interrelated books having the effect of double-entry bookkeeping because items listed in the *cargo* of one account are in the *data* of another.

Audit Copies

Few of the original books have been preserved. In their place we have the copies made for auditing. Written up at the local level while the first audit was underway, the audit copy was then sent to the accountants (*contadores mayores*) of the Council of the Indies, who reviewed the entries, allowing or disallowing those accepted by the local level and making their own extensive notes on each person who received goods or funds from the account in question. Those records, like the accountants' lists of expenditures authorized by the council and king, were used to check the accounts of such secondary persons, if and when they gave an accounting. Entries accepted by the Council's auditors were rubriced in the margin; those questioned or to be noted for some other use were the subjects of marginalia. Occasional audit copies of the accounts also preserve some of the working papers of the accountants with their notes and calculations (carried out in arabic numerals in most cases). Once the audit was completed by the accountants, the Council of the Indies could give quittance (*finiquito*) or demand satisfaction of outstanding balances due to the crown. After no further use was anticipated, the copy was tied up and archived.[3] These documents today form most of the papers in the Contaduría section of the Archivo General de Indias. Seventeenth- and eighteenth-century accounts are found in the *audiencia* sections of that same archive and in the respective national archives in Latin America.

The auditing sequence outlined above remained the same until the establishment of the accounting tribunals (*Tribunales de Cuentas*) in 1605. However, auditing techniques within that sequence underwent numerous minor and two major modifications during the period of this study. The minor modifications dealt mostly with how the first or local audit was to be conducted. Most of these changes arose from local problems and do not effect the form or general quality of the accounts as sources, and so do not need to be considered here. The major changes in the frequency of audits and in the format of the audit copy did have an impact on the general reliability of the accounts as a group of sources. The reasons for these changes are bound up with the history of the American treasuries. Without going into extensive detail, the story may be told as follows.[4]

History of Auditing Standards

When first created, the royal treasury in America was a branch of the treasury of Castile staffed by deputies of the *contadores mayores* of the Council of Castile.[5] This arrangement remained in force from 1493 until 1502 when Fray Nicolás de Ovando took the first independent or proprietary treasury officials (treasurer, accountant, factor) with him to Española. The following year the Casa de Contratación was founded, to be followed within two years by the transformation of the empire from a royal trading monopoly into an empire of private exploitation taxed by the crown. Like the officials sent to Española, those of the Casa enjoyed commissions in their own right, not those of lieutenants of the *Contadores Mayores de Castilla*. But only in 1524, when the Council of the Indies was finally created, did the supervision of the treasury personnel pass from the hands of the *Contadores Mayores de Castilla*.[6]

During this early period, accounting was irregular. No complete audit of the books in the Indies occurred until 1500, when Francisco de Bobadilla began investigations into the Columbus government. Because of the contract of 1492, Columbus' personal affairs were intermixed with those of the crown. Columbus' agent, Rafael Catano, was still in Santo Domingo working on the accounts as late as 1504. They were resolved during 1505, and the disputes arising from them passed to the law courts for settlement.[7] Following this unhappy experience, the crown ordered a yearly rendering of accounts by the officials of the Casa and in the Indies.[8] Compliance with this order is not recorded.

The accountants of the Council of the Indies remained the nominal supervisors of the accounting process during the rest of the sixteenth century, except for the brief attempt of 1559–1562 to merge the accounting of the American and Peninsular portions of the empire under the control of the Council of Finance (*Hacienda*) and its accountants. The roots of this experiment in unified accounting may be traced to the unsatisfactory state of the empire's finances and bookkeeping in the early 1550s.

As has been noted, prior to 1554 accounts were rendered infrequently, and often only upon the death of the official or when a special *visitador* or accountant was dispatched to check on the affairs of a particular treasury.[9] Because of this irregular auditing, the average length of the accounting period during the reign of Charles I for five treasuries (the Casa de Contratación, Santo Domingo, Cuba, Tierra Firme, and Cartagena) used in this study was four years and some months. A more detailed study of the accounting would show that many audits revealed scandalous abuses of the royal funds. By the early 1550s, too, the accountant of the Council of the Indies was being overworked and accounts due from Seville were almost a decade in arrears. Within the administration of Castile similar problems existed at the same time.[10]

In 1554 the crown attempted to reform both the Castilian and the American accounting procedures by obtaining more frequent audits, in the evident hope that more money would be produced by the prevention of frauds in the use of royal funds and by the collection of balances (*alcances*) due to the crown. For the Americas that reform took the form of a general order setting out in detail the procedures to be followed in auditing the books of each treasury at the beginning of each year.[11] Like its predecessor of 1508, this order had no immediate impact on the habits of the treasury officials.

Because of the continuation of the unsatisfactory state of the treasury and the accounting machinery in all parts of the empire, the crown embarked on a bold experiment in 1559. It attempted to merge the American revenues and their accounting with that of its Spanish funds. Peru was chosen as a test case. Accountants representing both the Council of the Indies and the Council of Finance were sent out to form a *Consejo de Cámara y Estado* at Lima with full powers over the accounting and auditing process. This reform soon failed because of the pretensions of the new board, various excesses committed by its members, and the unworkability of having two councils issue orders for the same subject. The experiment was abandoned in 1562.[12]

For the rest of the empire, the rules of 1554 remained in effect. To help ensure compliance, in 1560 the *audiencias* were ordered to undertake the audits of the treasury books at the first of each year.[13] But again nothing seems to have been done, probably because of the confusion surrounding the attempt to merge the accountants of the Council of the Indies with those of the Council of Finance. Once that roadblock had been removed, the regulations of 1554 were reissued in 1564.[14] This time compliance was forthcoming.

By 1570 most treasuries were rendering yearly accounts. Cuba fell in line by 1574 as a result of a request by the treasury officials for yearly audits by the governor.[15] But like many other governor-audited accounts, the Cuban ones soon fell back into a pattern of less than yearly auditing. However, only in exceptional cases did the delay in accounting approach the previous average of four years plus. The Casa de Contratación, the Indies Fleet, and the treasury of Florida remained exceptions to this general trend throughout the years of this study. The Casa was probably not required to render yearly accounts because of the delay this would have produced in its administration of trade and the king's other business. The Indies Fleet's logical accounting period was the voyage, which might vary in length. The Fleet's accounts also tended to be audited only when a new treasurer was named. Florida's accounts, which were tied to the Indies Fleet from 1570 to 1574, were subject thereafter to the disinterest of the governors in strict accounting and the difficulty of rendering yearly audits in a place funded by a subsidy whose collection was irregular under the best of conditions.[16] Of these three exceptional treasuries, only Florida's accounts are less reliable because of infrequent auditing.

Related to the problem of securing an up-to-date accounting was the problem of knowing precisely what various revenues had yielded and what various types of expenditure had amounted to. Of interest for itself, such precision was also an aid in detecting irregularities by highlighting unusual changes in general patterns of expenditure. Subdivision of the accounts was thus an important tool for improving fiscal administration. It also makes the accounts easier to use.

The introduction of *ramos* or subdivisions within the general division of *cargo* or *data* was less universal and harder to document than the change to yearly accounts. By the early 1560s Cartagena's accounts, the Casa's accounts, and New Galicia's accounts for 1544–1558 had begun to use subdivisions according to types of revenue (tribute, *quinto*, *almojarifazgo*, etc.) and units of account (*pesos de plata corriente*, *pesos de oro*, etc.). In September 1565 the crown made such subdivisions mandatory, but the order was not widely complied with until the 1570s.[17]

A second type of division was to specify not only the types of revenues and accounting units, but also the classes of expenditure. The order of September 1565 noted above apparently intended this sort of division, but only the Mexican accounts seem to have used it prior to 1570, and they were probably rewritten about that time. Cuban accounts taken in 1576 introduce such a division of expenditures, as do the Casa's accounts taken in 1578. Lima's accounts for 1578 also show these divisions. Perhaps the earliest use was at Tierra Firme in 1574. In short, on the basis of internal evidence it is clear that the full system of subdividing the accounts by *ramos* did not come into general use until after 1575. It was, however, well established by 1580.

Reliability and Completeness of Records

Helpful as these two major changes in accounting technique were in allowing the crown to keep watch over its servants and its finances on a nearly up-to-date basis, they did not prevent fraud or always ensure its early detection. So tempting was the king's purse that one student of a related topic has spoken of the "atmosphere of fraud" that surrounded all transactions involving the treasury.[18] Other scholars have made the same observation on the basis of the abundant documentation about fraud to be found in letters, the accounts themselves, and in the texts of *residencias* and *visitas*.

A close examination of scholarly opinion on the problem of fraud shows that much of it is formed during considerations of the income side of the ledgers. There were numerous ingenious forms of tax evasion, and many royal officials found opportunities to keep the royal revenues outside of the strongbox for private use and, if necessary, to cover their losses with fraudulent bookkeeping.[19] Unless blessed with detailed contemporary investigations that reveal whether the accounts were accurate and, if not, what the true figures should be, the historian of the crown's income can use his data as only minimal indicators of economic reality.

It would be a mistake to assert that expenditures were not also falsified or subject to fraud such as overpricing or the purchase of unneeded items.[20] Yet it is also true that the spending of funds was hedged about with an elaborate procedure that served to minimize frauds in a way not possible with the collection of revenue. Each expenditure had to be approved by competent authorities,[21] have a proper draft (*libranza*) drawn, have records made of that and the authorization, have payment made before witnesses and a notary and recorded by a notarized receipt (*carta de pago*), have that in turn recorded in the books of the treasurer and the accountant and signed by them, and then undergo audit at two levels. In the local audit the basic documentation of the expenditure (authorization, *libranza*, *carta de pago*) was collated with the account entry. The review audit by the accountants of the Council of the Indies double-checked on the authorization(s). Frauds that escaped detection in this procedure simply became costs of government so far as contemporaries were concerned. Thus, unlike frauds involving revenues, those undetected in the expense data do not prevent the construction of statistical series whose figures accurately reflect the transactions that occurred.[22] This is particularly true if, as has been done in this study, all entries questioned by the auditors are excluded from the data.

In short, although there undoubtedly were frauds in the spending of the royal funds, procedural safeguards kept them to a minimum. Combined with improvements in auditing techniques, procedure produced accounts of high, and improving, reliability so far as the *data* are concerned.

Granting the high reliability of the data entries of the accounts, what of their completeness? Completeness involves two questions: did all expenditures get recorded? and, what accounts were preserved for scholarly use? The first of these questions is easily disposed of. Because the officials were liable for any surplus in the royal favor over and above what was found in the strongbox, they were careful to include every possible expenditure in their accounts, especially when the income of the treasury exceeded its authorized expenses. In many of the early accounts it was not uncommon for the royal officials to present the auditors with documentation of additional expenditures after a preliminary audit had revealed a large balance in the king's favor not covered by the money on hand.[23] In the other case, when expenses exceeded income, the officials would also fully report on their expenditures, since the money presumedly came from their own pockets and they would naturally wish to be repaid. The system thus had a built-in motiviation for the officials to report everything they spent.

Preservation of the records against possible future use in planning or lawsuits was a feature of the Spanish system. From the 1520s on, bureaucratic paper no longer needed for daily operations was sent to Simancas for storage in the castle. Until the eighteenth century few persons other than the custodians of the archive or special agents of the government used the papers. There were no fires, insect damage was minimal, and the only major deterioration was due to viral and fungal action or to the excess acidity of inks. In 1784 Juan Baptista Muñoz persuaded the crown to move the papers dealing with the American empire to the old Casa Lonja in Seville. There they remain, with additions from Simancas and other sources, as the Archivo General de Indias.

Among the papers shipped to Seville were the accounts of the royal treasuries during the sixteenth century. These became the core of the Contaduría section. Again fortune smiled and no major damage occurred until 1924. In that year there was a fire in the Contaduría papers. Hardest hit were some of the accounts for Mexico, Florida, and the Central American provinces (*Legajos* in the 940s, 960s, 970s, and a few of the 980s). In a number of cases the *cargo* sections were burned beyond recovery, with less damage to the *data* sections. In other cases, the accounts were damaged by chemicals used to fight the fire; in still others the *legajos* were not put back together correctly after the fire was out. The latter problem is being corrected, but the former is beyond repair except as expensive modern lamination techniques might preserve the brittle paper. In all, however, the loss of expenditure data because of this fire is not serious.[24]

Illustration 13 is a representation of the completeness of the account series used in this study. Gaps in the accounts for treasuries other than those damaged in 1924 seem to arise from the appropriation of the accounts for other uses, especially as part of the documentation of *visitas* and of lawsuits. I did not locate accounts thus used.

The most important gaps in the records involve the accounts of Cuba and Vera Cruz. For Cuba before 1572, there is little of interest for this study in the missing papers.[25] The absence of the Vera Cruz accounts is more important since construction of the fort at San Juan de Ulúa was underway during the 1570s. Originals may still exist in Mexico. Because of these gaps, Cuba's accounts are 41 percent complete, and Vera Cruz's are 62 percent complete. They are thus at one extreme among the more important accounts, with the Casa's perfectly preserved accounts at the other. Over all, the treasury records are 70 percent complete for the years 1535–1585, a situation that compares favorably to that of many correspondence series and is in some respects superior to that for the opinions (*consultas*) of the Council of the Indies. The records are certainly adequate for the construction of time series data on defense costs.

Method

After preliminary experimentation with hand-tabulation of data from the treasury accounts, I decided that the amount of material and the number of computations to be performed on each item made computerization profitable. Equipped with a beginner's knowledge of Fortran IV, Kenneth Janda's book on data processing,[26] and some general ideas about what I hoped to accomplish, I set out to devise the codes and programs that would perform the routine tasks involved in aggregating the treasury data. Now, a number of years later, I have finished a project that took a number of false turns as I learned about computers and the problems of manipulating large amounts of data.

Illustration 13. Years Covered by Treasury Records Used.

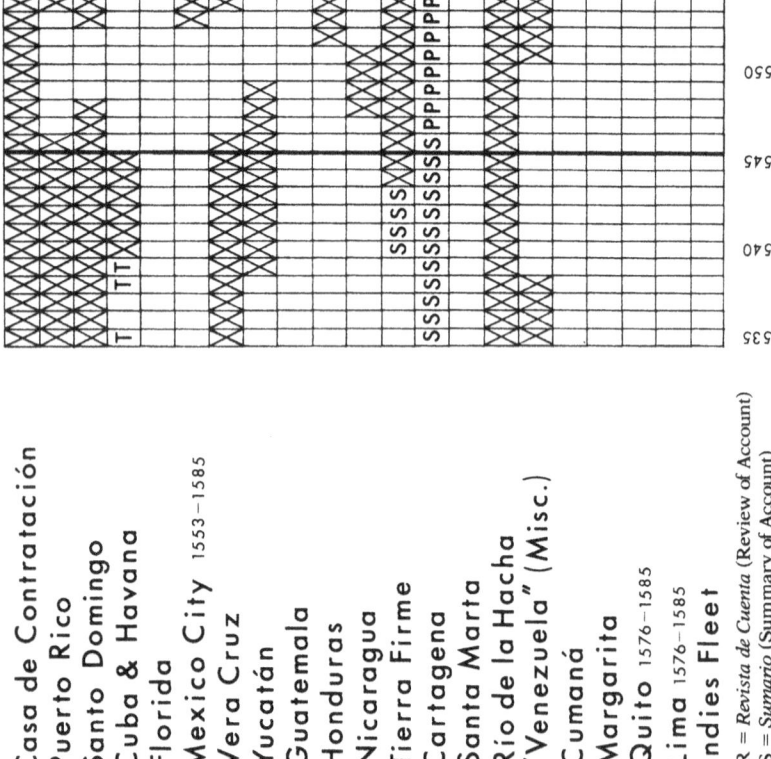

R = *Revista de Cuenta* (Review of Account)
S = *Sumario* (Summary of Account)
T = *Tanteo de Cuenta* (Estimate of Account)
P = Partial account, lacking one or more sections
X = Complete account for that year

Topical Analysis

The topical analysis of this work was inspired by the Planning, Programming, and Budgeting System (PPBS) introduced into the management of the United States Department of Defense (DoD) by Secretary of Defense Robert S. McNamara. Originating in private industry during the 1920s, PPBS had reached a high state of conceptual perfection by 1960 and was a powerful tool for planning, thanks to the development of computers.[27]

As a tool for historical analysis, PPBS had the attractive features of stressing rational analysis, highlighting alternative approaches, and being computer oriented. The comparative and counterfactual possibilities of the technique did not prove of interest for my work, the first because of the lack of data for other periods and the necessary limitation of my initial study, the latter because the problem was not one requiring negative verification of a thesis. For my purposes the rational analytical scheme and the computer orientation of the DoD PPBS were what mattered. I liberally copied the first and used my programming knowledge to implement the second. The result is a six-digit, hierarchical code developed for Fortran IV programs. However, only three of the digits were used, except for a detailed study of the manpower category. My experience thus ran parallel to that of the DoD, which found that its original PPBS system was frequently too sophisticated for the problems it had to handle.[28]

The Program Budget is based on two concepts: the *program* and the *program element*. A *program* is any objective or function of the "firm." A *program element* is "an integrated activity, a combination of men, equipment, and facilities which together constitute an identifiable ... capability or activity."[29] Program elements should be so defined that the set of them that makes up each major program, and each program element if there is more than one level of specification, contains an implicit statement of alternative means for achieving the objective in question. The ideal program budget would thus contain program elements within program elements, and so on through the various levels of specification within programs. Each element would be a self-contained grouping of men, equipment, and facilities performing a specific job or jobs. In practice, the application of the program element concept often breaks down as the analytical scheme moves from the program and the first program element into more specific examination of the means to be used to carry out the program. This breakdown arises from the need of planners, and historical analysts, to look at "capabilities and activities" in more descriptive terms than the program element concept permits.

The program considered here is the Spanish crown's defense of its American empire, 1535–1585. As noted in the Introduction, "defense" means protecting the empire, its sea-lanes, and navigation laws from the hostile activity of other Europeans. It does not include frontier wars with the Indians, the suppression of slave revolts, or campaigns against Cimarron Negroes except where, as on the Isthmus of Panamá in 1577–1580, those communities were allied with Europeans who may be said to be the main objective of the military operation in question.

The first specification of alternative means of defense involves the program elements "Land Defense" and "Naval Defense."[30] These elements are defined in reference to the surface or materials on which operations occur, not the objective of those operations. Land Defense thus is that grouping of men, matériel, and facilities (including auxiliary shipping) used on dry land for the defense of the empire or some part thereof. Naval Defense includes the men, matériel, and facilities (including those ashore) used on the high seas and in coastal waters to obtain the same objective. The data generated for both categories are limited by the number and quality of the treasury accounts used; that is, they do not include values of items from inventories because inventory accounts were not used, nor do they include costs listed in treasuries in Spain other than those of the Casa de Contratación.

The second level of specification involves the following categories: Under *Land Defense*: Manpower, Fortifications, Artillery, Other Installations, Support Activities Not Otherwise Classified; Under *Naval Defense*: General Purpose Squadrons, Convoy Escort Costs, Coastal and Riverine Patrols, and Auxiliary Craft and Forces Not Otherwise Classified. Each of these headings was originally developed to be a program element. Sixteenth-century men viewed armies, artillery trains, and fortifications as alternative means of defense, just as the naval categories suggest alternatives, however unequal in effectiveness.

Application of the program element concept to these categories and of them to the data resulted in the loss of a meaningful breakdown of the land defense costs. Almost all the expenditures had to be placed under "Fortifications" because that was where the few garrisons and most of the artillery were actually grouped. Continuation of the analysis under such conditions would have made it a pointless exercise. This difficulty might have been overcome by further elaboration of the coding scheme, but the quality of the data, the author's programming skills at the time, and considerations of publication problems dictated that the program element concept be partially abandoned in the land defense categories.[31] The naval categories remain program elements.

Because of the problem just noted, the land defense categories were made more descriptive by the application of two rules. The first was to combine under one heading the costs of all military personnel, regardless of which of the alternative "arms systems" utilized their services. Thus wardens of forts (*alcaides*), regular and militia troops, and artillerymen are specified as types under the heading "Manpower." Had the program element definition remained in force, only costs for the regular and militia troops not attached to forts, together with the costs of their weapons, supplies, and auxiliary personnel (if any), would have been included in that category. The category resulting from this rule therefore combines program element aggregations of costs (regular and militia troops, which are alternative means to the same end) with simple salary and training expenses (wardens and artillerymen). While not conceptually rigorous, the "Manpower" costs resulting are what the layman would assume the title to mean.

The application of rule one involved a distinction between troops and those auxiliary personnel whose function was to support the weapon or to make it, rather than the men who actually used it. Such auxiliary personnel remain assigned to the weapon category. For example, the slaves and journeymen who formed part of the personnel of the fort at Havana, 1558–1580, but whose jobs were primarily to build and maintain the fort, are included under "Fortifications," even though they formed a part of the garrison in times of extreme emergency and were occasionally employed to produce supplies for it.

The second rule was to separate artillery and its associated munitions and support personnel from the other categories, even when artillery was in fact an integral part of the "groupings of men, weapons, and facilities" that made up the "identifiable capability." This rule affected the category "Fortifications" more frequently than it did "Manpower" because relatively few militia or garrison units used field artillery, whereas all forts had some cannon.

There follows, then, brief definitions of each of these categories or program elements as they are used in this study. The reader is also referred to Table 26.

Manpower: All expenditures for the recruitment, outfitting, continued supply of, feeding, salary payment, housing, and other expenses of all military personnel who might have engaged in land combat. Also included are the expenses for auxiliary personnel such as drummers and chaplains. Militia and regular soldiers are included, with provision for the segregation of their respective costs.

Artillery: The costs of acquiring, maintaining, and providing munitions for artillery pieces regardless of where they were used ashore. Note, however, that the value of items taken from inventories is not included unless the original purchase for inventory was recorded under the "Central Supply" level of the coding system.

Table 26 **Category Codes**

Numerical Code	Content
3 0 0	Defense Expenditure
3 1 0	Land Defense Expenditure
3 1 1	Combat and Garrison Troops (Militia costs add a 7 in col. 20)
3 1 3	Artillery Park
3 1 5	Fortifications
3 1 9	Support Forces and Miscellaneous
3 3 0	Naval Defense Expenditure
3 3 1	General Purpose Naval Forces (If expenditure is for Convoy Duty, add 4 in col. 20; if for Coastal Patrol, add 3 in col. 20).
3 3 3	Convoy Escorts (excluding those by General Purpose Forces).
3 3 5	Coastal Patrols (excluding those by General Purpose Forces)
3 3 7	Miscellaneous Expenses, Naval
3 7 0	Central Supply Expenditure
3 7 1	Small Arms
3 7 3	Artillery
3 7 5	Munitions
3 7 7	Other Supplies
3 7 9	Costs of Maintaining Central Supply Depot

"col. 20" refers to column 20 of the punched card, see Table 28.

Fortifications: The costs of building and maintaining defensive structures of various types and of equipping them with permanent equipment not included in one of the other categories—for example, flags for ceremonial occasions, and pots and pans for the use of the wardens.

Other Installations: A category for buildings not otherwise classified. River and harbor booms and powder houses are the only items included.

Support Activities Not Otherwise Classified: A self-evident category.

General Purpose Squadrons: The costs of acquisition, maintenance, and use of those naval units not classified under another category, and specifically, the costs of the Indies Fleet. As used here, the category includes all the costs of the Indies Fleet, even where some of those costs were allocated to other categories (see Introduction).

Convoy Escort Costs: The costs of acquiring, maintaining, and using naval units whose primary task is escorting the convoys. In many years, the costs listed are *only* the crown's contribution to the *avería*; for other years the costs include the services of the Indies Fleet (see Introduction, Table 1).

Coastal and Riverine Patrols: The costs of those units engaged primarily in patrolling coastal zones or restricted zones of the ocean adjacent thereto, such as the Triangle.

Auxiliary Craft and Forces Not Otherwise Classified: Self-evident.

The analytical scheme was further developed into a fourth and a fifth level of specification, which display the same necessity of mixing descriptive and analytical (program element) categories. As these were not used in the data series, they do not require further discussion; most of the data were coded using the full coding scheme, to five places.

Geographic Categories

The DoD's program budgets do not utilize separate geographic categories as analytical tools. Because such categories were required for this study, a six-digit, hierarchical scheme was developed using the principles suggested by the PPBS approach and the coding conventions discussed by Janda. Again, the tool proved more powerful than the data warranted and only four of the six levels of specification were employed.

The first digit of the code specifies that part of the Spanish empire being considered—in this case the Atlantic or American empire. The second digit subdivides the Atlantic empire into its eastern, Caribbean,

Table 27   **Geographic Categories**

Numerical Code	Content
4 0 0 0	The Americas and the Sea-Lanes to Them
4 1 0 0	The Atlantic Triangle (Azores-Gibraltar-Canaries)
4 2 0 0	The Caribbean and Western Atlantic
4 2 1 0	The Greater Antilles
4 2 1 1	Puerto Rico
4 2 1 3	Española
4 2 1 5	Cuba
4 2 1 7	Jamaica
4 2 2 0–4 2 7 0	Total Non-Antilles Caribbean (computed, not coded)
4 2 2 0	The Floridas
4 2 3 0	Louisiana and Texas
4 2 4 0	New Spain
4 2 5 0	Central America (Gulfo Dulce to northern border of Veragua)
4 2 6 0	The Main (Isthmus of Panama to Guajira Peninsula)
4 2 6 1	Tierra Firme Province (Panamá)
4 2 6 3	Darién Province
4 2 6 5	Cartagena Province
4 2 6 7	Santa Marta Province
4 2 7 0	Guajira Peninsula to Guianas (*i.e.*, Venezuela), and Lesser Antilles (including off-shore islands)

Pacific, and other parts. The third specifies subregions within these regions.[32] A fourth digit delimits the province. The fifth was provided to allow specification of the cities, parishes, or other subdivisions of the province. The sixth and last digit provides specification of location within the preceding subdivision. It would thus be possible to code not only the city of San Juan de Puerto Rico, but also a particular *barrio* or fortification within that city.

The geographic codes used in this study are outlined in Table 27. All defintions are those used at the time, a necessary if imprecise way of handling the problem of "Florida" or the extent of New Spain. Precise definition of boundaries was not necessary because no objects of interest were in disputed areas.

Computation

Having developed the coding schemes and the converter codes for units of account and coin (to be discussed below), coding sheets and computer cards were laid out in the way specified in Table 28.

Table 28   **Computer Card Layout**

Columns	Contents
1–3	Year of Payment (omitting the 1)
4–5	Month of Payment
6–7	Day of Payment
8–9	Treasury Code
10–13	Blanks
14–19	Topical Analysis Code (Table 26)
20	Special code to indicate transfers of funds to other treasuries (9) and militia costs (7).
21–26	Geographic Code (Table 27)
27–42	Blanks (intended for special codings of manpower and goods types)
43–44	Currency Code (Tables 29–31)
45–54	Units, Currency
55–56	First sub-unit, Currency
57–58	Second sub-unit, Currency
59–61	Year of *Libranza* (Omitting the 1)
62–80	Blanks

Data Preparation: Various techniques were used in preparing the data for coding. Following the initial "discovery" of the treasury records, notes were taken on entries using mimeographed eight-and-one-half by eleven-inch forms. Later, note cards were used for direct transcription of notes from microfilm copies of the account entries. In both cases the data had to be entered again on the coding sheets. Finally, the data were encoded directly on the sheets from microfilms of the accounts. This technique is the fastest because even with the addition of notes on other cards for use in writing, it used less time and involved less duplication than the earlier techniques.

Following the coding on the sheets, the data were punched using the self-programming features of the keypunch to skip over the blanks. The duplicator key was used when possible, with a saving of time. Verification was done by hand and corrections made as needed.

Data preparation proved to be the most time-consuming portion of the project, although earlier use of the final technique for coding would have lessened the man-hours required. By comparison, the problems of programming were quickly resolved, despite having to adjust the program to three different computers.

254 APPENDIX I

Currency Conversion: The first step in computation was to convert the various units of account and currency found in the treasury entries to their common base, the maravedí. Maravedís figures were subsequently converted into ducats (375 maravedís), a unit selected for this study because of the availability of some comparative data from Europe stated in that unit.

Manuel Moreyra Paz-Soldan has noted that a unique feature of the Spanish monetary system was its use of the maravedí as the basis for figuring the value of gold and silver coins and units of account.[33] Because of this base, changes in the bimetallic ratio could be accommodated by the device of adjusting the maravedí value of gold upwards without changing the silver content of the real and other silver coins. The investigator is thus spared the problem of trying to figure out what silver coins were worth in constant units of gold or silver content. During the years of interest for this study, the value of the maravedí in silver (approximately 0.1 gram of pure silver) remained constant, making it unnecessary to adjust the maravedí to keep it constant.[34]

Table 29 lists the various units of account and currency found in the treasury accounts and their values in maravedís as officially stated. With the exception of the Casa de Contratación, which always recorded its accounts in maravedís, most of the early accounts use the *peso de oro fino* (OF) or the *peso de buen oro* (BO) as the unit of account equal to 450 maravedís. This was a fictitious unit based on the unit of weight, the *castellano* (4.6009 grams).

During the 1550s and the 1560s many of the treasuries switched their accounts to real units of currency such as the real (34 maravedís), the *peso de plata corriente* (PC, value varied), and the *peso de cuartos* (MC)—a particularly troublesome form of vellon minted at Santo Domingo and used there and on the island of Puerto Rico. The Isthmian accounts also used the *peso de plata ensayada* (PE) or assayed silver peso, a fictional unit of account pegged at 450 maravedís and used to replace the *peso de oro fino*, which was then worth more than 450 maravedís.

With the late 1570s various treasuries began to record their accounts in maravedís, an innovation decreed by the crown to avoid the fraud of being repaid in units of coin worth less (in terms of bullion) than those in which debts had been contracted. This reform was first instituted on the island of Española as part of the effort to deal with the vellon coinage problem (1578),[35] but later spread to other areas where it helped to

Table 29   **Units of Account and Currency, Values in Maravedís**

Unit	Place	Value
Gold		
Escudo	Castile	350 maravedís
Ducat	Castile	375 maravedís
Peso de Oro Bajo (OB)	New Granada	272 maravedís
Peso de Oro Común (OC)	New Spain	300 maravedís
Peso de Oro, Mejor Que Común	New Spain	360 maravedís
Peso de Oro, Ensayado de Tributo	Peru	425 maravedís
Peso de Oro de Ley Perfecta	New Spain	
Peso de Oro de Minas	New Spain	450 maravedís to 1578
Peso de Oro Bueno (OBo)		556 maravedís after 1578
Peso de Oro Fino (OF)		
Peso de Oro Fino o de Polvo	New Granada	490 maravedís
Gold or Silver		
Peso de Oro de Tepuzque	New Spain	272 maravedís
(Also called *Oro Común*, 1572–77)		
The famous *Real de a Ocho*		
Silver		
Real		34 maravedís
Peso de doze reales, ensayada	Peru	408 maravedís
Peso de Plata Ensayada (PE)	The Main	450 maravedís
Peso de a onze, Corriente 20%vis PE	The Main	375 maravedís
Peso de a onze, Corriente 25%vis PE	The Main	360 maravedís
Peso de a onze, Corriente 30% vis PE	The Main	346 maravedís
Peso de a diez, Corriente 35% vis PE	The Main	333.3 maravedís
Peso de a diez, Corriente 38% vis PE	The Main	326 maravedís
Peso de a diez, Corriente 40% vis PE	The Main	321 maravedís
Peso de a diez, Corriente 43% vis PE	The Main	314 maravedís
Peso de a diez, Corriente 45% vis PE	The Main	310 maravedís
(other discounts possible)		
Peso de a nueve (?), Corriente 50% vis PE	The Main	300 maravedís
Peso de a diez reales	Puerto Rico	350 maravedís

The range of possible discounts of *plata corriente* vis-à-vis *plata ensayada* is not limited to just these discounts, but since they were the only ones in use in the accounts studied, they are given here.

counteract not only fraud but also changes in the value of gold and fluctuations in the quality of the circulating coinage.

Perhaps the most difficult of the units of account and coin used in the records were the *peso de cuartos* from Española and the *pesos de plata corriente* as discounted against the *peso de plata ensayada*. The other units had defined values that changed infrequently.

The accounts of Cartagena and Tierra Firme use the *peso de plata ensayada* as a unit of account. The circulating coinage (PC) was a mixture of eleven, ten, and nine real pieces from various mints in the Viceroyalty of Peru.[36] When payment was made in such coins, rather than in assayed silver bars, the accounts usually record the ratio, or discount, between such pesos and the *peso de plata ensayada* (450 maravedís). Thus *pesos de once reales* in perfect condition had a discount of 20 percent against the *peso PE*, because the *peso de once* was nominally worth 374 maravedís (11 reales times 34 maravedís), which is 80 percent of 450 maravedís. Stated another way, it took 120 *pesos de once reales* to equal the value of 100 *pesos PE*. The *peso de diez reales* would have a nominal discount of 32 percent; the *peso de nueve reales* a discount of 47 percent.

But because few coins reaching the Main were up to par in terms of silver content and weight, a given batch of *pesos corriente* would have to be further discounted according to the actual weight of the coins and the judgment of the merchant or royal official as to the fidelity of the minting to the standard. In addition, there seems to have been a trade in the coins for the purpose of melting them for their silver content, which was then exported to Europe in bar form. Market forces of this type operated in ways that await documentation, but probably lowered the value of the coins for exchange purposes. The consequence of this combination of factors is a series of discount rates for each type of peso.

The accounts usually state the discount rate being used, but in a few instances it had to be interpolated from other entries of the same year or month (the latter being preferable since the rate often fluctuated within the year). In the very few cases where no rate was stated, I have used the 40 percent rate, which is associated with the ten real coin, apparently the most common form of the *peso PC* along the Main.

The *peso de cuartos* was a form of vellon coinage produced by the Santo Domingo mint between 1542 and 1578. Because of market manipulations that drove the value of the coins below their intrinsic worth and then below the value of their bullion content, they became known as "bad money" or *mala moneda*.[37]

In summary, the process of devaluation worked as follows. When first issued after 1542, the peso consisted of 112.5 cuartos, each worth four maravedís, for a total of 450 maravedís. The real was pegged at 44 maravedís, or eleven cuartos. In 1544 the crown ordered that effective in 1547 the real would be pegged at 34 maravedís, the value it had in other parts of the empire; but this order was not implemented until about 1552. Merchants and creditors, however, refused to accept cuartos for reals except at the old rate of eleven cuartos to the real, thus devaluing the cuarto and making a peso of 112.5 cuartos worth 337.5 maravedís, slightly more than its intrinsic worth of 331 maravedís. A 5.5 percent discount or exchange charge was then applied, and the peso fell to 318.71 maravedís, less than its intrinsic worth. By degrees in each subsequent trading season the merchants further discounted the cuartos until in 1559 the exchange value of the *peso de cuartos* (still 112.5 cuartos) fell below the value of the metals in the coins—that is, below 222 maravedís. From then on the merchants and other interested parties were able to drive the rate down until it hit a low of 24 maravedís early in 1578. To prevent further devaluation and the extraction of the coins from the islands for melting, the Audiencia moved in May of that year to peg the *peso de cuartos* at 39 maravedís. Shortly afterwards the crown's accounts were switched to maravedís.

The slow decline of the *peso de cuartos* on the Santo Domingo market was recorded in the books of a merchant (?), Francisco de Amaro, from which the crown obtained a summary. This was used to prepare a table listing the month-by-month changes in the rate from 1554 to 1578 (Table 30).

For Puerto Rico, where the *peso de cuartos* also circulated at increasing discounts, the exchange rate was worked out from the records of adjustments made in the governors' salaries. These were paid in the *mala moneda*, but adjusted so as to preserve a constant value in "good money"—that is, currency of Spain. These rates are listed for each year except 1565–1570, where monthly rates are available. For 1574–1577 no rates are given in the accounts, but figures were supplied by interpolation from a graph, whose end point (1578) is the value of the *peso*

Table 30 Maravedí Value of the *Peso de Cuartos* at Santo Domingo, 1554–1578

	All Year	Jan.	Feb.	Mar.	Apr.	May	June	July	Aug.	Sept.	Oct.	Nov.	Dec.
1554	306.45	318.71	318.71	318.71	318.71	318.71	318.71	294.19	294.19	294.19	294.19	294.19	294.19
1555	273.26	273.26	273.26	273.26	273.26	273.26	273.26	273.26	273.26	273.26	273.26	273.26	273.26
1556	273.26	273.26	273.26	273.26	273.26	273.26	273.26	273.26	273.26	273.26	273.26	273.26	273.26
1557	251.78	272.03	272.03	272.03	272.03	272.03	272.03	231.86	231.86	231.86	231.86	231.86	231.86
1558	231.86	231.86	231.86	231.86	231.86	231.86	231.86	231.86	231.86	231.86	231.86	231.86	231.86
1559	215.27	231.86	231.86	231.86	231.86	231.86	231.86	198.68	198.68	198.68	198.68	198.68	198.68
1560	172.02	173.81	173.81	173.81	173.81	173.81	173.81	169.99	169.99	169.99	173.81	173.81	173.81
1561	146.08	156.15	156.15	156.15	156.15	156.15	156.15	136.01	136.01	136.01	136.01	136.01	136.01
1562	124.27	136.01	136.01	136.01	136.01	136.01	115.88	115.88	115.88	115.88	115.88	115.88	115.88
1563	86.40	90.79	90.79	90.79	90.79	90.79	90.79	82.01	82.01	82.01	82.01	82.01	82.01
1564	102.58	82.01	82.01	115.88	115.88	104.40	104.40	104.40	104.40	104.40	104.40	104.40	104.40
1565	85.67	90.79	90.79	90.79	90.79	90.79	82.01	82.01	82.01	82.01	82.01	82.01	82.01
1566	81.56	82.01	82.01	82.01	82.01	82.01	82.01	81.11	81.11	81.11	81.11	81.11	81.11
1567	76.73	77.85	77.85	77.85	77.85	77.85	77.85	75.60	75.60	75.60	75.60	75.60	75.60
1568	65.14	66.26	66.26	66.26	66.26	66.26	66.26	64.01	64.01	64.01	64.01	64.01	64.01
1569	56.54	57.26	57.26	57.26	57.26	57.26	56.03	56.03	56.03	56.03	56.03	56.03	56.03
1570	42.72	45.34	45.34	45.34	41.85	41.85	41.85	41.85	41.85	41.85	41.85	41.85	41.85
1571	42.70	43.54	43.54	41.18	41.18	41.18	41.85	41.85	41.85	43.54	43.54	43.54	43.54
1572	44.89	43.54	43.54	43.54	45.34	45.34	45.34	45.34	45.34	45.34	45.34	45.34	45.34
1573	39.75	40.28	40.28	40.28	40.28	40.28	38.93	38.93	38.93	39.71	39.71	39.71	39.71
1574	38.93	38.93	38.93	38.93	38.93	38.93	38.93	38.93	38.93	38.93	38.93	38.93	38.93
1575	38.93	38.93	38.93	38.93	38.93	38.93	38.93	38.93	38.93	38.93	38.93	38.93	38.93
1576	33.55	38.93	38.93	38.93	38.93	38.93	36.34	36.34	36.34	24.75	24.75	24.75	24.75
1577	27.96	30.26	30.26	30.26	30.26	30.26	30.26	30.26	24.75	24.75	24.75	24.75	24.75
1578	34.08	24.75	24.75	24.75		39.00	39.00	39.00	39.00	39.00	39.00	39.00	39.00

Table 31   Maravedí Value of the *Peso de Cuartos* at Puerto Rico, 1554–1578

Year	All Year	Jan.	Feb.	Mar.	Apr.	May	June	July	Aug.	Sept.	Oct.	Nov.	Dec.
1554	306.45												
1555	273.26												
1556	273.26												
1557	251.78												
1558	231.86												
1559	215.27												
1560	182.14												
1561	182.14												
1562	159.41												
1563	149.96												
1564	90.68												
1565	84.87	90.68	90.68	90.68	90.68	81.79	81.79	81.79	81.79	81.79	81.79	81.79	81.79
1566	78.02	86.96	86.96	86.96	73.24	73.24	73.24	73.24	73.24	77.29	77.29	77.29	77.29
1567	60.43	59.29	60.53	60.53	60.53	60.53	60.53	60.53	60.53	60.53	60.53	60.53	60.53
1568	61.69	60.53	60.53	60.53	60.53	60.53	60.53	60.53	60.53	64.01	64.01	64.01	64.01
1569	60.53	60.53	60.53	60.53	60.53	60.53	60.53	60.53	60.53	60.53	60.53	60.53	60.53
1570	54.20	54.45	54.45	54.45	54.45	54.45					45.34	45.34	45.34
1571	45.34												
1572	45.34												
1573	45.34												
1574	40.50												
1575	35.00												
1576	30.00												
1577	24.75												
1578	34.08												

de cuartos at Santo Domingo in early 1578. For the 1554–1560 period, the rate was taken from the Santo Domingo accounts because the Puerto Rican adjustments do not cover those years in detail (Table 31).

The use of these exchange rates for the *peso de cuartos*, instead of their official value, was decided upon as part of the effort to determine what defense actually cost on a year-to-year basis. In this case, the question is what would the crown have had to pay if it had had good money available. The merchants' manipulation of the exchange rates had the effect of adjusting prices of goods and services for rising costs due to scarcity, while keeping the nominal prices of some items more or less constant. It is thus appropriate to inquire what the prices would have been if they were stated in maravedís rather than *pesos de cuartos*. The validity of this method is shown by the crown's adoption of the maravedí as the unit of account in 1578 and by the consistency of the figures after that date with those before. If the method was wrong, one would expect to find a sharp change in the magnitude of the numbers as real prices were again reflected in the accounts. That did not occur.

Following conversion of the data items to maravedís, each entry was stored on tape for use in the aggregation programs.

Aggregation and Computation of Statistics: The data were aggregated into topical tables, which were each analyzed for straight-line trends over the entire fifty-one years studied and for two twenty-five year periods (1535–1559, 1561–1578). Each table was then stored on tape and used as the basis for the compilation of the mean yearly figures given in the text tables. At the same time that those figures were computed, mean yearly percentages (obtained by dividing the mean yearly figures into each other) were also computed. Other aggregations were made of data in the Manpower category according to its various subdivisions and for all categories and geographic areas in terms of the year in which the item or service was obtained (year of *libranza*), as distinguished from the year in which it was paid for. Still other treatments of moving averages, trends, and so on are possible given the data and the aggregate tables; but because no important insights were likely to result from game-playing with the machine, beyond the determination of the shifting patterns of royal spending that constitute the skeleton of this book, no further analysis was undertaken.

Appendix II
Raw Data on Available Militia Manpower Pools

	Island of Puerto Rico	*Island of Española*
1530	50 married *vecinos*, 20 single *vecinos*, San Juan; 30 *vecinos* resident outside of the city of San Juan	
1537		170 horse, 500 foot, Santo Domingo
1538	30 horse, San Germán	200 horse, 1,300–1,500 foot potential (for entire island?)
1541	40 *vecinos*, San Juan, many old	
1552		150 horse, Santo Domingo
1554	60 horse, San Juan	
1557	102 foot, 46 horse, San Juan	
1559	180 men total, San Juan	
1561		1 company horse, 3 companies of foot, Santo Domingo
1562	200 men total, San Juan—*i.e.*, 50 horse, 80 matchlocks, 70 with other weapons	
1563		70–120 horse, northern coast
1565		sent 200 men to Florida, mostly from Santo Domingo (?)
1566		500 *vecinos*, Santo Domingo
1568	10 *vecinos*, San Germán	100 *vecinos*, La Yaguana; up to 500 *vecinos*, Santo Domingo;

		up to 130 *vecinos*, central towns; 30–40 *vecinos*, Puerto Plata; more than 20 *vecinos*, Puerto Real
1570	80 men, San Juan	1,000 men claimed, Santo Domingo
1571	100 men available, San Juan, but only 50 normally in town	
1572	120 men in all the island, with 20 horse among them	
1574	200 *vecinos*, San Juan	500 *vecinos*, Santo Domingo
	50 *vecinos*, Guadianilla	262 *vecinos*, in other towns
1575	110 foot, 12 horse, San Juan	
1577	40–50 men show for muster, San Juan	150 horse, 500 foot, Santo Domingo
1579		300 men, 500 *vecinos*, Santo Domingo; 300 other *vecinos* on the island
1580		700 foot, 1 company of horse, Santo Domingo
1582		2,000 Spanish on the island
1583	100–150 men, San Juan; 221 men, muster of June 6, San Juan	500 foot, 100 horse, 200 seamen, 400–500 slaves, Santo Domingo
1586	160 men, San Juan	470 men in city, 39 with horses, Santo Domingo

	Island of Cuba	*Coasts of New Spain*
1535	about 200 men, Santiago	
1544	about 200 men, Santiago	
1555	30–50 *vecinos*, Havana	
1558		24–60 men, San Juan de Ulúa (?)
1559	over 160 men, Havana	
1561		25 men, Campeche
1565	70 matchlockmen, Havana	
1570	200 men in all, 100 of them available for militia duty, Havana. 130–150 have matchlocks	
1574	60 *vecinos*, Havana; 30 *vecinos*, Santiago; 327 *vecinos*, all towns	200 *vecinos*, Vera Cruz; (100 *vecinos*, Trujillo, Honduras)
1575	20 *vecinos*, Santiago	
1577	200 men, Havana. 150 foot, 22 horse, rest without weapons	

MANPOWER POOLS 263

1578	80 men, Santiago	
1582	305 men and boys; 57 Hispanized Indians from Guanabacóa; Havana muster, December	
1586	258 men, Havana residents; 208 men from other parts of the island	100 men at Campeche

	Tierra Firme and Cartagena	Santa Marta and Eastward
1538		30 horse, 70 foot, 40 *vecinos*, Cubagua
1543	300 foot, 40 horse, Isthmus	6–8 *vecinos*, Cubagua; 10–12 *vecinos*, Santa Marta
1554	30 horse, 300 foot, Nombre de Dios; 30 horse, 400 foot, Panamá	
1559	40 horse, 300 foot, 500 Indians Cartagena (exaggerated?)	
1560	100 men, Cartagena	
1561	fewer than 80 men when convoy not in port, Nombre de Dios	
1562		80–100 *vecinos*, Margarita
1566	200 foot, 40 horse, Cartagena	
1567	200 foot, 100 with matchlocks, Cartagena	60 men, Río de la Hacha
1572	200–300 slaves can be armed, Cartagena	
1574	150–200 houses, Nombre de Dios, but few permanent residents; 400 *vecinos*, Panamá; 800 men, 250 *vecinos*, Cartagena	25 *vecinos*, Santa Marta; 60 *vecinos*, Margarita
1575	14 *vecinos*, Veragua; 15 permanent residents, Nombre de Dios; 250 foot, 60 horse at Cartagena	
1577	30 *vecinos*, Nombre de Dios; 500 men, including 50 horse, Panamá	

Glossary

Adelantado. Literally, "the advancer." A title given to the commander of a column of soldiers and settlers entering a new area in order to secure it for the crown. Economic and some governmental privileges were usually conveyed with the title. For a discussion see Lyon, *The Enterprise of Florida*, 1–4.

Alcaldes. Often translated as "justices of the peace," the term refers to the two justices (also styled *alcaldes ordinarios*) elected each year from among the members of a town council. These justices had jurisdiction over misdemeanors, felony cases (if no superior justice was resident in the town), and the enforcement of municipal ordinances. They are not to be confused with the modern term *alcalde*, which means "mayor."

Almiranta. The ship on which the "admiral" or second-in-command of a fleet sailed. This ship normally brought up the rear of a fleet and its commander was responsible for keeping track of the other ships and aiding any that were in distress.

Averia. Literally, "average." A levy, figured as a percentage of value, collected from the members of a group or class of persons or goods to pay a common expense—in this case the expense of outfitting warships to escort merchantmen in areas of danger from corsairs. Guillermo Céspedes argues that it was not a tax, but rather a type of insurance premium. Common usage describes it as a tax or impost, which was what it became during the seventeenth century when it was divorced from calculations of the value of goods shipped in the Indies commerce.

Capitana. The ship on which the captain-general or commander of a fleet sailed. It normally led the sailing order, especially at night when its stern lantern served to guide the other ships. Equivalent to the flagship in modern navies.

Corsair. From the Spanish *corsario*, meaning "one who cruises." Any ship and crew, or member of that crew, sailing in the Spanish Indies without license from the Casa de Contratación at Seville, or sailing to attack Spanish shipping off the Iberian Peninsula.

Encomendero. The holder of a grant entitling him to a portion of the tribute paid by a group of Indians in exchange for which he had obligations to see to their material and spiritual well being (including conversion to Christianity) and to keep and bear arms when called upon to do so in the king's name. The Indians were "commended" to his care.

Frigate. A three-masted, one-deck ship of from 80 to 200 *toneladas* capacity used as a warship or freighter. As a warship it often accompanied larger warships as a scouting and utility craft. Square-rigged except for the mizzen (which was lateen-rigged), they typically carried main and top sails on the fore and main masts. Some frigates were equipped with sweeps.

Licenciado. A title indicating that its holder had earned this university degree, which was superior to the bachelor's degree but inferior to the doctorate. Usually held in law by judges of the *audiencias*. Also used as an honorific for any lawyer.

Pasamuro. An iron cannon reinforced so that it could throw a heavy ball. Literally "a wall-passer," the type was used to batter down walls. Size and weight of shot vary.

Patache. A two-masted open boat often fitted with oars or sweeps, varying in number from ten to eighteen to a side, with a total of from twenty to thirty-six. Ranging in size from 60 to 200 *toneladas* burden, they were very swift under sail or oar and were used as tenders for larger ships. The name seems to be derived from an Arabic adjective meaning "rapid, active."

Quinto. The royalty of 20 percent (the fifth part) levied on all minerals and precious and semi-precious gems extracted by private persons in the New World. Because all subsurface wealth was said to belong to the crown, private persons had to pay a royalty if they mined it. In the Peninsula the levy was as much as two-thirds of the value, but the rate was reduced to 20 percent in the New World to encourage exploitation.

Ribadoquin. A small iron cannon firing a 1- to 2-pound shot, weighing 700-900 pounds, and used for wall defense. Similar to the falconet, a type whose name and design replace the *ribadoquin* by 1550.

Saetía. A Mediterranean ship-type of fifty to sixty feet, slender, deckless, and equipped with ten to fifteen benches for rowers and two masts, lateen-rigged. Used in the Mediterranean as a scouting vessel for galley fleets and for other uses requiring speed. Name derived from *sagitta*, meaning "arrow." Similar to the brigantine and *fusta*.

Tonelada. A unit for measuring the carrying capacity of a ship. Defined as 1.4 m^3 in 1552 on the basis of Andalusian practice, by the 1570s it had become 1.686 m^3, the Biscayan unit. Both were replaced in 1590 by a *tonelada* of 2.6 m^3 that measured the displacement of the ship rather than just its cargo space. The English displacement ton is 2.83 m^3.

Urca. A general name for a Flemish ship-type characterized by large carrying capacity but relatively cheap construction and manning requirements. Often translated "hulk." The predecessor of the famous Dutch "flyboat" of the seventeenth century. Banned from the Indies trade during most of the period studied, although sometimes used when no other ships were available, as for example in 1568 when two were sent to Florida with supplies for the garrison.

Verso. An iron or bronze cannon fitted with removable breech blocks into which the powder, wad, and shot were loaded. Used on shipboard and as a wall piece in fortresses. Fired a one-half to one-pound shot. Swivel mounted.

Zabra. A small, three-masted, one-deck ship of Cantabrian design. Probably the predecessor of the frigate, it had a keel-to-beam ratio of at least three to one, was generally race-built, and was noted for its speed. Often equipped with sweeps or oars for shallow-water maneuvering.

A Note on the Citation of Archival Sources

THE COLLECTIONS of the Archivo General de Indias (AGI), Seville, Spain—known to the English-speaking world as the Archive of the Indies—are divided into sixteen major record groups or *secciones*. Of interest for this study are Sección I, *Patronato* or, roughly, Patrimony; Sección II, *Contaduría* or Accounting; Sección III, *Contratación* or House of Trade of Seville; Sección IV, *Justicia* or Justice; Sección V, *Gobierno* or Government; Sección VI, *Escribania de Cámara*, another group of judicial records dating after 1570; and Sección XVI, *Mapas, Planos, Dibujos y Estampas*, or Maps and Plans. Within Sección V, *Gobierno*, are fourteen subcollections organized according to the *audiencia* or appeals court district from which the documents came or to which they refer. The subcollections denominated Santo Domingo, México, Guatemala, Panamá, Lima, and Santa Fe de Bogatá were used for this study. The fifteenth subcollection within Sección V is known as *Indiferente General* or General Miscellaneous. It consists of papers retained by the Council of the Indies until the nineteenth century.

Within each subcollection (where a *sección* is divided into subcollections) each *legajo* or bundle is assigned a number. Bound books within a *legajo* often retain their original numeration and are generally folio numbered. Loose papers used to be left in whatever order the most recent user had adopted, but since the mid-1960s the staff of the Archive has been systematically organizing them according to archival principles (usually by date), assigning sequential numeration (*números*) to all documents, and then subdividing the *legajos* into *ramos* or parts. This began with the earliest documentation in Sección V and has now reached the seventeenth century for most of the subcollections in that group. The numeration of documents within the *legajos* has made it possible to cite a document by its *legajo* number, *ramo* number, and individual number.

The consequences are a great saving of time for the researcher wishing to check the work of others and a great reduction in the wear and tear on the documents.

In record groups other than Sección V, the system of numbering all documents in a *legajo* and then dividing them into conveniently sized sections (*ramos*) is often followed but with a change in the nomenclature. In previous centuries it was thought appropriate to have *números* (numbers) and then *ramos* (parts), especially for collections such as those in Sección I, *Patronato*, and Sección IV, *Justicia*. The uninitiated may find this difference in terminological convention confusing at first, but in practice there is no problem because researchers in the field understand the changes that have occurred and work with each group's internal ordering as it is.

Somewhat similar conventions for numbering documents within *legajos* and *legajos* within subcollections and *secciones* are followed at the Archivo General de Simancas or General Archive, Simancas. The chief difference is that at Simancas a document is given a "folio number" instead of a document number. Recently, these numbers have begun to be called document numbers.

Thanks to the numbering of specific documents within the *legajo*, it is no longer necessary to give the full, ponderous form of citation traditionally used. Thus the names of the correspondents, the place, and the date have been omitted from all notes in this book except where a document was not numbered at the time the research using it was done. The only information given, except in the cases just noted, is a citation of the archive, the name of the *sección* or subcollection, the number of the *legajo*, information on the part of the *legajo*, if any, and the document number. In a few cases I have supplied additional information that a worker at the archive might need to distinguish the document I used from others. My form of citation is thus the conventional one in the field of Latin American colonial history once one gets past the description of the document and arrives at the information on its location.

There follow some examples of the form of citation used here, with their interpretations for the benefit of the nonspecialist. Example 1: AGI, Santo Domingo 10, R. 2, No. 25. This somewhat cryptic message (often made more so by the use of fairly standard abbreviations for the group or subcollection title) simply means: Archive of the Indies, subcollection Audiencia de Santo Domingo (we omit the record group name for Sección V because it is unimportant), *Legajo* 10, Part 2, Document 25. This same document could also be cited as AGI, Santo Domingo 10, No. 25, but I prefer to include the *ramo* because it is the intention of the Archive that papers in these subcollections of Sección V will eventually be served by *ramo* rather than by *legajo*, as is now the case. Example 2: AGI, Justicia 3, No. 3, which indicates the third document in the third *legajo* of Sección IV—in this case a law suit of 90 folios bound together. Example 3: AGI, Patronato 258, "Ríos, Martín de los," R. 1, which uses the man's name for the *número* and so indicates the first document (here called a *ramo*) or group of documents (both could be the case) within the subdivision or part bearing this name in *Legajo* 258 of Sección I.

A NOTE ON THE CITATION OF ARCHIVAL SOURCES 269

There follows a list of the abbreviations used in the notes.

Archival Abbreviations

AGI Archivo General de Indias, or Archive of the Indies, Seville, Spain.
AGS Archivo General de Simancas, or General Archive of Simancas, Simancas, Valladolid, Spain.

Other Abbreviations

R. *Ramo*. Usually means *part*, and designates the first subdivision within a *legajo*, but in some *secciones* in the AGI it designates a document number or special subset of documents within a part (designated *número* in such cases) of a *legajo*.
No. *Número* or number. Usually the number of a particular document within a *legajo*, but in some *secciones* in the AGI it means *part* and is followed by a *ramo* number.
bk Book.
doc. Document. A designation assigned by me in my notes to indicate which of several documents within a *ramo* or *número* is meant where the official numeration of the documents does not embrace all of them.
fol. Folio. The recto side of a leaf in bound volumes or in other documents numbered within themselves on the recto of each sheet. *At Simancas the folio number is the equivalent of the document number.*
vto *Vuelto*. Spanish for *verso* or the back of a leaf or sheet numbered only on the recto. In copy books letters often begin on the back of leaves and continue onto the back of subsequent leaves, hence the need for this information to cite the document in question.
(Stetson) Indicates that the document in question was used in photocopy form in the John B. Stetson, Jr., Collection, P. K. Yonge Library of Florida History, University of Florida.

Other Conventions

IV:4
353:3 These designations indicate a signature (roman numeral) or folded sheet (*pliego*) that is numbered on the first page but not on the others. The first number is that found on the document, the second is one I assigned in my notes by simply counting the pages, beginning with number 1 in that signature or folded sheet. Thus: signature IV, page 4, and folded sheet 353, page 3. These designations are used primarily for treasury records that have not been given folio numbers.

Abbreviations for Printed Collections of Documents

DII   *Colección de documentos inéditos relativos al descubrimiento, conquista, y organización de las antiguas posesiones españoles de América y Oceaniá, sacados de los archivos del reino, y muy especialmente del de Indias.* Edited by Joaquín F. Pacheco, Francisco de Cardenas, and Luís Torres de Mendoza. 42 vols. Madrid, 1864–1884.

DIU   *Colección de documentos inéditos relativos al descubrimiento, conquista, y organización de las antiguas posesiones españoles de ultramar.* Edited by Joaquín F. Pacheco, Francisco de Cardenas, and Luís Torres de Mendoza. 25 vols. Madrid, 1885–1932.

Notes

Chapter I

1. Roland D. Hussey, "Spanish Reaction to Foreign Aggression in the Caribbean to about 1680," *Hispanic American Historical Review*, V (1927), 287.
2. Cesáreo Fernández Duro, *Armada Española desde la unión de los reinos de Castilla y de León* (9 vols.; Madrid, 1895–1903), esp. Vols. I–II; Clarence H. Haring, *Trade and Navigation Between Spain and the Indies in the Time of the Hapsburgs* (1918; reprint ed., Gloucester, Mass., 1964); Gervasio de Artiñano y de Galdácano, *Historia del comercio con las Indias durante el dominio de los austrias* (Barcelona, 1917); James A. Williamson, *Sir John Hawkins: The Times and the Man* (Oxford, 1927); Antonio de Herrera y Tordesillas, *Historia general de los hechos de los Castellanos en las islas y tierrafirme del mar océano* (17 vols.; 1601–15; reprint ed., Madrid, 1956); Joseph de Veitia Linage, *Norte de la Contratación de las Indias Occidentales* (1671; reprint ed., Buenos Aires, 1945).
3. Herbert E. Bolton, *The Colonization of North America, 1492–1783* (New York, 1920); Woodbury Lowery, *The Spanish Settlements Within the Present Limits of the United States* (2 vols.; 1901–1905; reprint ed., New York, 1959); Irene A. Wright, *The Early History of Cuba, 1492–1586* (New York, 1916).
4. Irene A. Wright (ed.), *Spanish Documents concerning English Voyages to the Caribbean, 1527–1568* (London, 1929), and *Documents concerning English Voyages to the Spanish Main, 1569–1580* (London, 1932); Arthur P. Newton, *The European Nations in the West Indies, 1493–1688* (1933; reprint ed., London, 1967).
5. Huguette and Pierre Chaunu, *Séville et l'Atlantique, 1504–1650* (8 vols. in 10; Paris, 1955–59).
6. Guillermo Céspedes de Castillo, "La Avería en el comercio de Indias," *Anuario de Estudios Americanos*, II (1945), 517–698; Enrique Marco Dorta, *Cartagena de Indias: La ciudad y sus monumentos* (Seville, 1951); José Antonio Calderon Quijano, *Historia de las fortificaciones en Nueva España* (Seville, 1953); Antonia M. Heredía Herrera, "Las fortificaciones de la isla Margarita en los siglos XVI, XVII, y XVIII," *Anuario de Estudios Americanos*, XV (1958), 429–514. A related work is Erwin Walter Palm, *Los monumentos arquitectónicos de la Española* (2 vols.; Ciudad Trujillo, 1955).
7. Compare Haring, *Trade and Navigation*, 68–73, 201–10; Newton, *European Nations in the West Indies*, 51–60; and Chaunu, *Séville et l'Atlantique*, II, 124–599, *passim*, and III, 8–12.

8. John H. Parry, *The Age of Reconnaissance* (London, 1963), and *The Spanish Seaborne Empire* (New York, 1966).
9. Kenneth R. Andrews, *The Spanish Caribbean: Trade and Plunder, 1530–1630* (New Haven, 1978).
10. E. G. R. Taylor, *The Haven-Finding Art* (London, 1958), 151–214, 245–51.
11. Chaunu, *Séville et l'Atlantique*, VIII, Pt. 1, 161–95.
12. Carlo M. Cipolla, *Guns, Sails and Empires: Technological Innovation and the Early Phases of European Expansion, 1400–1700* (New York, 1965), 28–35, 81–89.
13. Michael Lewis, *Armada Guns* (London, 1961), 193–99.
14. Two criteria were used to determine periodizations. For the period before the development of undeclared war in the Americas, 1535-1563, the return to zero costs or nearly zero costs is the most appropriate determination of periods because it reflects the way contemporaries thought about wars and their accompanying costs. Once war in the Caribbean became a permanent fact of life, defense spending also became a permanent fact. Under these conditions, the "return to zero" test for a periodization point makes no sense. Instead, the reaching of a new high in spending seems more important. No attempt was made to correlate the fluctuations in defense spending (dependent variable) and corsair activity (independent variable). It is obvious that there was a general relationship between the two, but so many other factors entered into the determination of defense spending besides the simple numbers of corsair attacks that the measure of unexplained variance in a multiple regression equation would be very large in the absence of more factors. The graphic display of the two series was thought adequate for the purpose at hand.
15. The date of receipt of a royal order or of an agreement by the officers of the Indies Fleet to begin fitting out for a particular cruise was used to determine when costs for that cruise began to occur. Once a cruise was ended or the fleet had begun to be put to another use, as determined by an officers' agreement or some other record, costs were allocated either to "general purpose" or to the next cruise, if its preparations began immediately upon the return of the fleet to port.

Chapter II

1. Paul E. Hoffman, "Diplomacy and the Papal Donation," *The Americas*, XXX (1973), 157–59; Antoine Perrenot de Granvelle, *Papiers d'état du cardinal de Granvelle, d'après les manuscrits de la bibliothèque de Besançon*, ed. Ch. Weiss (9 vols.; Paris, 1841–52), II, 404.
2. Archivo General de Indias (hereafter AGI), Indiferente General 1962, bk 4, fols. 60vto–62vto; Casa de Contratación to Crown, February 12, 1537, AGI, Indiferente General 1092; AGI, Patronato 194, No. 1, R. 39, doc. 2. The gloom in Seville in 1537 was due to the fact that corsairs captured eighteen ships, or 26 percent of those recorded as entering and leaving Seville for the Indies in that year. Chaunu, *Séville et l'Atlantique*, II, 278–85.
3. Figures for Spanish losses of ships to corsairs given in this book are considerably higher than those given by the Chaunus in their tables 624, 625, 628, 629, 632, 652–67. Chaunu, *Séville et l'Atlantique*, VI, 900–903, 909, 911, 917, 919, 958–73.
4. AGI, Santo Domingo 10, R. 1, No. 18.
5. AGI, Panamá 30, R. 1, No. 2; AGI, Panamá 39, R. 1, No. 14.
6. *Colección de documentos inéditos relativos al desubrimiento, conquista, y organización de las antiguas posesiones españoles de ultramar*, ed. Joaquín F. Pacheco, Francisco de Cardenas, Luís Torres de Mendoza (25 vols.; Madrid, 1885–1932), IX, 143–49 (hereafter *DIU*); AGI, Indiferente General 420, bk 9, fol. 17; Fernández Duro, *Armada Española*, I, 202–204; Herrera, *Historia general*, VII, 480. Santo Domingo was designated as the assembly point in 1526 because the route through the new Bahama Channel was not approved until 1541. Irene A. Wright, *Historia documentada de San Cristóbal de la Habana en el siglo XVI* (2 vols.; Havana, 1927), I, 14.
7. Luís Fernández de Álfaro to Crown, Seville, February 17, March 2, 12, 20, 1535, AGI, Indiferente General 1092.
8. AGI, Indiferente General 1962, bk 4, fols. 60vto–88, 107, 147–65, 183–84, *passim*,

NOTES TO PAGES 29–34 273

and bk 5, fols. 68, 135vto–139, 146; Chaunu, *Séville et l'Atlantique*, II, 268, note 1, which has details of the Perea voyage wrong; Lic. Carvajal to Crown, August 18, 1536, AGI, Indiferente General 1092; Pedro de Girón, *Crónica del Emperador Carlos V*, ed. Juan Sánchez Montes (Madrid, 1963), 70, gives a figure of 150,000 ducats for the loss; Fernández Duro, *Armada Española*, I, 426.

9. AGI, Indiferente General 1962, bk 5, fols. 304vto–313vto, 328vto–330vto.

10. Documentation for the Núñez Vela fleet is voluminous. See AGI, Indiferente General 1962, bk 5; AGI, Indiferente General 1092; and the Casa's treasury records for 1537–38. See also *Colección de documentos inéditos relativos al descubrimiento, conquista, y organización de las antiguas posesiones españoles de América y Océania, sacados de los archivos del reino, y muy especialmente del de Indias*, ed. Joaquín F. Pacheco, Francisco de Cardenas, Luís Torres de Mendoza (42 vols.; Madrid, 1864–84), XXXXII, 147–51 (hereafter *DII*); AGI, Santo Domingo 74, R. 1, No. 40; AGI, Contaduría 1051, No. 1 (a), fol. 230; AGI, Patronato 194, No. 1, R. 42; Haring, *Trade and Navigation*, 170. Chaunu, *Séville et l'Atlantique*, II, 280–81, Addenda to Table 1537A, and note 1, p. 280, estimates the tonnage. Treasury records show it was 2133 *toneladas*.

11. For details except those concerning the Núñez Vela fleet, see AGI, Indiferente General 1962, bk 5, fols. 287vto–288, 301vto–302, 329vto–331vto, and bk 6, fols. 1vto–2vto, 8–9vto, 33, 35vto–36.

12. AGI, Patronato 258, "Núñez Vela," R. 2, doc. 2; also in *DII*, XXXII, 47, 52–53.

13. AGI, Indiferente General 1962, bk 5, fols. 198vto–201vto, and AGI, Indiferente General 1963, bk 6, fols. 1–2vto; AGI, Indiferente General 1963, bk 7, fols. 109–10; Fernández Duro, *Armada Española*, I, 427–28; Hoffman, "Diplomacy and the Papal Donation," 160–62.

14. AGI, Indiferente General 1963, bk 7, 195vto–197; Opinion (*consulta*) of Council of Indies, n.d. [March 1541], AGI, Patronato 267, No. 13, in Henri P. Biggar (comp.), *A Collection of Documents Relating to Jacques Cartier and the Sieur de Roberval* (Ottawa, 1930), 244–53. For the preparations of the squadron, see AGI, Indiferente General 1963, bks 7 and 8; AGI, Contratación 5010; and AGI, Contratación 4677, bk C, signature IV, fols. 9, 15–16, 17–17vto, 21vto–22vto, signature V, fols. 22vto–23, and signature VI, fols. 5–10vto.

15. Crown to Casa, August 30, 1542, AGI, Contratación 5010; AGI, Indiferente General 1963, bk 8, fols. 160vto–168, *passim*.

16. Casa to Crown, November 30, December 12, 1542, AGI, Indiferente General 1093; Chaunu, *Séville et l'Atlantique*, II, 339; AGI, Indiferente General 1963, bk 8, fols. 153–54, 166vto–171, 182–83; AGI, Patronato 251, No. 1, R. 43, doc. 1.

17. AGI, Patronato 251, No. 1, R. 43, doc. 1.

18. AGI, Indiferente General 1963, bk 8, fols. 182–83; AGI, Patronato 258, "Ríos, Martín de los," R. 1; Fernández Duro, *Armada Española*, I, 430; Chaunu, *Séville et l'Atlantique*, II, 353.

19. AGI, Patronato 251, No. 1, R. 43, doc. 3; AGI, Indiferente General 1963, bk 8, fols. 189, 207–210vto.

20. AGI, Indiferente General 1963, bk 8, fols. 275–277vto; Fernández Duro, *Armada Española*, I, 430–31; Haring, *Trade and Navigation*, 201–202.

21. Ernesto Schäfer, *El consejo real y supremo de las Indias: su historia, organización, y labor administrativa hasta la terminación de la casa de Austria* (2 vols.; Seville, 1935–47), I, 90, note 1; Fernández Duro, *Armada Española*, I, 430. The administrative motive seems to have far outweighed any other. Thus Robert S. Smith's comment that the founding of the Consulado was a *quid pro quo* caused by the "increasing dependence" of the crown on the merchants for defense seems only partially correct. Robert S. Smith, *The Spanish Guild Merchant: A History of the Consulado, 1250–1700* (Durham, N.C., 1940), 91.

22. AGI, Patronato 251, No. 1, R. 43, doc. 2; AGI, Indiferente General 1963, bk 9, fols. 5vto–6, and bk 8, fols. 286vto–287vto.

23. AGI, Indiferente General 1963, bk 9, fols. 1–2; *DIU*, XIV, 231; Schäfer, *El consejo real*, II, 368; Fernández Duro, *Armada Española*, I, 431; AGI, Santo Domingo 868, bk 2, fols. 206vto–207.

24. AGI, Indiferente General 1963, bk 9, fols. 54vto, 63–63vto, 112–115vto; Francisco

Tello to Prince, April 24, 1544, and Casa to Prince, August 30, 1544, AGI, Indiferente General 1093.

25. AGI, Indiferente General 1963, bk 9, fols. 63-63vto, 80vto; AGI Santo Domingo 868, bk 2, fols. 215vto-216; *DIU*, XIV, 231; Schäfer, *El consejo real*, II, 368. No narrative of this voyage has been found.

26. Duarte to Crown, September 15, 1544, and Casa to Crown, September 19, 1544, AGI, Indiferente General 1093; AGI, Indiferente General 1963, bk 9, fols. 124-125vto, 133vto-134, 150vto; Ship list in AGI, Contratación 4792.

27. AGI, Indiferente General 1963, bk 9, fols. 325-327vto; AGI, Indiferente General 1964, bk 1, fols. 56-56vto, 86, 105, 125-26.

28. AGI, Indiferente General 1964, bk 1, fols. 86, 125vto-126, 138-138vto.

29. AGI, Indiferente General 1964, bk 1, fols. 155vto-157, 182vto-184, 201vto-202, 224vto-230, 299vto-301.

30. AGI, Indiferente General 1964, bk 1, fols. 183vto-88vto, 195-96.

31. AGI, Indiferente General 1964, bk 1, fols. 339vto-340.

32. Saturnino Ullivarri, *Piratas y corsarios de Cuba: Ensayo histórico* (Havana, 1931), 36-39; AGI, Patronato 194, No. 1, R. 39, doc. 3; *DIU*, IV, 440.

33. AGI, Santo Domingo 77, R. 4, No. 104. The Windward Passage was still an important route from the Main to Spain. Ullivarri, *Piratas y corsarios de Cuba*, 45-46. The tax apparently ended after de Soto built the fort to protect the town and its anchorage.

34. Fernández Duro, *Armada Española*, I, 427-28; *DII*, I, 581; AGI, Santo Domingo 868, bk 2, fols. 71vto-75vto; AGI, Santo Domingo 74, R. 1, No. 54; AGI, Contaduría 1051, No. 1 (c), fol. 34, and No. 2, fol. 8vto.

35. Fernández Duro, *Armada Española*, I, 430; AGI, Santo Domingo 182, R. 3, No. 62; AGI, Panamá 30, R. 1, No. 2; AGI, Contaduría 1562, fols. 322vto-323.

36. AGI, Santo Domingo 74, R. 2, No. 16.

37. Juan de Solorzano y Pereyra, *Política Indiana* (5 vols.; 1647; reprint ed., Madrid and Buenos Aires, 1930), II, 288-89. For a complaint of *encomenderos* who found militia service taxing, see Cabildo to Crown, Cartagena, n.d. [post-1553], AGI, Sante Fe 187, bk 1, fols. 100vto-101. Dr. Antonio Gonçalez to Crown, March 18, 1571, AGI, Guatemala 9, notes that the *encomenderos* kept arms but that the other residents of the Spanish towns could not be armed.

38. Esteban de Pasamonte to Crown, Santo Domingo, November 3, 1528, *DII*, XXX, 398-417. Herrera, *Historia general*, VIII, 407, incorrectly dates this event as 1529.

39. AGI, Santo Domingo 868, bk 1, fols. 275vto-77vto, printed in *DIU*, X, 527-28, and Diego de Encinas, *Cedulario Indiano* (4 vols.; 1596; facsimile ed., Madrid, 1945-46), IV, 38; AGI, Indiferente General 1963, bk 8, fols. 196vto-197. Alfonso García Gallo, "El servicio militar en Indias," *Anuario de historia de derecho español*, XXVI (1956), 501, claims that the first orders establishing militias date from 1562. He apparently overlooked Encinas.

40. For examples, see AGI, Panamá 236, bk 9, fol. 123; AGI, Santa Fe 987, bk 3, fol. 92vto; AGI, Santo Domingo 899, bk 1, fols. 63-63vto; AGI, Santa Fe 187, bk 1, fol. 157; Town Council to Crown, Nombre de Dios, August 2, 1561, AGI, Panamá 39; AGI, Santo Domingo 899, bk 1, fols. 252vto-253 (the order to which García Gallo refers in "El servicio militar en Indias," 501); AGI, Santo Domingo 168, R. 4, No. 175.

41. Havana, Ayuntamiento, *Actas capitulares del Ayuntamiento de la Habana* (3 vols. in 5; Havana, 1937-40), I, pt. 2, pp. 9, 25, 46-47, 88, 134, 197-98, II, 197-98, and III, 12; AGI, Santo Domingo 168, R. 2, No. 58; "Percivimientos de guerra ...," Puerto Rico, June 5, 1557, AGI, Indiferente General 2661; AGI, Patronato 267, No. 1, R. 34, doc. 4; AGI, Santo Domingo 71, bk 2, fols. 431-432vto; AGI, Santo Domingo 73, R. 2, No. 59a; Cabildo to Crown, Veragua, April 13, 1575, AGI, Panamá 32.

42. Juan López de Velasco, *Geografía y descripción universal de las Indias* (1574; reprint ed., Madrid, 1894), *passim*.

43. Havana, Ayuntamiento, *Actas*, I, pt. 2, 78-79.

44. "Percivimientos de Guerra," Puerto Rico, June 5, 1557, AGI, Indiferente General 2661; AGI, Patronato 267, No. 1, R. 34, doc. 4; AGI, Patronato 270, No. 1, R. 2; AGI, Santo Domingo 51, R. 1, No. 83.
45. Fernández Duro, *Armada Española*, I, 436; AGI, Santo Domingo 79, R. 2, No. 19.
46. Solorzano, *Política Indiana*, V, 26, commenting on laws in Encinas, *Cedulario Indiano*, IV, 33–36; AGI, Indiferente General 739, R. 7, No. 330. For the Santo Domingo contracts, see AGI, Santo Domingo 868, bk 1, fol. 52; and AGI, Santo Domingo 899, bk 1, fols. 307–307vto. For the contract for Panamá, see AGI, Panamá 235, bk 6, fol. 191. For the contract for Peru, see AGI, Panamá 236, bk 9, fol. 102.
47. In 1539 the king ordered the Casa to send weapons to Santiago de Cuba for the militia to use against the Indians. As of 1542, they had not arrived; it was 1557 before the governor, during a tour of inspection, gave the militia some firearms. AGI, Santo Domingo 1121, bk 2, fols. 130vto–131; King to Casa, April 4, 1542, AGI, Contratación 5010.
48. AGI, Santo Domingo 166, R. 1, No. 48.
49. At Santiago, the militia had 50 matchlocks, 100 pikes, and a few *versos*. AGI, Santo Domingo 115, fol. 31. Puerto Rico had 44 matchlocks, 17–18 men with sword and shield, 7 men with crossbows, and 31 men with pikes. Thirty-six of 46 horsemen were armed with lances, the other 10 with swords and daggers. "Percivimientos de Guerra," June 5, 1557, AGI, Indiferente General 2661.
50. Havana, Ayuntamiento, *Actas*, I, Pt. 2, pp. 25, 46–47, 88–89, 134–35, 197–98.
51. AGI, Contaduría 1051, No. 5, fol. 75vto; Luís de Guzmán to Crown, Panamá, Aug. 30, 1563, AGI, Panamá 29. These watchmen are not to be confused with the "sea guards" hired by the treasury in most ports to prevent nocturnal smuggling.
52. AGI, Patronato 258, "Núñez Vela," R. 1, doc. 3. The use of temporary armies was a feature of European warfare at this time. Ramón Carande Thovar, *Carlos V y sus banqueros* (3 vols.; Madrid, 1959–67), I, 19–20.
53. AGI, Patronato 267, No. 1, R. 13, doc. 5.
54. AGI, Santo Domingo 155, R. 1, No. 4; AGI, Patronato 174, No. 1, R. 36, doc. 1 (March 30, 1528); AGI, Santo Domingo 164, R. 1, No. 7; AGI, Santo Domingo 2280, bk 1, fols. 169–169vto. For a popular history of the forts of San Juan, see Albert Manucy and Ricardo Torres-Reyes, *Puerto Rico and the Forts of Old San Juan* (Riverside, Conn., 1973), 29–36.
55. *DII*, I, 505–506, 509–21.
56. Mendoza's instruction is in *DII*, XXIII, 438–44.
57. For Cumaná see AGI, Santo Domingo 1121, bk 3, fols. 19vto–21; and AGI, Santo Domingo 180, R. 4, No. 154. For Margarita see AGI, Santo Domingo 182, R. 3, No. 57. For Cubagua see AGI, Santo Domingo 182, R. 3, No. 56. For Santo Domingo see AGI, Contaduría 1050, No. 4, fols. 21–22vto.
58. For Nombre de Dios see AGI, Patronato 194, No. 1, Rs. 39, 41, 44; and Fernández Duro, *Armada Española*, I, 426. For Santo Domingo see *DII*, I, 506–13; and AGI, Santo Domingo 77, R. 4, No. 102.
59. For Nombre de Dios see AGI, Panamá 235, bk 6, fols. 117vto–118, 190vto, 194vto–195. For Havana see AGI, Santo Domingo 1121, bk 2, fol. 112. For Cartagena see AGI, Santa Fe 987, bk 2, fols. 32–32vto, 37.
60. For Santiago de Cuba see AGI, Santo Domingo 10, R. 1, No. 24; and AGI, Santo Domingo 116, R. 1, No. 26. For Puerto Rico see AGI, Santo Domingo 164, R. 1, No. 16; AGI, Santo Domingo 868, bk 1, fols. 139vto–140; AGI, Santo Domingo 2280, bk 2, fol. 144vto; and AGI Contaduría 1073, No. 1, No. 5, B, fols. 54vto–55. For Santo Domingo see AGI, Contaduría 1051, No. 1, A, fol. 251.
61. *DIU*, VI, 73–74; AGI, Santo Domingo 1121, bk 2, fols. 125–27; AGI, Santo Domingo 74, R. 1, No. 52.
62. AGI, Indiferente General, bk 6, fols. 27vto–28, 53; AGI, Santo Domingo 1121, bk 2, fol. 113vto; AGI, Santo Domingo 118, R. 1, No. 71; AGI, Santo Domingo 74, R. 1, No. 52. Description of 1545 in Irene A. Wright, *The Early History of Cuba, 1492–1586* (New York,

1916), 222. See also Wright, *Historia documentada de San Cristóbal de la Habana*, I, 184.
  63. AGI, Santa Fe 80, R. 1, No. 10.
  64. AGI, Patronato 258, "Núñez Vela," R. 1, doc. 3.
  65. For Cartagena see AGI, Santa Fe 987, bk 2, fol. 76-76vto; for Panamá see AGI, Panamá 235, bk 7, fols. 42vto-44. Samano to ?, n.d., in Buckingham Smith (ed.), *Colección de varios documentos para la historia de la Florida y tierras adyacentes* (London, 1857), 106. Vaca de Castro wrote the crown that another man whom "the bishop was bringing with him" had drowned in a shipwreck. He could find no masons or stonecutters on the Isthmus. AGI, Patronato 194, No. 1, R. 62. See also AGI, Patronato 267, No. 1, R. 13, doc. 5.
  66. For Española see AGI, Santo Domingo 868, bk 1, fols. 273vto-274, and bk 2, fols. 7-7vto, 28-29; and AGI, Santo Domingo 73, R. 1, No. 34. For Cartagena see AGI, Santa Fe 987, bk 2, fol. 130. For Santa Marta see AGI, Santa Fe 1174, bk 2, fols. 205vto-206. For orders to the Casa see AGI, Santo Domingo 868, bk 3, fols. 27vto-28. For orders to Vaca de Castro see AGI, Panamá 235, bk 7, fols. 172vto-173.
  67. AGI, Santo Domingo 868, bk 2, fols. 62-66vto.
  68. For Cartagena see Marco Dorta, *Cartagena de Indias*, 38; AGI, Santa Fe 80, R. 1, No. 15; and AGI, Santa Fe 70, No. 1, R. 1, No. 6. Regarding the forts at Puerto Plata, Azua, and La Yaguana, see AGI, Santo Domingo 74, R. 1, No. 53; AGI, Santo Domingo 73, R. 1, No. 34; and AGI, Santo Domingo 868, bk 2, fols. 132vto-133vto.
  69. AGI, Patronato 267, No. 1, R. 13; doc. 5; Town Council to Crown, Nombre de Dios, March 6, 1544, AGI, Panamá 32; AGI, Panamá 39, R. 1, No. 8; AGI, Panamá 235, bk 8, fols. 116-116vto, 201.
  70. AGI, Santo Domingo 166, R. 1, Nos. 40, 47; AGI, Santo Domingo 164, R. 1, No. 26; AGI, Santo Domingo 10, R. 2, No. 56; AGI, Patronato 175, R. 30.
  71. Wright, *Historia documentada de San Cristóbal de la Habana*, I, 186; *DIU*, III, 248.
  72. AGI, Contaduría 876, No. 2; Fernández Duro, *Armada Española*, I, 433.
  73. AGI, Santo Domingo 166, R. 1, No. 48; AGI, Contaduría 1073, No. 1, No. 5B, fols. 81-90, *passim*.
  74. AGI, Santo Domingo 868, bk 1, fol. 140vto; AGI, Santo Domingo 74, R. 1, No. 53.
  75. AGI, Santo Domingo 73, R. 1, No. 28; AGI, Santo Domingo 868, bk 2, fols. 132vto-133vto; "Una carta inédita de Gonçalo Fernández de Oviedo," ed. Enrique Otte, *Revista de Indias*, XVI, No. 65 (July-September 1956), 442-43.
  76. AGI, Contaduría 1051, No. 1A, fols. 376-77; AGI, Santo Domingo 868, bk 2, fols. 350vto-51.
  77. For Santo Domingo see AGI, Santo Domingo 72, R. 1, No. 13; *DII*, I, 44; and AGI, Contratación 4676, *Data*, Section E, fols. 206vto-207. For Puerto Rico see AGI, Santo Domingo 164, R. 1, No. 10, fol. 6, paragraph 23; AGI, Santo Domingo 2280, bk 2, fols. 59-59vto; and AGI, Contratación 4676, *Data*, fol. 205vto.
  78. AGI, Santo Domingo 1121, bk 3, fols. 47-47vto; AGI, Santo Domingo 183, R. 4, No. 139; AGI, Santo Domingo 182, R. 3, No. 57; Casa to Crown, November 29, 1535, AGI, Indiferente General 1092; AGI, Contratación 4676, *Data*, fols. 206-206vto.
  79. AGI, Santo Domingo 74, R. 1, No. 38; AGI, Indiferente General 1962, bk 5, fol. 76vto; AGI, Contratación 4676, *Data*, fol. 213vto. For the salvage, see Lorenzo García to Casa, Cadiz, July 1, 1537, and following dates, in AGI, Contratación 5103.
  80. Account of the *Serafín*, AGI, Contaduría 552, No. 5; AGI, Indiferente General 1962, bk 6, fols. 143-143vto; AGI, Santo Domingo 1121, bk 3, fols. 108vto-109.
  81. AGI, Santo Domingo 73, R. 1, No. 38; AGI, Santo Domingo 71, bk 1, fol. 24.
  82. For Nombre de Dios see AGI, Patronato 194, No. 1, R. 39. For Santiago de Cuba see *DIU*, VI, 73-74; and AGI, Santo Domingo 1121, bk 2, fols. 124-27, 128-31. For Santa Marta see AGI, Santa Fe 66, R. 1, No. 9; and AGI, Santa Fe 1174, bk 2, fol. 218. For Cabo de la Vela see AGI, Panamá 39, R. 1, No. 14; and King to Audiencia of Lima, August 9, 1550, AGI, Santo Domingo 1121, bk 3, unnumbered.
  83. Wright, *Historia documentada de San Cristóbal de la Habana*, I, 18, 186; and *DIU*, VI, 181, and III, 248. For purchase details, see AGI, Contaduría 274, No. 1, fols. 492-93;

and AGI, Contaduría 275, No. 1, fols. 166-71. The original bill was drawn against Tierra Firme, but the officials there refused to pay it in 1547 and again in early 1548 on the grounds that they had no funds.

84. AGI, Panamá 39, R. 1, No. 8; and AGI, Santo Domingo 99, R. 1, No. 25.

85. AGI, Indiferente General 1962, bk 6, fol. 143-143vto; AGI, Santo Domingo 2280, bk 2, fols. 158-158vto; AGI, Santo Domingo 166, R. 1, Nos. 40, 47, 48, 51; AGI, Santo Domingo 168, R. 1, No. 45; AGI, Contaduría 1073, No. 1, and No. 5B, fols. 81-83. List of Artillery in the Atarazanas of Seville, n.d. [ca. 1541], AGI, Patronato 173, R. 10, doc. 1.

86. In 1537 the Casa complained that it could not get together the powder ordered for Santo Domingo because Seville manufacturers lacked saltpeter. It recommended that powder be brought from Málaga, as it eventually was. Casa to Crown, February 25, 1537, AGI, Indiferente General 1092. Powder being prepared with considerable difficulty in 1541 was taken for the los Ríos fleet. AGI, Indiferente General 1963, bk 8, fols. 83-84; and AGI, Contratación 4677, *Data* (Section C), IV, fol. 9, entry for October 31, 1541.

87. See AGI, Contratación 5010, for correspondence about the guns cast in Málaga. AGI, Contaduría 291, No. 7, and AGI, Contaduría 292, contain lists of the Casa's gun holdings during this period. Regarding the guns made with Cuban copper, see AGI, Indiferente General 1964, bk 1, fol. 5, and AGI, Contaduría 275, No. 1, *Data*, fol. 141vto.

Chapter III

1. Text in Jean Dumont (ed.), *Corps universal diplomatique du droit des gens* . . . (8 vols.; Amsterdam, 1726-31), IV, pt. 2, pp. 280, 281.

2. Hoffman, "Diplomacy and the Papal Donation," 160-65.

3. Charles G. M. B. de la Roncière, *Histoire de la marine française* (6 vols.; Paris, 1899-1932), III, 303-305.

4. AGI, Patronato 267, No. 1, R. 24; and AGI, Santo Domingo 49, R. 3, No. 137.

5. AGI, Santo Domingo 49, R. 3, No. 129; Fernández Duro, *Armada Española*, I, 438-39; AGI, Santo Domingo 49, R. 3, No. 129; and Santo Domingo 71, bk 2, fols. 28-30vto. Writing from Cartagena in 1553, Pedro de Heredía reported a French *patache* operating in the Windward Passage and another, with only forty men as crew, off Cartagena. He went on to comment that "it is a great shame that a row boat [*patache*] like this, with such a despicable [*ruín*] crew, should dare to sail from France and come to these Indies and return loaded with gold and silver from what has been stolen." AGI, Santa Fe 187, bk 1, fol. 61. Chaunu, *Séville et l'Atlantique*, II, 450, calls this combination "le couple traditionnal de l'époque."

6. AGI, Panamá 29, R. 3, No. 182; AGI, Santo Domingo 49, R. 3, No. 150; and AGI, Santo Domingo 71, bk 2, fols. 28-30vto.

7. For a discussion of the type and its historical evolution, see Auguste Jal, *Archéologie Navale* (2 vols.; Paris, 1840), I, 452-53; AGI, Santo Domingo 71, bk 2, fols. 28-30vto.

8. AGI, Indiferente General 1964, bk 2, fols. 2vto-3; AGI, Santo Domingo 49, R. 3, No. 122; and AGI, Santo Domingo 77, R. 5, No. 132.

9. The currency manipulation is discussed in Appendix I. See Cipriano de Utrera, *La moneda provincial de la isla Española, Documentos* (Ciudad Trujillo, 1951), *passim*.

10. Chaunu, *Séville et l'Atlantique*, II, 512.

11. AGI, Santo Domingo 899, bk 1, fol. 127.

12. By law only 10,000 ducats could be shipped on any merchant ship, an apparent attempt to reduce losses due to shipwreck and capture by corsairs. Chaunu's incomplete figures show identified returns from New Spain as 1 ship for 1545, 6 of 65 in 1546, 8 of 75 in 1547, although some of the unidentified ports of origin of the returning ships may have been in New Spain. Chaunu, *Séville et l'Atlantique*, II, 382-85, 394-99, 406-11; Cobos to Casa, June 12 and June 28, 1548, AGI, Contratación 5010.

13. AGI, Indiferente General 1964, bk 2, fols. 4vto-5, 12vto-13, 68vto-70, 81-82, 108vto, 132-33, Crown to Casa, January 18, February 7, 18, 22, June 8, August 2, 1549, in AGI, Contratación 5010; and "Inquiry," Villanueva de Portimão, December 2, 1548, AGI, In-

diferente General 1208. For the refitting, see AGI, Contaduría 275, No. 1, fols. 299vto–300.

14. Fernández Duro, *Armada Española*, I, 438; Crown to Casa, March 30, 1549, AGI, Contratación 5010; *Maximiliano de Austria, governador de Carlos V en España: Cartas al Emperador*, ed. Rafaela Rodríguez Raso (Madrid, 1963), 129–30, cited hereafter as *Maximiliano ... Cartas al Emperador*.

15. Crown to Casa, June 27, August 2, 1549, AGI, Contratación 5010; Crown to Casa, October 16, 1549, AGI, Indiferente General 1093; AGI, Contaduría 275, No. 2, fols. 206–209vto.

16. Fernández Duro, *Armada Española*, I, 439, Wright, *Early History of Cuba*, 259–60, asserts that the squadron was sent because the crown was concerned about illegal trade. The evidence of Roelas' letter, just cited, and his course suggest that this was not the case. Illegal trade had only just begun to involve Frenchmen; the crown did not as yet know much about the trade of the Portuguese.

17. Wright, *Historia documentada de San Cristóbal de la Habana*, I, 22, and document 3, p. 188; Crown to Casa, May 1550, AGI, Contratación 5010.

18. *Maximiliano ... Cartas al Emperador*, 148–49, 157, 159–60, 180–81; and Fernández Duro, *Armada Española*, I, 440. The contract with Bazán, February 14, 1550, is in *Colección de documentos inéditos para la historia de España*, ed. Martín Fernández de Navarette, et al. (113 vols.; Madrid, 1842–95), L, 265.

19. Crown to Casa, January 24, March 29, May 22, June 10, 1550, AGI, Contratación 5010.

20. *Maximiliano ... Cartas al Emperador*, 191–201, 239–40, and Fernández Duro, *Armada Española*, I, 440–41.

21. Prince to Casa, Nava de Roa, August 29, 1551, AGI, Contratación 5010, reports that 120,000 *pesos de oro* had been brought back under the restriction that only 10,000 pesos could be carried in each ship. Some 335,000 pesos remained. For the La Gasca squadron, see AGI, Contaduría 1452, "1544–1549," X:20vto; and AGI, Contaduría 1453, "1549–1552," fol. 96. For plans to arm ships, see Crown to Casa, June 26, July 10, August 29, December 25, 1551, March 2, 1555, in AGI, Contratación 5010; and AGI, Contaduría 275, No. 2, fols. 240vto, 256, 272–73, 287, 291vto–292. The total cost, exclusive of freight charges, was 516 ducats.

22. Prince to Casa, February 16, 20, March 2, July 11, 1552, AGI, Contratación 5010; and AGI, Contratación 4678, *Data*, bk E, fols. 195vto–196vto.

23. Prince to Casa, February 13, 1552, AGI, Contratación 5010; Encinas *Cedulario Indiano*, IV, 127–30.

24. AGI, Santo Domingo 39, R. 3, Nos. 126, 127, 129, 131; AGI, Santa Fe 80, R. 1, No. 25, paragraph 13 (which also mentions the possibility of a patrol on the Main); AGI, Patronato 267, No. 1, R. 24; and AGI, Santo Domingo 71, bk 1, fol. 10vto.

25. Prince to Casa, March 1, April 5, May 1, 1552, and Council of Indies to Casa, August 17, 1552, AGI, Contratación 5010, and AGI, Patronato 197, R. 26; Chaunu, *Séville et l'Atlantique*, II, 488.

26. Prince to Casa, July 11, 1552, and Council of Indies to Casa, August 17, 1552, AGI, Contratación 5010. The Council of the Indies wanted the squadron increased by two ships, apparently at the expense of the *avería*, but the project never got beyond the talking stage. The reason for the suggested increase was the report of additional French ships sailing for the Azores.

27. AGI, Santo Domingo 71, bk 2, fols. 3–3vto, 9vto–10, 22–22vto; and Prince to Casa, March 2, 1552, AGI, Contratación 5010.

28. AGI, Santo Domingo 71, bk 1, fols. 28–34vto; and AGI, Santo Domingo 49, R. 3, No. 145.

29. AGI, Santo Domingo 71, bk 1, fols. 30–31.

30. Fernández Duro, *Armada Española*, I, 443.

31. Prince to Casa, March 11, May 31, July 29, 1554, and Princess to Casa, December 9, 1554, AGI, Contratación 5010.

32. Prince to Casa, August 24, October 24, November 9, December 26, 1553, AGI, Contratación 5010; and Fernández Duro, *Armada Española*, I, 445–46.
33. AGI, Santo Domingo 49, R. 3, No. 148; AGI, Santo Domingo 73, R. 1, No. 49; Prince to Casa, January 19, 1554, AGI, Contratación 5010.
34. The memorial from the officials at Santo Domingo has escaped my investigations to the date of this writing, but its content is partially revealed by the "memorials" that Pedro Menéndez submitted to the crown, probably at Valladolid in February 1554, found in AGI, Santo Domingo 71, bk 1, fols. 290–94, with supporting letters in fols. 44–44vto and 46–47; AGI, Santa Fe 187, bk 1, fols. 60vto–61; AGI, Santa Fe 80, R. 1, No. 25; and Fernández Duro, *Armada Española*, I, 443.
35. Chaunu, *Séville et l'Atlantique*, II, 510; Prince to Casa, April 9, 1554, and Princess to Casa, August 9, 15, September 9, 1554, AGI, Contratación 5010. The *avería* issue involved costs. If the Consulado's plan had been approved, the crown would have paid more *avería* on its funds than if the costs were figured separately, because it would have paid for the outbound as well as the inbound cost of the convoy.
36. Princess to Casa, September 9, 1554, AGI, Contratación 5010.
37. One caravel was bought at Santo Domingo, the other built at Puerto Rico. AGI, Santo Domingo 49, R. 3, No. 158; AGI, Contaduría 1051, No. 5, fols. 78vto–81vto; AGI, Santo Domingo 78, R. 1, No. 12b; AGI, Santo Domingo 166, R. 2, No. 62; and AGI Santo Domingo 155, R. 1, No. 12.
38. Princess to Casa, December 1, 1554, AGI, Contratación 5010; and Fernández Duro, *Armada Española*, I, 449.
39. Princess to Casa, February 18, 1555, AGI, Contratación 5010.
40. Princess to Casa, March 16, April 5, 1555, AGI, Contratación 5010. It must be said in the Casa's defense that it had its hands full trying to get the convoy dispatched, sending supplies to Carvajal's and Bazán's squadrons, and trying to get its books for the 1548–1550 coastal patrols audited.
41. Princess to Casa, August 2, September 29, 1555, February 18, 26, April 30, July 29, 1556, in AGI, Contratación 5010; Chaunu, *Séville et l'Atlantique*, II, 524, 536–37; and accounts of the Casa.
42. Princess to the Casa, April 30, 1556, AGI, Contratación 5010, stating that "during this time [of the truce] it seems good that the trade of the Indies be more frequent than before and that the ships come and go very frequently [*muy a menudo*] and that they not await such large numbers for a group [*flota*] as they did during the war."
43. Princess to Casa, December 4, 1555, February 9, March 5, April 30, May 6, September 21, December 5, 1556, all in AGI, Contratación 5010; AGI, Indiferente General 737, R. 5, No. 149; AGI, Santo Domingo 899, bk 1, fols. 12vto–14; AGI, Contratación 4678, bk E, fols. 412–13; Ship list, October 9, 1557, AGI, Contaduría 1051, No. 5, fols. 128.
44. AGI, Indiferente General 737, R. 5, No. 149; AGI, Patronato 251, No. 1, R. 54; Chaunu, *Séville et l'Atlantique*, II, 537.
45. AGI, Santo Domingo 899, bk 1, fols. 72–86vto.
46. AGI, Santo Domingo 168, R. 2, No. 55.
47. AGI, Santo Domingo 168, R. 2, No. 58. I have not found any narratives of these expeditions. Information on their outfitting is found in AGI, Contaduría 1051, No. 5, fols. 88vto, 90–91vto, 94–96vto.
48. Princess to Casa, November 23, 1557, January 23, April 2, June 6, September 15, November 28, December 9, 1558, all in AGI, Contratación 5010. See also Chaunu, *Séville et l'Atlantique*, II, 552, 565, 568–69. Chaunu says that Bazán sailed to escort the Roelas convoy in February 1558, but this is unlikely and seems to be based on a misreading of one of Fernández Duro's notes in *Armada Española*, II, 462–63.
49. AGI, Santo Domingo 71, bk 1, fols. 94–94vto.
50. AGI, Contaduría 1051, No. 5, fols. 131vto, 138; AGI, Santo Domingo, 166, R. 2, No. 65.
51. AGI, Santo Domingo 71, bk 1, fols. 102–104, 106–107, 112–114vto.

52. AGI, Santo Domingo 71, bk 1, fols. 102–104, 108–108vto; AGI, Santo Domingo 168, R. 2, No. 62.
53. AGI, Santo Domingo 71, bk 1, fols. 112–114vto, and bk 2, fols. 122–123; Princess to Casa, November 23, 1558, AGI, Contratación 5011.
54. AGI, Santo Domingo 899, bk 1, fols. 123vto–127vto.
55. For example, AGI, Santo Domingo 155, R. 1, No. 17; AGI, Santo Domingo 115, fols. 35–38, and AGI, Contaduría 1051, No. 5, fol. 143 and following.
56. AGI, Santa Fe 187, bk 1, fols. 116–116vto.
57. AGI, Contaduría 1051, No. 5, fols. 160–64; AGI, Santo Domingo 899, bk 1, fol. 179; Princess to Casa, February 22, July 9, 1559, and King to Casa, September 17, October 16, December 28, 1559, and March 10, 1561, all in AGI, Contratación 5011.
58. For details see Paul E. Hoffman, "The Defense of the Indies, 1535–1574: A Study in the Modernization of the Spanish State" (Ph.D. dissertation, University of Florida, 1969), 201–205, and Table 5, p. 205.
59. AGI, Justicia 1160, No. 8, R. 1, contains all the relevant documentation.
60. Chaunu, *Séville et l'Atlantique*, VIII, pt. 1, 397–405. For the standard treatments of the operation of the convoy system, see Veitia Linage, *Norte de la contratación de las Indias*; Haring, *Trade and Navigation*; Artiñano y de Galdácano, *Historia del comercio con las Indias*; Chaunu, *Séville et l'Atlantique*; and August A. Thomazi, *Les flottes de l'or: Histoire de galions d'Espagne* (Paris, 1937).
61. AGI, Patronato 267, No. 1, R. 34, doc. 4, fols. 4–26; AGI, Santo Domingo 71, bk 2, fols. 236–39.
62. AGI, Patronato 194, No. 1, R. 91, doc. 1; AGI, Panamá 236, bk 9, fols. 36vto, 197–98; and Sancho de Clavijo to Crown, Panamá, December 12, 1550, and Álvaro de Sousa to Crown, Panamá, August 20, 1555, both in AGI, Panamá 29. The building of the bulwark is outlined in AGI, Contaduría 1452, "1549–1552," V, fols. 3vto–4vto, and again in fols. 105vto–106.
63. AGI, Santo Domingo 1121, bk 3, fols. 223–223vto; AGI, Santa Fe 187, bk 1, fol. 61; AGI, Patronato 197, R. 26; AGI, Santo Domingo 49, R. 3, Nos. 129, 137; and AGI, Santo Domingo 71, bk 2, fols. 3–3vto, 10–11vto, 28–30vto, 78–79.
64. Wright, *Historia documentada de San Cristóbal de la Habana*, I, 22, 188–91. The bailey was 156 feet (*pies*) on a side with a keep 31 feet square and 37 feet high. For other details see AGI, Santo Domingo 115, fols. 13–13vto, 11vto; AGI, Santo Domingo 49, R. 3, No. 150; and Havana, Ayuntamiento, *Actas*, I, pt. 2, pp. 76–79.
65. AGI, Santo Domingo 71, bk 2, fols. 28–30vto.
66. To be exact, 45,689 ducats from a total of 61,010 ducats, or 74.9 percent. For details of the events and sources see Wright, *Historia documentada de San Cristóbal de la Habana*, I, *passim*. Unfortunately, her citations are in the pre-1929 numbers from the AGI.
67. There was an initial shortage in 1552, which was so severe that the crown had to ask the grandees of Andalusia to lend their few remaining pieces. Prince to Casa, March 2, 1552, AGI, Contratación 5010. Guns had been sent from Málaga in 1548. A shipment of 200 pieces from Flanders arrived in 1555, to be followed by German guns from 1557 onwards. Most of these weapons found their ways onto ships in the patrol squadrons or the convoys. See AGI, Contaduría 291, 292, and 301.
68. AGI, Santo Domingo 11, R. 1, No. 7; and AGI, Santo Domingo 164, R. 2, Nos. 40, 42. Princess to Casa, February 9, March 5, 1556, AGI, Contratación 5010.
69. For example, Nombre de Dios. AGI, Panamá 39, R. 1, No. 34.
70. For Puerto Rico see AGI, Santo Domingo 168, R. 1, No. 36, and R. 2, No. 62; and AGI, Santo Domingo 155, R. 1, Nos. 15, 20. For Havana see Wright, *Historia documentada de San Cristóbal de la Habana* I, 190–91; and Havana, Ayuntamiento, *Actas*, I, pt. 2, 29–50, 80. For the Isthmus see City Council to Crown, Panamá, August 2, 1561, AGI, Panamá 39. For Santiago de Cuba see AGI, Santo Domingo 11, R. 2, No. 27. For Santo Domingo see AGI, Santo Domingo 73, R. 1, No. 38; AGI, Santo Domingo 71, bk 1, fol. 24; AGI, Santo Domingo 49, R. 3, No. 155; Princess to Casa, September 5, 1556, AGI, Contratación 5010; and AGI, Santo Domingo 899, bk 1, fols. 232–232vto.

71. This fact is partly explained by the decline in the value of the *peso de cuartos*, the "bad money" (*mala moneda*) coined at Santo Domingo and used to pay the warden and his men. The figures used in this study discount that money to its equivalent in "good" or Castilian money at the going merchant rate. See Appendix I.
72. AGI, Santo Domingo 71, bk 2, fols. 28–30vto, 42–42vto, 46vto; and AGI Contaduría 1051, No. 5, fol. 77.
73. It is not clear when they were discharged. See AGI, Santo Domingo 71, bk 2, fols. 64–64vto, for marginal comments containing the crown's reaction.
74. Wright, *Early History of Cuba*, 235–41; *DII*, XII, 49–82; Fernández Duro, *Armada Española*, I, 211; Havana, Ayuntamiento, *Actas*, I, pt. 2, p. 113; "Pedro Menéndez a Consejo de Indias," April 29, 1556, in *Boletín del Archivo General de la Nación (República Dominicana)*, IV (1941), 147.
75. Examples of such squadrons are the eight ships reported in the fall of 1552 and Jacques Le Clerc's squadrons of the spring and fall of 1554. Fernández Duro, *Armada Española*, I, 443, 446, 448. A group of ten ships was reported off the Capes in August 1557, but it is not clear that they were under single command. Chaunu, *Séville et l'Atlantique*, I, 568. Le Clerc, known to the Spanish as Wooden Foot (*Pie de Palo*), did have one success for his backers: the raid of Las Palmas, Grand Canary Island, in June 1553. Chaunu, *Séville et l'Atlantique*, II, 500–501. For a discussion of Jean de Ango, one of the backers of French corsairs in this period, see Édoward H. Gosselin, *Documents authentiques et inédits pour servir à l'histoire de la marine normande et du commerce rouennais pendant les XVI*e *et XVII*e *siècles* (Rouen, 1876), 21–26. For a discussion of the commercial motives behind some of the English corsairs, see Kenneth R. Andrews, *Drake's Voyages: A Reassessment of Their Place in Elizabethan Maritime Expansion* (New York and London, 1967).
76. One ship was taken at Nombre de Dios in 1552 (Fernández Duro, *Armada Española*, I, 443–49). Five were captured in the Triangle in 1555 (Chaunu, *Séville et l'Atlantique*, I, 524). Two more were captured after the Truce of 1556, again in the Triangle (Princess to Casa, April 30, 1556, AGI, Contratación 5010). Four French were killed off Cuba in April 1552 (Ullivarri, *Piratas y corsarios de Cuba*, 55). Five were killed near La Yaguana in 1550 (AGI, Santo Domingo 49, R. 3, No. 129). Seven Frenchmen were captured near Cartagena in June 1553 (AGI, Santa Fe 187, bk 1, fol. 60vto). Fourteen Frenchmen were captured after a shipwreck on the Andalusian coast in 1555 (Princess to Casa, January 23, 1555, AGI, Contratación 5010). Several were killed at Havana in 1555 (Ullivarri, *Piratas y corsarios de Cuba*, 61–78).
77. Archivo General de Simancas, Guerra Antigua 65, fol. 26; and Chaunu, *Séville et l'Atlantique*, II, 568. Archivo General de Simancas cited hereafter as AGS.
78. Ullivarri, *Piratas y corsarios de Cuba*, 86–87; Lic. Vayllo to Crown, Guatemala, December 20, 1559, AGI, Guatemala 39; AGI, Santa Fe 187, bk 1, fol. 116.
79. Text in Frances G. Davenport (ed.), *European Treaties Bearing on the History of the United States and Its Dependencies* . . . (4 vols.; Washington, D.C., 1917–37), I, 217. Philip was then king of England by virtue of his marriage to Mary Tudor. See also Granvelle, *Papiers d'État*, IV, 541.
80. AGI, Indiferente General 738, R. 3, No. 41; Granvelle, *Papiers d'État*, V, 285–86, 546, 564; and Henry Folmer, *Franco-Spanish Rivalry in North America, 1524–1763* (Glendale, 1953), 68–69.
81. Text in Dumont (ed.), *Corps Universel*, V, pt. 1, 35.
82. Academia de la Historia (Madrid), *Negociaciones con Francia* (11 vols. to 1960; Madrid, 1950–60), III, 217, and VII, 421–23. Philip subsequently tightened the regulations on trade and specifically warned governors in the Indies not to allow the French to trade unless they had licenses from the House of Trade (Casa de Contratación). Encinas, *Cedulario Indiano*, I, 446; and AGI, Santa Fe 987, bk 3, fol. 200.
83. Academia, *Negociaciones con Francia*, I, 37–43.
84. *Ibid.*, I, 39, 44, 49.
85. *Ibid.*, I, 74, 128–29. It should be noted that the Spanish and French were probably not as far apart as these exchanges would suggest. The Spanish apparently believed that

the areas they had explored included North America to 40° North, some point on the northern coast of Brazil, and the Río de la Plata area. *Ibid.*, I, 421–23, lists the explorers of North America as Ponce de León, Narváez, de Soto, Arrellano, Villafaña, Vázquez de Ayllon (II), and Pedro Menéndez de Avilés. The first three gave Spain a general claim to the area south of 40° N, and Menédez de Avilés specifically tried to settle at, or had received orders to settle at, Santa Elena (32° 20′ N). This evidence suggests that the Spanish would have drawn their line somewhere between 37° N—the area of Cape Hatteras—and 40°N—the presumed upper limit of the Chesapeake Bay. Their line would have left a large part of North America to the French but would not have given them all of the coast that Verrazzano had explored for France in 1524 (from below 34° northward). More documentation of the Spanish position in 1559 is needed to settle just where they expected to draw the line.

86. Herbert I. Priestly (ed. and trans.), *The Luna Papers: Documents Relating to the Expedition of Don Tristan de Luna y Arellano for the Conquest of La Florida in 1559–1561* (2 vols.; Deland, Fla., 1928), II, 15, 16. The Luna colonies were the result of lobbying by religious authorities in New Spain who were interested in the Gulf Coast as far east as Mobile. However, Philip's orders of 1557 added Santa Elena, for reasons that are not stated. Priestly attempts to explain this by reference to the order of 1559 but provides no documents from 1557 to support his case. The relationship between this colony and contemporary diplomatic events awaits explanation. *Ibid.*, I, xxiii.

87. Academia, *Negociaciones con Francia*, I, 157–58.

88. *Ibid.*, I, 174–75.

89. Lowery, *Spanish Settlements*, I, 354–80. For details of the failure of the Luna colony, see Priestly (ed. and trans.), *The Luna Papers, passim* and his "Historical Introduction." See also, Academia, *Negociaciones con Francia*, III, 172, 294, and IV, 15. The French claimed that the *Dauphine* under command of Vincent Tiran and Grangean Bucier had found twenty-nine pounds of gold at some point between Cape Florida and Norembega, an Indian town on the Penobscot River in Maine that figures prominently in the lore of North American discovery.

90. AGI, Patronato 170, R. 44, points 1 and 4.

91. Encinas, *Cedulario Indiano*, III, 248–51; AGI, Patronato 170, R. 55.

92. Encinas, *Cedulario Indiano*, III, 337, and 248–51. See also Appendix I.

Chapter IV

1. Lowery, *Spanish Settlements*, II, 44–48; Academia, *Negociaciones con Francia*, V, 51–52, 84. For additional details about this colony, see the testimony of French witnesses in AGI, Justicia 212, No. 6, *pieza* 4, and AGI, Justicia 881, No. 6. The Ribault account is Jean Ribault, *The Whole and True Discoverye of Terra Florida* (1563; reprint ed., Gainesville, Florida, 1964).

2. Hoffman, "Diplomacy and the Papal Donation," 155–56, based largely on Gordon Connell-Smith, *Forerunners of Drake: A Study of English Trade with Spain in the Early Tudor Period* (London and New York, 1954), *passim*, and xiv. See also Connell-Smith's "English Merchants Trading to the New World in the Early Sixteenth Century," London University, Institute of Historical Research, *Bulletin*, XXIII, No. 67 (May 1950), 53–67.

3. James A. Williamson, *Hawkins of Plymouth: A New History of Sir John Hawkins and of the Other Members of His Family Prominent in Tudor England* (London, 1949), 49–55. The case against Pedro de Ponte is in AGI, Justicia 999, No. 2, R. 2.

4. Great Britain, Public Records Office, *Calendar of Letters and State Papers Relating to English Affairs Preserved Principally in the Archives of Simancas, Elizabeth, 1558–1603*, ed. Martin A. S. Hume (4 vols.; 1892–99; reprint ed., Nendeln, 1971), II, 139–40, 168, 178, 194–95, 251, 419–20, 537–38, cited hereafter as PRO, *Calendar*. An agreement, known as the Alva-Cobham Agreement, was reached in December 1575. See Pauline Croft, "Englishmen and the Spanish Inquisition, 1558–1625," *English Historical Review*, LXXXVII, No. 1343 (April 1972), 254–55.

5. Francisco Duarte to Casa, May 31, 1572, AGI, Contratación 5105. Statistics for this

third period of corsair activity (1563–1577) are less satisfactory than for earlier periods. The number and general quality of reports on corsair raids decline and for some areas, particularly the eastern Main, almost cease to exist by 1570. Even where the record is abundant, for example for the western Main in 1568–1574, it is often exasperatingly vague as to specific numbers of corsairs and prizes taken by them. The data in Table 15 are, therefore, only suggestive of the true extent of corsair activity. They do agree with contemporary evaluations of the problem and by that test would seem to be fairly reliable.

6. However, successful raiding was more apt to happen in the Antilles (87 percent successful) than on the Main (ca. 60 percent successful). This is explained by the fact that raids on the Main were generally on towns, whereas those in the Antilles tended to be on ranches and sugar plantations whose residents were less able to defend themselves.

7. Most of the discussion of illegal trade that follows is drawn from Gerónimo de Torres, "Representación," Madrid, May 29, 1577, AGI, Patronato 259, No. 1, R. 67. Torres was a notary and resident of La Yaguana for many years before the date of his statement. Cited hereafter as Torres, "Representación," with pagination.

8. *Ibid.*, 1.

9. AGI, Santo Domingo 115, fols. 147vto–148; and AGI, Santo Domingo 11, R. 3, No. 52; AGI, Santo Domingo 79, R. 2, No. 19; Williamson, *Sir John Hawkins*, 104–109; and Williamson, *Hawkins of Plymouth*, 75–84.

10. Torres, "Representación," 12; Concepción Hernández Tapía, "Despoblación de la isla de Santo Domingo en el XVII," *Anuario de Estudios Americanos*, XXVII (1970), 281–320; Richard H. Boulind, "The Strength and Weakness of Spanish Control of the Caribbean, 1520–1650: The Case for the *Armada de Barlovento*" (Ph.D. dissertation; Clare College, Cambridge University, England, 1965), 735–40.

11. AGI, Justicia 21, No. 2, R. 1; AGI, Justicia 41, No. 3, R. 1; Wright, *Early History of Cuba*, 278–80; and Irene A. Wright, "Rescates, with Special Reference to Cuba, 1599–1610," *Hispanic American Historical Review*, III (1920), 336–37.

12. Torres, "Representación," 7–8; AGI, Santo Domingo 71, bk 2, fols. 483–84.

13. Hussey, "Spanish Reaction to Foreign Aggression in the Caribbean," 286; AGI, Santo Domingo 168, R. 2, No. 81; AGI, Santa Fe 187, bk 2, fols. 169–169vto; King to Audiencia of New Granada [*sic*], January 19, 1576, Biblioteca Nacional (Madrid), MS 3045, Item 144, fols. 350vto–351; Robert Ricard, "Los portugueses en las Indias españolas," *Revista de Historia de América* (Mexico), No. 34 (December, 1952), 449–56.

14. AGI, Santo Domingo 51, R. 1, No. 6; AGI, Santo Domingo 79, R. 2, No. 36, and R. 3, No. 46.

15. AGI, Santo Domingo 71, bk 1, fols. 587–587vto, and bk 2, fols. 484, 514vto–515, 592vto–593, 618–19.

16. It cannot be stressed enough that the development of this illegal trade was the result of a number of factors, most of them connected with the war of 1552–1559 and the peculiar nature of the islands' commerce, which exported items of great bulk but relatively low value. Earlier writers such as Irene A. Wright and Clarence Haring allowed their devotion to classical economics to blind them to the multiple factors producing this trade. Only after commerce raiding, wartime dislocations of trade patterns, business cycles, the dynamics of the international hide and sugar trades, and similar factors had done their work did the monopolistic instincts of the Seville merchants make a bad situation irretrievably worse. It may be that when the full background for the various steps in creating the monopoly are known, we shall see that the monopoly was a rational, if traditional, response to the economic realities of the times.

17. Question 9 and responses to it, Inquiry, Nombre de Dios, May 6, 1569, AGI, Panamá 32, *passim*.

18. The type was patterned after small galleasses in use on the Bay of Biscay since the 1550s. The galleons were fifty-two feet long on the keel, eighteen feet in the beam (a 3 to 1 ratio), had two decks, the first six feet from the keel and the second six feet nine inches above that, and a gunwale of three feet. They were originally race-built with three masts. Artillery and oars were supposed to be worked between decks. The hatches on the lower

part of the hold could be sealed, making the lower section, which was below the waterline, a compartment that would prevent the ship from sinking regardless of the damage it suffered above the waterline. "Relación de Rodrigo de Vargas," n.d. [1577?], AGI, Patronato 260, R. 2, No. 34, which also gives details of the maiden voyage.

19. King to Casa, September 19, 1568, AGI, Contratación 5012. The investigation of the loss of the galleons has not been found.

20. AGI, Contaduría 1052, No. 1, No. 2, fols. 27vto–30.

21. AGI, Panamá 13, R. 1, Nos. 11 and 12; AGI, Patronato 267, No. 1, R. 46.

22. For the squadron of 1561 see Ullivarri, *Piratas y corsarios de Cuba*, 87–88; and Wright, *Historia documentada de San Cristóbal de la Habana*, I, 36. For 1565 and 1566 see Ullivarri, *Piratas y corsarios de Cuba*, 89–90. For 1567 see Diego Flores de Valdés to Crown, Nombre de Dios, August 6, 1567, AGI, Panamá 39.

23. AGI, Santo Domingo 71, bk 1, fols. 418–19; AGI, Panamá 33, R. 1, No. 45.

24. Wright (ed.), *Documents Concerning English Voyages . . . 1569–1580*, 16–19, 29–30; Diego Flores de Valdés to Casa, March 14, 1571, AGI, Contratación 5101.

25. AGI, Santo Domingo 79, R. 1, Nos. 9 and 10.

26. AGI, Santo Domingo 74, R. 2, No. 79; AGI, Santo Domingo 79, R. 2, No. 19.

27. Esteban de las Alas to Casa, Cartagena, April 17, 1572, AGI, Contratación 5105; documents in AGI, Santa Fe 187, bk 2, fols. 279, 176–176vto; and AGI, Patronato 254, "Alas," R. 2.

28. AGI, Santa Fe 187, bk 2, fol. 280; AGI, Patronato 270, No. 1, R. 2.

29. King to Casa, July 7, 1572, August 7, 1573, in AGI, Contratación 5013; Ortega de Melgosa to Casa, San Lúcar, August 30, 1572, AGI, Contratación 5105, reporting that he had turned the ships over to Diego Flores de Valdés, captain-general of the Tierra Firme convoy.

30. AGI, Contaduría 449, No. 2, No.4; and No. 1, No. 3C. AGI, Santo Domingo 71, bk 3, fols. 227–227vto; testimony in an inquiry, Cartagena, January 15 to February 6, 1576, AGI, Patronato 257, "Menéndez Marques" (Stetson).

31. AGI, Santa Fe 187, bk 2, fols. 67–69vto; Agreement, Cartagena, April 14, 1575, AGI, Contaduría 484, No. 2; AGI, Patronato 254, "Alas," R. 3, [doc. 9]; AGI, Patronato 255, "Eraso, C," R. 7, [doc. 2]; Instruction for Miguel de Eraso, Nombre de Dios, July 30, 1576, AGI, Contaduría 474, No. 5C.

32. Royal Officials to Crown, Havana, January 14, 1577, AGI, Santo Domingo 118 (Stetson); Wright (ed.), *Documents Concerning English Voyages . . . 1569–1580*, 125–28.

33. Officials of the Fleet to the Crown, Seville, August 29, 1577, AGI, Indiferente General 1094; AGI, Indiferente General 739, R. 1, No. 32; Agreement, Seville, December 11, 1577, AGI, Contaduría 484, No. 5.

34. Opinion of the Galley Committee, October 22, 1577, AGS, Guerra Antigua 82, fol. 169.

35. AGI, Indiferente General 2495, bk 2, fols. 49–53.

36. Chaunu, *Séville et l'Atlantique*, III, 28–29, 40–42; King to Casa, June 11, 1562, February 18, March 21, April ?, 1563, AGI, Contratación 5011; AGI, Indiferente General 738, R. 6, No. 70; AGI, Contaduría 310 B, No. 12, 481:2–482:4, which deals with the *chalupas* of 1564.

37. AGI, Indiferente General 1967, bk 16, fols. 26–28, 36vto–37vto, 46vto–47, 58vto–60, 117vto–118vto.

38. For 1567 see Fernández Duro, *Armada Española*, II, 107; and Chaunu, *Séville et l'Atlantique*, III, 112–13. For 1568 see Chaunu, *Séville et l'Atlantique*, III, 127. For 1569 see Chaunu, *Séville et l'Atlantique*, III, 138. For 1570 see King to Casa, July 25, 1570, AGI, Contratación 5012. For 1572 see AGI, Indiferente General 1968, bk 19, fols. 10vto–11; and Chaunu, *Séville et l'Atlantique*, III, 183. For 1574 see Delgado to Crown, n.d. [1574], AGS, Guerra Antigua 78, fol. 255. For 1575 see Chaunu, *Séville et l'Atlantique*, III, 216–18. For 1576 see AGI, Indiferente General 738, R. 16, No. 199; and Delgado to King, n.d. [after June 2, 1576], AGS, Guerra Antigua 82, fol. 99. For 1577 see King to Casa, June 8 and 26, 1577, AGI, Contratación 5013. For 1578 see AGI, Indiferente General 739, R. 3, No. 105; and King to Casa, July 11, 1578, AGI, Contratación 5013.

39. Don Juan de Borja to Crown, February 23, 1571, ? to Casa, Lisbon, May 19, 1571, and Don Juan de Borja to Casa, Lisbon, September 5, 1571, all in AGI, Contratación 5105. See also Gracian to Delgado, July 28, 1571, AGS, Guerra Antigua 75, fols. 104, 105; and Visconte de Santarém, *Quadro Elementar das relações políticas e diplomáticas de Portugal* . . . (18 vols. in 13; Paris, 1842–76), II, 113–14.

40. Copies of Don Juan de Sylva to Crown, Lisbon, May 1, and June 27, 1576, AGI, Contratación 5105; AGI, Indiferente General 738, R. 16, pt. II, No. 207; and Chaunu, *Séville et l'Atlantique*, III, 228–29.

41. AGI, Indiferente General 739, R. 3, Nos. 97 and 105.

42. AGI, Santo Domingo 899, bk 1, fols. 400–400vto; AGI, Contaduría 1074, No. 3, fols. 19–21; Havana, Ayuntamiento, *Actas*, I, pt. 2, 295; AGI, Contaduría 310 B, No. 2, No. 12, 431:2–473:1.

43. Eugene Lyon, *The Enterprise of Florida* (Gainesville, Fla., 1976), 33–99. I am endebted to Dr. Lyon for allowing me to use the manuscript of his book and for a number of the citations that follow in connection with the Florida colony.

44. AGI, Santo Domingo 899, bk 1, fols. 406–407; AGI, Indiferente General 738, R. 7, No. 79; AGI, Contratación 2932, No. 1; AGI, Contaduría 294, No. 2 B, 3:4–6:2.

45. Paul E. Hoffman, "The Narrow Waters Strategies of Pedro Menéndez," *Florida Historical Quarterly*, XLV (1966), 13.

46. King to Menéndez, Madrid, March 21, 1566, copy, AGI, Patronato 275 (Stetson).

47. AGI, Justicia 1001, No. 4, R. 3, which contains the claims of the heirs of Pedro Lorenzo, Menéndez' agent at Puerto Plata. Álvaro Cavallero and Baltasar García served as his agents at Santo Domingo, while Juan Ponce de León was his agent at San Juan de Puerto Rico. AGI, Santo Domingo 71, bk 1, fols. 314–15. See also AGI, Santo Domingo 115, fols. 191–93, for the role of Francisco de Parada at Santiago de Cuba.

48. AGI, Contratación 3908 and 3909, *passim*; AGI, Santo Domingo 71, bk 1, fols. 341–344vto, and bk 2, fols. 455–57.

49. For Puerto Rico see AGI, Santo Domingo 155, R. 1, No. 31; and AGI, Santo Domingo 164, R. 2, No. 51. For Puerto Plata, AGI, Justicia 1001, No. 4, R. 3; AGI, Santo Domingo 899, bk 2, fols. 64–65vto; and AGI, Contaduría 1052, No. 1, No. 3, fol. 16vto, and No. 1, No. 7, fols. 20vto–21. For Havana see AGI, Contaduría 1174, (1574), fols. 9, 12, 14, 187.

50. AGI, Santo Domingo 2280, bk 3, fols. 12–12vto; AGI, Santo Domingo 899, bk 2, fols. 64–65vto.

51. AGI, Santo Domingo 899, bk 2, fols. 64–65; AGI, Justicia 900, No. 5, question 8 of the interrogatory of Captain Juan de Garibay de Aguirre; Petition of Juan Tisol, Puerto Rico, 1577, AGI, Santo Domingo 168 (Stetson); AGI, Contaduría 548.

52. Order of July 15, 1568, in order of June 17, 1570, AGI, Contaduría 548.

53. Text is incorporated in the accounts of Tierra Firme, AGI, Contaduría 1454, fols. 1117vto–1119.

54. Havana, Ayuntamiento, *Actas*, II, 141–42, 146–47; AGI, Santo Domingo 99, R. 1, No. 41; and Wright, *Historia documentada de San Cristóbal de la Habana*, I, 206–207.

55. AGI, Santo Domingo 1122, bk 4, fol. 251; and Wright, *Historia documentada de San Cristóbal de la Habana*, I, 207–208.

56. For Santa Marta see AGI, Contaduría 1509, No. 1, fols. 50vto, 56vto, 58–58vto, 65, 68vto, 69. For Trujillo see AGI, Contaduría 988, R. 9 (1571), fols. 24–24vto.

57. AGI, Contaduría 1454, "1550–1572," fols. 712vto, 1045vto–1047vto; Wright (ed.), *Documents Concerning English Voyages . . . 1569–1580*, 9–10.

58. AGI, Contaduría 1454, "1550–1572," fols. 1120vto–1123; AGI, Contaduría 1455, "1572," fol. 37, and "1573," fols. 24–25vto, 30vto, 32–36.

59. AGI, Patronato 267, No. 1, R. 40; La Roncière, *Histoire de la marine française*, IV, 127–28.

60. AGI, Santo Domingo 155, R. 1, No. 28; AGI, Santo Domingo 71, bk 2, fols. 405–411vto; AGI, Santa Fe 987, bk 3, fols. 271–72.

61. For Puerto Plata see AGI, Santo Domingo 13, No. 4; AGI, Santo Domingo 868, bk 3,

fol. 42vto; AGI, Santo Domingo 79, R. 5, No. 148; Rengifo de Angulo to Crown, June 8, 1582, AGI, Indiferente General 1887; documents from Santo Domingo 2677, No. b. For Yucatán see King to Casa, October 6, 1573, AGI, Contratación 5013. Other requests are found in AGI, Santo Domingo 155, R. 2, No. 64bis; AGI, Santo Domingo 99, R. 3, No. 102; AGI, Santo Domingo 51, R. 2, No. 6.

62. AGI, Santo Domingo 155, R. 2, No. 38; AGI, Santo Domingo 99, R. 3, No. 102; AGI, Santo Domingo 71, bk 2, fol. 587vto.

63. AGI, Indiferente General 1967, bk 18, fol. 310–11; AGI, Indiferente General 1887, No. 29 b.

64. King to Casa, June 11, 1573, AGI, Contratación 5013; AGI, Santo Domingo 99, R. 3, No. 78; AGI, Santo Domingo 116, R. 2, No. 79; AGI, Santo Domingo 171, bk 1, No. 10; AGI, Santo Domingo 2280, bk 3, fols. 78vto–79vto; AGI, Santo Domingo 164, R. 4, No. 89; AGI, Contaduría 310 B, No. 2, No. 12, 387:2–4.

65. AGI, Santo Domingo 868, bk 3, fol. 114; AGI, Indiferente General 1887, doc. 20.

66. Documents sewn together and labeled "1582 y 1586" in AGI, Contratación 2939, No. 5.

67. Cost figures for these forts are not available for the 1574–1580 period because of the loss of detailed accounts for the Vera Cruz treasury. In all probability, they cost as much as the fort at Havana.

68. AGI, Santo Domingo 168, R. 2, Nos. 55, 58, 62; AGI, Santo Domingo 155, R. 1, No. 17.

69. AGI, Santo Domingo 71, bk 1, fols. 341–344vto; AGI, Santo Domingo 166, R. 2, No. 69; AGI, Santo Domingo 1122, bk 5, fols. 1vto–2vto; AGI, Santo Domingo 155, R. 2, No. 56.

70. Treasury officials to Crown, July 20, September 14, 1577, AGI, Santo Domingo 166; AGI, Santo Domingo 2280, bk 3, fols. 84–84vto.

71. AGI, Santo Domingo 899, bk 1, fols. 374, 413–14, and bk 2, fol. 126; AGI, Santo Domingo 71, bk 1, fol. 593, and bk 2, fols. 341–344vto, 431–432vto, 492; AGI, Contaduría 1052, No. 1, No. 2, fols. 18vto–19.

72. AGI, Santo Domingo 71, bk 3, fol. 41–51; AGI, Santo Domingo 73, R. 2, No. 59 a.

73. AGI, Santo Domingo 71, bk 2, fols. 315–316vto.

74. AGI, Santo Domingo 79, R. 3, No. 49; AGI, Santo Domingo 79, R. 5, No. 148; AGI, Santo Domingo 74, R. 3, No. 102; AGI, Santo Domingo 51, R. 1, No. 38.

75. AGI, Santo Domingo 80, R. 1, No. 14, and R. 2, No. 73 b.

76. Wright, *Early History of Cuba*, 278–80.

77. AGI, Santo Domingo 99, R. 3, Nos. 59 and 92; AGI, Santo Domingo 1122, bk 5, fols. 37–37vto; AGI, Santo Domingo 13, No. 30; AGI, Indiferente General 739, R. 4, No. 142.

78. Wright, *Historia documentada de San Cristóbal de la Habana*, I, *passim*.

79. Havana, Ayuntamiento, *Actas*, I, pt. 2, p. 80; Wright, *Historia documentada de San Cristóbal de la Habana*, I, 121–22.

80. Domingo de León to Crown, October 1584, AGI, Santo Domingo 231, as quoted in Louis Andre Vigneras, "Las fortificaciones de la Florida," *Anuario de Estudios Americanos*, XVI (1959), 543.

81. Vigneras, "Fortificaciones de la Florida," 533–44; Jeannette T. Connor, "The Nine Old Wooden Forts of St. Augustine," *Florida Historical Society Quarterly*, IV (1925–26), 103–10; Inquiry, St. Augustine, June 30, 1586, AGI, Contaduría 943, No. 3.

82. Vigneras, "Fortificaciones de la Florida," 546–52; AGI, Santo Domingo 231, No. 64, fols. 11–29vto.

83. AGI, México 19, R. 1, No. 17; Calderon Quijano, *Historia de las fortificaciones en Nueva España*, 8.

84. Calderon Quijano, *Historia de las fortificaciones en Nueva España*, 6–11; Juan Manuel Zapatero, "Una traza inédita de ciudadela-castillo para la isla de San Juan de Ulúa," *Anuario de Estudios Americanos*, XXIII (1966), 658, figure 2, and 647–68; AGI, México 19, R. 2, No. 55; AGI, México 1090, bk C–6, fols. 71–72vto.

85. AGI, Patronato 258, "Villavicéncia," R. 3.
86. Licenciado Landecho to Bishop Las Casas, December 27, 1559, AGI Guatemala 9; AGI, Contaduría 988, R. 1, (1557–59), fols. 103–104; Dr. Villalobos to Crown, Guatemala, March 2, 1574, March 17, 1578, and Town Council to Crown, May 16, 1583, all in AGI, Guatemala 10. See also Diego López to Crown, Trujillo, December 29, 1577, AGI, Guatemala 39.
87. AGI, Panamá 236, bk 9, fols. 197–98, 218vto–219vto, 305, and bk 10, fols. 384vto–385; AGI, Contaduría 1454, "1550–1572," fols. 908vto–909vto, 921, 932vto–933; Lucas de Guzmán to Crown, Panamá, November 24, 1562, AGI, Panamá 29; AGI, Patronato 267, No. 1, R. 46; AGI, Panamá, 13, R. 1, doc. 2.
88. AGI, Santa Fe 187, bk 1, fols. 189, 252–252vto, 269; AGI, Patronato 195, No. 1, R. 28; AGI, Santa Fe 987, bk 3, fols. 299–300, 362vto–363.
89. AGI, Patronato 195, No. 1, R. 28, doc. 5 b; Marco Dorta, *Cartagena de Indias*, 30.
90. AGI, Santa Fe 187, bk 1, fols. 345vto–346, 280; Marco Dorta, *Cartagena de Indias*, 31, 35–37.
91. AGI, Patronato 270, No. 1, R. 2; AGI, Santa Fe 988, bk 4, fols. 20–20vto, 74–74vto, 146vto–147, 150–150vto, 187–187vto.
92. For Veragua see Inquiry, Veragua, March 30, 1575, AGI, Panamá 32; and AGI, Patronato 270, No. 1, R. 6. For Santa Marta see AGI, Santa Fe 1174, bk 3, fols. 2–2vto. For Margarita see AGI, Santo Domingo 182, R. 1, No. 2; and Heredía Herrera, "Las fortificaciones de la isla Margarita," 446–48; and AGI, Santo Domingo 180, R. 1, No. 2. For Río de la Hacha see Wright (ed.), *Spanish Documents Concerning English Voyages . . . 1527–1568*, 95–99, 120.
93. For Havana's pieces see AGI, Contaduría 299, No. 2, 44:3–45:4, 52:2. For the distribution of the guns sent with Menéndez see AGI, Contaduría 301 and Contratación 3908 and 3909, *passim*. For the losses of Puerto Rico and Santo Domingo see AGI, Santo Domingo 71, bk 2, fols. 431–32, and bk 1, fols. 314–15. For the guns for San Juan de Ulúa see AGI, Contaduría 299, No. 2, 85:1, 98:3–4, 113:4; AGI, Contaduría 890, No. 1, 22:3. For the Cartagena pieces see AGI, Contaduría 310 B, No. 2, No. 12, 374:1–377:4.
94. AGI, Contaduría 304, No. 1, 84:4, 89:2–3, 102:1–2; AGI, Indiferente General 1967, bk 18, fols. 358vto–359, 369vto; AGI, Indiferente General 1956, bk 1, fols. 101, 116vto–117. For the merchant's guns see Francisco Duarte to Crown, Seville, July 26, 1573, AGI, Indiferente General 1094; Licenciado Gamboa to Crown, January 31, 1578, AGI, Indiferente General 1095.
95. For Margarita see AGI, Santo Domingo 182, R. 1, No. 3. For Trujillo see Licenciado Ortíz to Crown, Trujillo, April 15, 1567, and Dr. Antonio Gonçalez to Crown, March 18, 1571, both in AGI, Guatemala 9; Governor Diego López de Herrera to Crown, Puerto Caballos, April 4, 1575, AGI, Guatemala 39. For Santiago de Cuba see AGI, Santo Domingo 99, R. 2, No. 59. For the king's order see AGI, Indiferente General 1967, bk 18, fols. 310–11. Concerning Veragua see AGI, Panamá 11, fols. 24–24vto; and Inquiry, Veragua, March 30, 1575, AGI, Panamá 32. For Santa Marta see AGI, Santa Fe 1174, bk 3, fol. 25vto.
96. For Havana see Wright, *Historia documentada de San Cristóbal de la Habana*, I, 221–23. For Puerto Rico see AGI, Indiferente General 1967, bk 16, fols. 317vto–318; AGI, Santo Domingo 155, R. 2, Nos. 38, 41, 46, 56; AGI, Santo Domingo, 2280, bk 3, fols. 26vto, 78, and bk 4, vols. 12vto–13.
97. AGI, Santa Fe 187, bk 1, fol. 252vto; AGI, Patronato 195, No. 1, R. 28; AGI, Santa Fe 987, bk 3, fols. 288vto–290vto; AGI, Patronato 270, No. 1, R. 2; AGI, Santa Fe 187, bk 2, fols. 16–16vto; AGI, Patronato 195, No. 1, R. 28; AGI, Santa Fe 988, bk 4, fol. 157.

Chapter V

1. The loss of the accounts of Vera Cruz and hence of records of payments to its garrison for the period May 1570 to April 1580 and after May 1582 would itself account for much of the drop in mean yearly expenditures. Another factor to be considered is the cost

of the troops at San Juan de Puerto Rico, who were not paid from the treasury except for two occasions, and then in very small amounts.
 2. Artinaño y de Galdacáno, *Historia del comercio con las Indias*, 103–104.
 3. Inquiry, Nombre de Dios, May 6, 1569, AGI, Panamá 32; AGI, Patronato 267, No. 1, R. 46, fol. 2vto; AGI, Santa Fe 187, bk 1, fol. 307vto.
 4. The *cédula* has not been found, but its date is given in a report from Nombre de Dios, AGI, Patronato 270, R. 1. The copies were apparently sent out in the convoy of 1570, arriving at their destinations late in that year and early the next. This leisurely pace suggests that the central authorities were not overly concerned about the matter. See also AGI, Santo Domingo 71, bk 3, fols. 559–559vto; AGI, México 19, R. 2, No. 58, paragraph 8; Audiencia to Crown, May 21, 1571, AGI, Panamá 13; AGI, Santa Fe 187, bk 1, fol. 345vto.
 5. AGI, Panamá 11, fols. 13–13vto. The *cédula* came after the 1571 convoy had sailed, apparently because of an oversight in Madrid, or perhaps because someone there forgot that he had already asked the Isthmanian officials for a report.
 6. AGI, Santa Fe 187, bk 2, fols. 211, 238–39, 242, 259, 280vto; AGI, Patronato 270, No. 1, Rs. 2, 3, and 4; AGI, Santa Fe 37, R. 1, No. 8; and Wright (ed.), *Documents Concerning English Voyages . . . 1569–1580*, 50; AGI, Santo Domingo 71, bk 3, fols. 196vto–197; AGI, Patronato 269, No. 2, R. 9.
 7. AGI, Santa Fe 988, bk 4, fol. 120.
 8. AGI, Indiferente General 1956, bk 1, fols. 262–262vto; AGI, Indiferente General 738, R. 15, No. 135.
 9. A brief history of the discussions of the committee from its formation until October 21, 1577, is Juan Delgado, "Relación de lo que a pasado en las Juntas . . . ," October 22, 1577, AGS, Guerra Antigua 82, fol. 168.
 10. AGI, Indiferente General 1956, bk 1, fols. 285–86; AGI, Santa Fe 187, bk 8, fols. 69–69vto; Inquiry, Nombre de Dios, April 19, 1575, AGI, Panamá 32; AGI, Panamá 11, fols. 55vto–56; AGI, Santa Fe 187, bk 2, fol. 34; AGI, Panamá 11, fols. 55vto–56, which is a letter from Dr. Criado de Castillo saying that the galleys should have higher bows and be more heavily timbered than those used in the Mediterranean.
 11. Antonio Enriquez Pimental to Crown, Seville, October 28, 1575, AGI, Indiferente General 1094; AGI, Indiferente General 738, R. 16, Nos. 197, 183.
 12. AGS, Guerra Antigua 82, fol. 168; AGI, Patronato 255, No. 3, "Flores de Valdés," R. 10; Fernández Duro, *Armada Española*, II, 293–94; AGI, Guerra Antigua 82, fol. 168.
 13. AGI, Guerra Antigua 82, fol. 168; AGI, Indiferente General 738, R. 16, pt. 2, No. 226; AGI, Indiferente General 1956, bk 1, fols. 354vto–355vto.
 14. For Santo Domingo see Report of the Audiencia, January 28 to February 2, 1577, AGI, Indiferente General 2661; AGI, Santo Domingo 79, R. 4, No. 99. For Panamá see Wright (ed.), *Documents Concerning English Voyages . . . 1569–1580*, 136–41. For Cartagena see Governor Bustos to Crown, May 15, 1577, copy in AGI, Indiferente General 1094; AGI, Patronato 270, No. 7, R. 5. For the views of Nombre de Dios see AGI, Patronato 255, "Eraso, C," R. 7. For Havana see AGI, Santo Domingo 13, R. 2, No. 42; AGI, Santo Domingo 73, R. 2, No. 76; memo of Hernán Manrrique de Rojas, 1576, enclosing a proposal of November 10, 1576, in AGI, Indiferente General 2661.
 15. AGS, Guerra Antigua 82, fol. 169.
 16. King to Gamboa, April 27, 1578, AGI, Contratación 5103. Terms of sale for the old ships are found in AGI, Contaduría 316, No. 2, No. 6, 83:2–84:1, 89:3–4; AGI, Contaduría 319, No. 3, No. 5, 70:3–4, 68:1–2. For the other fiscal problems of the Fleet see Agreements of the Royal Officials of the Fleet, December 11, 1577, January 4, 29, 31, 1578, in AGI, Contaduría 484, Nos. 5 and 6.
 17. Andrés de Eguino to Crown, Cartagena, February 1, 1579, AGI, Indiferente General 1095; Cristóbal de Eraso to Crown, February 4, 1579, AGI, Indiferente General 2661; AGI, Santo Domingo 79, R. 5, No. 151; Martín Perez de Olacaval to Crown, Cartagena, January 30, 1579, AGI, Indiferente General 1095.
 18. Chaunu, *Séville et l'Atlantique*, III, 252–54; AGI, Panamá 33, R. 1, No. 71; Wright

(ed.), *Documents Concerning English Voyages* . . . *1569-1580*, 212, 230; AGI, Patronato 270, No. 1, R. 11.

19. Agreement, Cartagena, October 28, 1578, AGI, Contaduría 484, No. 6. For a discussion of the sailing qualities of the *saetía* see "Información de Capt. Castañeda," Cartagena, October 16, 1578, AGI, Indiferente General 1095; AGI, Patronato 270, No. 1, R. 9; AGI, Patronato 270, No. 1, R. 8; Instructions, Cartagena, October 29, 1578, AGI, Contaduría 484, No. 6.

20. Officials of the Fleet to the Crown, April 24, 1579, AGI, Indiferente General 1095; AGI, Indiferente General 739, R. 5, Nos. 206, 207; Zelia Nuttall (ed. and trans.), *New Light on Drake: A Collection of Documents Relating to His Voyage of Circumnavigation, 1577-1580* (London, 1914), 123-27; AGI, Patronato 255, "Eraso, C.," R. 14, doc. 2.

21. AGI, Santo Domingo 79, R. 5, No. 165; Eraso to Crown, San Lúcar, November 27, 1579, AGI, Indiferente General 2661; Officers of the Fleet to Crown, and Casa to Crown, both December 9, 1579, AGI, Indiferente General 1095.

22. AGI, Indiferente General 739, R. 7, Nos. 306, 310.

23. AGI, Patronato 270, No. 1, R. 9; AGI, Patronato 255, "Eraso, C.," R. 16; AGI, Indiferente General 2495, bk 3, fol. 41; AGI, Indiferente General 740, R. 2, No. 64.

24. AGI, Patronato 270, No. 1, Rs. 9, 13; AGI, Santo Domingo 79, R. 5, No. 165; AGI, Indiferente General 2495, bk 3, fol. 46vto; AGI, Indiferente General 1956, bk 3, fols. 45-45vto; AGI, Patronato 241, Único, doc. 52; AGI, Contaduría 550, No 1, No. 2.

25. AGI, Patronato 270, No. 1, R. 9; AGI, Indiferente General 2495, bk 3, fols. 27-28vto, 42vto-43, 47vto-48; AGI, Indiferente General 1956, bk 3, fol. 129; AGI, Contaduría 316, No. 2, No. 19, 242:1-2; AGI, Contaduría 319, No. 13, 235:1.

26. Andrés de Eguino to Crown, February 1, 1579, Martín Perez de Olacaval to Crown, January 30, 1579, and Officers of the Fleet to Crown, April 24, 1579, all in AGI, Indiferente General 1095; AGI, Indiferente General 739, R. 9, No. 389; AGI, Indiferente General 740, R. 2, No. 45; AGI, Patronato 247, Único, doc. 86 a; Álvaro de Bazán to Casa, May 7, 1583, and Fernándo de Benavides to Casa, May 8, 1583, in AGI, Indiferente General 1096.

27. AGI, Santo Domingo 184, R. 1, No. 7; AGI, Patronato 259, No. 1, R. 78; AGI, Patronato 247, Único, doc. 89; AGI, Santo Domingo 155, R. 2, No. 70.

28. AGI, Santo Domingo 50, R. 3, No. 77; AGI, Patronato 269, No. 2, R. 1; AGI, Patronato 257, No. 1, R. 67; AGI, Santo Domingo 168, R. 3, No. 131; AGI, Santo Domingo 73, R. 2, No. 87; AGI, Santo Domingo 51, R. 1, No. 61; "Relación . . . cerca poner galeras," n.d. [1580], AGI, Indiferente General 1096; AGI, Indiferente General 739, R. 7, No. 306; AGI, Patronato 255, "Eraso, C.," R. 17, doc. 2.

29. AGI, Santo Domingo 70, R. 1, No. 13; AGI, Santo Domingo 51, R. 1, No. 61; AGI, Santo Domingo 80, R. 1, No. 19; AGI, Indiferente General 739, R. 9, No. 373.

30. AGI, Indiferente General 740, R. 1, No. 8, and R. 2, Nos. 60, 64, 74; AGI, Patronato 269, No. 2, R. 5; Casa to Crown, July 11, 1582, AGI, Indiferente General 1096; AGI, Patronato 258, "Urbide Apallua," R. 2.

31. AGI, Santo Domingo 80, R. 2, Nos. 46, 46 a, 56, 55; AGI, Santo Domingo 70, R. 1, No. 21, fols. 10-10vto.

32. AGI, Santo Domingo 169, R. 1, Nos. 2, 4.

33. AGI, Santo Domingo 73, R. 2, No. 98; AGI, Indiferente General 740, R. 2, No. 64; AGI, Santo Domingo 169, R. 1, No. 4; AGI, Santo Domingo 168, R. 4, No. 175; AGI, Santo Domingo 51, R. 1, No. 77; AGI, Santo Domingo 80, R. 2, No. 55.

34. AGI, Patronato 269, No. 2, R. 7; Richard Boulind, "Shipwreck and Mutiny in Spain's Galleys on the Santo Domingo Station, 1583," *Mariners Mirror*, LVIII (1972), 302-12, which is a translation of the document in AGI, Patronato 269.

35. AGI, Santo Domingo 51, R. 1, No. 77, and R. 2, No. 89; AGI, Santo Domingo 72, R. 1, No. 5 a; AGI, Santo Domingo 80, R. 2, Nos. 73, 74, 78; AGI, Patronato 269, No. 2, R. 5.

36. File of documents dating December 12-20, 1583, AGI, Indiferente General 1187, doc. 23; Boulind, "Shipwreck and Mutiny," *passim*; Antonio de Eraso to ?, February 1 and 11, 1584, and Secretary of Council of Indies to Jorge Manrique, July 15, 1584, all in AGI, Indiferente General 2661; AGI, Santo Domingo 80, R. 3, No. 86.

37. Casa to Crown, August 19, 1583, AGI, Indiferente General 1096; AGI, Santo Domingo 184, R. 1, No. 11; AGI, Santa Fe 1, R. 1, No. 47.
38. AGI, Patronato 270, No. 1, R. 13, doc. 3; AGI, Santa Fe 991, bk 1, fol. 68; AGI, Santa Fe 1, R. 1, No. 47; AGI, Santo Domingo 184, R. 1, No. 11.
39. AGI, Patronato 270, No. 1, R. 14; AGI, Santo Domingo 183, R. 1, No. 18.
40. Vique to Crown, Cartagena, June 29, 1585, AGI, Contratación 5101.
41. AGI, Patronato 270, No. 1, R. 14; AGI, Santa Fe 991, bk 1, fol. 68.
42. Gerónimo de Rojas y Avellaneda to Crown, Havana, n.d. [1577], AGI, Santo Domingo 127 (Stetson); AGI, Santo Domingo 99, R. 3, Nos. 80, 112; and memo of a letter, duque de Medina Sidonia to Crown, October 14, 1583, and record of a committee, Seville, February 27, 1584, both in AGI, Indiferente General 2661; AGI, Indiferente General 741, R. 1, No. 15.
43. AGI, Indiferente General 739, R. 7, No. 330; AGI, Patronato 247, Único, Nos. 45, 12, 16.
44. AGI, Indiferente General 739, R. 8, No. 366.
45. AGI, Indiferente General 739, R. 9, No. 397; AGI, Indiferente General 740, R. 1, No. 31, and R. 3, Nos. 82 a, 82 b, and R. 4, No. 132. Accounts are found in AGI, Contaduría 529B, No. 5, No. 2, *datas*.
46. AGI, Indiferente General 740, R. 6, No. 199 a; and marqués de Santa Cruz to Lic. Gasca, November 1, 1583, AGI, Indiferente General 1096; AGI, Indiferente General 740, R. 6, No. 212. Duarte's accounts are AGI, Contaduría 323, No. 11.
47. Santa Cruz to Lic. Gasca, November 1, 1583, AGI, Indiferente General 1096; Antonio de Eraso to ?, February 1, 1584, AGI, Indiferente General 2661.
48. Recalde to Crown, July 4, 1584, Secretary of Council to Recalde, July 15, 1584, and Memo of Antonio de Eraso, July 21, 1584, all in AGI, Indiferente General 2661; Chaunu, *Séville et l'Atlantique*, III, 358.
49. AGI, Justicia 1002, No. 5, fol. 7; AGI, Contaduría 462, No. 9; AGI, Contratación 3917; Proceedings, Havana 1579–80, AGI, Contaduría 944, No. 8; AGI, Santo Domingo 2528, fols. 112vto–114vto.
50. AGI, México 20, R. 1, No. 68, fol. 9; Alonso de Herrera Guzmán to Crown, San Juan de Ulúa, May 2, 1583, AGI, Indiferente General 1096; AGI, Santo Domingo 868, bk 3, fol. 95; AGI, Santo Domingo 1122, bk 5, fols. 63–65.
51. Irene A. Wright (ed.), *Further English Voyages to Spanish America, 1583–1594* (London, 1951), 125–28, 154–57. Cited hereafter as Wright (ed.), *Further English Voyages*.
52. Memo of Secretary Delgado on a meeting of the committee, ?, 15, 1578 [before April 19], AGI, Indiferente General 1094; AGI, Panamá 237, bk 11, fols. 12vto–14; AGI, Contaduría 1457, No. 3, fols. 41, 149; letters from Cristóbal de Eraso to Crown, Seville, April 19, May 6, May 26, 1578, in AGI, Indiferente General 1095. The soldiers recruited for Florida did not want to serve there, but were willing to serve in the Cimarron war.
53. AGI, Contaduría 1459, (1583), fols. 247–55; AGI, Contaduría 1460, "1584," fols. 223–223vto.
54. AGI, Santo Domingo 5, R. 1, No. 11; AGI, Patronato 247, Único, docs. 5, 45; AGI, Santo Domingo 99, R. 3, No. 105; Captain Rodrigo de Vargas to Crown, Angra, Tercera, August 11, 1583, AGI, Indiferente General 1096; Copy, Antonio de Eraso to Lic. Gasca de Salazar, Lisbon, April 9, 1582, AGI, Indiferente General 1096.
55. AGI, México 20, R. 1, No. 96; Wright, *Historia documentada de San Cristóbal de la Habana*, II, 7–14; AGI, Santo Domingo 99, R. 4, No. 128; AGI, Contaduría 683, No. 1, "Extraordinário," 5:4–7:1, 8:2, 9:1–2. See also Wright, *Historia documentada de San Cristóbal de la Habana*, I, 94; AGI, Santo Domingo 118, R. 3, No. 165 a, 179; AGI, Santo Domingo 99, R. 3, No. 166; AGI, Indiferente General 740, R. 4, No. 124; AGI, Panamá 33, R. 2, No. 99, claiming that the officials of Havana had to send them a receipt and thus accept the risk for the money once put on a ship. The treasury officials at Havana did not want to assume that risk, and so the matter was thrown into the crown's lap, but it was not resolved before 1586.
56. AGI, Santo Domingo 164, R. 4, No. 99; AGI, Patronato 175, R. 38, doc. 13; AGI,

Santo Domingo 155, R. 2, No. 70; AGI, Patronato 175, R. 38, doc. 9; and Menéndez de Valdés to Crown, January 12, 1583, AGI, Indiferente General 1887; AGI, Santo Domingo 155, R. 2, No. 70; Menéndez de Valdés to Hernándo de Viedma, January 5, 1585, AGI, Indiferente General 1887; AGI, Santo Domingo 169, R. 1, No. 11.

57. AGI, Santo Domingo 80, R. 2, No. 58; AGI, Santo Domingo 51, R. 2, No 84.

58. For the voyage of William Hawkins see AGI, Santo Domingo 184, R. 1, No. 11; AGI, Santo Domingo 169, R. 1, No. 9; and Wright (ed.), *Further English Voyages*, xviii–xxi. For the Granvelle and Drake voyages see Diego de Alcega to Crown, Havana, June 22, 1585, and Álvaro de Bazán to Casa, October 23, 1585, both in AGI, Contratación 5101; AGI, Santo Domingo 51, R. 2, No. 96; and Wright (ed.), *Further English Voyages*, xxii–xxv.

59. AGI, Santo Domingo 899, bk 2, fols. 161vto–162; AGI, Santo Domingo 71, bk 2, fols. 551vto–552. Cartagena made an eloquent statement of this burden in 1572: "hasta agora no havía en estas partes tierra de V. Md. a donde los vecinos y moradores hayan sido mas cargados de contribuciones para polvora, municiones, artilleria, officiales, velas, centinales, barcos de aviso, y otros gastos que de ordinario ha avido, estando siempre en acto de guerra con las armas en la mano," AGI, Santa Fe 187, bk 2, fols. 208–208vto. Santo Domingo continued to employ paid watchmen at Punta de Cauzedo when it had the money (AGI, Santo Domingo 50, R. 3, No. 89). Santiago de Cuba had an excise tax for that purpose (AGI, Santo Domingo 116, R. 2, No. 79). Santa Marta occasionally paid watchmen from the royal treasury (AGI, Contaduría 1509, No. 1, fols. 70vto–71vto).

60. AGI, Patronato 13, R. 1, No. 12; Inquiry, Nombre de Dios, May 6, 1569, AGI, Panamá 32; AGI, Santo Domingo 115, fols. 204–205; AGI, Patronato 270, No. 1, R. 2.

61. The warden of the Puerto Plata fort, Pedro Rengifo de Angulo, while apparently zealous in defending his port and even claiming (without any supporting documentation) to have led several raids on small parties of corsairs filling water casks along the coast, was also charged with trading with corsairs. AGI, Santo Domingo 79, R. 5, No. 148; AGI, Santo Domingo 80, R. 2, Nos. 30, 74; AGI, Santo Domcngo 51, R. 2, No. 96.

62. For San Juan de Ulúa see AGI, Patronato 258, "Villavicénica," R. 3; AGI, México 20, R. 1, Nos. 68, 113; Calderón Quijano, *Historia de las fortificaciones en Nueva España*, 11–12. For Santo Domingo see AGI, Santo Domingo 70, R. 1, No. 10, paragraph 35; AGI, Santo Domingo 51, R. 2, No. 86. For the Isthmus see AGI, Panamá 237, bk 11, fols. 95vto–96.

63. AGI, Patronato 260, No. 2, R. 48.

64. For Santiago de Cuba see AGI, Santo Domingo 116, R. 2, No. 79. For Florida see AGI, Santo Domingo 99, R. 3, No. 106. For Panamá see AGI, Panamá 30, R. 1, No. 18, point 3; AGI, Panamá 237, bk 11, fols. 122–23. For Trujillo see Captain Diego López to Crown, Trujillo, May 16, 1580, AGI, Guatemala 39.

65. AGI, Santo Domingo 168, R. 4, Nos. 163, 183; AGI, Santo Domingo 164, R. 4, No. 99; AGI, Santo Domingo 2280, bk 4, fols. 23–23vto; AGI, Santo Domingo 169, R. 1, No. 9.

66. AGI, Santo Domingo 168, R. 3, Nos. 135, 151; AGI, Santo Domingo 2280, bk 4, fols. 14vto–15, 24–24vto; Opinion of Don Francés de Alava, n.d. [fall of 1583], AGI, Indiferente General 1887, No. 39, with No. 20 a; AGI, Patronato 269, No. 2, No. 3; AGI, Santo Domingo 155, R. 2, No. 79.

67. AGI, Santo Domingo 155, R. 2, No. 76.

68. AGI, Santo Domingo 99, R. 3, No. 80; AGI, Patronato 260, No. 2, R. 48; AGI, Santo Domingo 118, R. 3, No. 154; AGI, Santo Domingo 99, R. 3, No. 101; AGI, Indiferente General 740, R. 1, No. 34.

69. AGI, Santo Domingo 99, R. 3, Nos. 112, 115, 116; AGI, Santo Domingo 116, R. 3, No. 94; AGI, Contaduría 1088, No. 3B, fol. 19.

70. AGI, Santa Fe 1174, bk 3, fols. 37–37vto; AGI, Santa Fe 988, bk 4, fols. 180–180vto, 188; AGI, Santo Domingo 1122, bk 5, fol. 43; AGI, Patronato 173, No. 1, R. 22; AGI, Santo Domingo 899, bk 3, fol. 47; AGI, Contaduría 310B, No. 2, No. 12, 486:3.

71. Pedro de Coronado Maldonado to Crown, Seville, January 1, 1579, AGI, Indiferente General 1095; AGI, Santa Fe 988, bk 4, fol. 222vto; AGI, Contaduría 316, No. 2 and No. 20, 246:2–3; AGI, Contaduría 319, No. 4, No. 14, 237:1; AGI, Santo Domingo 70, R. 1, No.

10, fols. 16, 18; AGI, Santo Domingo 180, R. 1, No. 22; AGI, Santo Domingo 51, R. 1, No. 65; AGI, Santo Domingo 80, R. 2, No. 58.

72. AGI, Santo Domingo 79, R. 5, No. 148; AGI, Santo Domingo 51, R. 1, No. 6; AGI, Santo Domingo 80, R. 2, Nos. 30, 74, 58.

73. Capt. Diego López to Crown, Trujillo, May 16, 1580, and Governor Rodrigo Ponce de León to Crown, May 26, 1584, both in AGI, Guatemala 39; Town Council to Crown, Trujillo, May 16, 1583, AGI, Guatemala 10; AGI, Santo Domingo 116, R. 2, No. 79; AGI, Santo Domingo 184, R. 1, No. 11.

74. AGI, Santo Domingo 155, R. 2, Nos. 64 bis, 68 a, 76, 79; AGI, Santo Domingo 164, R. 4, Nos. 89, 99; AGI, Santo Domingo 2280, bk 4, fol. 19vto, and bk 3, fols. 130–130vto; AGI, Santo Domingo 168, R. 4, No. 163; AGI, Santo Domingo 169, R. 1, No. 9.

75. AGI, Santo Domingo 99, R. 3, Nos. 93, 112; AGI, Santo Domingo 118, R. 2, No. 140, and R. 3, No. 154; AGI, Santo Domingo 51, R. 1, Nos. 78, 83.

76. Alonso de Herrera Guzmán to Crown, San Juan de Ulúa, May 2, 1583, AGI, Indiferente General 1096; AGI, México 20, R. 2, Nos. 110, 113; AGI, Panamá 30, R. 1, No. 18; AGI, Panamá 229, bk 1, fol. 90vto; Inquiry, 1584, AGI, Panamá 32 (regarding artillery for Nombre de Dios).

77. AGI, Indiferente General 1968, bk 21, fols. 96vto–99; AGI, Indiferente General 1956, bk 2, fols. 49vto–50vto. For an example of needs referred to Alava, see Council of Indies to Casa, March 15, 1577, Contratación 5013.

78. AGI, Panamá 229, bk 1, fol. 90vto; AGI, Santa Fe 991, bk 1, fols. 69vto–70; AGI, Indiferente General 1956, bk 3, fols. 55–55vto, ordering the borrowing of twenty-five pieces for the galleys of Spain; Prior and Consuls to Crown, December 29, 1583, AGI, Indiferente General 1096, complaining about guns taken for the fleet to the Straits of Magellan; Opinion of the Council of War, appended to a memorial of Don Francés de Alava to Council of War, April 28, 1578, AGI, Indiferente General 1883.

79. AGI, Santo Domingo 70, R. 1, Nos. 16, 17, 19, 21; Wright (ed.), *Further English Voyages*, xxiv.; AGI, Santo Domingo 99, R. 4, No. 128.

Chapter VI

1. The estimate of 1536 was 15,000 ducats for mails. AGS, Estado, Armadas y Galeras 439, fol. 186.

2. The absolute decrease is due to delays in paying subsidies.

3. The cities were forewarned by a matter of weeks, but the crown was unable to send more than a small quantity of munitions. Agreement of the Casa, November 25, 1585, AGI, Contratación 4312, No. 6. For the account of one of the dispatch boats carrying arms, see AGI, Contratación 2939, No. 5.

4. Sociedad de Bibliofilos Españoles, *Nobiliária de conquistadores de Indias* (Madrid, 1892), 280–81, for the shield and accompanying royal order, dated December 23, 1574.

5. AGI, Santo Domingo 99, R. 3, No. 115, paragraph 36.

6. John Francis Guilmartin, Jr., *Gunpowder and Galleys: Changing Technology and Mediterranean Warfare at Sea in the Sixteenth Century* (New York, 1975).

7. John L. Phelan, *The Kingdom of Quito in the Seventeenth Century: Bureaucratic Politics in the Spanish Empire* (Madison, 1967), 330–36.

8. AGI, Santo Domingo 168, R. 3, No. 95.

9. Granvelle, *Papiers d'État*, VI, 156–65; Geoffrey Parker, *The Army of Flanders and the Spanish Road, 1567–1659* (Cambridge, 1972), 241, and Tables 21–23.

Appendix I

1. For a discussion of the principles underlying this form of accounting see Sybill M. Jack, "An Historical Defense of Single Entry Bookkeeping," *Abacus*, II (1966), 137–58, esp. 149–50, 158. See also Ananias C. Littleton, *Essays on Accountancy* (Urbana, 1961), 36–40; and Basil S. Yamey, "Some Topics in the History of Financial Accounting in England, 1500–1900," in William T. Baxter and Sidney Davidson (eds.), *Studies in Accounting*

NOTES TO PAGES 238-242   293

Theory (2nd ed.; London, 1962), 15-18. For a discussion of the eighteenth-century Spanish rejection of double-entry bookkeeping for their treasury accounts, see P. Santos Martínez, "Reforma de la contabilidad colonial en el siglo XVIII (el método de partido doble)," *Anuario de Estudios Americanos*, XVII (1960), 525-36. There are numerous published studies of English accounts of this type from the thirteenth century onwards.

2. The format was first laid down in the Ordinances of the Casa issued in 1503, *DIU*, V, 31. Martín Fernández de Navarrete (ed.), *Colección de los viages y descubrimientos que hicieron por mar los Españoles desde fines del siglo XV* . . . (5 vols.; Madrid, 1825-37), II, 286. See also AGI, Indiferente General 418. The persistence of the use of roman numerals has been ascribed to the difficulty of changing them once written and, more probably, to the use of the abacus as a device for tallying. Jack, "An Historical Defense of Single Entry Bookkeeping," 146. Examples of the Casa's books are AGI, Contratación 4678.

3. The laws governing auditing are found in Encinas, *Cedulario Indiano*, III, 248-81. For a discussion, see Ismael Sánchez-Bella, *La organización financiera de las Indias (Siglo XVI)* (Seville, 1968), 269-81.

4. It should be noted that Haring's call of 1919 for a history of the treasury has only been partially filled by Sánchez-Bella's recent study. The remarks that follow are thus necessarily limited in their documentation. Clarence H. Haring, "Ledgers of the Royal Treasuries in Spanish America in the Sixteenth Century," *Hispanic American Historical Review*, II (1919), 173-87, esp. 187; Sánchez-Bella, *Organización financiera de las Indias*, 9-58, and *passim*.

5. "Instrucción del Rey y de la Reina para D. Cristóbal Colón, May 29, 1493, *DIU*, V, xv-xvii. Also in Navarette (ed.), *Colección*, II, 66-73; Crown to Treasurer of the Indies, Burgos, April 23, 1497, *ibid.*, II, 189.

6. Ursula Lamb, *Frey Nicolás de Ovando, governador de Indias, 1501-1509* (Madrid, 1956), 201-203; Juan Perez de Tudela, *Las armadas de Indias y los origines de la política de colonización, 1492-1505* (Madrid, 1956).

7. Crown to Bobadilla, May 30, 1500, in Navarrete (ed.), *Colección*, II, 242-43; Crown to Ovando, September 27, 1501, *ibid.*, II, 275-78; Crown to Ovando, January 8, 1504, *DIU*, V, 67-70.

8. Ordinances of the Casa de Contratación, January 30, 1503, AGI; Indiferente General 418, bk 3, fol. 4, printed in the *DIU*, V, 36. King to Ovando, July 13, 1508, *DIU*, V, 148-49.

9. Schäfer, *El consejo real*, I, 172-73.

10. *Maximiliano . . . Cartas al Emperador*, 210-11. Prince to Casa, September 3, 1551, and October 9, 1553, in AGI, Contratación 5010, both complaining of the failure of the Casa to complete the accounts from the squadrons of the 1540s. The Casa claimed that it was too busy with other matters and that the one notary entrusted with the task could not complete the work any faster. See also AGI, Contaduría 3, No. 10, for a group of documents generated by the accountants about various accounts from 1529 to 1550, documents probably produced during the early 1550s in an effort to regain control over the accounting process. For a discussion of accounting problems in Castile, see Francisco Gallardo y Fernández, *Origen, progresos, y estado de las rentas de la corona de España, su govierno y administración* (7 vols.; Madrid, 1805-1806), I, 29-30.

11. The text was subsequently incorporated in a *sobrecédula* of July 9, 1564, in Encinas, *Cedulario Indiano*, III, 248-51. For a summary of its provisions, see also Solorzano, *Política Indiana*, X, 95.

12. Ismael Sánchez-Bella, "El govierno del Peru, 1556-1564," *Anuario de Estudios Americanos*, XVII (1960), 464-67, 472-80, 507-13; Solorzano, *Política Indiana*, V, 76-77. This was not the end of it, though, because the Council of Finance continued to intervene in American affairs on occasion thereafter.

13. *Cédula*, July 29, 1560, in Encinas, *Cedulario Indiana*, III, 246.

14. *Sobrecédula*, July 9, 1564, in *ibid.*, III, 248-49.

15. AGI, Santo Domingo 1122, bk 5, fol. 4-6.

16. For a detailed discussion of the quality of the Florida accounts, see Paul E. Hoffman,

"A Study of Florida Defense Costs, 1565–1585: A Quantification of Florida History," *Florida Historical Quarterly*, LI (1973), 403–408.

17. Cartagena: AGI, Contaduría 1379, No. 2. Casa: AGI, Contaduría 299, as an example. New Galicia's accounts are noted in King to Audiencia of New Galicia, January 18, 1562, in Encinas, *Cedulario Indiano*, III, 267. For royal orders making these subdivisions mandatory, see King to Audiencia of Panama, September 13, 1565, reproduced in *sobrecédula*, October 4, 1569, in Encinas, *Cedulario Indiano*, III, 252–54; King to Audiencia of Mexico, September 27, 1565, in *ibid.*, III, 259–62; King to Audiencia of Lima, October 19, 1565, in *ibid.*, III, 256–58. See the accounts for the 1570s, as listed in the bibliography.

18. Chaunu, *Séville et l'Atlantique*, I, 97–110.

19. *Ibid.*, I, 97–110; Sánchez-Bella, *Organización financiera de las Indias*, 204–50, *passim*. Besides outright tax evasion, the revenue side of the ledger involved frauds having to do with the collection of one type of money while crediting the accounts with another of lesser value, the collection of old debts in money worth less than that involved in the original debt, or the use of royal funds for private speculations. It is thus nearly impossible to know what should have been collected; the same is true of what was collected, but not recorded. That such practices were common knowledge is indisputable. An amusing and informative sidelight on the matter is provided by the detailed report from the Casa de Contratación to the crown in 1579 on ways to export money and other items from the Indies to Spain and Europe without passing through Seville. Casa to Crown, April 10, 1579, AGI, Indiferente General 1095.

20. An example that shows the vulnerability of the system is found in the will of Diego Ruíz, St. Augustine, January 28, 1574, AGI, Escribanía de Cámera 154A, fols. 765–80, in which he admits having made various false statements of fact while performing his duties. Diego de Valle, who was notary in Florida, 1565–1570(?), testified under oath that he had been asked to make false statements of expense by the *adelantado* and, having refused, ended up first under arrest in Florida and then in Guatemala, whence he made his way to Spain without most of his notarial records, which had been taken from him by Pedro Menéndez Marques at Havana, apparently to prevent a true record of events from reaching Spain and royal authorities (AGI, Justicia 1160, No. 13).

21. Normally both the treasury officials and the highest local administrator of the crown had to agree on expenses, although only the treasury officials were liable for amounts incorrectly spent. This tended to prevent expenditures not authorized by the crown. After 1565 no new expenditures could be made without prior authorization from Spain, except in cases where an *audiencia* found that waiting for such authorization would work irreparable harm, as in the face of an enemy attack.

22. It should be pointed out that absolute figures are not required for most problems. Figures of the correct order of magnitude (*e.g.*, 1000s rather than 100s) that are accurate to three or four digits are generally as much as can be expected in any statistical study, even those done from twentieth-century sources. Figures based on the expenditure data from the royal accounts have this sort of accuracy. The problem with the income side of the ledger is that it is almost impossible to determine whether the computed figures are accurate to three places; sometimes it may also be difficult to be sure that they are of the correct order of magnitude.

23. This is both evidence of intent to defraud and of the less-than-perfect state of records accumulated over a number of years. The latter was usually accepted as the reason for the presentation of items not properly recorded in books of accounts.

24. Continued use of these accounts, especially those of Mexico, without some form of lamination to preserve them will result in the loss of much of the remaining text as the edges flake away, taking parts of entries with them.

25. All the remissions of funds from New Spain for the fort at Havana can be documented from non-Cuban or nonaccounting sources. Except for some activity regarding Florida during the 1560s, there was no other major defense activity on the island except for the fort.

26. Kenneth Janda, *Data Processing: Applications to Political Research* (Evanston, 1965).

Since 1970 a number of books aimed at the historian who wishes to use quantification have appeared. Among the better ones are Edward Shorter, *The Historian and the Computer* (Englewood Cliffs, N.J., 1970), and Charles Dollar and Richard Jensen, *Historian's Guide to Statistics: Quantitative Analysis and Historical Research* (New York, 1971).

27. George Steiner, "Program Budgeting: Business Contribution to Government Management," *Business Horizons*, VIII (1965), 43–52. For somewhat less perceptive remarks, see my earlier statements in "The Program Budget as a Tool of Historical Analysis," *Historical Methods Newsletter*, III (1970), 14–18.

28. Compare the original statements on PPBS contained in U.S. Department of Defense, Office of the Secretary, *Study Report, Programming System for the Office of the Secretary of Defense* (Washington, 1963), with those in U.S. Department of Defense, *Significant Documents on PPBS in the Department of Defense* (Washington, DC, 1969).

29. Department of Defense, *Study Report*, Part II, p. 1.

30. A third category of secondary specification was developed during the course of the work as "Central Supply." With descriptive subdivisions, this set of categories was intended to take care of those few items that could not be included in the land and naval coding scheme because their use was not clear. Data from this category was incorporated into the Total Cost figures.

31. The program element concept can be reapplied to the data for land defense by totaling the figures, except for those for militia expenses. It should be noted that other periods of colonial history do not suffer from this problem because the military organization was sufficiently complex to provide data for a strictly program element analysis without loss of meaning because of overaggregation.

32. It was found after the study was too far advanced for recoding that there were not enough alternative subregions provided within the Caribbean region. Besides a basic comparison between the Antilles and the Main, the study also needed a comparison of the Antilles and all other areas on the littoral of the Caribbean-Gulf of Mexico. This need was met during aggregation by adding a slot to the geographic category matrix and instituting corresponding changes in the geographic subroutine.

33. Manuel Moreyra Paz-Soldan, "La técnica de la moneda colonial: Unidades, pesos, medidas y Relaciones," *Revista de Historia de América*, No. 20 (1945), 347–69, esp. 357–58. This is a fundamental article for any student of colonial finance or economic history.

34. Figure 4, in Fernand P. Braudel and F. Spooner, "Prices in Europe from 1450 to 1750," in E. E. Rich and C. H. Wilson (eds.), *The Economy of Expanding Europe in the Sixteenth and Seventeenth Centuries* (Cambridge 1967), Vol. IV of *The Cambridge Economic History of Europe*, 458.

35. *Sobrecédula*, July 23, 1583, AGI, Contaduría 1075, fols. 890–94. The accounts begin to be kept in maravedís with 1578.

36. Dr. Alonso Criado de Castillo to Crown, May 8, 1575, AGI, Panamá 29, fol. 161, states "en éste reyno de Tierra Firme solía correr plata en tejuelos que llaman plata corriente que es como la moneda que corre en Castilla. Solía ser buena plata refinada. Quando querían comprar barras, valían a quince por ciento de la mas ruín plata y estos tejuelos se llevaban a Castilla y no se perdía nada en ellos. Aviendo aqui ésto a tanta corrupción ya sea la plata tan mala y que es cobre y plomo que vale a interés de las barras por ser estos tejuelos tan malos a quarenta y cinco por ciento de cuya causa se an perdido muchos hombres que tienen tiendas porque todo lo que compran en junto es con plata ensayada y ellos venden en corriente y como a subido tanto el interés de lo ensayado por ser tan malo lo corriente han perdido sus caudales. Será necesario que V. Md. con rigor mande que no baje plata corriente de Peru sino toda la moneda hecha barras ensayada por que desta manera entender sea el valor que tiene y no que el corriente ande por dos mil y docientos y cinquenta maravedís el marco, no teniendo a quatrocientas maravedís en fundiendolo y ensayando la."

37. Antonio Enriquez Pimental to Crown, Seville, October 28, 1575, AGI, Indiferente General 1094, speaking as the agent of the islands of Española and San Juan, charged that the decline in the value of the money during the preceding two years was due to "la

industria de algunos mercaderes y personas particulares interesantes," who numbered fifteen to twenty at most. For the documentation of how this was done, see Cipriano de Utrera, *La moneda provincial de la isla Española*, esp. 53–59 for the accounts of Francisco de Amaro.

Bibliography

Manuscript Sources

Archivo General de Indias

Patronato: Legajos 19, 170–177, 179, 181–182, 193–195, 197, 247, 251, 254–260, 267, 269–271.
Contaduría: Legajos 3, 274–275, 286, 291–296, 298–299, 301, 304–306, 310, 312, 314, 316, 319–321, 323, 326, 438, 442, 448–450, 454, 459–460, 462–465, 474, 476–477, 479, 483–485, 500, 502, 508, 513–517, 521, 529B, 530–531, 533, 548, 550, 552, 666–667, 671, 675, 677–681, 683–687, 809, 876–879, 890, 911A, 941, 944, 967–968, 984, 987–989, 1050–1054, 1073–1075, 1088–1089, 1174, 1379–1380, 1382, 1384, 1452–1455, 1457–1460, 1463–1465, 1485, 1509, 1536, 1562–1565, 1609, 1649, 1664A, 1688–1689, 1692–1694.
Contratación: Legajos 2929, 2932, 2939, 3281, 3908–3909, 3917, 4307, 4555, 4675A, 4676, 4677, 4685, 5010–5014, 5101, 5103, 5105.
Santo Domingo: Legajos 10–14, 24, 49–51, 70–74, 77–80, 99, 115–116, 118, 155, 164, 166, 168–169, 180, 182–184, 868, 899–900, 1121–1122, 2070, 2280, 2528.
México: Legajos 19–20, 257, 350–351, 1090–1091.
Guatemala: Legajos 9–10, 39.
Panamá: Legajos 11, 13, 29–30, 32–33, 39, 229, 235–237.
Santa Fe de Bogotá: Legajos 1, 37, 49, 56, 62, 65–66, 70, 72, 80, 124, 187, 419, 533–535, 987–988, 991, 1174.
Lima: Legajo 207.
Indiferente General: Legajos 737–741, 984, 989, 1013, 1092–1096, 1219–1220, 1866, 1883–1884, 1887, 1956, 1962–1965, 1967–1969, 2006, 2495, 2535, 2661.

Escribania de Cámara: Legajos 154 A, 967, 1024.
Justicia: Legajos 21, 394, 817, 899–909, 917–918, 979–980, 982, 984, 999, 1000–1003, 1121, 1160, 1166.

Archivo General de Simancas
 Consejo de Estado: Legajos 439, 806–808, 816, 818.
 Guerra Antigua: Legajos 1, 12, 18–19, 22–24, 30, 35, 44, 52, 57, 59, 61, 82.

Biblioteca Nacional, Madrid. MS 3045.

John B. Stetson, Jr., Collection. P. K. Yonge Library of Florida History, University of Florida, Gainesville, Florida. A collection of photostats of documents in the Archivo General de Indias.

Printed Collections of Documents

Academia de la Historia, Madrid. *Negociaciones con Francia.* 11 vols. to 1960. Madrid, 1950–?.

Biggar, Henri P., comp. *A Collection of Documents Relating to Jacques Cartier and the Sieur de Roberval.* Ottawa: Public Archives of Canada, 1930.

Colección de documentos inéditos para la historia de España. Edited by Martín Fernández de Navarrete, *et al.* 113 vols. Madrid: Imprente de la Viuda de Calero, 1842–1895.

Colección de documentos inéditos relativos al descubrimiento, conquista, y organización de las antiguas posesiones españoles de América y Oceanía, sacados de los archivos del reino, y muy especialmente del de Indias. Edited by Joaquín F. Pacheco, Francisco de Cardenas, and Luís Torres de Mendoza. 42 vols. Madrid: Imprenta de Quirós and others, 1864–1884.

Colección de documentos inéditos relativos al descubrimiento, conquista, y organización de las antiguas posesiones españoles de ultramar. Edited by Joaquín F. Pacheco, Francisco de Cardenas, and Luís Torres de Mendoza. 25 vols. Madrid: Sucesores de Rivadeneyra, 1885–1932.

Davenport, Frances G., ed. *European Treaties Bearing on the History of the United States and Its Dependencies.* 4 vols. Washington, D. C.: Carnegie Institution of Washington, 1917–1937.

Dumont, Jean, ed. *Corps universel diplomatique du droit des gens* . . . 8 vols. Amsterdam: Chez P. Brunel, R. et G. Wetstein, and others, 1726–1731.

Gosselin, Édoward H. *Documents authentiques et inédits pour servir à l'histoire de la marine normande et du commerce rouennais pendant les XVIe et XVIIe siècles.* Rouen: Imprimerie de H. Boissel, 1876.

Granvelle, Antoine Perrenot de. *Papiers d'état du cardinal de Granvelle, d'après les manuscrits de la bibliothèque de Besançon.* Edited by Ch. Weiss. 9 vols. Paris: Imprimerie Royale, 1841–1852.

Great Britain. Public Records Office. *Calendar of Letters and State Papers Relating to English Affairs Preserved Principally in the Archives of Simancas, Elizabeth, 1558–1603.* Edited by Martin A. S. Hume. 4 vols. 1892–1896. Reprint. Nendeln: Kraus Reprint, 1971.

Havana. Ayuntamiento. *Actas capituares del Ayuntamiento de la Habana*. Preface and preliminary study by Emilio Roig de Leuschenring. 3 vols. in 5. Havana: Municipio de la Habana, 1937–1940.

Markham, Sir Clements R., ed. *Early Spanish Voyages to the Strait of Magellan*. London: Hakluyt Society, 1911.

Maximiliano de Austria, Governador de Carlos V en España: Cartas al Emperador. Edited by Rafaela Rodríguez Raso. Madrid: CSIC, Escuela de Historia Moderna, 1963.

Menéndez de Avilés, Pedro. *Letters of Pedro Menéndez de Avilés and Other Documents Relating to His Career, 1555–1574*. Translated by Edward W. Lawson. Typescript. 2 vols. St. Augustine, 1955. (Copy at P. K. Yonge Library of Florida History, University of Florida.)

Navarrete, Martín Fernández, ed. *Colección de los viages y descubrimientos que hicieron por mar los Españoles desde fines del siglo XV* . . . 5 vols. Madrid: Imprenta Real, 1825–1837.

Nuttal, Zelia, ed. and trans. *New Light on Drake: A Collection of Documents Relating to His Voyage of Circumnavigation, 1577–1580*. London: Hakluyt Society, 1914.

Paso y Troncoso, Francisco del. *Epistulario de Nueva España, 1505–1818*. 16 vols. México: Antigua Librería Robredo, de J. Porrúa y Hijos, 1939–1942.

"Pedro Menéndez a Consejo de Indias, 29 Abril 1556," *Boletín del Archivo General de la Nación (República Dominicana)*, IV (1941), 147.

Priestly, Herbert I., ed. and trans. *The Luna Papers: Documents Relating to the Expedition of Don Tristan de Luna y Arellano for the Conquest of La Florida in 1559–1561*. 2 vols. Deland, Fla.: Florida State Historical Society, 1928.

Ruidiaz y Caravia, Eugenio, comp. *La Florida: Su conquista y colonización por Pedro Menéndez de Avilés*. 2 vols. Madrid: Imprenta de los Hijos de J. A. García, 1893.

Smith, Buckingham, ed. *Colección de varios documentos para la historia de la Florida y tierra adyacentes*. London: Trubner and Company 1857.

Wright, Irene A., ed. *Documents Concerning English Voyages to the Spanish Main, 1569–1580*. London: Hakluyt Society, 1932. Library of Congress author classification is: Spain. Archivo General de Indias.

―――, ed. and trans. *Further English Voyages to Spanish America, 1583–1594*. London: Hakluyt Society, 1951.

―――, ed. and trans. *Spanish Documents Concerning English Voyages to the Spanish Main, 1527–1568*. London: Hakluyt Society, 1929.

Books Cited

Andrews, Kenneth R. *Drake's Voyages: A Re-assessment of Their Place in Elizabethan Maritime Expansion*. New York and London: Weidenfeld and Nicolson, 1967.

―――. *The Spanish Caribbean: Trade and Plunder, 1530–1630*. New Haven: Yale University Press, 1978.

Artiñano y de Galdácano, Gervasio. *Historia del comercio con las Indias durante el dominio de los Austrias*. Barcelona: Talleres de Oliva de Vilanova, 1917.
Barrientos, Bartolomé de. *Pedro Menéndez de Avilés, Founder of Florida*. Translated with Introduction by Anthony Kerrigan. Gainesville: University of Florida Press, 1965.
Bigges, Walter. *A Summarie and True Discourse of Sir Frances Drakes West Indian Voyage*. London: Richard Field, 1589.
Bolton, Herbert E. *The Colonization of North America, 1492-1783*. New York: Macmillan, 1920.
Calderon Qijano, José Antonio. *Historia de las fortificaciones en Nueva España*. Seville: Escuela de Estudios Hispano-Americanos, 1953.
Carande Thovar, Ramón. *Carlos V y sus banqueros*. 3 vols. Madrid: Sociedad de Estudios y Publicaciones, 1959-1967.
Chaunu, Huguette and Pierre. *Séville et l'Atlantique, 1504-1650*. 8 vols. in 10. Paris: Librairie Armand Colin, 1955-1959.
Cipolla, Carlo M. *Guns, Sails and Empires: Technological Innovation and the Early Phases of European Expansion, 1400-1700*. New York: Pantheon, 1965.
Connell-Smith, Gordon. *Forerunners of Drake: A Study of English Trade with Spain in the Early Tudor Period*. London and New York: Longmans, Green, 1954.
Dollar, Charles, and Richard Jensen. *Historian's Guide to Statistics: Quantitative Analysis and Historical Research*. New York: Krieger, 1971.
Encinas, Diego de. *Cedulario Indiano*. 4 vols. 1596. Facsimile edition. Madrid: Ediciones Cultura Hispánica, 1945-1946.
Fernández Duro, Cesáreo. *La Armada Española desde la unión de los reinos de Castilla y de Aragón*. 9 vols. 1895-1903. Reprint. Madrid: Museo Naval, 1972-1973.
Folmer, Henry. *Franco-Spanish Rivalry in North America, 1524-1673*. Glendale, Cal.: A. H. Clark Co., 1953.
Gallardo y Fernández, Francisco. *Origen, progresos, y estado de las rentas de la corona de España, su govierno y administración*. 7 vols. Madrid: Imprenta Real, 1805-1808.
Girón, Pedro de. *Crónica del Emperador Carlos V*. Edited by Juan Sánchez Montes. Madrid: CSIC, Escuela de Historia Moderna, 1964.
Guilmartin, John Francis, Jr. *Gunpowder and Galleys: Changing Technology and Mediterranean Warfare at Sea in the Sixteenth Century*. New York: Cambridge University Press, 1975.
Hakluyt, Richard. *Principal Navigations, Voyages, Traffiques, and Discoveries by the English Nation made by Sea or Over-land to the Remote and Farthest Distant Quarters of the Earth at any Time Within the Compass of These 1600 Yeares*. 12 vols. Glasgow: J. MacLehose and Sons, 1903.
Haring, Clarence H. *Trade and Navigation between Spain and the Indies in the Times of the Hapsburgs*. Cambridge, Mass.: Harvard University Press, 1918.

Heckscher, Eli F. *Merchantilism*. Authorized translation by Mendel Shapiro. 2 vols. London: Allen and Unwin, 1935.
Herrera y Tordesillas, Antonio de. *Historia general de los hechos de los Castellanos en las islas y tierrafirme del Mar Océano*. 17 vols. 1601–1615. Reprint. Madrid: Tipografía de Archivos, 1934–37.
Jal, Auguste. *Archéologie Navale*. 2 vols. Paris: Arthus Bertrand, 1840.
Janda, Kenneth. *Data Processing: Applications to Political Research*. Evanston, Ill.: Northwestern University Press, 1965.
Lamb, Ursula. *Frey Nicolás de Ovando, Governador de Indias, 1501–1509*. Madrid: CSIC, Instituto Gonçalo Fernández de Oviedo, 1956.
La Roncière, Charles G. M. B. de. *Histoire de la marine française*. 6 vols. Paris: E. Pon Nourriett, 1899–1932.
Lewis, Michael A. *Armada Guns*. London: Allen and Unwin, 1961.
Littleton, Ananias C. *Essays on Accountancy*. Urbana: University of Illinois Press, 1961.
López de Velasco, Juan. *Geografía y descripción universal de las Indias*. 1574. Reprint. Madrid: Fortanet, 1894.
Lowery, Woodbury. *Spanish Settlements Within the Present Limits of the United States*. 2 vols. 1901–1905. Reprint. New York: Russell and Russell, 1959.
Lyon, Eugene. *The Enterprise of Florida*. Gainesville, Fla.: University of Florida Press, 1976.
Manucy, Albert, and Ricardo Torres-Reyes. *Puerto Rico and the Forts of Old San Juan*. Riverside, Conn.: The Chatham Press, 1973.
Marco Dorta, Enrique. *Cartagena de Indias: La Ciudad y sus monumentos*. Seville: Escuela de Estudios Hispano-Americanos, 1951.
Morales Padrón, Francisco. *Jamaica Española*. Seville: Escuela de Estudios Hispano-Americanos, 1952.
Newton, Arthur P. *The European Nations in the West Indies, 1493–1688*. 1933. Reprint. London: Adam and Charles Black, 1966.
Palm, Erwin Walter. *Los monumentos arquitectónicos de la Española*. 2 vols. Ciudad Trujillo: Universidad de Santo Domingo, 1955.
Parker, Geoffrey. *The Army of Flanders and the Spanish Road, 1567–1659*. Cambridge: Cambridge Unversity Press, 1972.
Parry, John H. *The Age of Reconnaissance*. London: Weidenfeld and Nicolson, 1963.
———. *The Spanish Seaborne Empire*. New York: Knopf, 1966.
Perez de Tudela, Juan. *Las armadas de Indias y los origines de la política de colonización, 1492–1505*. Madrid: Instituto Gonçalo Fernández de Oviedo, 1956.
Perez Martínez, Hector. *Piraterias en Campeche (Siglos XVI, XVII, XVIII)*. México: Porrúa Hermanos, 1937.
Phelan, John L. *The Kingdom of Quito in the Seventeenth Century: Bureaucratic Politics in the Spanish Empire*. Madison: University of Wisconsin Press, 1967.

Ribault, Jean. *The Whole and True Discoverye of Terra Florida*. 1563. Facsimile ed. Introduction by David W. Doud. Gainesville: University of Florida Press, 1964.
Sánchez-Bella, Ismael. *La organización financiera de las Indias (Siglo XVI)*. Seville: Escuela de Estudios Hispano-Americanos, 1968.
Santarém, Viscont de. *Quadro elementar das relações políticas e diplomáticas de Portugal com as diversas potencias do mundo, desde o principio da monarchia portugueza até aos nossos dias*. 18 vols. in 13. Paris: J. P. Aillaud, and others, 1842–1876.
Schäfer, Ernest. *El consejo real y supremo de las Indias: Su historia, organización, y labor administrativa hasta la terminación de la casa de Austria*. 2 vols. Seville: M. Carmona and Escuela de Estudios Hispano-Americanos, 1935–1947.
Shorter, Edward. *The Historian and the Computer: A Practical Guide*. Englewood Cliffs, N.J.: Prentice-Hall, Inc., 1970.
Smith, Robert S. *The Spanish Guild Merchant: A History of the Consulado, 1250–1700*. Durham: Duke University Press, 1940.
Sociedad de Bibliófilos Españoles. *Nobiliária de conquistadores de Indias*. Madrid, 1892.
Solís de Merás, Gonçalo. *Pedro Menéndez de Avilés*. Translated by Jeannette Thurbor Conner. Introduction by Lyle N. McAlister. Gainesville: University of Florida Press, 1964.
Solorzano y Pereyra, Juan de. *Política Indiana*. 5 vols. 1647. Reprint. Madrid and Buenos Aires: Compania Ibero-Americana de Publicaciones, 1930.
Taylor, E. G. R. *The Haven-Finding Art*. London: Hollis and Carter, 1958.
Thomazi, August A. *Les flottes de l'or: Histoire des galions d'Espagne*. Paris: Payot, 1937.
Ullivarri, Saturnino. *Piratas y corsarios de Cuba: Ensayo histórico*. Havana: Maza, Caso y Cia., 1931.
U.S. Department of Defense. *Significant Documents on PPBS in the Department of Defense*. Washington, D.C.: U. S. Government Printing Office, 1969.
———. Office of the Secretary. *Study Report, Programming System for the Office of the Secretary of Defense*. Washington, D.C.: U. S. Government Printing Office, 1963.
Utrera, Cipriano de. *La moneda provincial de la isla Española, Documentos*. Ciudad Trujillo: Tipografía Franciscana, 1951.
Veitía Linage, Joseph de. *Norte de la Contratación de las Indias*. 1672. Reprint. Buenos Aires: Comisión Argentina de Fomento Interamericano, 1945.
Williamson, James A. *Hawkins of Plymouth: A New History of Sir John Hawkins and of the Other Members of His Family Prominent in Tudor England*. London: Black, 1949.
———. *Sir John Hawkins: The Time and the Man*. Oxford: Clarendon Press, 1927.
Wright, Irene A. *The Early History of Cuba, 1492–1586*. New York: Macmillan, 1916.

———. *Historia documentada de San Cristóbal de la Habana en el siglo XVI.* 2 vols. Havana: Imprenta El Siglo XX, 1927.
Wright, J. Leitch, Jr. *Anglo-Spanish Rivalry in North America.* Athens: University of Georgia, 1971.

Articles Cited

Boulind, Richard. "Shipwreck and Mutiny in Spain's Galleys on the Santo Domingo Station, 1583." *Mariners Mirror,* LVIII (1972), 297–330.
Braudel, Fernand P., and F. Spooner. "Prices in Europe from 1450 to 1750." Chapter VII of *The Economy of Expanding Europe in the Sixteenth and Seventeenth Centuries.* Vol. 4. *Cambridge Economic History of Europe.* Edited by E. E. Rich and C. H. Wilson. Cambridge: Cambridge University Press, 1967.
Céspedes del Castillo, Guillermo. "La Avería en el comercio de Indias." *Anuario de Estudios Americanos,* II (1945), 517–698.
Connell-Smith, Gordon. "English Merchants Trading to the New World in the Early Sixteenth Century." London University, Institute of Historical Research, *Bulletin,* XXIII, No. 67 (May 1950), 53–67.
Connor, Jeannette T. "The Nine Old Wooden Forts of St. Augustine." *Florida Historical Society Quarterly,* IV (1925–26), 103–40.
Croft, Pauline. "Englishmen and the Spanish Inquisition, 1558–1625." *English Historical Review,* LXXXVII (1972), 249–68.
García Gallo, Alfonso. "El servicio militar en Indias." *Anuario de historia de derecho español,* XXVI (1956), 447–515.
Haring, Clarence H. "Ledgers of the Royal Treasuries in Spanish America in the Sixteenth Century." *Hispanic American Historical Review,* II (1919), 173–87.
Heredía Herrera, Antonia. "Las fortificaciones de la isla Margarita en los siglos XVI, XVII, y XVIII." *Anuario de Estudios Americanos,* XV (1958), 429–514.
Hernandez Tapía, Concepción. "Despoblación de la isla de Santo Domingo en el XVII." *Anuario de Estudios Americanos,* XXVII (1970), 281–320.
Hoffman, Paul E. "A Study of Florida Defense Costs, 1565–1585: A Quantification of Florida History." *Florida Historical Quarterly,* LI (1973), 401–22.
———. "Diplomacy and the Papal Donation." *The Americas,* XXX (1973), 151–83.
———. "The Narrow Waters Strategies of Pedro Menéndez." *Florida Historical Quarterly,* XLV (1966), 12–17.
———. "The Program Budget as a Tool of Historical Analysis." *Historical Methods Newsletter,* III (1970), 14–18.
Hussey, Roland D. "Spanish Reaction to Foreign Aggression in the Caribbean to About 1680." *Hispanic American Historical Review,* V (1929), 286–302.
Jack, Sybill M. "An Historical Defense of Single Entry Bookkeeping." *Abacus,* II (1966), 137–58.
Konetzke, Richard. "Legislación sobre immigración de extrangeros en América

durante la época colonial." *Revista Internacional de Sociología* (Madrid), XI–XII (1945), 269–99.

Lyon, Eugene. "Captives of Florida." *Florida Historical Quarterly*, L (1971), 1–24.

Martínez, P. Santos. "Reforma de la contabilidad colonial en el siglo XVIII (el método de partido doble)." *Anuario de Estudios Americanos*, XVII (1960), 525–36.

Moreyra Paz-Soldan, Manuel. "La técnica de la moneda colonial: Unidades, pesos, medidas y relaciones." *Revista de Historia de América* (México), No. 20 (1945), 347–69.

Otte, Enrique, ed. "Una carta inédita de Gonçalo Fernández de Oviedo." *Revista de Indias*, No. 65 (1956), 437–58.

Ricard, Robert. "Los portugueses en las Indias españolas." *Revista de Historia de América* (México), No. 34 (December 1952), 449–56.

Sánchez-Bella, Ismael. "El govierno del Peru, 1556–1564." *Anuario de Estudios Americanos*, XVII (1960), 407–524.

Steiner, George. "Program Budgeting: Business Contribution to Government Management." *Business Horizons*, VIII (1965), 43–52.

Vigneras, Louis André. "Las fortificaciones de la Florida." *Anuario de Estudios Americanos*, XVI (1959), 533–52.

Wright, Irene A. "Rescates, with Special Reference to Cuba, 1599–1610." *Hispanic American Historical Review*, III (1920), 336–72.

Wright, J. Leitch, Jr. "Sixteenth Century English-Spanish Rivalry in La Florida." *Florida Historical Quarterly*, XXXVIII (1960), 265–79.

Yamey, Basil S. "Some Topics in the History of Financial Accounting in England, 1500–1900," in William T. Baxter and Sidney Davidson, eds., *Studies in Accounting Theory*. 2nd Edition. London: Sweet and Maxwell, 1962.

Zapatero, Juan Manuel. "Una traza inédita de ciudadela-castillo para la isla de San Juan de Ulúa." *Anuario de Estudios Americanos*, XXIII (1966), 647–68.

Dissertations

Boulind, Richard H. "The Strength and Weakness of Spanish Control of the Caribbean, 1520–1650: The Case for the *Armada de Barlovento*." Ph.D. dissertation, Clare College, Cambridge University, 1965.

Hoffman, Paul E. "The Defense of the Indies, 1535–1574: A Study in the Modernization of the Spanish State." Ph.D. dissertation, University of Florida, 1969.

Index

Acla, 133, 197
Alas, Martín de las, 136, 166
Alava, Francés de, 204, 209
Alba, duque de, 111
Alonso de los Ríos, Martín, 31, 32, 61, 268
Amaro, Francisco de, 257
Andagoya, Pascual de, 53, 54
Andrews, Kenneth R.: book discussed, 3–4, 228
Ango, Jean de, 281n75
Antilles: corsair actions in, 25, 26, 66, 113, 211, 216, 217, 283n6; patrol squadrons in, 38, 79, 109, 216, 217; militia actions in, 47, 201; temporary garrisons, 140, 141, 218; mentioned, 5, 24, 126, 216. See also Española Squadron, Indies Fleet, Galleys of Santo Domingo
Antonio, Pretender to the Portuguese throne, 196, 198, 206, 207
Araya, 38
Archiniega, Sancho de, 140
Archivo General de Indias, 269; Contaduría section, 239, 244
Archivo General de Simancas, 268, 269
Arenas Gordas, 127
Arquello, Antonio de, 56
Artillery: effect of technology of, on defenses, 8, 170; geographic distribution of, 61–62, 101, 179; supply of, 79, 100, 169, 209, 280n67; costs of, 22, 72, 123, 124, 176, 178, 214; as category in analysis, 249, 250; mentioned, 8, 59, 208, 213, 219

Artiñano y de Galdácano, Gervasio: work noted, 2, 127
Atlantic Triangle: defined, 7; patrol squadrons in, 21, 28, 29, 30, 32, 33, 35, 74, 78, 79, 81, 86, 87, 88, 89–90, 94, 136–38, 193, 195, 213, 216; corsair activities in, 24, 25, 26, 35, 63, 64, 66, 113, 137–38, 188, 211, 216; defense of commerce in, 29, 30, 31, 34, 35, 112; corsairs captured in, 281n76
Auxiliary craft and forces: analytical category defined, 251
Avería, 3, 16, 17, 21, 28, 30, 32, 35, 79, 83, 94, 102, 127, 136, 138, 191, 210
Azeituno, Juan de, 54
Azores: as navigational aid, 6, 7; as gathering place for ships, 88; corsairs in, 94, 278n26; mentioned, 5, 30, 81
Azua: fort proposed, 52, 55, 56, 97; mentioned, 118

Bahama Channel, 5, 119
Bahamond de Lugo, Francisco, 167
Baracoa (Cuba), 172
Barbudo, Gonçalo, 116
Barreda, Captain Baltasar, 144
Barros, Cristóbal de, 136
Bastides, Rodrigo de, 211
Bayahá: as check on illegal trade, 119, 212; settlement of, 121, 157
Bazán, Alvaro de (the elder): proposes Indies fleet, 75–78 passim; commands patrols in the Triangle, 84

Bazán, Alvaro de (marqués de Santa Cruz): commands patrol squadrons in Triangle, 86, 94, 136; captures French ships, 88, 89; views on galleys for Caribbean, 190
Bejar, duque de, 60
Bermuda, 52
Bilbao, 127, 222
Blas, Hernándo, 32
Bobadilla, Francisco de, 240
Bohemia, Kings of, 77
Bolton, Herbert E.: work noted, 2
Bonaire, 116
Bontemps, Jean, 116, 122, 172
Brazil, 27, 35, 70, 104, 218
Bucier, Grangean, 282n89
Burburata, 70, 114
Bureaucratization: hampers defense, 206, 209

Caballos, Francisco de, 157
Cabo de la Vela, 27, 38, 60, 69
Cabo Verde, 86
Cádiz, 7, 29, 128
Calona, Francisco de, 98, 158
Camacho, Antón, 85
Campeche, 114, 115; militia strength, 42, 262, 263
Canary Islands: as navigational aid, 6, 7; trade with Indies, 27, 94, 141; corsairs at, 29, 32, 88, 172
Cardona, Nicolás de, 131
Caribbean, 97, 115, 198, 216, 218, 220, 272n*14*
Carreño, Bartolomé, 81
Carreño, Francisco, 133, 170, 181, 182
Carrión, Captain Eugenio de, 38
Carta de pago, 238, 243
Cartagena: Drake's attack on, 1, 167, 168, 195, 226; politics of defense of, 10, 152, 165, 181–83; corsair attacks on, 25, 42, 47, 50, 55, 194, 200; munitions for, 44, 150, 151; militia, 45, 102, 149, 179; garrison, 48, 147, 148, 199, 219; fortifications, 52, 54, 55, 97, 153, 165–67, 171, 203, 227; wall, 55, 56, 166, 227; artillery, 60, 169, 170, 171, 207, 222; naval patrol squadron, 84, 93, 96, 128, 132, 181; cost of living, 189; lacks passive defenses, 227; provides for own defense, 227; 291n59; treasury records, 240, 242; corsairs reported off, 277n5; corsairs killed near, 281n76; mentioned, 132, 179, 213

Cartier, Jacques, 20, 24–25, 31, 49–50, 64
Carvajal, Luís de, 86, 87
Casa de la Contratación: history of, 33, 239; supplier of war matériel, 40, 43, 55, 150, 171, 207, 217, 222, 223–24, 226, 234, 236; artillery inventories, 62, 171; work load and efficiency, 89, 217, 226, 279n*40*, 293n*10*; role in shaping defense history, 219; treasurer's accounts, 238, 240, 241, 242, 245, 248, 254; reports on illegal export of money, 294n*19*; mentioned, 27, 265
Castellanos, Juan de, 56, 59
Castellanos, Miguel de, 115
Castile: cost of mail service, 213
Catano, Rafael, 240
Cateau-Cambrésis, Treaty of (1559), 65, 105
Caucedo, Point, 46, 291n59
Cavallero, Alvaro, 57, 285n*46*
Cavallero, Diego, 38
Central America, 126, 244; militias in, 45, 47, 201; corsairs in, 66, 67, 113, 211. *See also* Honduras, Puerto Caballos, Trujillo
Céspedes, Guillermo, 3, 264
Chagres River, 52, 122, 186
Chantone, sieur de (Tomás Perrenot), 106
Charles I, King of Spain, 20, 63, 232, 240
Chaunu, Huguette and Pierre: work discussed, 3, 4, 127
Cimarrons (of Panamá), 18, 147, 165, 170, 196, 197, 223, 248, 290n52
Coastal patrols: cost data, 17, 19, 21, 23, 24, 73, 122, 123, 125, 177, 214, 216; analytical term defined, 251. *See also* Indies Fleet, Galleys
Coco River, 118
Coligny, Gaspard de, 106
Colón, Cristóbal, 81, 240
Colón, Luís de, 121
Commerce, defense of: examples of, 27–28, 29, 31, 33, 35, 36, 39, 80, 93, 96, 173, 216; ship armament rules, 28, 33, 79, 213; use of group sailings in, 30, 78, 88, 213
Consulado of Seville: and defense of commerce, 20, 21, 32, 34, 35, 71, 75, 83, 85, 128, 234; reason for creation, 33, 273n*21*; political power of, 94; uses convoy for economic ends, 128–29
Convicts: for galleys, 188
Convoy system: definition of, 16, 251; costs to crown, 17, 19, 23, 71, 73, 122, 125, 127, 177, 178, 214; history of, 28, 30, 33, 34–37 *passim*, 73, 76, 78, 79, 81, 83, 87,

INDEX 307

88, 94, 126–27, 215; effects on commerce, 36, 83, 94–95, 104; evaluated, 37, 74, 126–27; effect on corsairs, 112, 128; from Santo Domingo to Spain, 193; routes, 228; mentioned, 3, 4, 6, 7, 109
Coro (Venezuela): fort proposed, 52
Corsairs: geographic and temporal patterns and statistics, 7, 8, 12, 13, 16, 25, 29, 46–47, 65–67, 68, 102–103, 112, 114, 117, 129, 210, 216, 217, 218, 220, 224, 225, 229, 272n2, 283n5; size of fleets, 25, 26, 65, 122, 172, 281n75; Spanish reactions to, 25, 67, 272n2; effects of defenses on, 65, 67, 92, 103, 188, 216; illegal trade of, 67, 69, 97, 210, 216, 217, 220, 229, 278n16, 281n75; ship types used by, 67, 180, 220; losses suffered by, 88, 89, 92, 103, 172, 190, 281n76; invasions threatened by, 101, 121, 193; aided by Indies residents, 221, 225; normal threat from, 224, 225; mentioned, 1, 94, 104, 265
Coruña, La, 84, 216
Council of the Indies: role in decisions, 31, 77, 188, 196, 232; role in auditing treasury accounts, 238, 239
Crépy-en-Laonnis, Treaty of (1544), 27, 35, 64, 105
Criado de Castillo, Alonso, 182
Crown, Spanish: use of various types of defenses, 2, 9–10, 28, 75, 79, 80, 93, 95, 147, 152, 173, 179, 204, 216, 219, 227, 228; view of own responsibilities for defense, 9–10, 21, 37, 43, 62, 75, 213, 233–34; parsimony of, 10–11, 36, 39, 85, 107–108, 213, 229, 234, 235; relationship to Consulado of Seville, 28, 32–33, 35, 78, 85, 95, 279n35; interests as shipper, 37, 78, 95, 216; and fiscal discretion of local officials, 64, 107, 108; view of illegal trade, 278n16
Cuba: munitions for, 44, 155; militia of, 45, 262; illegal trade with, 70; supply of Florida, 141; treasury records of, 240–42, 245
Cubagua, 25, 38, 52, 60, 203; militia of, 40, 42, 263
Cumaná, 48, 52, 53, 59, 114–15
Curaçao, 41, 116, 172, 185

Defense: general strategies of, 2, 204, 213, 219; costs of, 2, 12, 14, 15, 22–23, 64, 71, 72–73, 110, 122, 123, 124–25, 126, 171, 175, 176–77, 212, 214, 215, 223, 235; geographic zones, 7, 8, 228; definition of, 18, 248; general evaluations of, 63, 194, 203–204, 212, 223, 225, 227, 235, 236; system after 1586, 120, 223, 231; limiting factors, 224, 231, 235; system compared to model systems, 229–31; as analytical category, 248
De Soto, Hernándo, 30, 53
Diplomacy: and definition of the Indies, 9, 104, 105, 217, 281n85; and terms of non-Spanish access to Indies, 9, 64, 109, 215; Franco-Spanish, 110–11, 217, 281n85, 282n86; Anglo-Spanish, 112; and Florida claims, 282n86
Dominica, 52, 185
Drake, Sir Francis, 1, 132, 147, 175, 186, 195, 197, 199, 200, 202, 224, 225, 235, 236
Ducat. *See* Units of account and currency
Dutch War (1621–48), 229

Elizabeth I, Queen of England, 111
England: corsairs from, 30–31, 74, 96, 116, 218; trade rights in Spanish empire, 65, 109, 111–12; Spanish ambassador in, 225
Encomendero: role in defense, 274n37
Enriquez, Martín, 163, 219
Enriquez Pimental, Antonio, 295n36
Eraso, Alonso de, 184, 185, 188
Eraso, Cristóbal de, 134, 135, 183, 184, 186
Eraso, Miguel de, 134, 184, 185
Escalante, García de, 89
Española: militia of, 45, 261; illegal trade on NW coast of, 70, 118, 192, 211; depopulation of NW coast of, proposed, 116; forts to check illegal trade with, 157
—Squadron of 1552, 81, 82
—Squadron of 1557–59: delays in fitting out, 82, 83, 84, 86, 87, 88, 89; history of, 87, 89–92; evaluation of, 92–93, 217. *See also* Indies Fleet, Santo Domingo

Fernández de Busto, Pedro, 167
Fernández de Oviedo, Gonçalo, 52, 58, 59
Fernández de Quiñones, Diego, 198, 206
Fernández Duro, Cesáreo: work mentioned, 2
Flemish: trading rights in Indies, 65
Flores, Álvaro, 134
Flores de Valdés, Diego, 131, 183
Florida: limits of, 107, 252; French colonies in, 110–11, 138–40, 172, 218,

282n86; corsairs raid, 113, 211; garrisons in, 123, 140, 142, 145, 178, 196, 219, 223, 261, 290n52; effect on defense costs, 126, 218, 223, 228; supply system, 139, 141, 145, 185, 196, 285n47, 294n25; fortifications in, 140, 153, 161, 162; abandonment of, proposed, 190; treasury records of, 241, 242, 244, 294n20; mentioned, 2, 65, 109, 110, 114, 129, 148, 181, 203, 234
—St. Augustine, 139, 146, 162, 195
—Santa Elena, 106, 107, 140, 142, 146, 282n86
—Straits of, 5, 6, 119, 129
Fortifications: designs and evaluations, 8, 51, 58, 96, 97, 110, 152–53, 161, 202, 203, 206, 227, 228; costs of, 16, 21, 22, 51, 71, 72, 123, 124, 153, 176, 178, 214; private builders of, 51, 153; geographic distribution of, 174, 179; as analytical category, 248–49, 251
France: illegal trade with Indies, 27, 65, 69, 105, 111, 116, 215, 281n82; plans to seize Caribbean, 140, 194, 218; interest in colonies, 215, 218, 282n89; mentioned, 65, 106, 216, 218
Francis I, King of France, 20, 65

Galicia, 191, 225
Galleys: costs of, 17, 175, 182; used off Spain, 109, 126; in Caribbean, 110, 135, 171, 175, 180, 181, 182, 189–90, 195, 221–22; mentioned, 13, 69, 88, 122, 235
—of Cartagena, 132, 180–86 *passim*, 188–89, 192, 221
—of Santo Domingo, 180, 182, 183, 184, 188–92 *passim*, 210, 222
—of Havana, 182, 183, 188, 193
García, Baltasar, 285n47
Garibay de Aguirre, Captain Juan, 144
Garrisons: costs of, 21, 123; caretaker, 49; full, 49, 50, 101, 179
Gatapenda, Rodrigo de, 31
General purpose squadrons: analytical category defined, 251
Geography: effects of on sailing routes, 5–8; analytical categories defined, 251–52
Godoy, Captain Francisco de, 119, 144
Grenville, Richard, 199
Guadalquivir River, 68
Guadianilla (Puerto Rico), 90, 118, 203, 262
Guanabacoa (Cuba), 263
Guanabara Bay, 106

Guanaïbes, 210
Guanalisbez, 119
Guarico, 119
Guatemala, 294n20
Guayanas, 4
Guilmartin, John: work noted, 230
Guise, Henri, duc de, 106
Gulfo Dulce, 114
Guzmán, Juan de, 89

Haring, Clarence: study of trade noted, 2, 127, 283n16, 293n4
Havana: second fort in, 9, 98, 100, 158–59, 160, 161, 202, 249; corsair raids on, 25, 41, 42, 47, 50, 63, 71, 200, 206; strategic location of, 33, 152, 234; local naval patrol of, 38, 133; militia of, 40, 46, 98; militia strength of, 41, 42, 262; munitions for, 44, 149, 150, 208; garrison of, 48, 50, 102, 110, 139, 141, 144, 146, 148, 196, 197, 198, 219, 223, 226, 235; first fort in, 52, 53, 54, 57, 58, 76, 97–98; corsairs off, 53, 128, 133; Morro fort, 54, 160, 161, 203, 205; artillery in, 60–61, 98, 100, 169, 170, 207, 208, 210; corsairs captured off, 92, 103, 172, 281n76; costs of second fort in, 96, 97, 98, 99, 100, 123, 153, 294n25; subsidy for garrison of, 146, 178, 198, 290n55
Hawkins, Sir John, 2, 111, 112, 115, 116, 120, 163, 171, 172, 197, 200, 219
Hawkins, William, 199
Henry II, King of France, 63, 65
Heredía, Pedro de, 277n5
Honduras, 42, 149, 151, 203, 216. *See also* Puerto Caballos, Trujillo
Huguenots, 106
Hussey, Roland: work noted, 2

Illegal trade in Caribbean, 8, 24, 26–27, 70, 102, 114–15, 200, 229, 283n16; persons involved in, 69–70, 116, 120; geographic pattern of, 114–15, 116, 119
Indies: definition of, 18
Indies Fleet, 127, 129, 136, 194, 196, 219, 221; costs of, 16–17, 19, 122, 135, 178, 184; as convoy escort, 19, 126, 128, 130, 132, 134, 184, 186; costs of patrols by, 19, 136, 221, 272n15; evaluation of, 126, 221, 224; design of ships for, 127, 194–95, 220, 222, 283n18; voyages of, 128, 130, 132–33, 134, 179–80, 184, 185, 235; patrols in Triangle by, 128, 195; ships of, named, 129, 135, 178, 184, 185;

captures corsairs, 132, 221; subsidy for, 182, 185, 186; and galleys, 183, 184; involved in smuggling, 186, 220; supply problems of, 194; mentioned, 9, 96, 145, 148, 173, 175
—Tierra Firme Squadron, 110, 126, 130, 132–33, 134, 181, 184, 185, 220
—Antilles Squadron, 130, 134, 184, 220
Intelligence system: role in defense, 112, 137, 190, 193, 225
Invasion: special case in defense planning, 212, 224, 225, 226
Isabela (Española), 119
Italy, 183

Jamaica, 52, 86, 119, 121, 185
Janda, Kenneth: work cited, 245
Jiménez de Peralta, Diego, 132
Junco, Captain Rodrigo de, 192
Junta de Puerto Rico, 208
Just titles, 65

La Gasca, Licenciado Pedro de, 36, 56, 60, 77, 278n*21*
Land defenses: costs of, 96, 97, 123, 178; characterized and evaluated, 123, 174, 196, 222. *See also* Artillery, Fortifications
Laudonnière, René de, 111
La Yaguana, 120, 203, 261; corsairs attack, 53, 91, 102; fortifications of, 55, 56, 97; illegal trade at, 69, 70, 118, 133, 190; visited by patrol squadrons, 91, 133, 190; corsairs captured near, 172, 190, 281n*76*
La Clerc, Jacques (Pie de Palo), 281n*75*
Leo XII, Pope, 20
Lima, 60, 242
Lisbon, 120
Lobera, Juan de, 60, 98
López, Licenciado Gregorio, 33, 36
López de Archuleta, Juan, 34
López de Isasti, Juan, 32, 33
López de las Roelas, Diego, 29, 74, 76, 77, 98, 278n*16*
López de las Roelas, Pedro, 75–76, 103, 136
Lorenzo, Pedro, 285n*47*
Lorraine, Cardinal of, 106
Louis of Nassau, Count: attack on Indies expected, 132, 147, 150, 155, 170, 231
Lowery, Woodbury: book noted, 2
Luís, Captain Francisco, 121
Luís de Cabrera, Antonio, 131
Luís de Lugo, Alonso, 60

Luna y Arellano, Tristan, 141, 282n*86*
Luxan, Gabriel de, 205
Lyon, Eugene: book noted, 139, 142, 264, 285n*43*

Macorís River, 118
Madeira, 31, 193
Magellan, Straits of, 18, 24, 52, 186, 204, 222
Mahan, Alfred T.: views noted, 229
Main, the Spanish: weather of, 7; corsair raids on, 25, 26, 38, 66, 67, 113, 114, 129, 133, 180, 211, 216, 283n*5*; militia actions along, 47, 201; defense costs of, 126, 223; mentioned, 5, 43, 132, 175, 180, 181, 185, 216, 220
Málaga, 29, 136, 209
Manpower: general costs of, 123, 178, 218, 281n*71*; defined as analytical category, 250; "sea guards" defined, 275n*51*
Manrique, Aldonça de, 121
Manrique de Rojas, Hernán, 183
Manzanillo, 119
Maravedí, 254
Margarita, 192, 233; raided by corsairs, 38, 114; requests patrol squadron, 39, 131, 188, 189; militia of, 42, 263; fortifications of, 53, 169, 203; illegal trade of, 70, 114–15, 118, 121, 211; artillery sought, 170, 207; mentioned, 132, 172
Mariel (Cuba), 128
Martín, Remón, 209
Martinez de Recalde, Juan, 194
Matanzas River (Florida), 139
Mazariegos, Diego de, 100, 161
McNamara, Robert S., 247
Medina del Campo, Treaty of (1490), 111–12
Medina Sidonia, duque de, 193
Menderichaga, Fray Juan de, 84, 86
Mendoza, Antonio de, 52
Mendoza, Martín de, 144
Menéndez de Avilés, Pedro: and Española squadron, 84, 279n*34*; Florida activities of, 111, 139, 145, 161, 220, 285n*47*; captain-general of Indies Fleet, 127, 130, 180, 219; grand strategy of, 129, 181, 220, 229; and Antilles garrisons and forts, 141, 144, 146, 152, 154, 155; mentioned, 102, 116, 132, 145, 148, 181, 196, 229
Menéndez de Valdés, Diego, 198, 204, 208
Menéndez de Valdés, Pedro. *See* Menéndez de Avilés, Pedro

Menéndez Marqués, Pedro, 143, 162, 196, 294n20
Messina, Straits of, 183
Methodology: role of statistics in, 11–12, 13, 16, 17, 18, 294n22; periodization, 16, 272n14; price data, 18; topical analysis codes, 245, 247–51, 295n30; use of Planning-Programming-Budgeting System (PPBS) concepts, 247–49; geographic categories and codes, 252; data preparation, 252, 253, 260
Militias, 39, 40, 41, 46, 47, 102, 199, 274n37; manpower base for, 11, 41, 42, 262–63; supplies of arms and munitions, 43, 148, 150, 152, 199, 219, 226; evaluation of, 46, 49, 199, 200–202; collapse of, 102, 226; mentioned, 21, 213
Miranda, Gutierre de, 162
Miranda, Hernándo de, 196
Mona Passage, 52, 90; corsairs in, 39, 66, 67, 68, 80, 86, 89, 91; mentioned, 5, 6, 25, 81, 103, 118, 128, 129
Monte Cristi, 91, 119, 120
Montejo, Juan de, 89
Moreyra Paz-Soldán, Manuel: work noted, 254
Moyano, Hernándo de, 143
Munitions: problems with supply of, 11, 150, 209, 277n86
Muñoz, Juan Baptista, 244

Naval patrols, 38, 71, 75, 76, 79, 82, 94, 116, 123, 222, 229. *See also* Galleys, Indies fleet
Navarro de Prado, Antonio, 202
Navigational techniques, 6
Navy, Spanish royal. *See* Indies Fleet, Española Squadron, Galleys
New Cádiz, 59
New Galicia, 242
New Spain: funds for Havana fort, 98, 99, 294n25; soldiers to Havana, 198, 226; treasury records of, 242, 244, 294n24; limits of, 252; militia data from, 262; mentioned, 74, 115, 126, 148, 180
Newton, Arthur P.: work cited, 3
Nice, Truce of (1538), 24, 30
Nombre de Dios: corsairs off, 24, 53, 114, 131, 132, 200, 208; militia of, 42, 44, 263; temporary garrison of, 50, 147, 197, 198; fortifications of, 52, 53, 55, 56, 97, 165, 202, 203; artillery in, 60, 61, 100, 208; patrol squadrons of, 82, 128, 131, 133, 181; corsairs captured at, 128, 281n76; raided by Drake, 132, 147, 165, 200; visited by galleys, 180, 183, 193
Norembega, 282n89
North African pirates, 64, 127, 137
Núñez Vela, Blasco: commands treasure fleet, 29, 34, 38, 273n10; defense strategies of, 30, 49, 54, 153, 194, 224, 228

Ocoa, 91, 118, 211
Oran, 88
Osorio, Diego, 191
Osorio, García, 144
Other installations: analytical category defined, 251
Ovando, Bernardino de, 211
Ovando, Fray Nicolás de, 239
Oxenham, John: raid mentioned, 18, 133, 147, 172, 185, 196, 197

Panamá (city): defenses of, 44, 197, 208; mentioned, 1, 24, 68
Panamá, Isthmus of: number of militiamen in, 41, 263
Parada, Francisco de, 285n47
Pardo, Captain Juan, 142
Pardo Osorio, Sancho, 134
Parry, John H.: work noted, 3
Patrimonialism, 9, 232. *See also* Political system
Pearl Islands (Panamá), 197
Penobscot River, 282n89
Peña, Alonso de la, 86
Perea, Miguel de, 29, 38
Perrenot, Antoine (Cardinal Granvelle), 20
Peru, 43, 197, 241
Peso de cuartos: tables of values, 258, 259
Pesos. *See* Units of account and currency
Pexón, Alonso, 81, 82, 84
Philip II, King of Spain, 84, 112, 216, 232
Pizarro, Gonçalo: rebellion of, mentioned, 36, 77, 101
Political system, 9, 10, 95, 150, 152, 173, 195, 205–206, 230, 232–34; examples of role of city councils in, 91, 152, 180, 181; examples of role of audiencias in, 152, 180, 181, 183; use of advocates in, 188, 190, 233
Ponce de León, Juan, 204, 205, 285n47
Ponte, Pedro de, 111
Portugal: royal navy in Triangle aids Spanish defenses, 29, 31, 34, 137; mentioned, 34–35, 138, 179
Portuguese: illegal trade by, in Caribbean,

INDEX   311

27, 69, 70, 116, 128, 216; resident in Caribbean, 120
Private persons: role in defense noted, 16, 62, 153, 173, 205, 213, 219, 222, 227, 234, 291n59
Puerto Belo, 52, 197
Puerto Caballos (Honduras), 50, 114, 203
Puerto de Mosquitos, 190
Puerto Francés, 119
Puerto Plata: garrison of, 48, 141, 144, 199; fort of, 52, 55, 56, 97, 119, 153, 157, 203; corsair raids on, 91, 200, 291n61; and illegal trade, 119, 210, 291n61; militia, 148, 262; artillery, 170, 207; mentioned, 120, 141, 152, 191
Puerto Real, 52, 97, 119, 120, 262
Puerto Rico: supply of arms and munitions in, 44, 150, 151, 207, 208; militias of, 45, 148; corsairs in, 70, 91, 154, 191, 194, 205; and patrol squadrons, 89, 91, 191; *peso de cuartos* used in, 257–58; mentioned, 6, 24, 25, 61, 141. *See also* Guadianilla, San Germán
—San Juan de: militia of, 41, 42, 43, 46, 200, 261, 275n49; garrison of, 48, 50, 110, 141, 144, 148, 178, 179, 196, 198, 199, 223, 288n1; fortifications of, 52, 53, 55, 57, 58, 97, 153, 154–55, 203, 204, 205, 222, 227, 275n54; artillery in, 59, 60, 61, 100, 169; political power of, 91, 152, 233, 252; residents of build defenses, 153, 205, 222; mentioned, 90, 179, 234

Rengifo de Angulo, Pedro, 121, 157, 211, 291n61
Ribault, Jean, 107, 109, 110, 139
Río de la Hacha, 50, 60, 96, 192, 233; militia strength of, 42, 263; forts in, 97, 169, 203; corsairs at, 114, 115, 200
Rivera, Diego de la, 146
Rivera, Licenciado, 190, 202, 212
Roberval, sieur de: voyage to New World noted, 24, 26, 31, 49, 64
Rodrígues Farfán, Cosmé, 79, 81, 85, 187
Ruidíaz de Mendoza, 191
Ruíz, Diego, 294n20

Saavedra, Lope de, 54
Sabana, 52, 119
Saint Nicolas, Cape, 119
San Antonio, Cape, 193, 210
San Germán: corsairs at or near, 38, 56, 69, 91, 92, 118; fortifications of, 52, 55, 56, 61; militia size of, 261; mentioned, 77, 90, 91
San Juan de Puerto Rico. *See* Puerto Rico
San Juan de Ulúa: garrison of, 48, 110, 147, 178, 196, 208, 219, 223, 287n1; fortifications of, 52, 55, 57, 153, 162–63, 164, 202, 219, 245, 286n67; artillery in, 60, 169; attacked, 112, 114, 172; militia size of, 262
San Lúcar de Barameda, 31, 81, 127
Sánchez, Bartolomé, 98
Sánchez Bella, Ismael: work noted, 293n4
Sánchez Quesada, Juan, 211
Santa Marta: corsairs at, 25, 39, 50, 55–56, 102; militia of, 41, 42, 45, 102, 149, 151, 263; temporary garrisons of, 50, 146; fortifications of, 52, 55, 56, 97, 167, 169, 203; artillery in, 60, 170, 207; mentioned, 96, 115, 185
Santiago de Cuba: raided by corsairs, 25, 50, 86, 102; militia of, 46, 262, 275n47, 275n49; temporary garrison of, 50, 141, 144, 158; artillery in, 53, 60, 61, 100, 169, 170; corsairs near, 53, 119; fortifications of, 53–54, 56–57, 158, 203; seeks munitions, 150, 207; mentioned, 61, 65
Santo Domingo: Drake's attack on, mentioned, 1, 195, 226, 236; use of political system by, 10, 233; local naval patrols of, 38, 39, 67, 86, 89, 96, 128, 129, 132; militia of, 40, 41, 42, 171, 199, 261; supply of arms and munitions in, 43, 44, 100, 149, 150, 151; garrison of, 46, 48, 50, 101, 141, 144, 199; fortifications of, 52, 53, 55, 57, 58, 155, 156, 202, 227; artillery in, 59, 60, 100, 207, 208; supplies Florida, 139, 141; use of *peso de cuartos* in, 254, 256–58; mentioned, 33, 57, 101, 120, 179, 194, 213, 217, 240
—Audiencia of, 121, 152; opinions on defenses, 76, 158, 183; political position of, 95, 96, 233
Saona, 82, 91, 94, 118, 192
São Tomé: slave ships from, 67, 70, 90
Ships: sizes allowed in Indies trade, 33; lead sheathing on, 38, 80
—named: *Dauphine*, 282n89; *La Gineta*, 88; *Nuestra Señora de Candelária*, 133; second of the name, 185; *Nuestra Señora de Guadalupe*, 185; *Ocasión*, 184, 189, 192; *Pantecras*, 140; *San Andrés*, 185; *San Cristóbal*, 186; *San Juan*, 88; *San Pedro*, 184; *San Salvador*, 184; *Santa Clara*, 184; *Santa Catalina*, 185; *Santiago*

(galley), 184; *Santiago* (ship), 88; *Santiago Mayor* (galleon), 184; *Santiago Menor* (galleon), 184; *Serafín*, 59
—types: general comments on, 6, 8–9; frigate, 129; fusta, 127, 185; galleass, 9, 75; galleon, 194–95, 222; galleyed galleon, 127, 220, 222, 283n*18*; patache: described, 68–69, 265, and role in raids, 32, 67, 79, 122, 180; saetía, 183, 265; urca, 266; zabra, 79, 266
Slaves, 41, 56, 57, 98, 115, 120, 121, 140, 158, 190, 205, 206, 208
Smuggling. *See* Illegal trade
Soco, 91
Solís, Francisco de, 233
Solorzano, Juan de: work cited, 39
Sores, Jacques de: Havana raid of, 42, 98, 106
Support activities: analytical category defined, 251

Tello de Guzmán, Juan, 85, 87, 103, 217, 221
Tercera: expedition to (1583), 194, 198
Tetuán, 136
Tiburón, Cape, 118
Tierra Firme Province: general data on militias of, 45, 149, 263; treasury records of, 240, 242
Tiran, Vicente, 282n*89*
Toledo, Francisco de, 147, 166
Tolú, 128, 132, 186, 207
Tordesillas, Treaty of (1494), 24
Torres, Geronimo de: work noted, 283n*7*
Tortuga, 119
Treasure fleets: crown-run, 21, 29, 31, 37, 213
Treasury records: 237–38, 242, 244; bookkeeping used in, 237, 238; auditing procedures of, 238, 241; fraud in, 242–43, 294n*19*, 294n*20*, 294n*21*
Troche, Captain Rodrigo, 144
Trujillo (Honduras): militia and caretaker garrison, 48, 147, 262; corsairs at, 103, 114; politics of defense of, 152; fortifications of, 163; artillery sought by, 170, 207
Tudor, Mary, Queen of England, 84

United States of America, Department of Defense: PPBS concepts, 247
Units of account and currency: discussed, 242, 254–55, 281n*71*; 295n*36*; tables of maravedí values of, 254, 255, 258, 259

Vaca de Castro, Licenciado, 55
Valdés, Pedro de, 130, 144, 161
Vallamo (Panamá), 147, 197. *See also* Cimarrons
Valle, Diego de, 294n*20*
Vallejera, Captain, 166
Varela, Pedro, 57
Vaucelles, Truce of (1555), 88, 104
Veitía Linage, Joseph: work noted, 2
Velasco, Diego de, 202
Vellon currency: manipulation of, in Antilles, 70, 257
Venezuela, 115, 211, 228
Venta de Chagres, mentioned, 122, 131
Vera Cruz: militia strength of, 42, 262; arms and munitions in, 44; treasury records of, 245, 286n*67*, 287n*1*
Veragua, 114, 115, 170, 172; forts sought by, 167, 169, 203
Verrazzano, Giovanni da: voyage of 1524, 282n*85*
Viedma, Sancho de, 77, 98
Vique y Manrique, Pedro, 150, 184, 185, 186, 188, 192, 193
Villafañe, Angel de, 141
Villavicéncio, Bartolomé, 163, 203
Vivero, Diego, 211

Williamson, James A.: work cited, 2
Windward Passage: corsairs in, 66, 68, 80, 277n*5*; illegal trade, 211; trade route, 274n*33*; mentioned, 5, 6, 129, 185
Wright, Irene A.: work mentioned, 2–3, 283n*16*

Yabaque, 118
Yacabo, 118–19
Yáquimo, 118
Yucatán, 115, 148
Yucatán Channel, 5, 6

Zorita, Alonso de, 81
Zorita, Captain Juan de, 144

www.ingramcontent.com/pod-product-compliance
Lightning Source LLC
Chambersburg PA
CBHW020637230426
43665CB00008B/210